The Complete Guide to DECKS

Updated 5th Edition

Plan & Build Your Dream Deck
Includes Complete Deck Plans

Creative Publishing international

MINNEAPOLIS, MINNESOTA
www.creativepub.com

400 First Avenue North, Suite 300
Minneapolis, Minnesota 55401
1-800-328-0590
www.creativepub.com

Printed in China

10 9 8 7 6 5 4 3 2 1

Library of Congress Cataloging-in-Publication Data

The complete guide to decks : plan & build your dream deck : includes complete deck plans. -- 5th ed.
p. cm. -- (Complete guide)
Includes index.
Summary: "Featuring the most-current and popular deck-building materials being used today, this book uses full-color, step-by-step photography to show homeowners how to build, maintain and customize a deck"--Provided by publisher.
ISBN 978-1-58923-659-2 (soft cover)
1. Decks (Architecture, Domestic)--Design and construction--Amateurs' manuals. I. Creative Publishing International. II. Title. III. Series.

TH4970.C645 2011
690'.893--dc23

2011036740

President/CEO: Ken Fund
Group Publisher: Bryan Trandem

Home Improvement Group

Associate Publisher: Mark Johanson
Managing Editor: Tracy Stanley
Editor: Jordan Wiklund

Creative Director: Michele Lanci
Art Direction/Design: Brad Springer, James Kegley, Kim Winscher, Brenda Canales

Lead Photographer: Corean Komarec
Set Builder: James Parmeter
Production Managers: Laura Hokkanen, Linda Halls

Contributing Editor: Chris Peterson
Page Layout Artist: Danielle Smith
Technical Editor: Eric Smith
Shop Help: Charles Boldt
Proofreader: Drew Siqveland

The Complete Guide to Decks
Created by: The Editors of Creative Publishing international, Inc., in cooperation with Black & Decker.

NOTICE TO READERS

For safety, use caution, care, and good judgment when following the procedures described in this book. The publisher and Black & Decker cannot assume responsibility for any damage to property or injury to persons as a result of misuse of the information provided.

The techniques shown in this book are general techniques for various applications. In some instances, additional techniques not shown in this book may be required. Always follow manufacturers' instructions included with products, since deviating from the directions may void warranties. The projects in this book vary widely as to skill levels required: some may not be appropriate for all do-it-yourselfers, and some may require professional help.

Consult your local building department for information on building permits, codes, and other laws as they apply to your project.

Contents

The Complete Guide to Decks

8

36

56

86

Contents (Cont.)

96

110

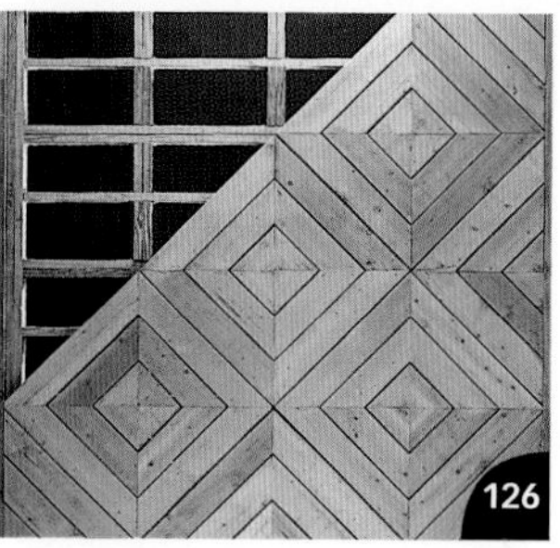
126

140

196

204

231

232

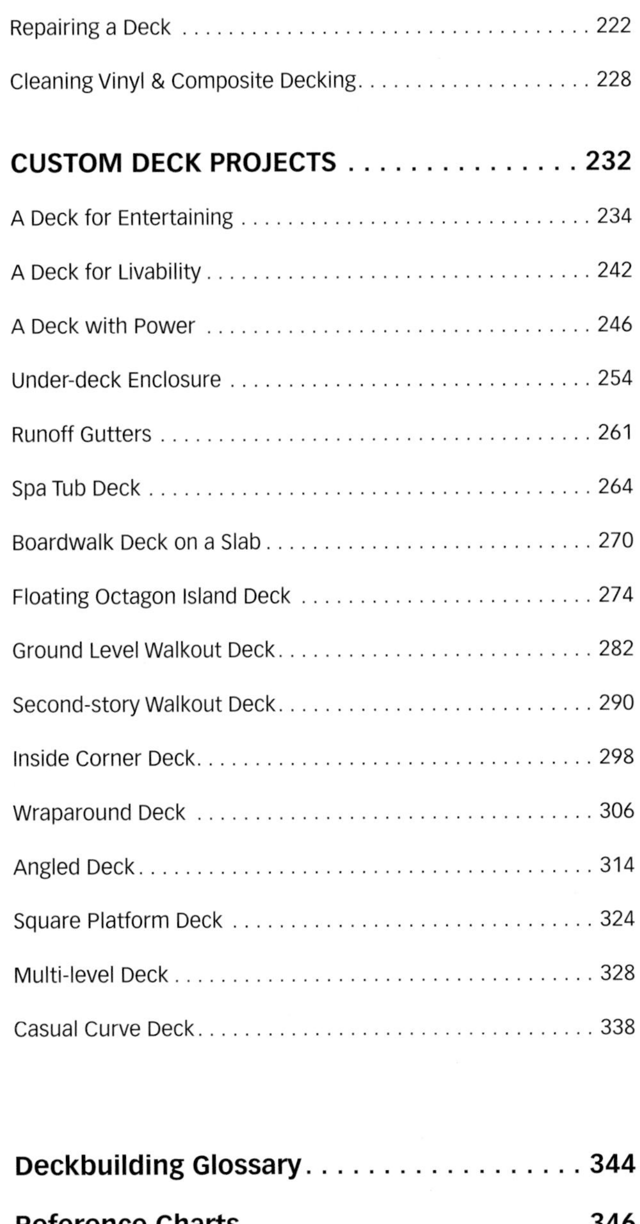

270

274

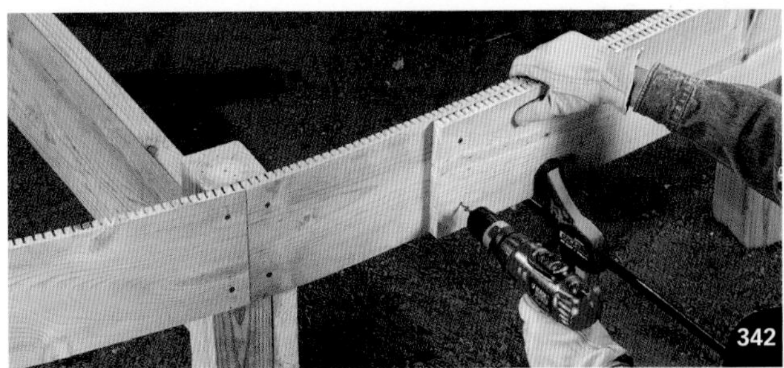
342

344

Introduction

The right deck can transform your yard, home, and life. It can extend your usable living space outside, provide a platform for relaxation, cooking, socializing, and much, much more. A deck can also add to your home's value for a relatively small investment—especially when you build it yourself.

Building a deck may seem like a daunting project, but it is really quite manageable if you have knowledge and guidance at your fingertips. That's where *The Complete Guide to Decks* comes in. This new edition of one of the bestselling deck books ever has been revised and updated with crucial new information, including changes to construction techniques, materials, and building codes. This version offers all the information you'll need to quickly and safely build the deck of your dreams.

Start with the gallery section that, along with photos throughout the book, will inspire you with examples of stunning decks of all sizes. These ideas set the stage for the essential sections on planning and design. There, we'll walk you step-by-step through the process of assessing your site and designing your deck. You'll learn about building codes and best practices that affect deck construction. We'll show you how to draft plan drawings that will be accepted by your local building department. You'll learn about all the fundamental techniques, tools, and materials that together form the art of deck-building.

Once we've covered the basics, we provide you with an in-depth, blow-by-blow guide to the entire deck construction process. Each chapter in the How to Build a Deck section focuses on an essential stage in the process, covering such topics as: building a sturdy foundation and structural support system; laying decking; constructing stairs and railings; installing lighting; and applying the perfect deck finish.

The last section of the book includes actual working plans, illustrations, and step-by-step instructions for a variety of decks. You can build any of these exactly as shown, or adapt a plan, modifying it to suit your own circumstances. You'll also find instructions and background information for adding any of a number of luxuries such as a spa tub, outdoor kitchen, seating, or a privacy screen.

Combine the comprehensive information in this book with a bit of time and work on your part (and maybe help from a friend or two), and you'll experience the overwhelming satisfaction that comes from building a spectacular deck. When you're done, you'll understand exactly why *The Complete Guide to Decks* is the deck-building manual for do-it-yourselfers and pros alike.

Gallery of Inspiring Decks

Like any major home improvement project, a deck should be designed to suit your family's lifestyle while it improves the value and beauty of your home. Realistically, you should build your deck with a budget in mind. But a budget doesn't have to squelch your freedom to dream about that ideal new outdoor space. As you begin to plan your project, let your imagination inspire its design. A deck doesn't have to be boring, even if you are a novice do-it-yourselfer or are working with limited finances. A curved metal railing, some attractive lighting, or common decking laid in an eye-catching geometric pattern can transform what might otherwise look like a boat dock on stilts into a compelling feature of your yard and neighborhood.

The following gallery of stunning decks is intended to help you explore the possibilities of what your deck could be. Granted, the bigger the deck the more it will cost, but even a small deck that doesn't suit your needs is an expensive investment if you never use it. So, whatever your budget may be, let these images serve as a way to gather ideas. Who knows... one small aspect of an elegant design could be just the key to unlocking the perfect deck plan for your home. Now is your chance to let any and all ideas be fair game.

Multi-level Decks

A basic, linear design such as this can make planning and building the complicated structure of multi-level decks far easier and quicker. Pressure-treated pine, as used throughout this deck, keeps costs to a minimum and ensures the longevity of the deck.

Multi-level deck designs are ideal for making the most of a slope. The redwood used in this deck is a traditional choice because the wood's appearance fits perfectly into the naturalistic surroundings, and it is inherently rot-resistant.

A multi-level deck can be a significant commitment in time, effort, and expense. Planning is crucial to ensure the deck is as usable as possible; make sure you know what activity each level of deck will accommodate. The layout should be logical. Here, cooking is done nearest the kitchen, with a social area down one platform. A hot tub is positioned underneath to keep it level with the pool.

Walkout Decks

An inside corner is the perfect place to nestle a quiet, cozy walkout deck. The type of thoughtful landscaping used around this platform helps it blend in with the house and yard. Use skirting as the builder did here to hide an unsightly supporting structure.

A basic, square walkout deck is one of the easiest to build. Dress it up with detailed railings (even if they aren't required by code) and enclosed stairs for a more polished look.

Jazz up a single-level walkout deck by designing it with an unusual shape. The shape of this outdoor entertaining area adds a little zest to a staid home design, and using white rails and lattice ties the deck in visually with the siding of the house—a technique that can be used with any deck.

Pool Decks

Make your deck conform to your needs, not the other way around. This simple platform attractively follows the shape of the pool and provides the perfect surface underfoot; always soft and forgiving, and cool when the sun is high.

Decks around pools often look best when coupled with natural materials such as the rock border shown here. The color of this deck was chosen to blend into the surroundings and let the allure of the pool itself really shine. When making decisions such as deck material and finish, always think about what the focal point of the deck will be.

Spa Decks

A spa tub can be a great experience day or night. That's why the broken shade of a pergola and a wind-stopping privacy screen are ideal additions to any spa tub in a deck. As this photo clearly shows, these features also add visual appeal.

Don't leave a spa tub alone. Creating nearby conversation or eating areas is a great way to spur party interaction and make the deck much more than just a platform for a spa tub.

Railings

One of the advantages of using composite decking is that composite materials can be formed to just about any shape. That means curving rails like this can be purchased ready-to-assemble, making a dynamic deck feature much easier to install.

Tube balusters are a wonderful choice for a wide range of deck designs. You can choose from enameled metal shown here, to copper, or stainless steel. Add a filigree ornamentation as the deck builder did to this railing, and you'll get even more bang for your buck.

Don't limit yourself to wood balusters—the choices for your railings are plentiful. The bent iron balusters and thick composite rails used here work perfectly with the stone posts to create an impression of solidity and permanence.

Handrail-mounted gates are a common code requirement for decks leading to a pool. They are also a chance to add a decorative highlight to plain railings. Gates like this add panache while increasing safety on an elevated deck platform.

A pure white rail is an excellent companion to glass railing inserts. The white creates a clean, bright look. Notice that rather than just suspending the inserts between two posts, the designer used detailed top and bottom rails that capture the glass and yet leave plenty of viewing space for watching the changeable water scene.

Built-in Features

Decking itself is often the most overlooked potential area for a built-in design focal point. Although the multi-shade herringbone pattern shown here may be a bit more involved than you want, you can still achieve an incredible look by simply running boards on a diagonal, or in four different directions meeting at a center point.

Pergolas are some of the most stunning built-in deck features. You can use them to create broken shade as the deck builder has here, or add a smaller version to your deck as a purely decorative feature. Either way, the structure is visually impactful.

Although gazebos are a significant built-in element, manufacturers provide complete kits to make building them much easier. Use them on any mid-size or large deck where you want a completely separate outdoor room to eat in or relax out of the sun.

Built-in Seating

You'll never regret planning seating into the deck design. Not only do benches serve an incredibly useful practical purpose, they can also be stylish focal points. The slotted seat versions here are popular—in straight runs or the more engaging angled forms featured on this deck—because the design allows for free flow of air and moisture, preventing mold and other detrimental conditions.

A straight and simple bench is easy to build, provides abundant seating, and in this case, creates a back border for the deck. It's the rare deck that won't be vastly improved with the addition of built-in benches. On low decks, they can even take the place of handrails.

INCHES
BRACING PARALLEL TO BEAM
American Wood Council
(1) 3/8" diameter
thru-bolt with
washers, typical
beam
2x4, typical

Deck Planning & Design

One of the benefits of building a deck is that you can create an impressive structure in a relatively short period of time, even with modest tools and skills. It's an exciting project to undertake, but don't let your energy and enthusiasm get the best of you. Without careful planning and design on the front end, your deck project could be frustrating to build, unnecessarily costly, or even dangerous to use when you're through. So, in order to put your best foot forward, plan to spend those first hours of the project at a desk developing a thorough plan.

As you begin the planning process, keep in mind that your deck needs to satisfy four goals: it should meet the functional needs of your household, contribute to your home's curb appeal and property value, fit your project budget, and satisfy local building codes for safety. This chapter will help you familiarize yourself with all four goals so you can build confidently and correctly, the first time. Be sure to spend some time reviewing the deck plans of this book, as well as other published deck plans. You may be able to find the perfect deck for your home without designing it from scratch or by making minor modifications to these plans.

In this chapter:

Evaluating Your Site

That overused real estate adage about "location, location, location" definitely applies to decks. Once you build your deck, it'll be there to stay, so choose your site carefully. A deck will be affected by sunlight and shade, prevailing winds and seasonal changes. Those natural factors will influence how and when you use your deck. There are other site-related issues to consider as well. An on-grade deck will reduce the size of your yard, which may or may not be an issue, depending on your desire for a garden, lawn, or play area. A raised deck could be perfect for entertaining friends, but it could also create unwanted shade in a flowerbed or darken a nearby living space.

The size and layout of your property will also impact your choice of deck sites. You may need to build a multi-level deck or a long run of steps to reach the ground of a sloping yard. Will your proposed deck site require you to remove a tree or two to accommodate it, or will you simply build around it? A tall deck could give you new vistas on the neighborhood, but will it encroach on your neighbor's window privacy or put you dangerously close to power lines? These are all factors to keep in mind when settling on the final location of your deck. Make sure the benefits of your deck site outweigh any compromises you may need to make.

The location of your deck is often dictated by the design and pre-existing features of your house. This home was built with a second-story sliding glass door in anticipation of an upper-level deck. However, you'll usually have more than one site to choose from, so consider all the options before you commit to a final location for your deck.

Deck Siting Considerations

Natural yard features, such as a steep slope, will impact a deck's layout and access. You may need to build a multi-level deck or a long staircase with a landing to accommodate the changing grade.

If you live in the midst of nature, you can go one of two ways with your deck design: blend in or stand out. Here, the homeowner has chosen the former, opting to build a modest lower deck around an existing evergreen using synthetic decking the exact color of the home's siding.

Before you build a second-floor deck, consider whether your site will compromise your neighbor's privacy, place you too close to power lines, or shade areas of the yard or windows beneath.

Built-ins and features you may want to use in conjunction with the deck, such as a swimming pool, will influence where and how you site the deck.

Deck Building Codes

Most decks are relatively simple structures, but even a basic deck project must conform to the requirements of building codes in your area. In fact, virtually every aspect of your new deck—from its location on your property, to the design you choose and the materials you buy to build it—must meet stringent guidelines for safety. Codes vary to some degree from state to state, but they are based on general regulations established by the International Residential Code. Your local building inspector can provide you with a list of the relevant deck codes and help you interpret them so you can create code-compliant plans for your deck project. You may also want to download a free PDF copy of the "Prescriptive Residential Deck Construction Guide" (see Resources, page 347).

The next few pages will provide a survey of some of the more common code requirements for decks, although it is by no means comprehensive. Use this section as a way to familiarize yourself with the code requirements you will probably face as you plan and build your new deck.

Footing diameter and depth is determined by your local codes, based on the estimated load of the deck and on the composition of your soil. In regions with cold winters, footings must extend a prescribed depth below the frost line. Minimum diameter for concrete footings is 8".

Metal flashings must be used to prevent moisture from penetrating between the ledger and the wall.

Beams may overhang posts by no more than 1 ft. Building regulations generally require that beams should rest on top of or be fully notched into posts, secured with metal post-beam caps or bolts.

Engineered beams, such as a laminated wood product or steel girder, should be used on decks with very long joist spans, where standard dimension lumber is not adequate for the load. Engineered beams for decks must be rated for exterior use.

Railings are required by local codes for decks more than 30" above the ground and must usually be at least 36" in height. Bottom rails must be positioned with no more than 4" of open space below them. Balusters, whether vertical or horizontal, can be spaced no more than 4" apart.

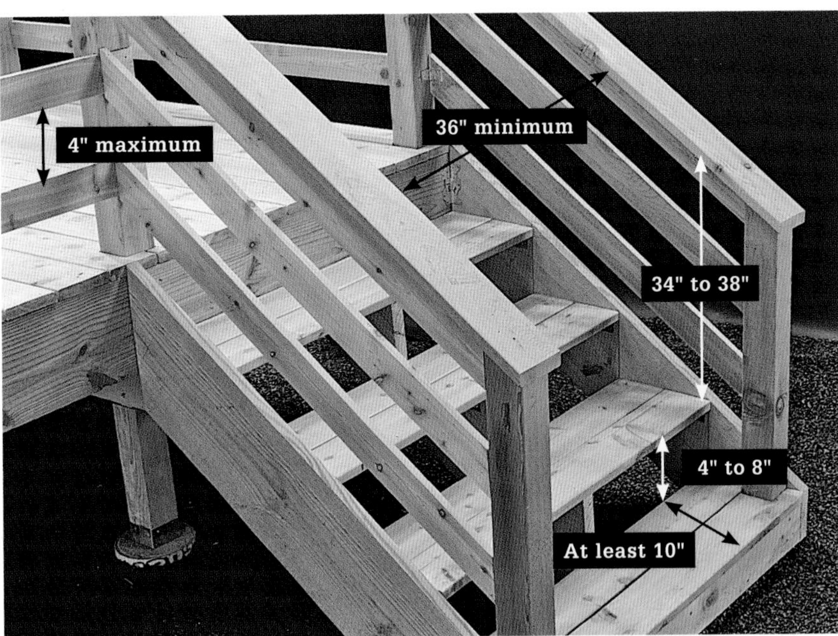

Stairs must be at least 36" wide. Vertical step risers must be between 4" and 7¾" and uniform in height within a staircase. Treads must have a horizontal run of at least 10" and be uniform in size within a staircase. Stair railings should be 34" to 38" above the noses of the step treads, and there should be no more than 6" of space between the bottom rail and the steps. The space between the rails or balusters should be no more than 4". *Note: Grippable handrails may be required for decks with four or more risers. Consult your local building inspector.*

Code violation. The International Building Code no longer allows joists to straddle the sides of a post fastened with through bolts, as shown here. It no longer endorses structural posts made of 4 × 4 lumber: 6 × 6 is the minimum size. Railing posts may be 4 × 4.

Beam assemblies. Deck beams made of 2× lumber must be fastened together with staggered rows of 10d galvanized common nails or 3" deck screws. If the wood components that make up the beam are spliced together, stagger the splices and locate them over beams for added strength.

Post-to-beam attachment. Deck posts, regardless of length or size of deck, should be made of minimum 6 × 6 structural lumber. Notch the posts so that beams can bear fully in the notch, and attach them with pairs of ½-in.-diameter galvanized through bolts and washers. Or, you can mount beams on top of posts with galvanized post cap hardware. Some codes prohibit the use of notched posts. Check with your local building department.

Ledgers and rim joists. When a ledger is fastened to a rim joist, the house siding must be removed prior to installation. Either ½-in.-diameter lag screws or through-bolts with washers can be used to make the connections.

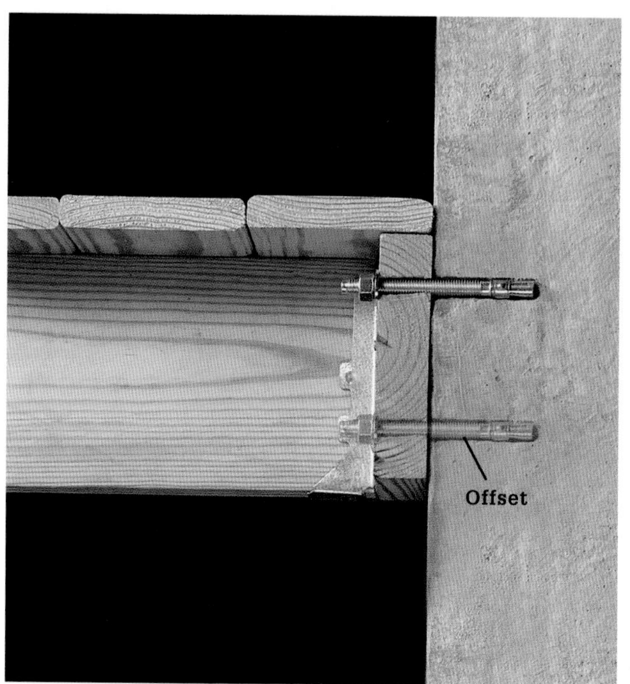

Ledgers and concrete walls. Ledgers fastened to solid concrete must be attached with bolts and washers driven into approved expansion, epoxy, or adhesive anchors.

Ledgers and block walls. When fastening ledgers to hollow concrete block walls, secure the attachment bolts to the wall with approved epoxy anchors (also called acrylic anchors).

No notched railing posts. Code no longer allows deck railing posts to be notched where they attach to the deck rim joists. Railing posts should be fastened to rim joists with pairs of ½-in.-diameter through bolts and washers. In some cases, hold-down anchor hardware may also be required.

Stair lighting. Deck stairs must be illuminated at night from a light located at the top of the landing. The light can be switch-controlled from inside the house, motion-controlled, or used in conjunction with a timer switch.

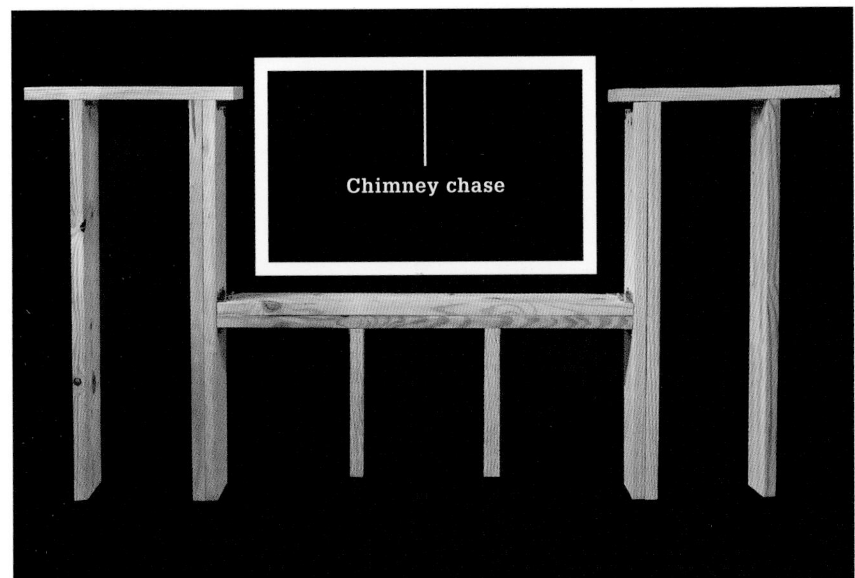

Chimney chases and bays. When framing a deck around a chimney or bay window, a suitable double header must be added where the ledger is spliced to accommodate the obstruction. The type of header shown here can span a maximum of 6 ft.

Rim joist connections. Attach rim joists to the end of each joist with five #10 × 3-in. minimum wood screws. Secure decking to the top of rim joists with #10 × 3-in. minimum wood screws, two per board.

Determining Lumber Size

A deck has seven major structural parts: the ledger, decking, joists, one or more beams, posts, stairway stringers, and stairway treads. To create a working design plan and choose the correct lumber size, you must know the span limits of each part of the deck. The ledger is attached directly to the house and does not have a span limit.

A span limit is the safe distance a board can cross without support from underneath. The maximum safe span depends on the size and wood species of the board. For example, 2 × 6 southern pine joists spaced 16" on-center can safely span 9'9", while 2 × 10 joists can span 16'1".

Composite, plastic, and aluminum decking all have their own span specifications, which are shorter than the standardized specifications for lumber. Always consult the manufacturer's recommendations when using non-wood decking. None of these materials are suitable for use in structural support.

Begin planning your deck by first choosing the size and pattern for the decking. Determine the actual layout of joists and beams by using the tables on the opposite page and information in the "Prescriptive Residential Deck Construction Guide" (see Resources, page 347). In general, a deck designed with larger lumber, such as 2 × 12 joists and beams, requires fewer pieces because the boards have a longer span limit. Finally, choose the stair and railing lumber that fits your plan, using the same tables.

Use the design plans to make a complete list of the quantities of each lumber size your deck requires. Add 10% to compensate for lumber flaws and construction errors. Full-service lumberyards have extensive selections of lumber, but prices may be higher than those at home improvement centers. The quality of lumber at home centers can vary, so inspect the wood and hand-pick the pieces you want or add a larger percentage to compensate for lumber flaws. Both lumberyards and home centers will deliver lumber for a small fee, and you can usually return unused, uncut lumber if you keep your receipts.

Meet or exceed all lumber size codes. For example, use lumber that is at least 6 × 6" for all deck posts, regardless of the size of the deck or the length of the post.

Dimension & Span Limit Tables for Deck Lumber ▸

Nominal vs. Actual Lumber Dimensions: When planning a deck, remember that the actual size of lumber is smaller than the nominal size by which lumber is sold. Use the actual dimensions when drawing a deck design plan.

NOMINAL	ACTUAL
1 × 4	¾" × 3½"
5/4 × 6	1" × 5½"
2 × 4	1½" × 3½"
2 × 6	1½" × 5½"
2 × 8	1½" × 7¼"
2 × 10	1½" × 9¼"
2 × 12	1½" × 11¼"
4 × 4	3½" × 3½"
6 × 6	5¼" × 5¼"

Recommended Decking Span Between Joists: Decking boards can be made from a variety of lumber sizes. For a basic deck use 2 × 4 or 2 × 6 lumber with joists spaced 16" apart.

DECKING BOARDS	RECOMMENDED SPAN
5/4 × 4 or 5/4 × 6, laid straight	16"
5/4 × 4 or 5/4 × 6, laid diagonal	12"
5/4 × 6 composite, laid straight	12"
5/4 × 6 composite, laid diagonal	Check manufacturer specifications
2 × 4 or 2 × 6, laid straight	16"
2 × 4 or 2 × 6, laid diagonal	12"
2 × 4, laid on edge	24"

Minimum Stair Stringer Sizes: Size of stair stringers depends on the span of the stairway. For example, if the bottom of the stairway lies 7 feet from the deck, build the stringers from 2 × 12s. Stringers should be spaced no more than 36" apart. Use of a center stringer is recommended for stairways with more than three steps.

SPAN OF STAIRWAY	STRINGER SIZE
Up to 6 ft.	2 × 10
More than 6 ft.	2 × 12

Recommended Railing Sizes: Sizes of posts, rails, and caps depend on the spacing of the railing posts. For example, if railing posts are spaced 6 feet apart, use 4 × 4 posts and 2 × 6 rails and caps.

SPACE BETWEEN RAILING POSTS	POST SIZE	CAP SIZE	RAIL SIZE
2 ft. to 3 ft.	2 × 4	2 × 4	2 × 4
3 ft. to 4 ft.	4 × 4	2 × 4	2 × 4
4 ft. to 6 ft.	4 × 4	2 × 6	2 × 6

Chart 1: Maximum Spans for Various Joist Sizes ▸

	SOUTHERN PINE			PONDEROSA PINE			WESTERN CEDAR		
Size	12" OC	16" OC	24" OC	12" OC	16" OC	24" OC	12" OC	16" OC	24 OC
2 × 6	10 ft. 9"	9 ft. 9"	8 ft. 6	9 ft. 2"	8 ft. 4"	7 ft. 0"	9 ft. 2"	8 ft. 4"	7 ft. 3"
2 × 8	14 ft. 2"	12 ft. 10"	11 ft. 0"	12 ft. 1"	10 ft. 10"	8 ft. 10"	12 ft. 1"	11 ft. 0"	9 ft. 2"
2 × 10	18 ft. 0"	16 ft. 1"	13 ft. 5"	15 ft. 4"	13 ft. 3"	10 ft. 10"	15 ft. 5"	13 ft. 9"	11 ft. 3"
2 × 12	21 ft. 9"	19 ft. 0"	15 ft. 4"	17 ft. 9"	15 ft. 5"	12 ft. 7"	18 ft. 5"	16 ft. 5"	13 ft. 0"

Understanding Loads

The supporting structural members of a deck—the posts, beams, and joists—must be sturdy enough to easily support the heaviest anticipated load on the deck. They must not only carry the substantial weight of the surface decking and railings, but also the weight of people, deck furnishings, and, in some climates, snow.

The charts and diagrams shown here will help you plan a deck so the size and spacing of the structural members are sufficient to support the load, assuming normal use. These recommendations are followed in most regions, but you should still check with your local building official for regulations that are unique to your area. In cases where the deck will support a hot tub or pool, you must consult your local building inspections office for load guidelines.

When choosing lumber for the structural members of your deck, select the diagram below that best matches your deck design, then follow the advice for applying the charts on the opposite page. Since different species of wood have different strengths, make sure to use the entries that match the type of lumber sold by your building center. When selecting the size for concrete footings, make sure to consider the composition of your soil; dense soils require footings with a larger diameter.

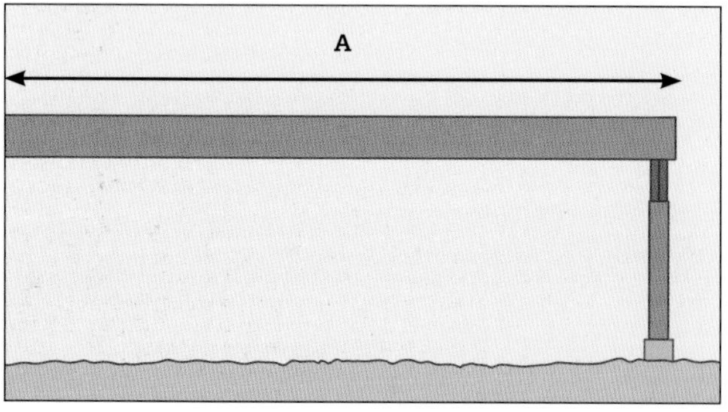

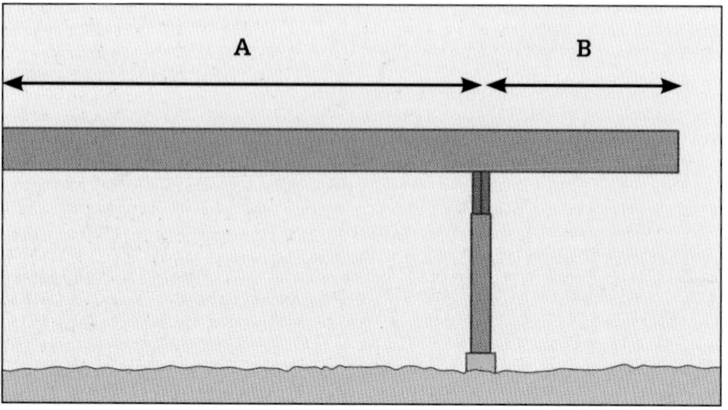

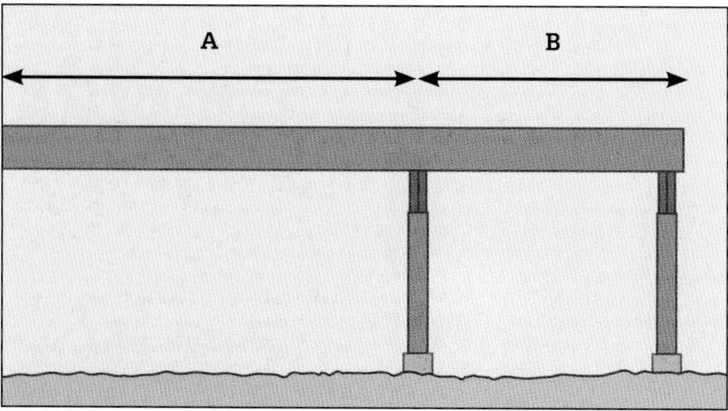

Post-and-beam deck: Using Chart 1, determine the proper size for your joists, based on the on-center (OC) spacing between joists and the overall length, or span, of the joists (A). For example, if you will be using southern pine joists to span a 12-ft. distance, you can use 2 × 8 lumber spaced no more than 16" apart, or 2 × 10 lumber spaced no more than 24" apart. Once you have determined allowable joist sizes, use Chart 2 to determine an appropriate beam size, post spacing, and footing size for your deck.

Cantilevered deck: Use the distance from the ledger to the beam (A) to determine minimum joist size, and use A + (2 × B) when choosing beam and footing sizes. For example, if your deck measures 9 ft. from ledger to beam, with an additional 3-ft. cantilevered overhang, use 9 ft. to choose a joist size from Chart 1 (2 × 6 southern pine joists spaced 16" apart, or 2 × 8 joists spaced 24" apart). Then, use A + (2 × B), or 15 ft., to find an appropriate beam size, post spacing, and footing size from Chart 2. *Note: If your deck cantilevers more than 18" beyond the support beam, add 1" to the recommended diameter for footings.*

Multiple-beam deck: Use distance A or B, whichever is larger, when determining joist size from Chart 1. For example, if your deck measures 8 ft. to beam #1 and another 4 ft. to beam #2, you can use 2 × 6 southern pine joists. Referring to Chart 2, use the total distance A + B to determine the size of beam #1, the spacing for the posts, and the size of the footings. Use joist length B to determine the size of beam #2, the post spacing, and footing size. For example, with an overall span of 12 ft. (8 ft. to the first beam, 4 ft. to the second), beam #1 could be made from two southern pine 2 × 8s; beam #2, from two 2 × 6s.

Chart 2: Diameters for Post Footing (inches) ▸

JOIST LENGTH		POST SPACING								
		4'	5'	6'	7'	8'	9'	10'	11'	12'
6'	Southern Pine Beam	1–2 × 6	1–2 × 6	1–2 × 6	2–2 × 6	2–2 × 6	2–2 × 6	2–2 × 8	2–2 × 8	2–2 × 10
	Ponderosa Pine Beam	1–2 × 6	1–2 × 6	1–2 × 8	2–2 × 8	2–2 × 8	2–2 × 8	2–2 × 10	2–2 × 10	2–2 × 12
	Corner Footing	6 5 4	7 6 5	7 6 5	8 7 6	9 7 6	9 7 6	10 8 7	10 8 7	10 9 7
	Intermediate Footing	9 8 7	10 8 7	10 9 7	11 9 8	12 10 9	13 10 9	14 11 10	14 12 10	15 12 10
7'	Southern Pine Beam	1–2 × 6	1–2 × 6	1–2 × 6	2–2 × 6	2–2 × 6	2–2 × 8	2–2 × 8	2–2 × 10	2–2 × 10
	Ponderosa Pine Beam	1–2 × 6	1–2 × 6	1–2 × 8	2–2 × 8	2–2 × 8	2–2 × 10	2–2 × 10	2–2 × 10	2–2 × 12
	Corner Footing	7 5 5	7 6 5	8 7 6	9 7 6	9 8 7	10 8 7	10 8 7	11 9 8	11 9 8
	Intermediate Footing	9 8 7	10 8 7	11 9 8	12 10 9	13 11 9	14 11 10	15 12 10	15 13 11	16 13 11
8'	Southern Pine Beam	1–2 × 6	1–2 × 6	2–2 × 6	2–2 × 6	2–2 × 8	2–2 × 8	2–2 × 8	2–2 × 10	2–2 × 10
	Ponderosa Pine Beam	1–2 × 6	2–2 × 6	2–2 × 8	2–2 × 8	2–2 × 8	2–2 × 10	2–2 × 10	2–2 × 10	3–2 × 10
	Corner Footing	7 6 5	8 6 6	9 7 6	9 8 7	10 8 7	10 8 7	11 9 8	11 9 8	12 10 9
	Intermediate Footing	10 8 7	11 9 8	12 10 9	13 11 9	14 11 10	15 12 10	16 13 11	16 13 12	17 14 12
9'	Southern Pine Beam	1–2 × 6	1–2 × 6	2–2 × 6	2–2 × 6	2–2 × 8	2–2 × 8	2–2 × 10	2–2 × 10	2–2 × 12
	Ponderosa Pine Beam	1–2 × 6	2–2 × 6	2–2 × 8	2–2 × 8	2–2 × 10	2–2 × 10	2–2 × 10	3–2 × 10	3–2 × 10
	Corner Footing	7 6 5	8 7 6	9 7 6	10 8 7	10 9 7	11 9 8	12 10 8	12 10 9	13 10 9
	Intermediate Footing	10 9 7	12 10 8	13 10 9	14 11 10	15 12 10	16 13 11	17 14 12	17 14 12	18 15 13
10'	Southern Pine Beam	1–2 × 6	1–2 × 6	2–2 × 6	2–2 × 6	2–2 × 8	2–2 × 8	2–2 × 10	2–2 × 12	2–2 × 12
	Ponderosa Pine Beam	1–2 × 6	1–2 × 6	2–2 × 8	2–2 × 8	2–2 × 10	2–2 × 10	2–2 × 12	3–2 × 10	3–2 × 12
	Corner Footing	8 6 6	9 7 6	10 8 7	10 8 7	11 9 8	12 10 8	12 10 9	13 11 9	14 11 10
	Intermediate Footing	11 9 8	12 10 9	14 11 10	15 12 10	16 13 11	17 14 12	17 14 12	18 15 13	19 16 14
11'	Southern Pine Beam	1–2 × 6	2–2 × 6	2–2 × 6	2–2 × 8	2–2 × 8	2–2 × 10	2–2 × 10	2–2 × 12	2–2 × 12
	Ponderosa Pine Beam	2–2 × 6	2–2 × 6	2–2 × 8	2–2 × 8	2–2 × 10	2–2 × 12	2–2 × 12	3–2 × 10	3–2 × 12
	Corner Footing	8 7 6	9 7 6	10 8 7	11 9 8	12 9 8	12 10 9	13 11 9	14 11 10	14 12 10
	Intermediate Footing	12 9 8	13 11 9	14 12 10	15 12 10	16 13 11	17 14 12	17 14 12	18 15 13	19 16 14
12'	Southern Pine Beam	1–2 × 6	2–2 × 6	2–2 × 6	2–2 × 8	2–2 × 8	2–2 × 10	2–2 × 10	2–2 × 12	3–2 × 10
	Ponderosa Pine Beam	2–2 × 6	2–2 × 6	2–2 × 8	2–2 × 10	2–2 × 10	2–2 × 12	2–2 × 12	3–2 × 12	3–2 × 12
	Corner Footing	9 7 6	10 8 7	10 9 7	11 9 8	12 10 9	13 10 9	14 11 10	14 12 10	15 12 10
	Intermediate Footing	12 10 9	14 11 10	15 12 10	16 13 11	17 14 12	18 15 13	19 16 14	20 16 14	21 17 15
13'	Southern Pine Beam	1–2 × 6	2–2 × 6	2–2 × 6	2–2 × 8	2–2 × 8	2–2 × 10	2–2 × 10	2–2 × 12	3–2 × 10
	Ponderosa Pine Beam	2–2 × 6	2–2 × 6	2–2 × 8	2–2 × 10	2–2 × 12	2–2 × 12	2–2 × 12	3–2 × 12	3–2 × 12
	Corner Footing	9 7 6	10 8 7	11 9 8	12 10 8	13 10 9	13 11 9	14 12 10	15 12 10	15 13 11
	Intermediate Footing	13 10 9	14 12 10	15 13 11	17 14 12	18 15 13	19 15 13	20 16 14	21 17 15	22 18 15
14'	Southern Pine Beam	1–2 × 6	2–2 × 6	2–2 × 6	2–2 × 8	2–2 × 10	2–2 × 10	2–2 × 12	3–2 × 10	3–2 × 12
	Ponderosa Pine Beam	2–2 × 6	2–2 × 8	2–2 × 8	2–2 × 10	2–2 × 12	3–2 × 10	3–2 × 12	3–2 × 12	Eng Bm
	Corner Footing	9 8 7	10 8 7	11 9 8	12 10 9	13 11 9	14 11 10	15 12 10	15 13 11	16 13 11
	Intermediate Footing	13 11 9	15 12 10	16 13 11	17 14 12	18 15 13	20 16 14	21 17 15	22 18 15	23 18 16
15'	Southern Pine Beam	2–2 × 6	2–2 × 6	2–2 × 8	2–2 × 8	2–2 × 10	2–2 × 12	2–2 × 12	3–2 × 10	3–2 × 12
	Ponderosa Pine Beam	2–2 × 6	2–2 × 8	2–2 × 8	2–2 × 10	3–2 × 10	3–2 × 10	3–2 × 12	3–2 × 12	Eng Bm
	Corner Footing	10 8 7	11 9 8	12 10 8	13 10 9	14 11 10	14 12 10	15 12 11	16 13 11	17 14 12
	Intermediate Footing	14 11 10	15 12 11	17 14 12	18 15 13	19 16 14	20 17 14	21 17 15	22 18 16	23 19 17

10 8 7
14 11 10

Soil composition: Clay Sand Gravel

Developing Your Deck Plan

A deck plan is more than just measured drawings. It needs to account for your deck's functional purposes as well as its dimensional form. Before you begin drawing plans, determine everything you want your deck to include. Here's where you'll focus on functional concerns. The size, shape, and location of your deck can be affected by several questions: Will the deck be used for entertaining? Will you cook on it? Do you need privacy? Consider how the features of the house and yard influence the deck design. Weather, time of day, and seasonal changes affect deck usage. For example, if your deck will be used mainly for summertime evening meals, look at the sun, shade, and wind patterns on the planned site during this time of day.

Of course, building plans also help you estimate lumber and hardware needs, and provide the measurements needed to lay out the deck and cut the lumber. You will need two types of drawings for your deck plans and to obtain a building permit. A plan view shows the parts of the deck as they are viewed from directly overhead. An elevation shows the deck parts as viewed from the side or front.

Calculator Conversion Chart ▸

8THS	16THS	DECIMAL
	1	.0625
1	2	.125
	3	.1875
2	4	.25
	5	.3125
3	6	.375
	7	.4375
4	8	.5
	9	.5625
5	10	.625
	11	.6875
6	12	.75
	13	.8125
7	14	.875
	15	.9375
8	16	1.0

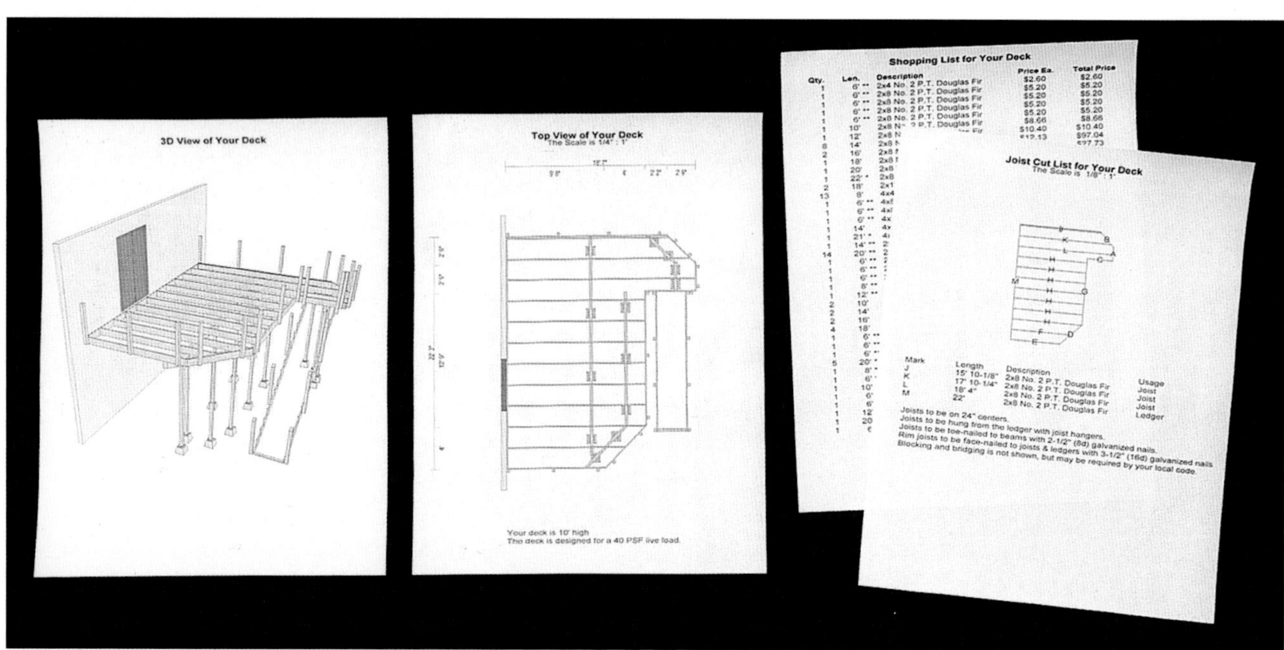

Many building centers will help you design and create deck plan drawings if you purchase your lumber and other deck materials from them. Their design capabilities include determining a detailed lumber and materials list based on the exact deck plan created.

How to Create Design Drawings

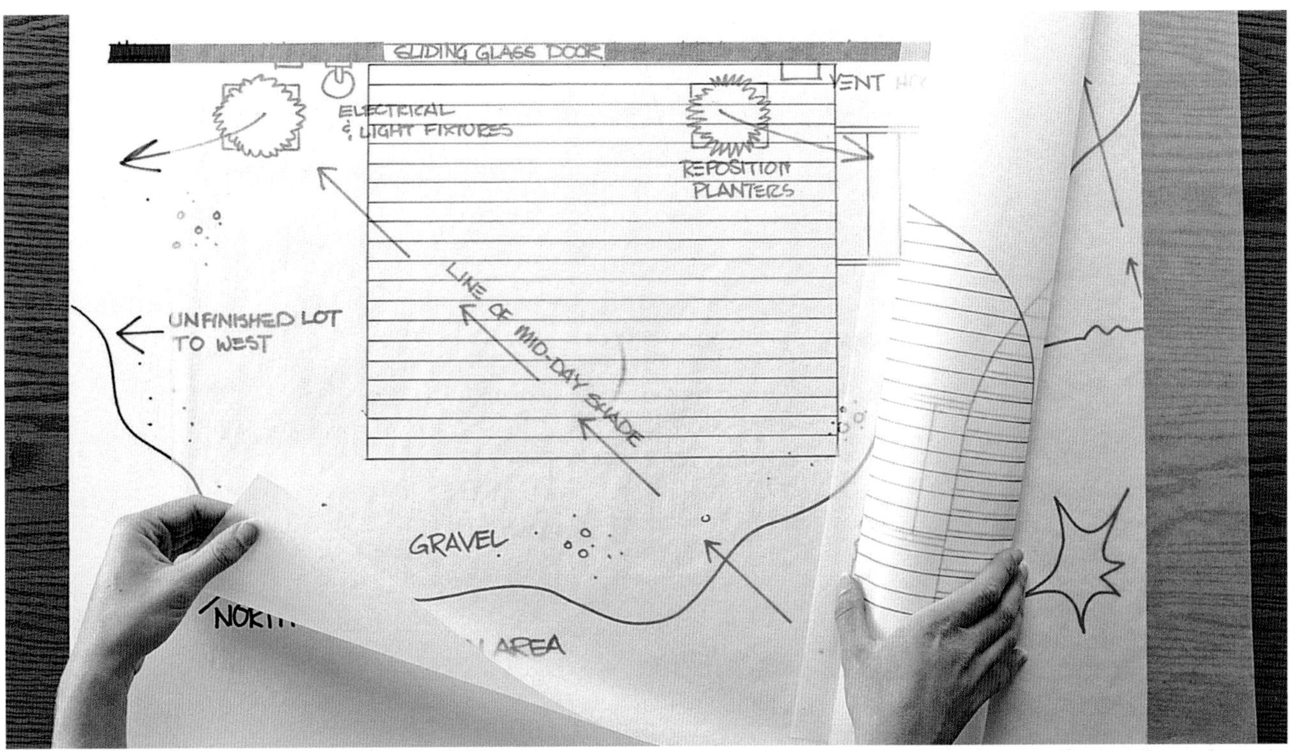

Use tracing paper to sketch different deck layouts. Then, test your ideas by overlaying the deck sketches onto a drawing of your building site. Make sure to consider sun patterns and the locations of existing landscape features when developing a deck plan.

Adapt an existing deck plan, either borrowed from a book or magazine, or purchased in blueprint form. Tracing paper, pens, and measuring tools are all you need to revise an existing deck plan.

Use drafting tools and graph paper if you are creating a deck plan from scratch. Use a generous scale, such as 1" equals 1 ft., that allows you to illustrate the deck in fine detail. Remember to create both overhead plan drawings and side elevation drawings of your project.

Using Deck Design CAD Software ▸

If you prefer working on computer to drafting by hand, you can choose from a number of different computer aided design (CAD) programs specifically developed to help the homeowner design his or her own deck and landscaping. Although most of these programs are sophisticated and powerful, they are generally easy to learn and use. Most include tutorials, and it generally only takes a few hours to become proficient with the software. These programs are loaded with features to help you envision and create a deck customized for your house. They include the ability to accurately re-create the exterior structure of your home and rough elements in the landscape. You can create and view both plan-view and elevation perspectives, and materials lists. The majority of these type of programs include the possibility of outputting drawings suitable for submission to building departments. But beyond the pragmatic uses, the best of these allow you to develop amazingly realistic renderings of material color and texturing, and give you the option of trying out different features such as cable railings or skirting. Some even offer 3-D perspectives that can be rotated on screen. Prices range from free to more than $200—buy the software that matches your needs and will work on your current computer.

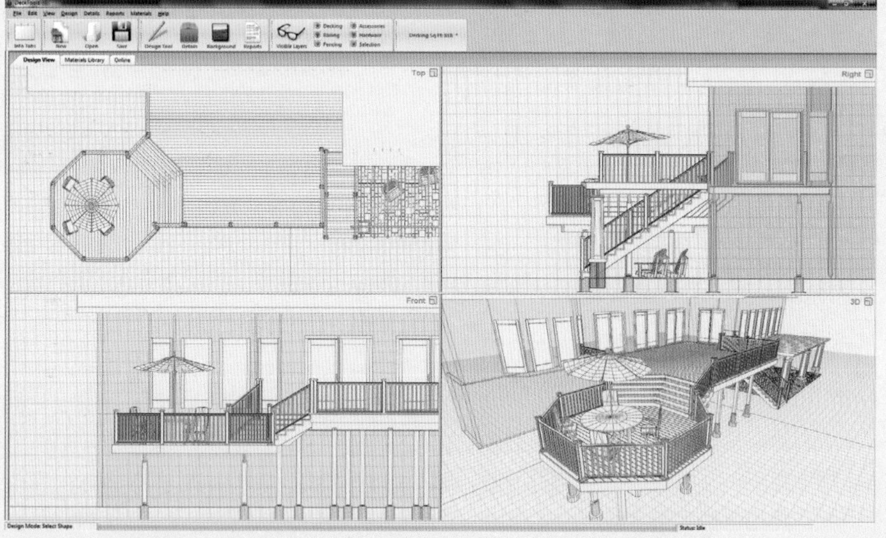

The plan drawings produced by some CAD programs are acceptable to many local building departments.

CAD programs have come a long way, and many can now show rotatable 3D versions of your deck design.

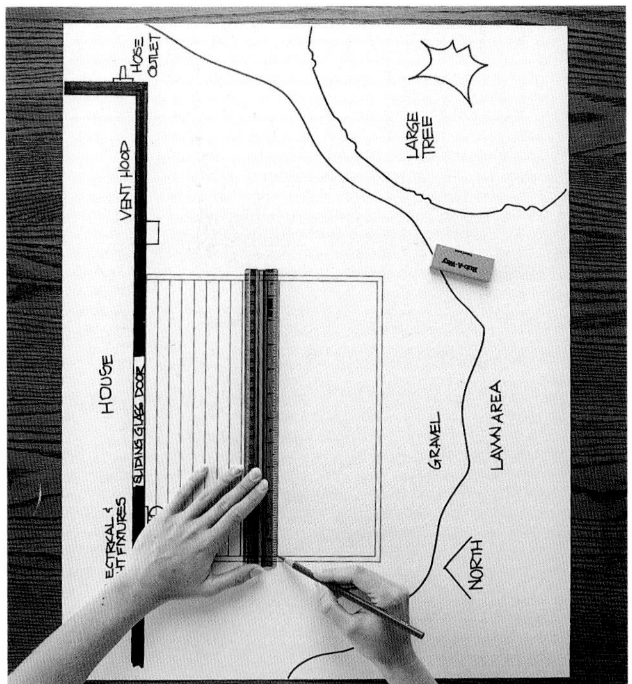

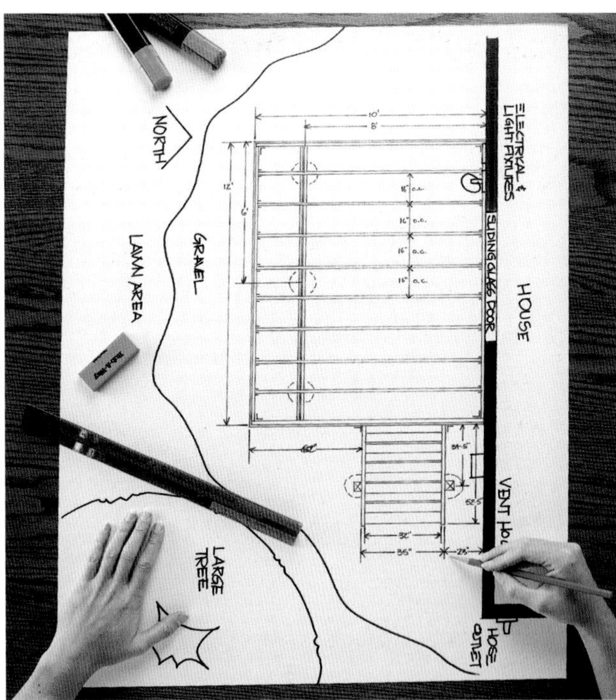

To avoid confusion, do not try to show all parts of the deck in a single plan view, especially for a complicated or multi-level deck. First, draw one plan view that shows the deck outline and the pattern of the decking boards. Then make another plan view (or more) that shows the underlying ledger, joists, beams, and posts.

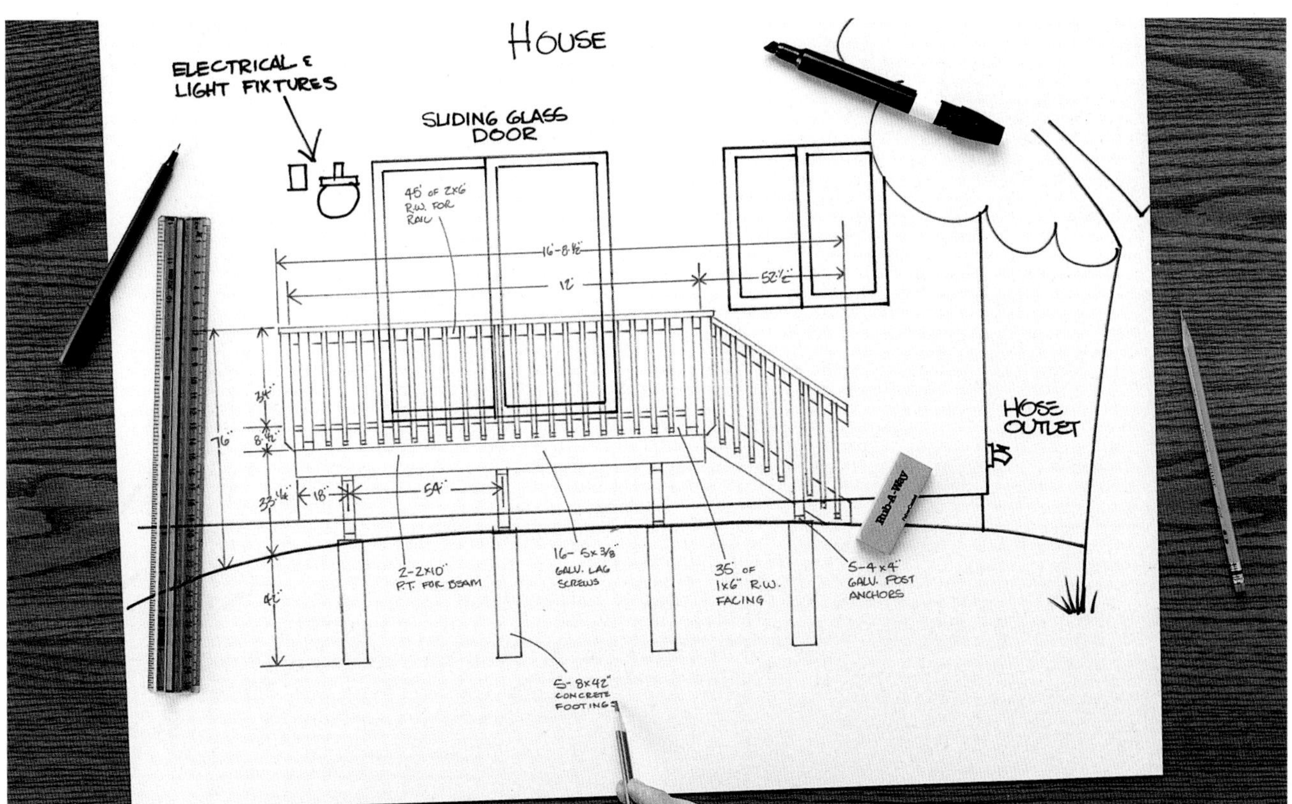

Elevation drawings must include deck dimensions, size and type of hardware to be used, beam sizes (if visible in drawing), and footing locations and their dimensions. Also indicate the grade of the ground in the deck area. Make multiple elevation drawings if necessary for complicated or multi-level decks.

Working with Building Inspectors

In most regions, you must have your plans reviewed and approved by a building official if your deck is attached to a permanent structure or if it is more than 30" high. The building official makes sure that your planned deck meets building code requirements for safe construction.

These pages show some of the most common code requirements for decks. But before you design your project, check with the building inspection division of your city office, since code regulations can vary from area to area. A valuable source of planning information, the building official may provide you with a free information sheet outlining the relevant requirements.

Once you have completed your deck plans, return to the building inspections office and have the official review them. Make certain you know how many copies of the plans they require before you go. If your plans meet code, you will be issued a building permit, usually for a small fee. This process often takes a few days. Regulations may require that a field inspector review the deck at specified stages in the building process. If so, make sure to allow for the review schedule in your project schedule.

While it might be tempting to forge ahead with your deck design and bypass the building inspector entirely, it's a big mistake. Building a deck without the proper permits can lead to fines, and you may even be required to tear the deck down or significantly rebuild it to satisfy local codes. Do the right thing: consider permits and inspections to be a necessary part of the construction process.

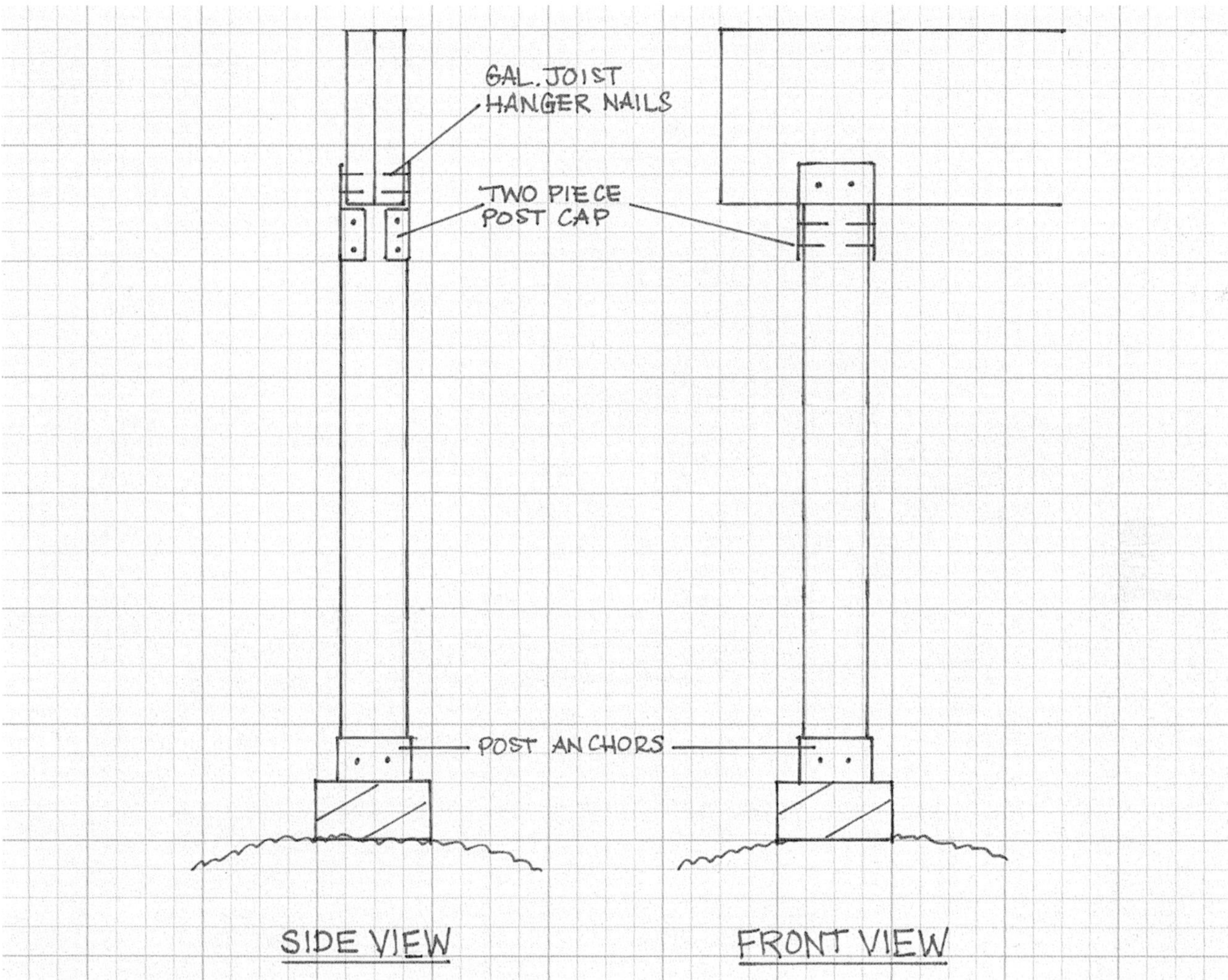

Draw detailed illustrations of the joinery methods you plan to use for all structural members of your deck. Your building official will want to see details on post-footing connections, post-beam joints, beam-joist joints, and ledger connections. Be prepared to make adjustments.

Plan-approval Checklist ▸

When the building official reviews your deck plans, he or she will look for the following details. Make sure your plan drawings include all this information.

- Overall size and shape of the deck.
- Position of the deck relative to buildings, property lines, and setbacks. Generally, a deck must be at least 5 ft. from the property line, although this varies locality to locality.
- Location of all beams and posts.
- Detailed drawings of joinery methods for all structural members of the deck.
- Size and on-center (OC) spacing of joists.
- Height of deck above grade.
- Thickness of deck boards—or profile of composite decking.
- Type of soil that will support the concrete post footings: sand, loam, or clay.
- Species of wood to be used, and/or type of composite material.
- Types of metal connectors and other hardware you plan to use in constructing the deck.
- Lighting and other electrical outlets or fixtures that will be wired into the deck.

BLACK&DECKER
BLACK&DECKER
AutoTape

Deck Materials & Tools

Constructing a deck requires a variety of building materials, and this chapter will introduce you to them. You'll need forms, concrete and gravel for making footings, treated posts and framing lumber for the deck's undercarriage, an assortment of connective hardware and fasteners, flashing supplies, decking, and materials for building railings and stairs. Get ready to make some long shopping lists! You may also want to acquaint yourself with the deck-building section of your local home center before you start your deck project. That way, you'll be able to find what you need quickly and easily when you really need it.

If you're a seasoned do-it-yourselfer or woodworker, you may already own most of the hand and power tools you'll need for building a deck. You'll also need a few masonry tools. Be sure to review the specialty tools (pages 54 and 55) that you may want to rent for your deck project. They may save you considerable time and effort.

In this chapter:

Footings & Structural Lumber

Generally, pressure-treated lumber is the preferred choice for deck posts, beams, and joist framing. It offers good resistance to decay and insect infestation, it's widely available in most parts of the country and it's a cheaper alternative to other rot-resistant wood species such as cedar or redwood. Treated lumber is milled in 4 × 4, 4 × 6, and 6 × 6 sizes for posts. Larger dimensions are available by special order. You'll need 2× treated lumber for beams and joists. Joists are usually 2 × 8 or larger. If your deck is particularly large or designed with oversized spans, you may need to use engineered beams instead of building beams from treated lumber. Make sure your engineered beams are rated for exterior use.

Select the flattest structural lumber you can find, free of splits, checks, and large loose knots. To prevent warping, stack and store it in a dry place or cover it with a tarp until you need it. Check the grade stamps or the stapled tags on your pressure-treated posts; they should be approved to a level of .40 retention for ground contact.

Chemical Formulations of Pressure-treated Lumber ▸

As of January 1, 2004, the lumber industry voluntarily discontinued the use of chromated copper arsenate (CCA) treated lumber for consumer uses. This was done in conjunction with the Environmental Protection Agency in an effort to help reduce the exposure to arsenic, a known carcinogen. Two alternative chemical treatments are now used instead: alkaline copper quaternary (ACQ) and copper boron azole (CBA). Both ACQ and CBA provide wood with the same protection from decay and insect attack as CCA, however the treatments are more corrosive to metals. Make sure to choose fasteners and connective hardware that are approved for use with ACQ- and CBA-treated lumber.

Treated lumber is available in common nominal sizes for use as deck beams and joists. Choose the clearest, flattest boards you can find, free of checks and splits. Use the correct post size for the deck you are building: 4 × 4s and 4 × 6s are still acceptable for railing and stair construction, but they do not meet requirements for deck posts. You'll need 6 × 6 or larger lumber for this purpose.

Lumber for Building Decks

Engineered beams that are rated for exterior use are a sturdy alternative to beams made from 2× lumber. They may be required if you are building a large deck with expansive or unusual spans. Your building inspector will help you make this determination.

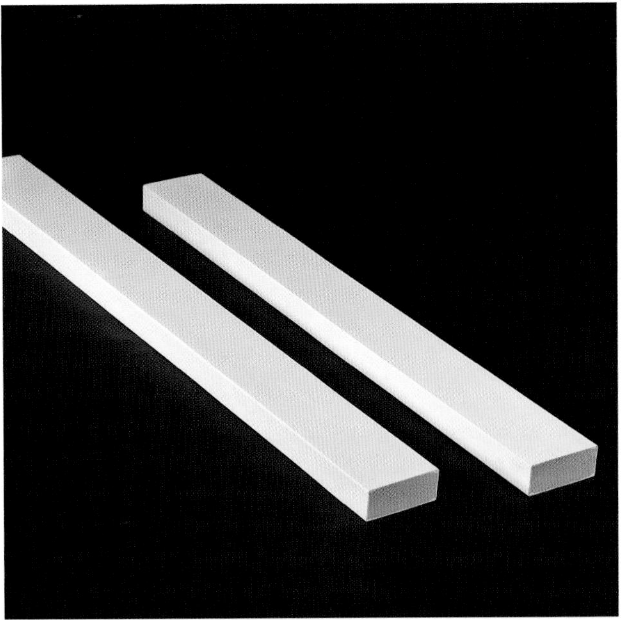

Composite lumber is widely used for non-structural purposes such as decking, skirting, and railing. Made from sawdust, recycled plastic, and binders, composite lumber is available in solid, hollow, and other profiles.

Sealing End Grain ▸

Seal cut edges of all lumber, including pressure-treated wood, by brushing on clear liquid sealer-preservative. Chemicals used in pressure treatment do not always penetrate completely. Sealer-preservative protects all types of wood from rot.

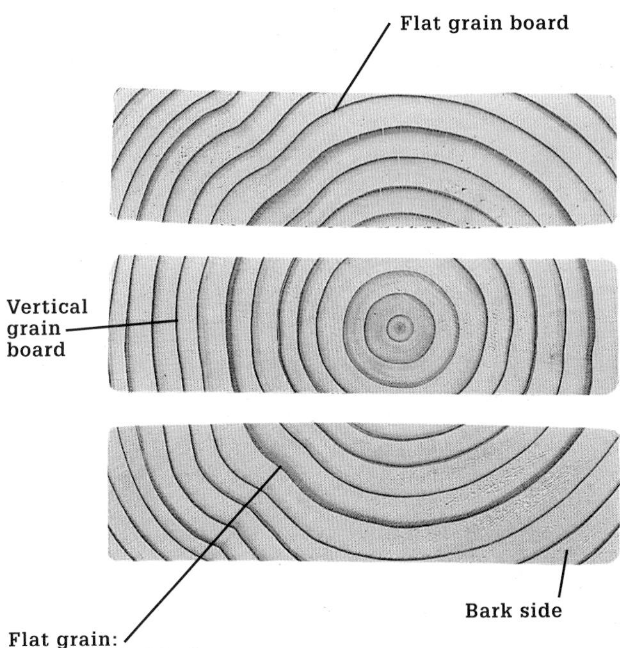

Check end grain of decking boards. Boards with flat grain tend to "cup," and can trap standing water if not installed properly. Research studies indicate that flat grain boards cup toward the bark side (not away from it, as was previously thought in the industry), and they should be installed so the bark side faces down.

Wood Decking

Wood continues to be the most popular choice among decking materials, due in large part to price. Pressure-treated decking remains the least expensive deck option, but other types of hardwoods and softwoods feature unique grain pattern and coloring that makes them consistently desirable. Wood of all types is easy to work with, and most softwoods take stain or paint well, allowing you to alter the appearance almost at will.

The two most popular choices for wood decking are pressure-treated and cedar. Depending on where you live, you may have other options as well. Redwood may still be available if you live on the West Coast, and cypress is common in the South. Redwood, cypress, and cedar are naturally resistant to decay and insects, which makes them excellent choices for decking. You can apply finish if you like, or leave them unfinished and they'll weather to a silvery gray color in a few years. If cost is less important than quality, you might consider covering your deck with mahogany, ipê, or any of several other exotic hardwoods grouped under the term "ironwood"—so-called because their cell structures are so dense the woods will sink in water.

For pressure-treated or cedar decking, you'll have to select a thickness that works for your budget and design. One option is to use 2× lumber. It will span wider joist spacing without flexing, but generally 2× lumber is made from lower-grade material that may contain more natural defects. Another choice is to use 5/4 decking, pronounced "five quarter." Its actual dry thickness is 1 inch and the edges are radiused to help minimize splinters. Often, 5/4 lumber is clearer than 2× lumber, but it's not as stiff. You may need to space your joists more closely with 5/4 decking. Either way, you can commonly find 2× or 5/4 decking in lengths up to 16 or even 20 ft. at most home centers.

Ipê

Cedar

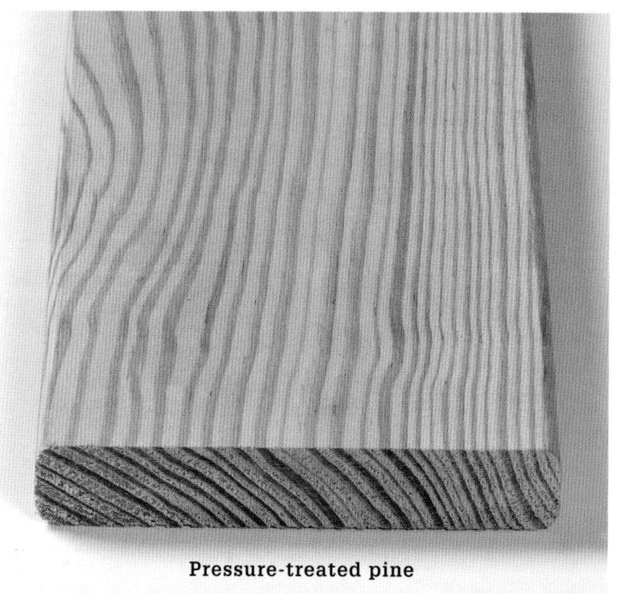

Pressure-treated pine

Wood Decking

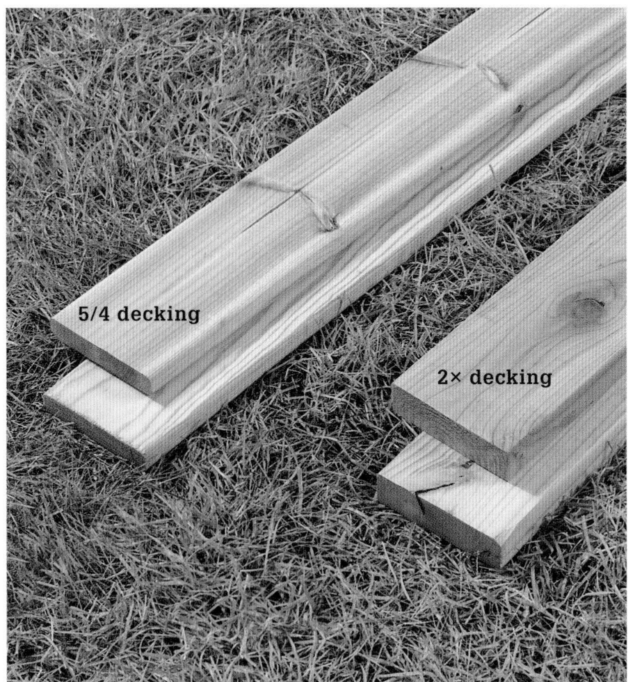

Both 2× and 5/4 lumber are suitable for use as decking. However, 5/4 will generally be of higher quality, and the radiused edges prevent splintering—an important consideration for bare feet or if you have young children.

If you hand-select each of your deck boards, look for pieces with vertical grain pattern (left in photo). They'll be less inclined to cup and warp than flat-grain lumber (right), but the wood tends to be significantly heavier.

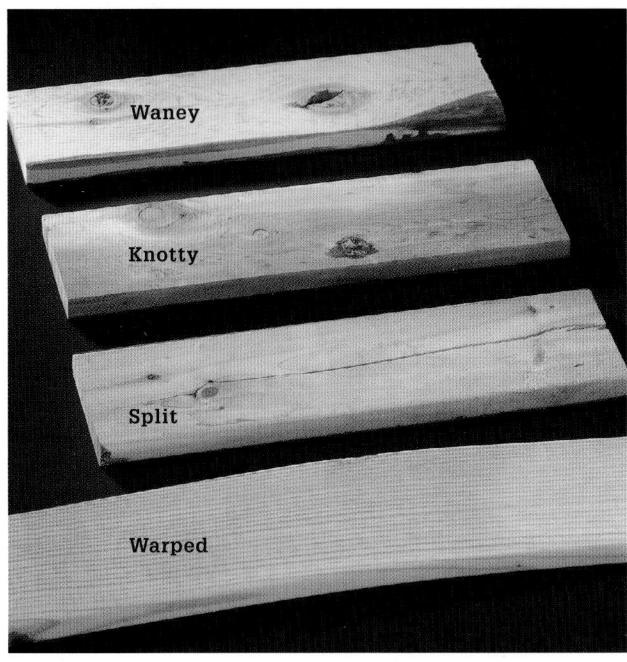

Be picky about the quality of the decking you buy. Natural defects in the wood could make the piece harder to install or deteriorate prematurely. Watch for soft pockets of sap in the wood. Sap will get sticky in warm weather, and the resin can bleed through wood finishes, leaving brown stains.

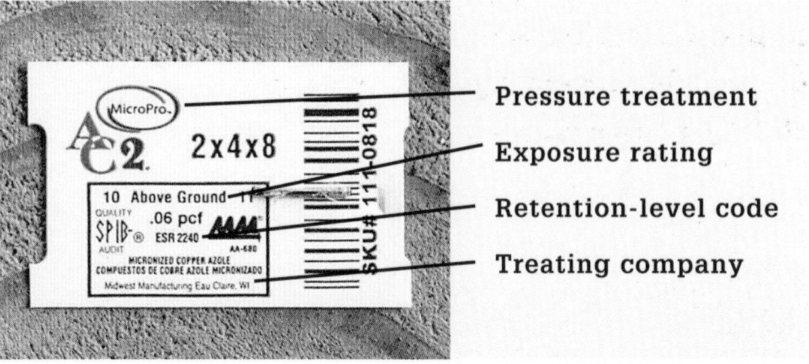

Pressure-treated lumber stamps list the type of preservative and the chemical retention level, as well as the exposure rating and the name and location of the treating company.

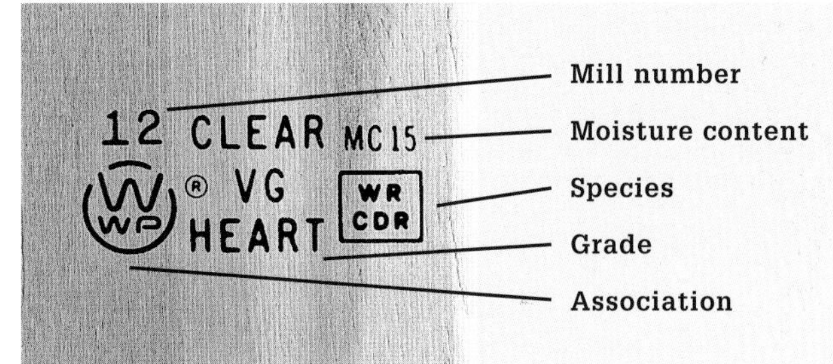

Cedar grade stamps list the mill number, moisture content, species, lumber grade, and membership association. Western red cedar (WRC) or incense cedar (INC) for decks should be heartwood (HEART) with a maximum moisture content of 15% (MC15).

Non-wood Decking

Decking made from non-wood materials such as composite lumber and PVC has taken over a large share of the decking market in recent years. Composite decking has only been around for a few decades, but it's a compelling option to consider for your deck. Most forms of composite decking are made from a blend of post-consumer plastic waste and wood pulp or non-wood fibers. The plastic component—polyethylene or polypropylene—makes the material impervious to rotting, and insects don't like it. Unlike solid wood, it has no grain, so it won't splinter or crack, and there are no knots or natural defects to cut away. Other formulations of synthetic decking contain no wood at all. These are made from polyethylene, PVC, polystyrene, or fiberglass blends. Composite decking comes with impressive warranties, which may last from 10 years to a lifetime, depending on the product. Some warranties are transferable from one homeowner to the next.

When composite lumber first hit the market, it didn't look anything like wood, and color choices were limited. Now, it's available in a range of wood textures and colors. Most products are non-toxic, easy to cut, drill, and fasten, and do not require finishing. Maintenance is usually limited to an occasional cleaning or spot removal. However, composite decking is more flexible than wood, so you may need to use closer joist spacing in your deck design. It's also heavier than wood and generally more expensive.

Composites ▸

Composite materials blend together wood fibers and recycled plastics to create a rigid product that, unlike wood, will not rot, splinter, warp, or crack. Painting or staining is unnecessary. Like wood, these deck boards can be cut to size, using a circular saw with a large-tooth blade.

PVC vinyl and plastic decking materials are shipped in kits that contain everything necessary to install the decking other than the deck screws. The kits are preordered to size, usually in multiples of the combined width of a deck board and the fasteners. The drawback of PVC vinyl decking is that it expands and contracts with freeze/thaw cycles.

Fiberglass reinforced plastic (FRP) decking will last a lifetime. Manufacturers claim that the material is three times as strong as wood and not affected by heat, sunlight, or severe weather. The decking is preordered to size but if necessary, it can be cut using a circular saw with a diamond-tip or masonry blade.

Surface patterns and textures of composite decking range from virtually smooth to intricate wood grain styles. Patterns and textures vary by manufacturer, but many offer varieties that convincingly mimic species of wood.

Composite decking colors cover the spectrum of wood tones, plus grays and white. The color is continuous throughout the material, but exposure to strong, direct sunlight may cause the surface color to fade.

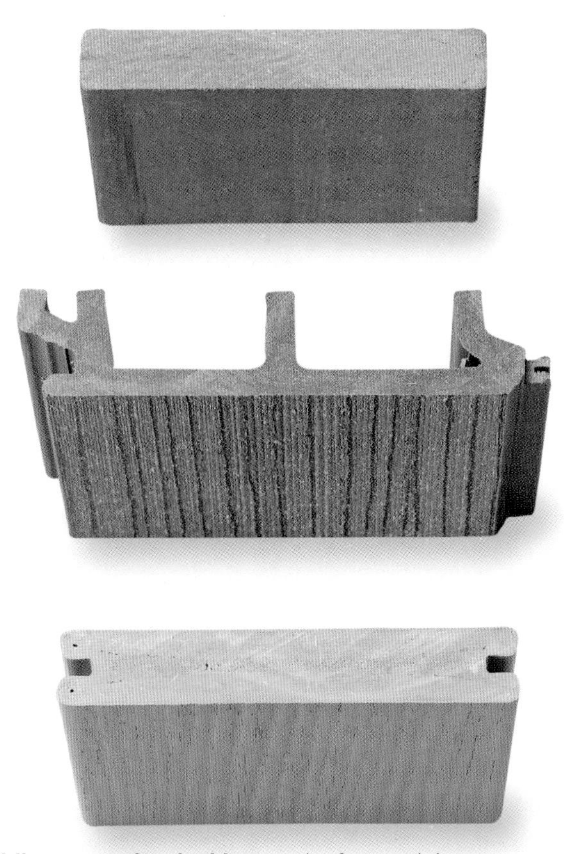

While composite decking can be fastened down conventionally with screws, you may be able to use various edge-fastening systems instead to avoid driving screws through the board faces. For more on these options, see pages 136 to 139.

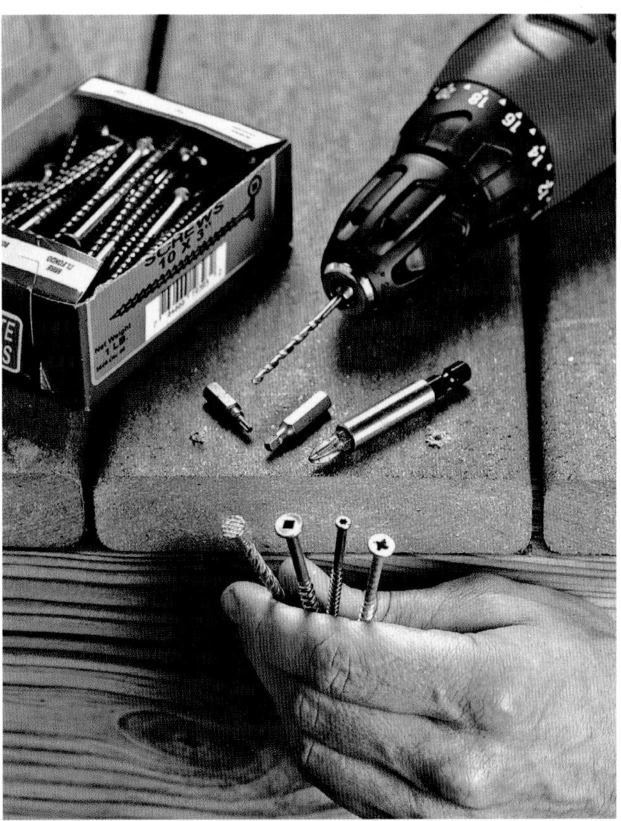

Composite and other non-wood decking often requires special fasteners that are designed to reduce "mushrooming" that occurs when the decking material bulges up around the screwhead. Pilot holes are recommended for some types as well.

Fasteners & Hardware

Certain structural connections of your deck will require the use of lag screws, through bolts, and concrete anchors to withstand the heavy loads and sheer forces applied to a deck. Attaching ledger boards to your home's band joist, fastening beams to posts, or anchoring posts to concrete footings are all areas where you'll need to step up to larger fasteners and anchors. Be sure to use hot-dipped galvanized or stainless steel hardware to prevent rusting or corrosion from pressure-treating chemicals. Building codes require that you install a washer beneath the heads of lag screws or bolts and another washer before attaching nuts. Washers prevent fasteners from tearing through wood and secure hardware under stress.

Another fastening option to consider is high-strength epoxy, applied from a syringe. If you are fastening deck posts or ledger boards to cured concrete, the epoxy will bond a threaded rod permanently in place without needing an additional metal anchor.

Here is an overview of the anchoring fasteners you may need for your project.

Galvanized or stainless steel lag bolts and washers are the correct fasteners for installing ledgers to the band joist of a house. You can also use them for making other wood-to-wood connections.

Anchoring Fasteners

Use ½"-diameter or larger through bolts, washers, and nuts for fastening beams to posts or railing posts to joists. They should be galvanized or made of stainless steel for corrosion resistance.

J-bolts, embedded in the wet concrete of deck footings, provide a secure connection for attaching concrete footings to metal connecting hardware.

Wedge or sleeve anchors draw a wedge through a hollow sleeve, expanding it to form a tight fit in solid concrete. A nut and threaded end hold the ledger boards in place.

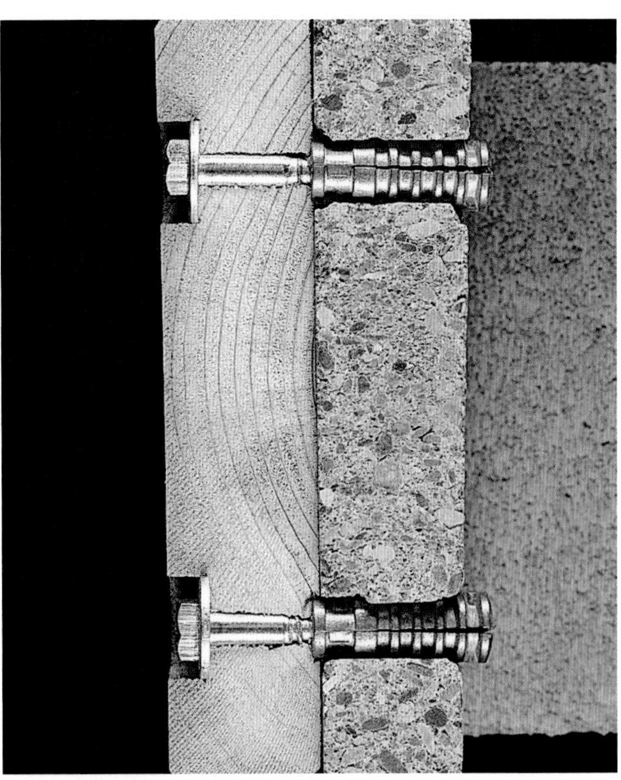

Soft metal shield anchors expand when lag screws are driven into them. They make suitable connections in either solid concrete or hollow block foundations.

A bolt driven through the foundation from the inside can be fitted with a washer and bolt to secure the ledger.

High strength epoxy and threaded rod are good options for attaching metal connecting hardware to concrete footings.

Metal Connecting Hardware

Sheet-metal connecting hardware comes in assorted shapes and styles. It is used to create strong wood-to-wood or wood-to-concrete joints quickly and easily. For instance, metal post anchors not only provide a simple way to attach posts and footings, they also create space between the two surfaces so post ends stay dry. Joist hangers are a fast way to hang long, heavy joists accurately. Post beam caps, T-straps, and angled joist hangers are ideal solutions for building stacked joints or when space doesn't allow you access to drive screws or nails from behind the joint.

Make sure to buy hot-dipped galvanized or stainless steel connecting hardware. Some styles are designed for interior use only and do not have adequate corrosion protection. The product label should identify whether or not the hardware is suitable for pressure-treated wood and outdoor use. Use joist hanger nails made from the same material as the hardware.

Deck post ties fasten stair or railing posts to stringers or joists without through bolts. Hardware is manufactured in 2 × 4 and 4 × 4 size options.

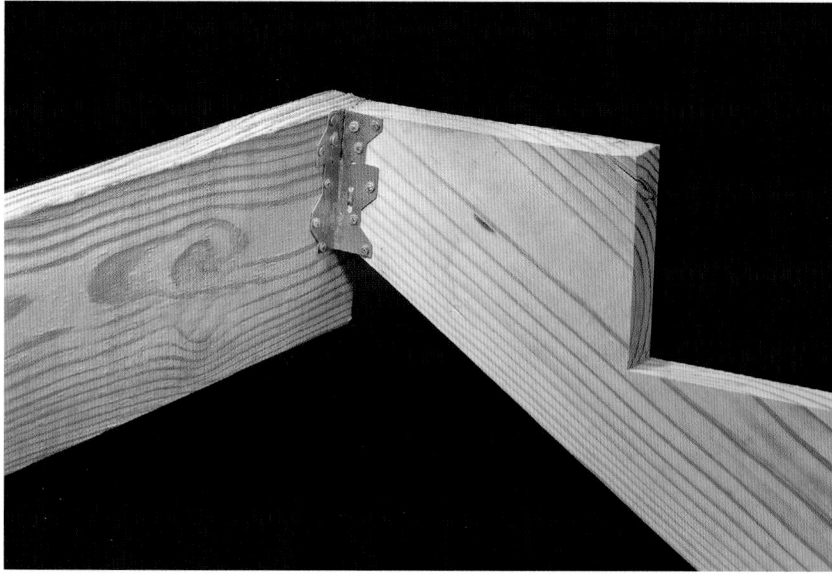

Framing anchors can be used to fasten rim joists together at corners or make other right-angle attachments, such as stair stringers to rim joists.

Hanger Hardware for Decks

Post anchors hold deck posts in place, and raise the base of the posts to help prevent water from entering the end grain of the post.

Angle brackets help reinforce header and outside joists. Angle brackets are also used to attach stair stringers to the deck.

Joist hangers are used to attach joists to the ledger and header joist. Double hangers are used when decking patterns require a double-width joist.

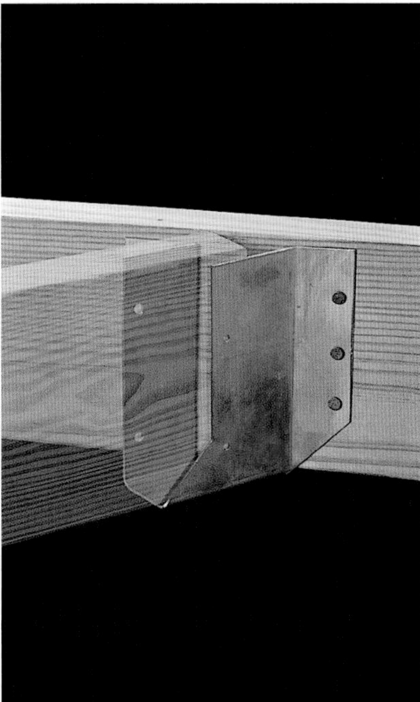

Angled joist hangers are used to frame decks that have unusual angles or decking patterns.

Stair cleats support the treads of deck steps. Cleats are attached to stair stringers with ¼ × 1¼" galvanized lag screws.

(continued)

Post-beam caps secure beams on top of posts and are available in one-piece or adjustable styles.

H-fit rafter ties attach 2× joists or rafters to the top of a beam between beam ends.

Seismic ties attach 2× joists or rafters to the top of a beam at its ends.

Skewable joist hangers attach 2× lumber, such as stair stringers, to the face of framing at an adjustable angle.

Skewable angle brackets reinforce framing connections at angles other than 90 degrees or at beam ends where 45-degree joist hangers won't fit.

Direct-bearing footing connectors attach beams directly to footings on low profile decks.

T-straps reinforce the connection between beam and post, particularly on long beams requiring spliced construction. Local building codes may also allow their use in place of post caps.

Strapping plates, also known as nailing plates or mending plates, are useful for a variety of reinforcement applications.

Screws & Nails

When you attach the beams and joists of your deck, and probably the decking as well, you'll need a collection of screws and/or nails to get these jobs done. It may not seem like screw and nail technology would ever change all that much, but in fact there are many new products available for making these essential connections. If you build your deck from pressure-treated lumber, be sure to use stainless, hot-dipped galvanized, or specially coated fasteners that are approved for use with the more corrosive ACQ and CBA wood preservatives. Spiral or ring-shank nails will offer better holding power than smooth nails. Use screws with auger tips and self-drilling heads to avoid drilling pilot holes. Some screws are specially designed for installing composite decking. They have a variable thread pattern that keeps the heads from mushrooming the surrounding material when driven flush.

If you are building a large deck, consider using a pneumatic nailer with collated nails instead of hand nailing. Collated screws are a faster way to lay deck boards than driving each screw individually. Here's an overview of your fastener options.

Whether you are fastening framing together or installing deck boards, your screw options include stainless steel or galvanized. You can also buy screws with colored coatings formulated to resist corrosion from pressure-treated wood. Stainless or coated screws will prevent black staining that can occur on cedar.

Screws & Nails for Decks

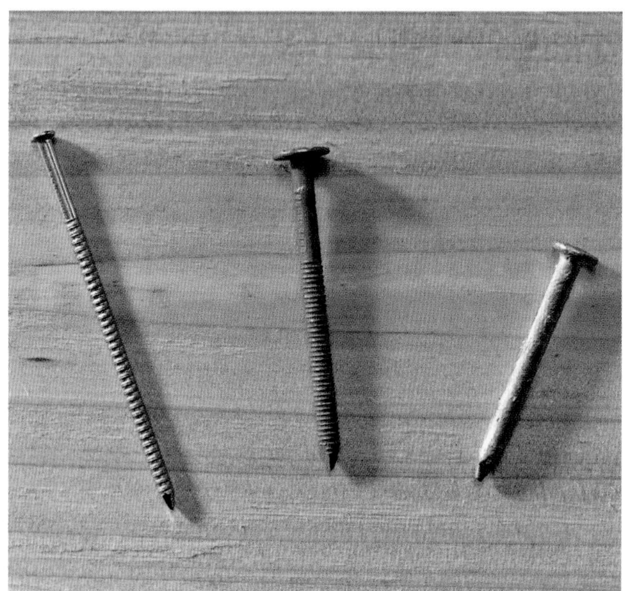

Use stainless steel or hot-dipped galvanized framing nails to assemble beams and joists. Install metal connector hardware with 8d or 10d hot-dipped galvanized metal connector nails.

For large deck projects, galvanized pneumatic nails or coated, collated screws are a faster way to fasten framing and decking than driving each nail or screw by hand.

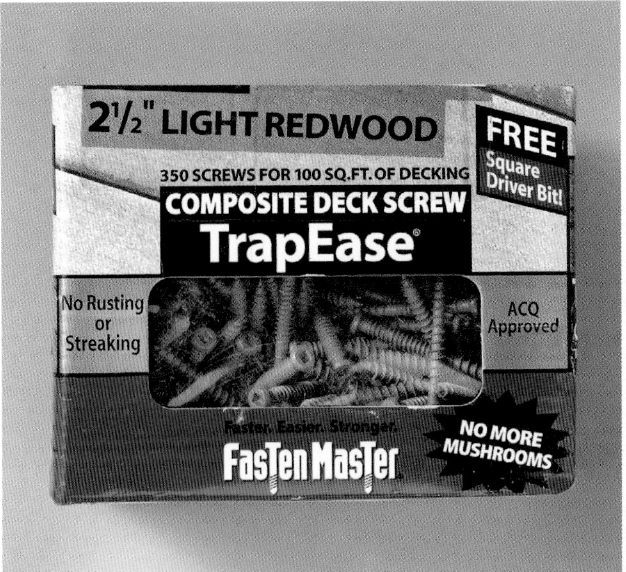

Make sure your fasteners will resist the corrosive effects of today's pressure-treating chemicals. Fastener manufacturers will usually provide this information on the product label.

Many composite decking manufacturers supply special screw types that hold the material in place better than ordinary screws would, and that are colored to match the decking boards.

If you'd prefer not to see screwheads in your decking but still want to drive them from the surface, you can buy screws with snap-off heads. A special tool breaks the head off after the screw is driven. The resulting hole is much smaller than a screwhead.

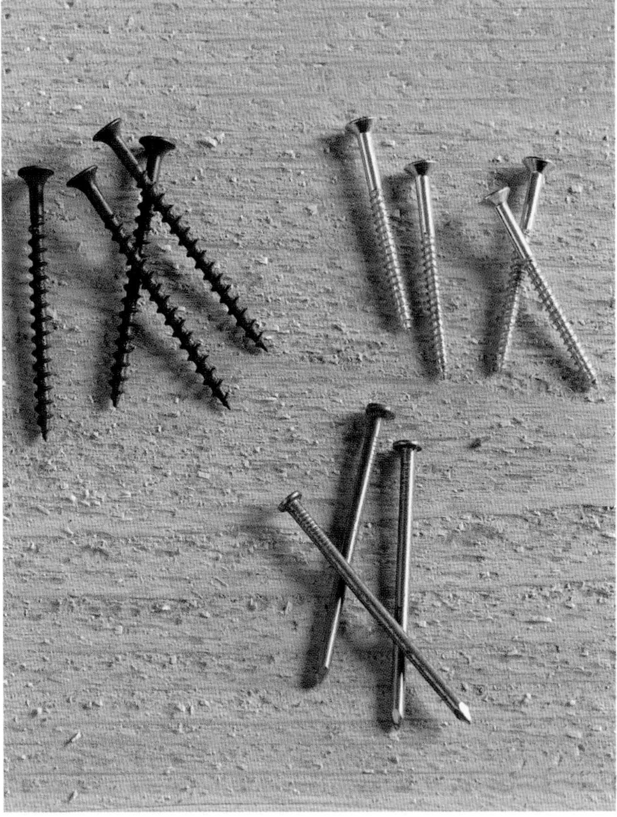

Choose your nails and screws carefully. Screws with "bright" or black-oxide coatings and uncoated nails will not stand up to exterior use or pressure-treating chemicals. Fasteners are as crucial to your deck's long-term durability as the quality of the framing lumber or decking.

Flashing

Building codes require that a deck's ledger board be attached directly to wall sheathing and house framing, and that a corrosion-resistant flashing material be used at any junction between a deck ledger and a house. If your home is sided, you'll need to remove the siding in the ledger board area before attaching the ledger to the house. Be sure to install 15# or 30# building paper or self-sealing, adhesive backed membrane behind the ledger to prevent moisture damage. Rotting in the area behind the ledger is one of the leading causes of premature deck deterioration. Flashing is particularly important if there's no housewrap behind the siding. Once the ledger is in place, cap it with a piece of galvanized Z-flashing, tucked behind the siding, for added protection.

Although building codes don't require it, you may also want to wrap the tops of beams and posts with self-sealing membrane to keep these areas dry and rot-free. Ledger flashing, self-sealing membrane, and building paper are available at most home centers and lumberyards. They're little details that can make a big difference to the longevity of your deck.

Building felt, also called building paper, is used behind house siding materials. Use it to replace felt damaged during a ledger installation. Ledger flashing, or Z-flashing, prevents moisture damage behind the deck ledger. Self-sealing membrane provides extra protection from moisture in damp climates or in areas where there is snow accumulation. It can be used over flashing or on top of beams and posts (see below left), and it self-seals around nails or screws that pierce it.

To apply self-sealing membrane, cut a piece to size and position it over the application area. Starting at one end, begin removing the thin plastic backing that protects the adhesive. Firmly press the membrane in place as you remove the backing, working along the installation area. To install long pieces of membrane, enlist the aid of a helper.

Install self-sealing membrane behind the ledger as extra protection from moisture. Apply the membrane over the house wrap or building felt, using the same method shown at left.

Footings

Footings, which are also called piers, anchor a deck to the ground and create a stable foundation for the posts. They transfer the weight of the deck into the soil and prevent it from heaving upward in climates where the ground freezes. Generally, footings are made from long, hollow tubes of fiber-reinforced paper in several diameters. Once a tube footing is set into the ground below the frostline, you backfill around the outside with soil, tamp it down firmly, and fill with concrete. Metal connective hardware imbedded in the concrete will attach the footings permanently to the deck posts.

For soils that have a poor bearing capacity, or if you are building a particularly large deck, you can also buy plastic footing tubes with flared bases that bear heavier loads. Or, you can attach a flared footing to the bottom of a conventional tube. For low-profile decks that aren't attached to a house, you may be able to use pre-cast concrete footings instead of buried piers. These footings simply rest on the surface of the soil.

Lumberyards and building centers will stock hollow footing forms in various diameters. The diameter you need will depend on the size and weight of your deck. Your building official will help you determine the correct size when you apply for a building permit.

Pre-cast concrete footings are usually acceptable for building low-profile, freestanding decks. Notches on top of the pier are designed to hold joists without fasteners or other hardware.

When building heavy decks or placing footings in unstable, loose soil, you may need to use piers with flared footings. Some styles are molded in one piece, or you can attach a flared footing to a conventional footing form with screws.

Specialty Tools

A big deck project can be labor-intensive and time consuming. Certain specialized tools, such as a power auger, hammer drill, or collated screw gun, can speed tasks along and save you some of the sweat equity involved. But these tools can be expensive, and they're hard to justify buying unless you plan to use them often. Renting them may be a better option. A wide assortment of tools, including the ones on these pages, are available at rental centers at a reasonable cost. Renting gives you an opportunity to try a tool that you're considering buying or use and return a tool you would never consider buying.

A collated screwgun speeds up the process of fastening decking to joists, and it can save wear and tear on your knees. These tools accept strips of exterior screws, and an advancing mechanism allows you to drive them one after the next without stopping. An adjustable clutch prevents the screws from being overdriven.

A laser level shines a continuous level line in a 360° plane. It's useful for striking off uniform post heights without measuring. Deck platforms should be flat and level in all directions. Posts should be plumb and located squarely on their footings. In order to achieve level and plumb, you'll probably need more than a carpenter's level in your tool collection. Consider buying a post speed level (top) and a laser level. Post-speed levels fasten in place with a rubber band and have three spirit levels to help you adjust posts quickly and accurately. They're handy for setting both deck and fence posts.

Hammer drills combine the usual rotary action with forward motion, similar to a tiny jackhammer. They make it much easier to drill large pilot holes in concrete or block walls for installing ledger board anchors.

If you have more than a few holes to dig for your deck footings, especially when they're deep, rent a power auger. Both one-person and two-person models are available. A gas-powered engine drives the auger to excavate these holes quickly.

Cordless impact drivers can make quick work of laborious tasks like driving lag screws. Because they have a percussive motion as well as high-torque spinning motion, they leverage two forces at once. They are excellent for driving lag screws as well as deck screws.

Tools for straightening deck boards are relatively inexpensive and can quickly pay for themselves by allowing you to install badly bowed boards.

BLACK&DECKER

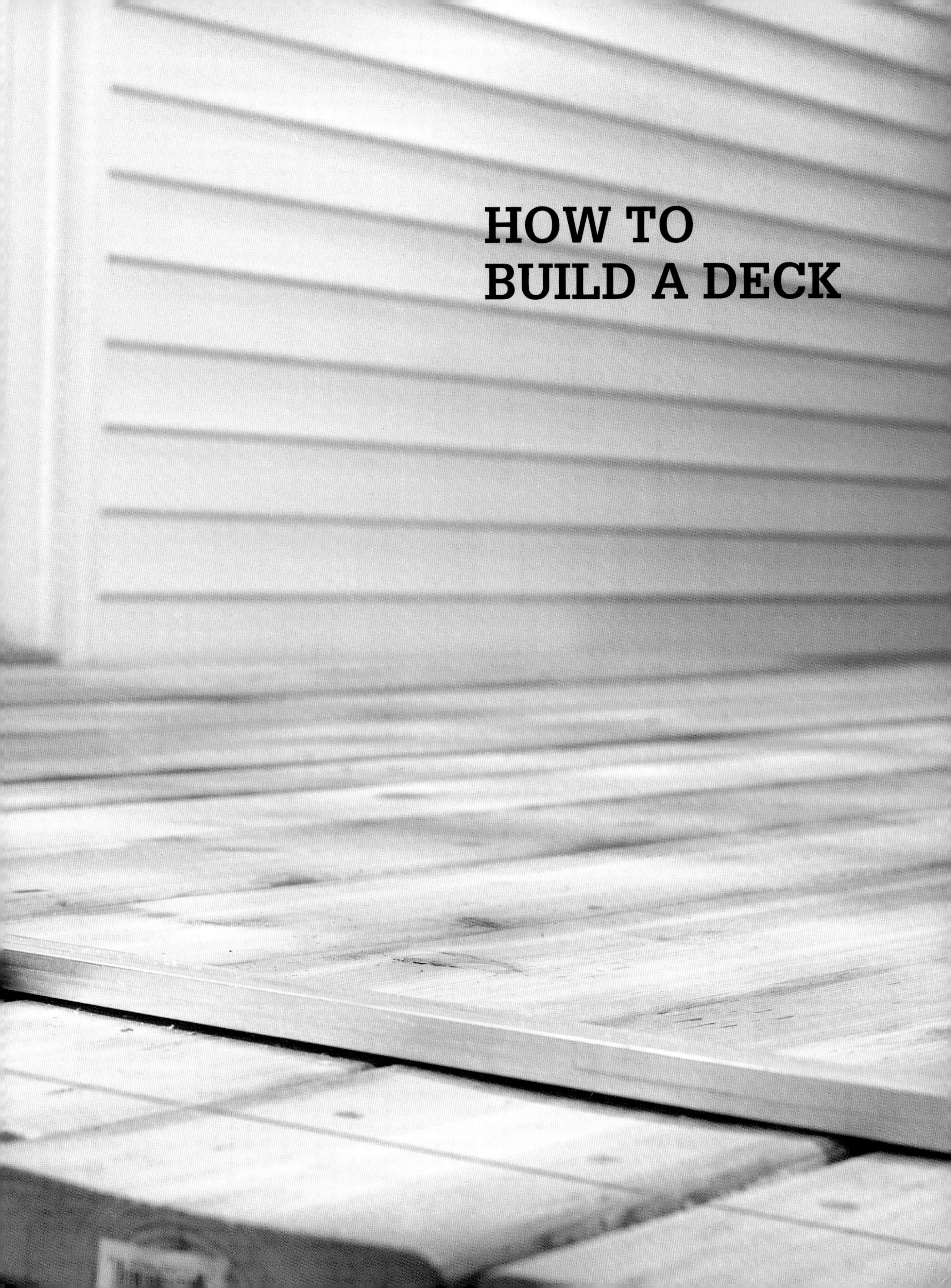

HOW TO BUILD A DECK

Building Decks: A Step-by-step Overview

Deck-building is a project you'll tackle in stages, no matter what design you choose. Before you begin construction, review the photos on these two pages. They outline the basic procedure you'll want to follow when building your deck. The chapters to follow will explore each of these stages extensively.

Be sure to gather your tools and materials before you begin the project, and arrange to have a helper available for the more difficult stages. Check with local utilities for the location of underground electrical, telephone, or water lines before digging the footings. Apply for a building permit, where required, and make sure a building inspector has approved the deck design before beginning work.

The time it takes to build a deck depends on the size and complexity of the design as well as your building skills. If you're comfortable using tools and start with thorough, accurate plans, you should be able to complete a single-level deck in a few weekends.

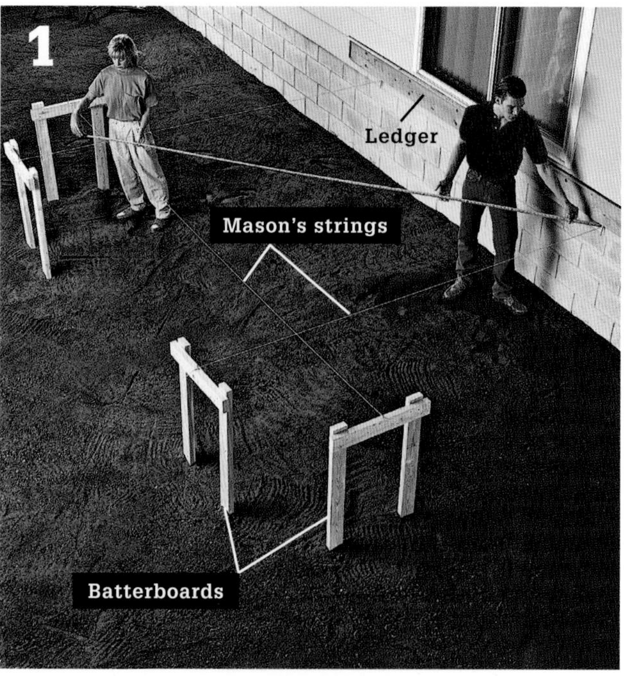

Install a ledger to anchor the deck to the house and to serve as reference for laying out footings (pages 70 to 75). Use batterboards and mason's strings to locate footings, and check for square by measuring diagonals (page 75).

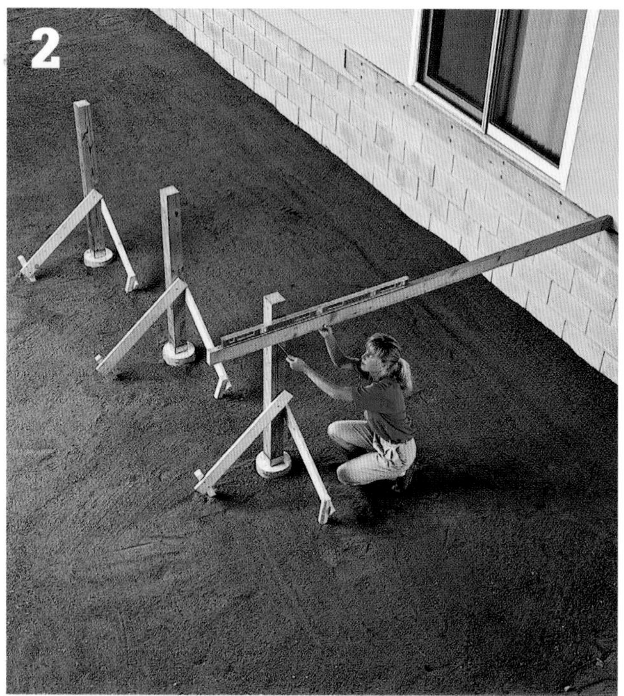

Pour concrete post footings (pages 76 to 79), and install metal post anchors (pages 81 to 83). Set and brace the posts, attach them to the post anchors, and mark posts to show where the beam will be attached (page 85).

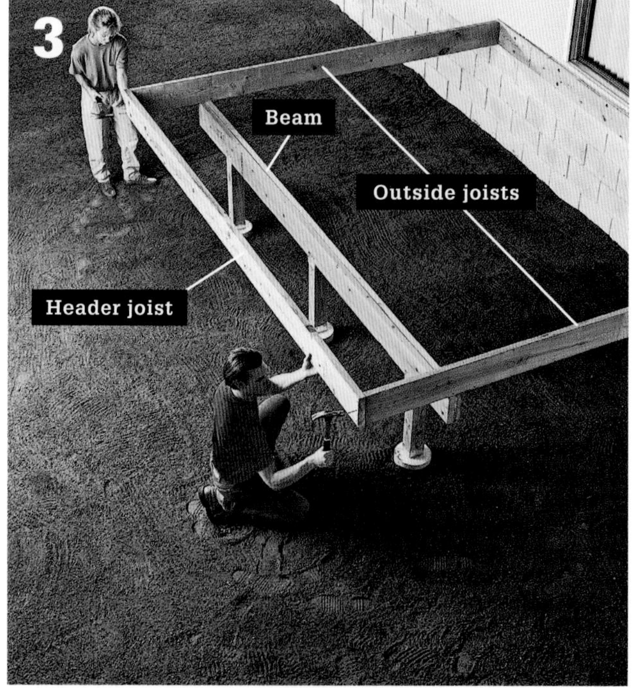

Fasten the beam to the posts (pages 86 to 89). Install the outside joists and header joist using galvanized nails (page 92).

Install metal joist hangers on the ledger and header joist, then hang the remaining joists (pages 90 to 95). Most decking patterns require joists that are spaced 16" on center.

Lay decking boards, and trim them with a circular saw (pages 128 to 139). If desired for appearance, cover pressure-treated header and outside joists with redwood or cedar facing boards (page 130).

Build the deck stairs. Stairs provide access to the deck and establish traffic patterns.

Install a railing around the deck and stairway (page 160). A railing adds a decorative touch and may be required on any deck that is more than 30" above the ground. If desired, finish the underside of the deck (page 210).

Structural Support

Regardless of the deck design you choose, every permanent deck has a fundamentally similar structure. Posts and footings anchored in the ground, working in tandem with a ledger board fastened to the house, support a framework of beams and joists that form a deck's undercarriage. Decking, railings, and steps are added to this platform to make it accessible and safe. There are proven techniques for installing each of these structural elements, and that's what you'll learn in this chapter. Once you get comfortable with these skills, you'll be able to apply them to any of the deck projects featured in this book—or create your own unique deck plans.

The end of the chapter will also show you important variations to basic techniques you may need to apply to your project, depending on the size, height, or location of your new deck or the topography of your yard.

In this chapter:

- Installing a Ledger
- Locating Post Footings
- Digging & Pouring Footings
- Installing Posts
- Installing Beams
- Hanging Joists
- Framing Low-profile Decks
- Framing Multi-level Decks
- Framing Decks on Steep Slopes
- Working with Angles
- Creating Curves
- Framing for Insets

Installing a Ledger

The first step in building an attached deck is to fasten the ledger to the house. The ledger anchors the deck and establishes a reference point for building the deck square and level. The ledger also supports one end of all the deck joists, so it must be attached securely to the framing members of the house.

If your deck's ledger is made from pressure-treated lumber, make sure to use hot-dipped, galvanized lag screws and washers to attach it to the house. Ordinary zinc-coated hardware will corrode and eventually fail if placed in contact with ACQ pressure-treating chemicals. For additional strength on large decks—and where the framing structure will permit it—use through bolts instead of lag screws, tightening down with a washer and nut on the opposite side.

Install the ledger so that the surface of the decking boards will be 1" below the indoor floor level. This height difference prevents rainwater or melted snow from seeping into the house.

Tools & Materials ▸

Pencil
Level
Circular saw with carbide blade
Chisel
Hammer
Metal snips
Caulk gun
Drill and bits (3/8" twist, 1 3/8" spade, 1/2" and 5/8–3/4" masonry)
Ratchet wrench
Awl
Rubber mallet
Pressure-treated lumber
Galvanized flashing
8d galvanized common nails
Silicone caulk
1/2 × 4" lag screws and 1 3/8" washers
Masonry anchors for 1/2" lag screws (for masonry walls)
2 × 4s for braces

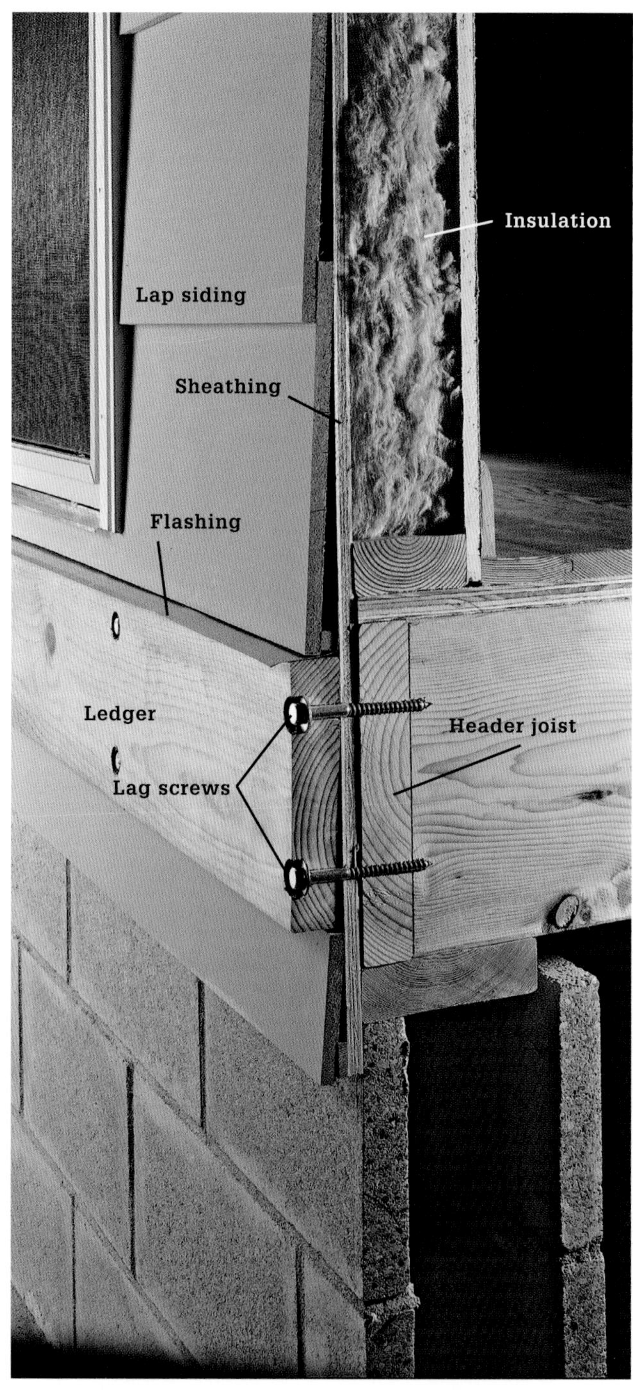

A deck ledger (shown in cross section) is usually made of pressure-treated lumber. Lap siding is cut away to expose sheathing and to provide a flat surface for attaching the ledger. Galvanized flashing tucked under siding prevents moisture damage to wood. Countersunk 1/2 × 4" lag screws hold ledger to header joist inside house. If there is access to the space behind the header joist, such as in an unfinished basement, attach the ledger with carriage bolts, washers, and nuts.

How to Attach a Ledger to Lap Siding

Draw an outline showing where the deck will fit against the house, using a level as a guide. Include the thickness of the outside joists and any decorative facing boards that will be installed.

Cut out the siding along the outline, using a circular saw. Set the blade depth to the same thickness as the siding, so that the blade does not cut into the sheathing.

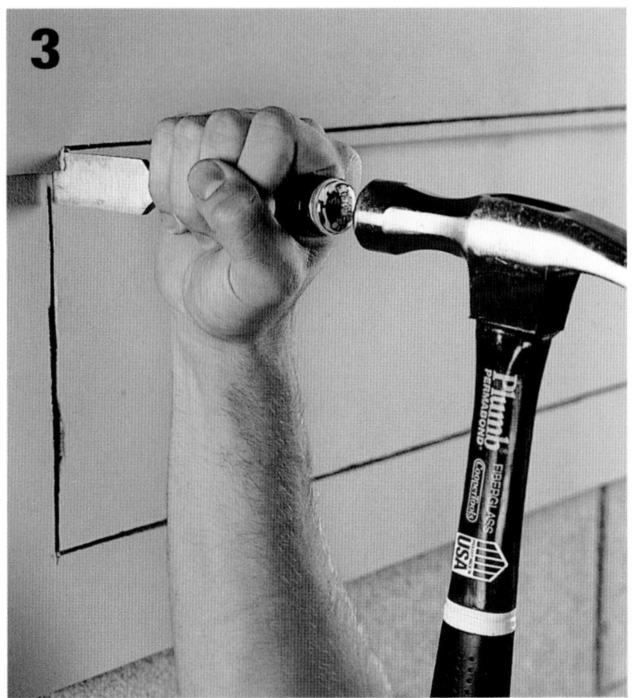

Use a chisel or oscillating saw to finish the cutout where the circular saw blade does not reach. Hold the chisel with the bevel-side in.

Measure and cut the ledger from pressure-treated lumber. Remember that the ledger will be shorter than the overall length of the cutout.

(continued)

Install the self-adhesive moisture barrier and cut galvanized flashing to match the length of the cutout, using metal snips. Slide the flashing up under the siding. Do not nail the flashing in place.

Center the ledger in the cutout, underneath the flashing. Brace in position, and tack the ledger into place with 8d galvanized nails. Apply a thick bead of silicone caulk to the space between the siding and flashing.

Drill pairs of ⅜" pilot holes through the ledger and sheathing, and into the house joist. Space the holes every 2 feet.

Counterbore each pilot hole to ½" depth, using a 1⅜" spade bit.

Attach the ledger to wall with ½ × 4" lag screws and washers, using a ratchet wrench or impact driver.

Seal lag screw heads with silicone caulk. Seal the crack between the wall and the sides and bottom of the ledger.

How to Attach a Ledger to Masonry

Measure and cut the ledger. The ledger will be shorter than the overall length of the outline. Drill pairs of pilot holes every 2 feet along the ledger. Counterbore each hole ½" deep, using a 1⅜" spade bit.

Draw an outline of the deck on the wall, using a level as a guide. Center the ledger in the outline, and brace in position. Mark the pilot-hole locations on the wall, using an awl or nail. Remove the ledger.

(continued)

Drill anchor holes 3" deep into the wall, using a masonry bit large enough for the anchors.

Drive lead masonry anchors for ½" lag screws into the holes, using a rubber mallet.

Attach the ledger to the wall with ½ × 4" lag screws and washers, using a ratchet wrench or impact driver. Tighten screws firmly, but do not overtighten.

Seal the cracks between the wall and ledger with silicone caulk. Also seal the lag screw heads.

How to Attach a Ledger to Stucco

Draw the outline of the deck on the wall, using a level as a guide. Measure and cut the ledger, and drill pilot holes. Brace the ledger against the wall, and mark hole locations, using a nail or awl.

Remove the ledger. Drill pilot holes through the stucco layer of the wall, using a ½" masonry bit.

Extend each pilot hole through the sheathing and into the header joist, using a ⅜" bit. Reposition the ledger and brace it in place.

Attach the ledger to the wall with ½ × 4" lag screws and washers, using a ratchet wrench. Seal the lag screw heads and the cracks between the wall and ledger with silicone caulk.

How to Attach a Ledger to Metal or Vinyl Siding

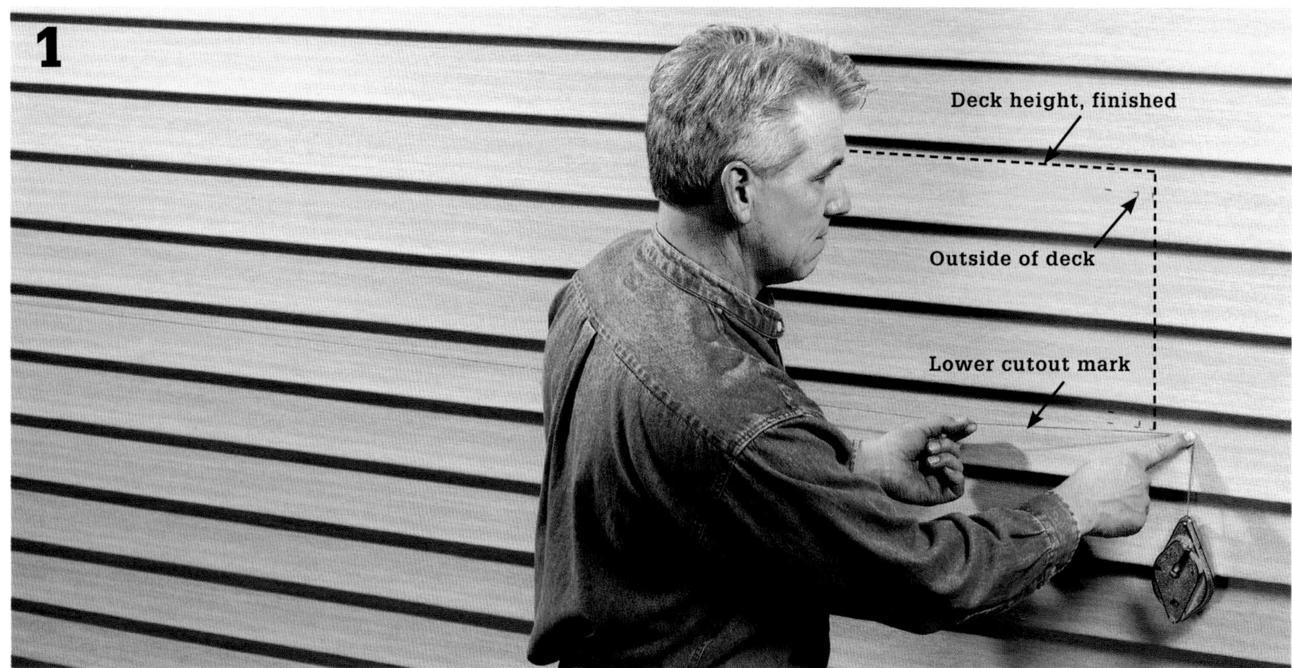

Mark the length of the ledger location, adding 1½" at each end to allow for the rim joists that will be installed later. Also allow for fascia board thickness if it will be added, and create space for metal rim-joist hangers. Then mark the top and bottom edges of the ledger at both ends of its location. Snap lines for the ledger position between the marks. Check the lines for level and adjust as necessary. You may be able to use the siding edges to help determine the ledger location, but only after checking to see if the edges are level. Don't assume siding is installed level.

Set the circular saw blade depth to cut through the siding. Use a metal cutting blade for metal siding; a 40-tooth carbide blade works well on vinyl siding. Cut on the outside of the lines along the top and sides of the ledger location, stopping the blade when it reaches a corner.

Snap a new level line ½" above the bottom line and make your final cut along this line. This leaves a small lip of siding that will fit under the ledger.

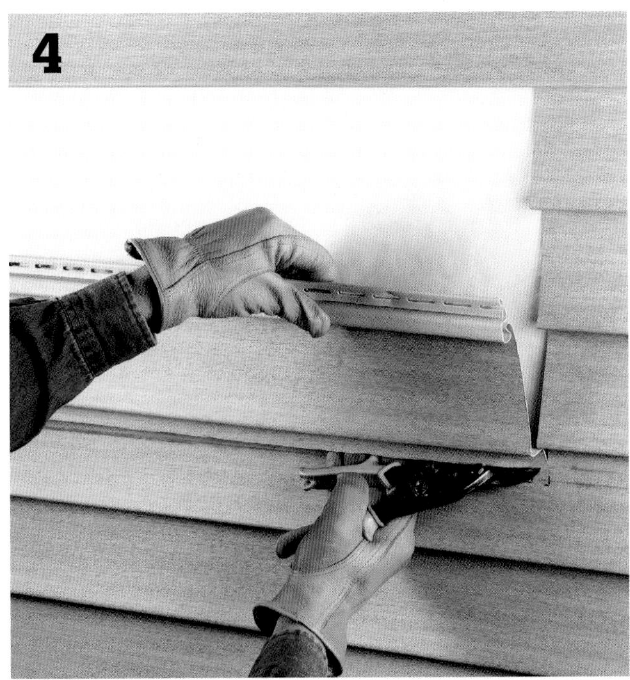

Complete the cuts in the corners, using tin snips on metal siding or a utility knife on vinyl siding. An oscillating saw also may be used.

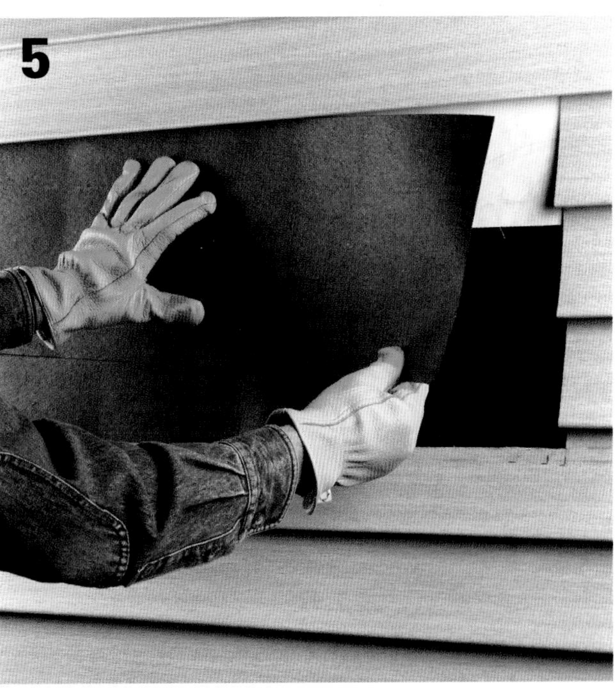

Insert building felt underneath the siding and over the existing felt that has been damaged by the cuts. It is easiest to cut and install two long strips. Cut and insert the first strip so it is underneath the siding at the ends and bottom edge of the cutout and attach it with staples. Cut and insert the second strip so it is underneath the siding at the ends and top edge of the cutout, so that it overlaps the first strip by at least 3".

Cut and insert galvanized flashing (also called Z-flashing) underneath the full length of the top edge of the cutout. Do not use fasteners; pressure will hold the flashing in place until the ledger is installed.

Cut and install the ledger board (see page 62).

Locating Post Footings

Establish the exact locations of all concrete footings by stretching mason's strings across the site. Use the ledger board as a starting point. These perpendicular layout strings will be used to locate holes for concrete footings and to position metal post anchors on the finished footings. Anchor the layout strings with temporary 2 × 4 supports, often called batterboards. You may want to leave the batterboards in place until after the footings are dug. That way, you can use the strings to accurately locate the J-bolts in the concrete.

Tools & Materials ▸

Tape measure
Felt-tipped pen
Circular saw
Screwgun
Framing square
Masonry hammer
Claw hammer
Line level
Plumb bob
2 × 4s
10d nails
2½" drywall screws
Mason's strings
Masking tape

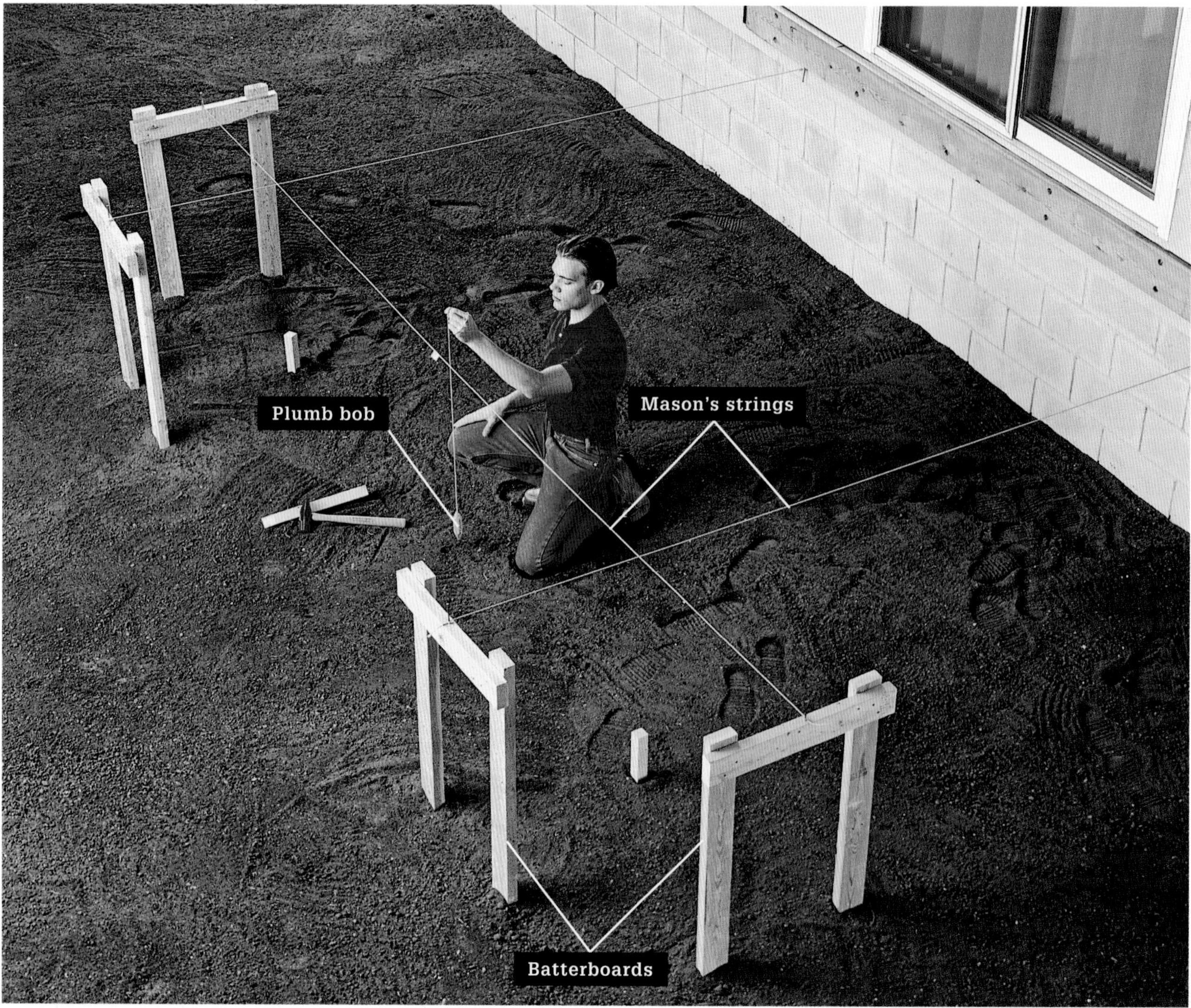

Mason's strings stretched between the ledger and the batterboards are used to position footings for deck posts. Use a plumb bob and stakes to mark the ground at the exact centerpoints of footings.

How to Locate Post Footings

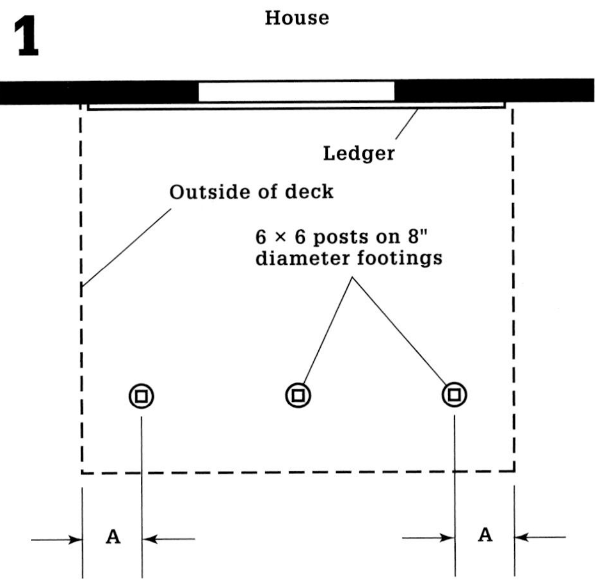

Use your design plan to find distance (A). Measure from the side of the deck to the center of each outside post. Use your elevation drawings to find the height of each deck post.

Cut 2 × 4 stakes for batterboards, each about 8" longer than post height. Trim one end of each stake to a point, using a circular saw. Cut 2 × 4 crosspieces, each about 2 ft. long.

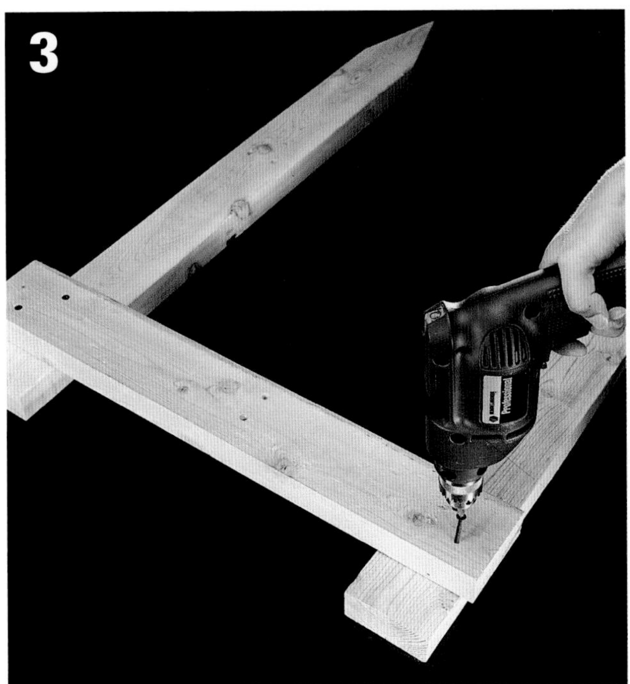

Assemble batterboards by attaching crosspieces to stakes with 2½" wallboard screws. Crosspieces should be about 2" below the tops of the stakes.

Transfer measurement A (step 1) to the ledger, and mark reference points at each end of the ledger. String lines will be stretched from these points on the ledger. When measuring, remember to allow for outside joists and facing that will be butted to the ends of the ledger.

(continued)

Drive a batterboard 6" into the ground, about 2 ft. past the post location. The crosspiece of the batterboard should be parallel to the ledger.

Drive a 10d nail into the bottom of the ledger at the reference point (step 4). Attach a mason's string to the nail.

Extend the mason's string so that it is taut and perpendicular to the ledger. Use a framing square as a guide. Secure the string temporarily by wrapping it several times around the batterboard.

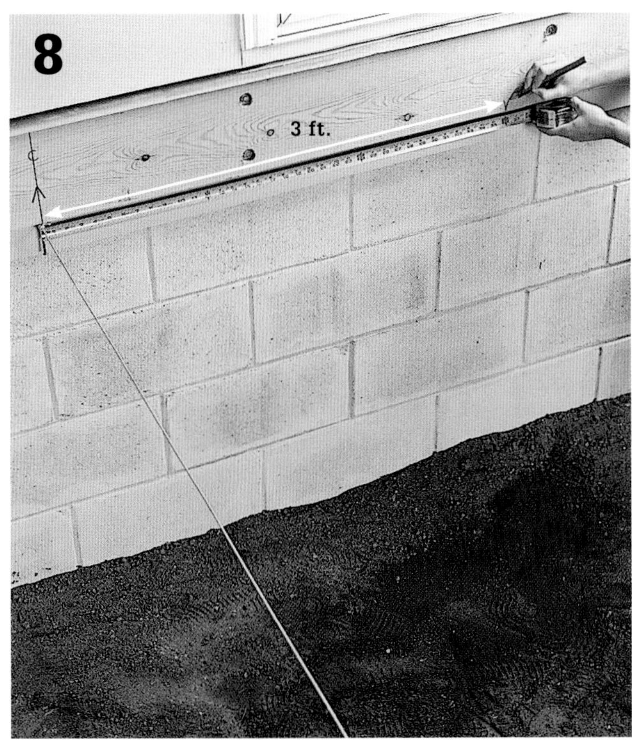

Check the mason's string for square using a "3-4-5 carpenter's triangle." First, measure along the ledger 3 ft. from the mason's string and mark a point, using a felt-tipped pen.

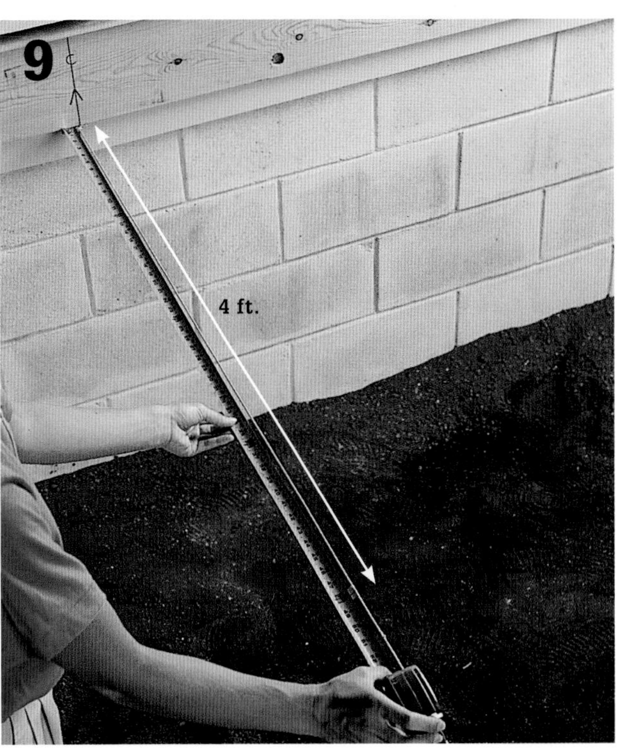

Measure the mason's string 4 ft. from the edge of the ledger, and mark with masking tape.

Measure the distance between the marks. If the string is perpendicular to the ledger, the distance will be exactly 5 ft. If necessary, move the string left or right on the batterboard until the distance between the marks is 5 ft.

Drive a 10d nail into the top of the batterboard at the string location. Leave about 2" of nail exposed. Tie the string to the nail.

(continued)

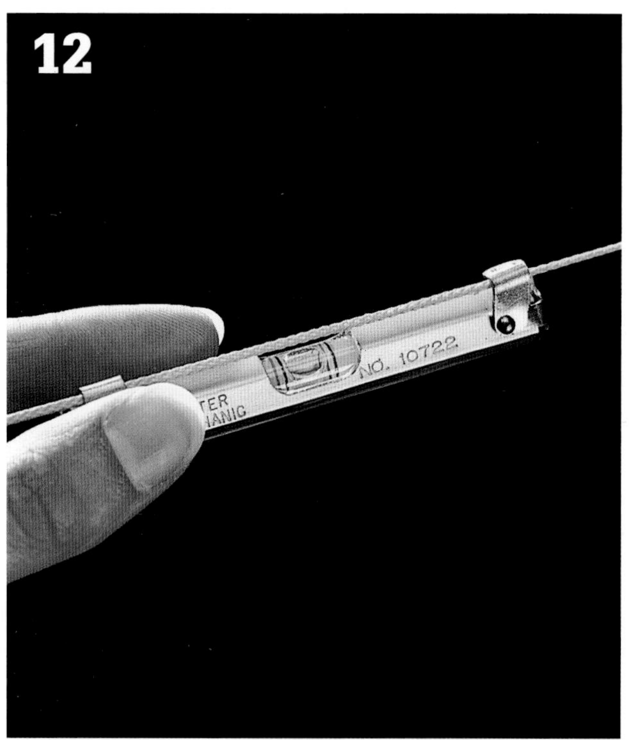

Hang a line level on the mason's string. Raise or lower the string until it is level. Locate the other outside post footing, repeating steps 5 to 12.

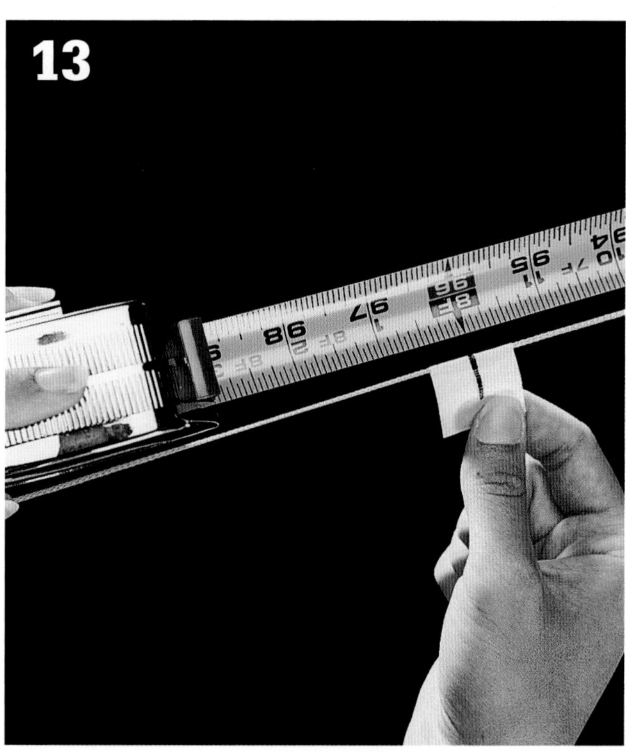

Measure along the mason's strings from the ledger to find the centerpoint of the posts. Mark the centerpoints on the strings, using masking tape.

Drive additional batterboards into the ground, about 2 ft. outside of the mason's strings and lined up with the post centerpoint marks (step 13).

Align a third cross string with the centerpoint marks on the first strings. Drive 10d nails in new batterboards, and tie off the cross strings on the nails. The cross string should be close to, but not touching, the first strings.

Check the strings for square by measuring distances A-B and C-D. Measure the diagonals A-D and B-C from the edge of the ledger to the opposite corners. If the strings are square, measurement A-B will be the same as C-D, and diagonal A-D will be the same as B-C. If necessary, adjust the strings on the batterboards until they are square.

Measure along the cross string and mark the centerpoints of any posts that will be installed between the outside posts.

Use a plumb bob to mark the post centerpoints on the ground, directly under the marks on the mason's strings. Drive a stake into the ground at each point. Remove the mason's strings before digging the footings.

Digging & Pouring Footings

Concrete footings hold deck posts in place and support the weight of the deck. Check local codes to determine the size and depth of footings required for your area. In cold climates, footings must be deeper than the soil frost line.

To help protect posts from water damage, footings are generally poured so that they are at least 2" above ground level. You can create footings by pouring concrete directly into a triangular hole with a form on top to create the aboveground portion, or turn to the more common solution of a tube-shaped form that allows you to pour the post you need quickly and easily. Mix your own cement to fill the form by combining Portland cement, sand, gravel, and water. You can also use premixed concrete, which is often a simpler solution.

As an alternative to inserting J-bolts into wet concrete, you can use masonry anchors, metal post brackets with pins, legs, or hooks, or install anchor bolts with an epoxy designed for deck footings and other masonry installations. The epoxy method provides you with more time to reset layout strings for locating bolt locations, and it eliminates the problem of J-bolts tilting or sinking into concrete that is too loose. Most building centers sell threaded rod, washers, nuts, and epoxy syringes, but you can also buy these items separately at most hardware centers.

Before digging, consult local utilities for location of any underground electrical, telephone, or water lines that might interfere with footings.

Tools & Materials ▸

- Power auger or clamshell posthole digger
- Tape measure
- Pruning saw
- Shovel
- Reciprocating saw or handsaw
- Torpedo level
- Hoe
- Trowel
- Shovel
- Old toothbrush
- Plumb bob
- Utility knife
- Concrete tube forms
- Portland cement
- Sand
- Gravel
- J-bolts
- Wheelbarrow
- Scrap 2 × 4

Power augers quickly dig holes for post footings. They are available at rental centers. Some models can be operated by one person, while others require two people.

How to Dig and Pour Post Footings

Dig holes for post footings with a clamshell digger or power auger, centering the holes on the layout stakes. For holes deeper than 35", use a power auger.

Measure hole depth. Local building codes specify depth of footings. Cut away tree roots, if necessary, using a pruning saw.

Pour 2" to 3" of loose gravel in the bottom of each footing hole. Gravel will provide drainage under concrete footings.

Add 2" to hole depth so that footings will be above ground level. Cut concrete tube forms to length, using a reciprocating saw or handsaw. Make sure the cuts are straight.

Insert the tubes into footing holes, leaving about 2" of the tube above ground level. Use a level to make sure the tops of the tubes are level. Pack soil around tubes to hold them in place.

(continued)

Mix the concrete using a basic formula of 4 parts gravel, 2 parts sand to 1 part cement. Mix the dry ingredients with a hoe.

Form a hollow in the center of the dry mix, and slowly pour a small amount of water into the hollow. Blend it in using the hoe.

Add more water gradually, mixing thoroughly until concrete is firm enough to hold its shape when sliced with a trowel.

Pour concrete slowly into the tube form, guiding concrete from the wheelbarrow with a shovel. Fill about half of the form, using a long stick to tamp the concrete, filling any air gaps in the footing. Then finish pouring and tamping concrete into the form.

Level the concrete by pulling a 2 × 4 across the top of the tube form, using a sawing motion. Add concrete to any low spots. Retie the mason's strings on the batterboards, and recheck measurements.

Insert a J-bolt at an angle into the wet concrete at the center of the footing.

Lower the J-bolt slowly into the concrete, wiggling it slightly to eliminate any air gaps.

Set the J-bolt so ¾" to 1" is exposed above the concrete. Brush away any wet concrete on the bolt threads with an old toothbrush.

Use a plumb bob to make sure the J-bolt is positioned exactly at the center of the post location.

Use a torpedo level to make sure the J-bolt is plumb. If necessary, adjust the bolt and repack the concrete. Let the concrete cure, then cut away the exposed portion of tube with a utility knife.

Installing Posts

Posts support the deck beams and transfer the weight of the deck, as well as everything on it, to the concrete footings. They create the above-ground foundation of your deck. Your building inspector will verify that the posts you plan to use are sized correctly to suit your deck design.

Choose post lumber carefully so the posts will be able to carry these substantial loads for the life of your deck. Pressure-treated lumber is your best defense against rot or insect damage. Select posts that are straight and free of deep cracks, large knots, or other natural defects that could compromise their strength. Try not to cut off the factory-treated ends when trimming the posts to length; they contain more of the treatment chemicals and generally last longer than cut ends. Face the factory ends down against the post hardware where water is more likely to accumulate.

Use galvanized metal post anchors to attach the posts to concrete footings. If posts are set directly on concrete, the ends won't dry properly. You'll also have a harder time making the necessary mechanical connection to the footings. Post anchors have drainage holes and pedestals that raise the ends of the wood above the footings and improve drainage. Make sure the posts are installed plumb for maximum strength.

Tools & Materials ▸

Pencil
Framing square
Ratchet wrench
Tape measure
Power miter saw or circular saw
Hammer
Screwgun
Level
Combination square
Metal post anchors
Nuts for J-bolts
Lumber for posts
6d galvanized common nails
2" drywall screws
Long, straight 2 × 4
1 × 4s
Pointed 2 × 2 stakes

How to Attach Post Anchors

Mark the top of each footing as a reference line for installing post anchors. Lay a long, straight 2 × 4 flat across two or three concrete footings, parallel to the ledger, with one edge tight against the J-bolts.

Draw a reference line across each concrete footing, using the edge of a 2 × 4 as a guide. Remove the 2 × 4.

Place a metal post anchor on each concrete footing, and center it over the J-bolt.

(continued)

Use a framing square to make sure the post anchor is positioned square to the reference line drawn on the footing.

Thread a nut over each J-bolt, and tighten it securely with a ratchet wrench or impact driver.

How to Set Posts

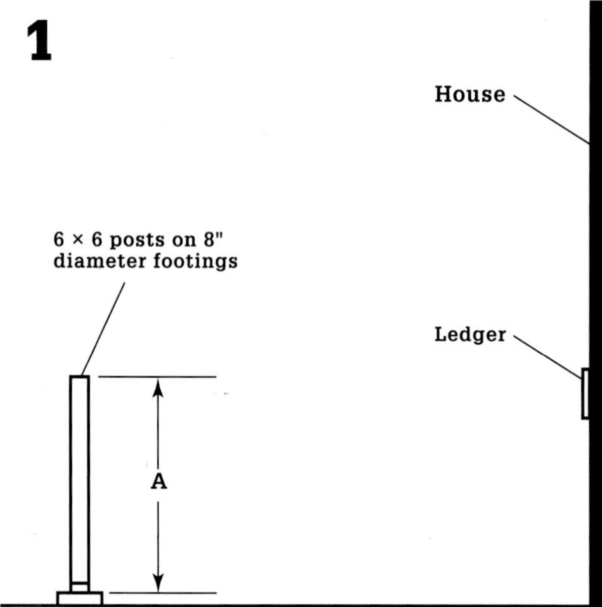

Use the elevation drawing from your design plan to find the length of each post (A). Add 6" to the length for a cutting margin.

Cut posts with a power miter saw or circular saw. Make sure factory-treated ends of posts are square. If necessary, square them by trimming with a power miter saw or circular saw.

Place the post in the anchor and tack it into place with a single 6d galvanized common nail. Do not drive the nail all the way in.

Brace the post with a 1 × 4. Place the 1 × 4 flat across the post so that it crosses the post at a 45° angle about halfway up.

Attach the brace to the post temporarily with a single 2" drywall screw.

Drive a pointed 2 × 2 stake into the ground next to the end of the brace.

(continued)

Use a level to make sure the post is plumb. Adjust the post, if necessary.

Attach the brace to the stake with two 2" drywall screws.

Plumb and brace the post on the side perpendicular to the first brace.

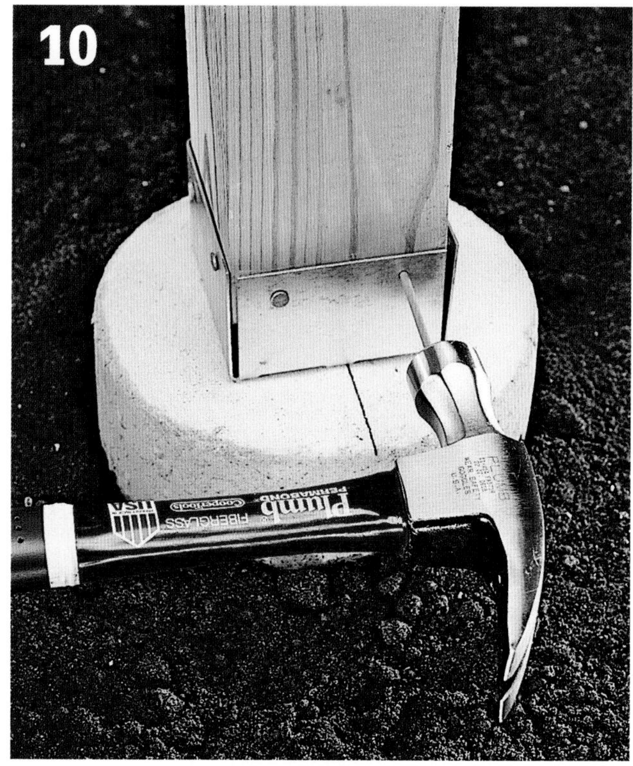

Attach the post to the post anchor with 10d galvanized joist hanger nails. (You can also mark the post and then remove it and cut it on the ground, then nail it in place.)

Position a straight 2 × 4 with one end on the ledger and the other end across the face of the post. Level the 2 × 4. Draw a line on the post along the bottom of the 2 × 4. This line indicates the top of the joists.

From the line shown in step 11, measure down and mark the posts a distance equal to the width of the joists.

Use a square to draw a line completely around the post. This line indicates the top of the beam. From this line, repeat steps 12 and 13 to determine the bottom of the beam.

Installing Beams

Deck beams attach to the posts to help support the weight of the joists and decking. Installation methods depend on the deck design and local codes, so check with a building inspector to determine what is acceptable in your area.

In a saddle beam deck, the beam is attached directly on top of the posts. Metal fasteners, called post-saddles, are used to align and strengthen the beam-to-post connection. The advantage is that the post bears the weight of the deck.

A notched-post deck requires 6 × 6 posts notched at the post top to accommodate the full size of the beam. The deck's weight is transferred to the posts, as in a post-and-beam deck.

In years past, a third style of beam construction, called sandwiching, was also generally acceptable for deck construction. (You can see an example of it on p. 23.) It consisted of two beams that straddled both sides of the post, connected by long through bolts. Because this method has less strength than the saddle or notched styles, it is no longer approved by most building codes.

Deck beams, resting in a notch on the tops of the posts and secured with through bolts and nuts, guarantee strong connections that will bear the weight of your deck.

Tools & Materials ▸

- Tape measure
- Pencil
- Circular saw
- Paint brush
- Combination square
- Screwgun
- Drill
- ½" auger bit
- 1⅜" spade bit
- Ratchet wrench
- Caulk gun
- Reciprocating saw or handsaw
- Pressure-treated lumber
- Clear sealer-preservative
- 2½" galvanized deck screws
- 10d joist hanger nails
- ½ × 8" carriage bolts with washers and nuts
- Silicone caulk

How to Fabricate a Beam

Select two straight boards of the same dimension (generally 2 × 8 or larger) and lay them face to face to see which alignment comes closest to flush on all sides. Apply exterior grade construction adhesive to one board and lay the mating board onto it. Drive a pair of 10d nails near the end of the assembly to pin the boards together.

Clamp the beam members together every 2–3 ft., forcing the boards into alignment as you go, if necessary. Drive 10d nails in a regular, staggered pattern every 12" to 16" or so. Flip the beam over and repeat the nailing pattern from the other side.

How to Mark Post Locations on a Beam

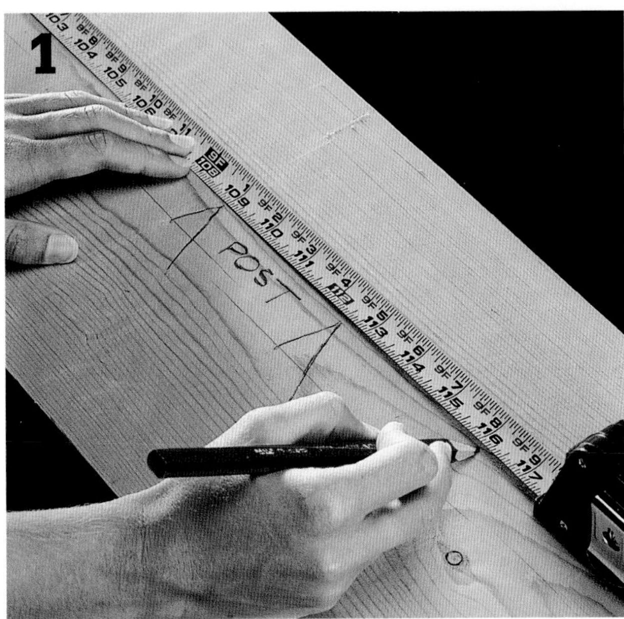

Measure along the beam to the post locations, making sure the ends of the boards of a doubled beam are flush. Mark both the near and far edges of the post onto the beam.

Use a combination square or speed square to transfer the post marks onto the top and then the other face of the beam, allowing you to make sure the post and post hardware align with both faces.

How to Install a Beam with a Post Saddle

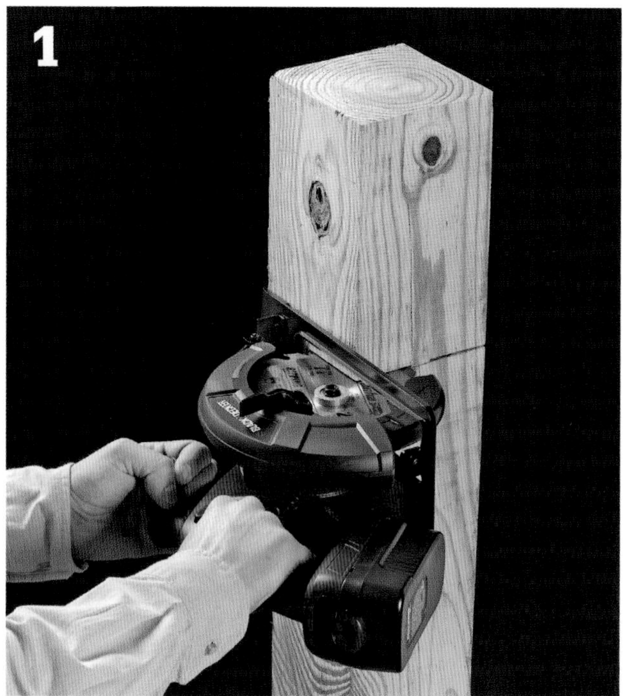

Cut the post to final height after securing it in place. Make two passes with a circular saw and finish with a reciprocating saw.

Attach the saddle hardware to the top of the post using joist hanger screws, 10d galvanized common nails, or joist hanger nails. You must drive a fastener at every predrilled hole in the saddle hardware.

Set the beam into the saddle, making sure the sides of the saddle align with the layout marks on the beam.

Secure the beam into the saddle by driving galvanized common nails or joist hanger screws through the predrilled holes in the top half of the saddle.

How to Install a Beam for a Notched-post Deck

Remove 6 × 6 posts from post anchors and cut to finished height. Measure and mark a notch at the top of each post, sized to fit the thickness and width of the beam. Trace the lines on all sides using a framing square.

Use a circular saw to rough-cut the notches, then switch to a reciprocating saw or hand saw to finish. Reattach posts to the post anchors, with the notch-side facing away from the deck.

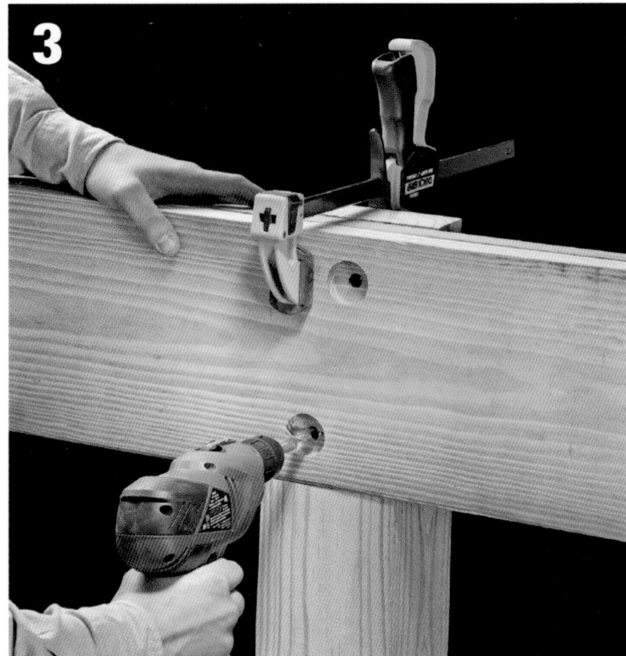

With someone's help, lift the beam (crown side up) into the notches. Align the beam and clamp it to the post. Counterbore two ½"-deep holes, using a 1 ⅜" spade bit, then drill ½" pilot holes through the beam and post, using a ½" auger bit.

Insert carriage bolts to each pilot hole. Add a washer and nut to the counterbore-side of each, and tighten using a ratchet. Seal both ends with silicone caulk. Apply self-sealing membrane to top surfaces of beam and posts if necessary (see page 52).

Hanging Joists

Joists provide support for the decking boards. They are attached to the ledger and header joist with galvanized metal joist hangers and are nailed or strapped to the top of the beam.

For strength and durability, use pressure-treated lumber for all joists. The exposed outside joists and header joist can be faced with composite or cedar boards for a more attractive appearance.

Tools & Materials ▸

- Tape measure
- Pencil
- Hammer
- Combination square
- Circular saw
- Paintbrush
- Drill
- Twist bits (1/8", 1/4")
- Pressure-treated lumber
- 10d joist hanger nails
- 10d and 16d galvanized common nails
- Clear sealer-preservative
- Joist angle brackets
- Galvanized metal joist hangers

Metal joist hangers attached to rim joists or ledgers are practically foolproof for hanging intermediate deck joists. Look for hanger hardware that is triple-dipped galvanized metal.

How to Hang Joists

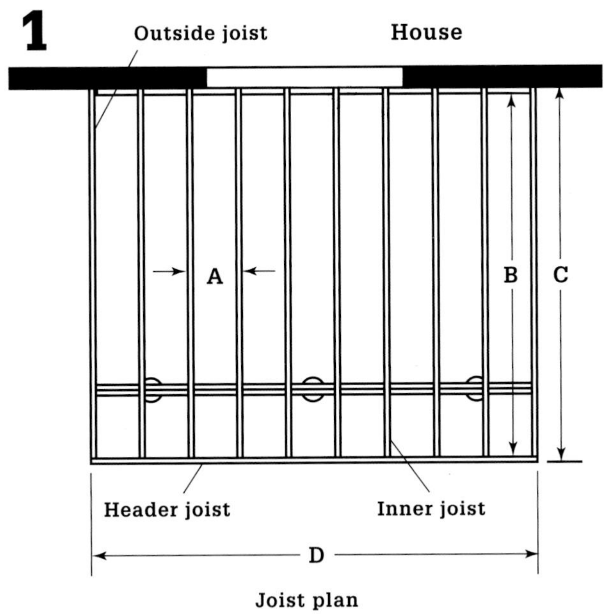

Use your deck plan to find the spacing (A) between joists, and the length of inner joists (B), outside joists (C), and header joist (D). Measure and mark lumber for outside joists, using a combination square as a guide. Cut joists with a miter or circular saw. Seal cut ends with clear sealer-preservative.

Attach joist hanger hardware near each end of the ledger board, according to your layout. Previous building codes allowed you to face nail the joists into the ends of the ledger, but this is no longer accepted practice. Attach only enough fasteners to hold the hanger in position while you square up the joist layout.

Attach the outside joists to the top of the beam by toenailing them with 10d galvanized common nails.

Trim off the ends of structural lumber to get a clean straight edge.

(continued)

Measure and cut the header joist. Seal cut ends with clear sealer-preservative. Drill ⅛" pilot holes at each end of the header joist. Attach the header to ends of outside joists with 16d galvanized common nails. For extra reinforcement, add metal corner brackets to the inside corner joints.

Finish nailing the end joist hangers, making sure you have a joist hanger nail in every punched hole in the hanger.

Measure along the ledger from the edge of the outside joist, and mark where the joists will be attached to the ledger.

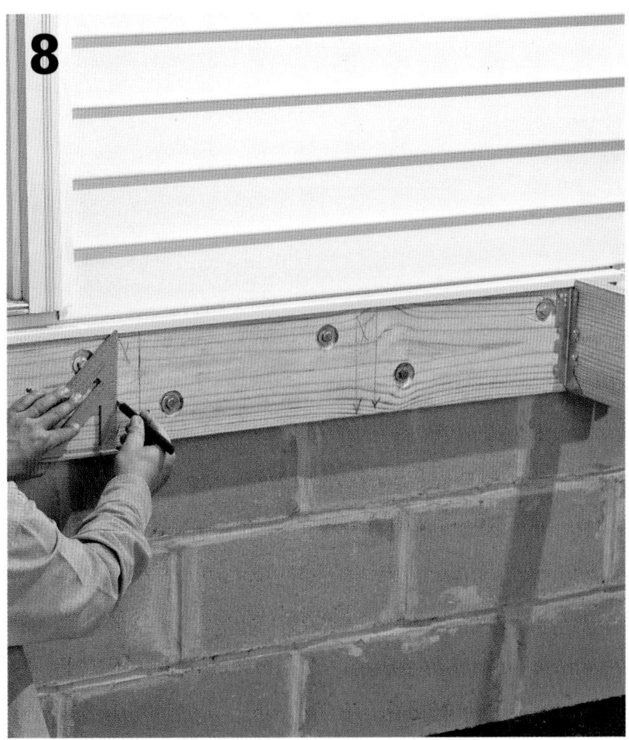

Draw the outline of each joist on the ledger, using a square as a guide.

Measure along the beam from the outside joist, and mark where joists will cross the beam. Draw the outlines across the top of both beam boards.

Measure along the header joist from the outside joist, and mark where joists will be attached to the header joist. Draw the outlines on the inside of the header, using a square as a guide.

Attach joist hangers to the ledger and to the header joist. Position each hanger so that one of the flanges is against the joist outline. Nail one flange to framing members with 10d galvanized joist hanger nails.

(continued)

Cut a scrap board to use as a spacer. Hold the spacer inside each joist hanger, then close the hanger around the spacer.

Nail the remaining side flange to the framing member with 10d joist hanger nails. Remove the spacer.

Measure and mark lumber for joists, using a combination square as a guide. Cut joists with a circular saw or power miter saw.

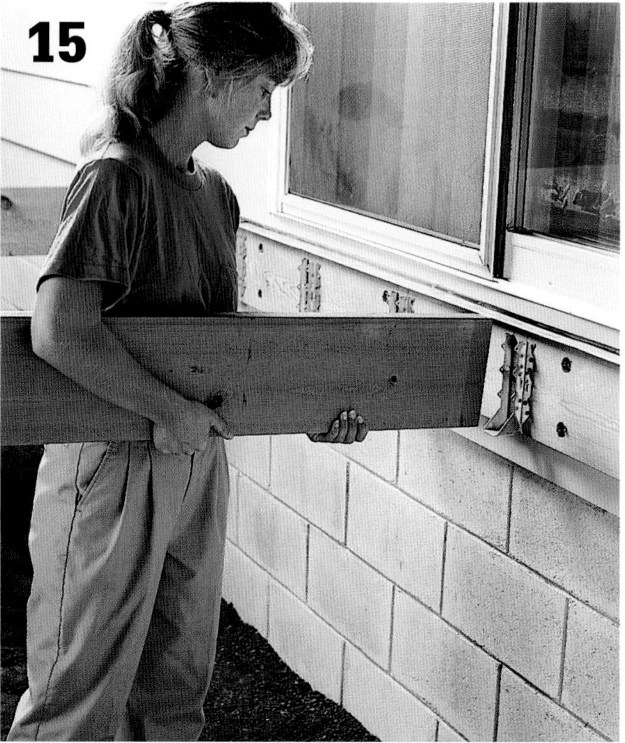

Seal cut ends with clear sealer-preservative. Place the joists in the hangers with crowned edge up.

Attach the ledger joist hangers to the joists with joist hanger nails. Drive nails into both sides of each joist.

Align the joists with the outlines drawn on the top of the beam. Anchor the joists to the beam by toenailing from both sides with 10d galvanized nails.

Alternate Method ▸

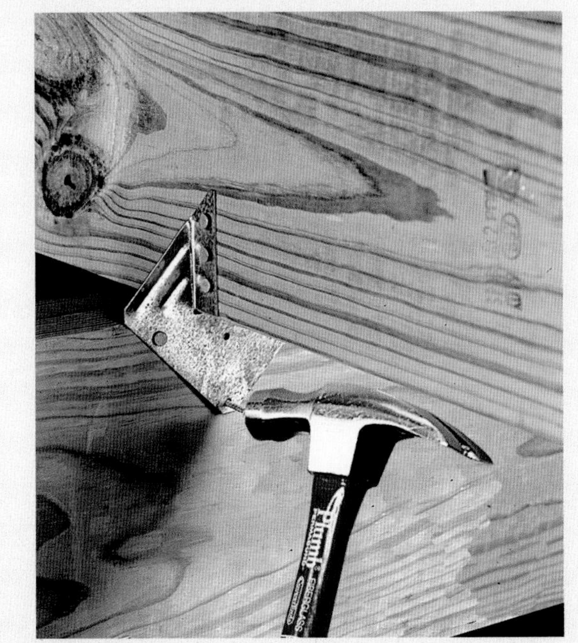

Fasten joists to beams using H-fit joist ties for strength and durability.

Attach the joists to the hangers on the joist with 10d joist hanger nails. Drive nails into both sides of each joist.

Framing Low-profile Decks

Building a deck that sits very close to the ground generally is easier than constructing a very high deck, but low-profile situations do require some design modifications. If the deck is extremely low (8" to 12" high), it is best to rest the beams directly on the concrete footings, since posts are not practical. The joists usually are hung on the faces of the beams rather than resting on top of the beams; cantilever designs are rarely used. Since the ledger is mounted so low on the house, it may need to be anchored to the foundation wall rather than to the rim joist (right).

A deck that is more than 12" above the ground should have at least one step, either box-frame style, or suspended from the deck.

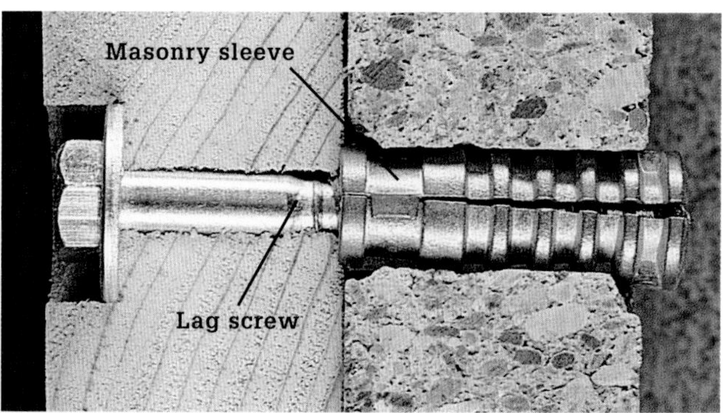

Masonry sleeves are used to attach a ledger to a masonry foundation. Drill 3"-deep guide holes for the sleeves, using a masonry bit, then drive sleeves for ½"-diameter lag screws into the holes. Position the ledger, then attach it with lag screws driven through the ledgers and into the masonry sleeves.

Beams for a low-profile deck often rest directly on concrete footings, with no posts. Because low-profile decks may require 2 × 8 or 2 × 6 joists, an intermediate beam may be required to provide adequate support for these narrower joists. At each end of the last beam, the outside timber must be 1½" longer than the inside timber, creating a recess where the end of the rim joist will fit.

How to Install Low-profile Beams and Joists

Install the ledger, then lay out and dig footings. If beams will rest directly on footings, use tube forms. Raise the tubes to the proper height and check them for plumb as you pour the concrete. Smooth off the surfaces of the footings, and insert direct-bearing hardware while the concrete is still wet, using layout strings to ensure that the hardware is aligned correctly.

Construct beams (page 23), then set the beams into the direct-bearing hardware. Drill pilot holes and use 4" through bolts to secure the beam to the hardware. Mark joist locations on the faces of the beams, then install joist hangers.

Cut and install all joists, attaching them with joist-hanger nails. Complete your deck, using standard deck-building techniques. Install a box-frame or suspended step, if desired (see page 145).

Framing Multi-level Decks

A multi-level deck has obvious advantages, but many do-it-yourselfers are wary of building such a deck, feeling that it is too complex. In reality, however, a multi-level deck is nothing more than two or more adjacent deck platforms set at different heights. You can build a multi-level deck with the same simple construction techniques used to build a standard deck—with one exception: For efficiency, multi-level decks usually are designed so the platforms share a single support beam on the side where they meet. For this reason, it is essential that the shared posts and beams be sturdy enough to carry the load of both platforms.

Except for the shared beam, the separate platforms on a multi-level deck are independent and can use different construction methods. For example, the upper level might use a post-and-beam design with decking boards installed perpendicular to the joists, while the lower level might use a curved cantilever design with decking laid at an angle. If your time and budget are limited, you can build your deck in phases, completing one platform at a time, at your convenience.

Remember to include railings and stairs where needed. Any deck platform more than 30" above the ground—or above a lower deck platform—requires a railing.

Creating structural support in a multi-level deck requires a bit of ingenuity and planning. For example, a sturdy support wall may be constructed on a lower deck to support an upper, as above. Note that new codes do not allow you to attach beams by mounting them to the sides of posts, even if you use metal hanger hardware.

Multi-level Support Options

The shared beam method has one beam supporting both platforms where they overlap. The upper platform rests directly on the beam, while the lower hangs from the face of the beam. This method is an economical choice, since only one beam is required, and it is well suited for relatively flat building sites where the deck levels are close together. See pages 100 to 101.

The support-wall method features a top platform supported by a stud wall that rests on the lower platform, directly over the beam and posts. Unlike the methods listed above, the support-wall method requires that the lower deck platform be built first. This method is a good choice when you want to use decorative wall materials, such as cedar siding, to cover the gap between the two platforms. The support-wall method also works well if you want to complete your deck in phases, delaying construction of the upper level. See pages 102 to 103.

How to Install Shared Beam Support

After laying out and installing the ledger and all posts and footings, mark the posts to indicate where the beam will rest. Use a straight 2 × 4 and a level to establish a point that is level with the top of the ledger, then measure down a distance equal to the height of the joists plus the height of the beam. Cut off the posts at this point, using a reciprocating saw.

Position a post-beam cap on each post. Construct a beam from 2 × 10 or 2 × 12 dimension lumber (page 23), then position the beam in the post-beam caps. If the beam is crowned, install it so the crowned side is up; if there is a gap between the middle cap and the beam, shim under the gap. Secure the post-beam caps to the posts and beam with joist hanger nails or screws.

Lay out joist locations for the upper platform on the ledger and on the top of the beam, then use a carpenter's square to transfer joist marks for the lower platform onto the face of the beam. Attach joist hangers at the joist layout lines on the ledger.

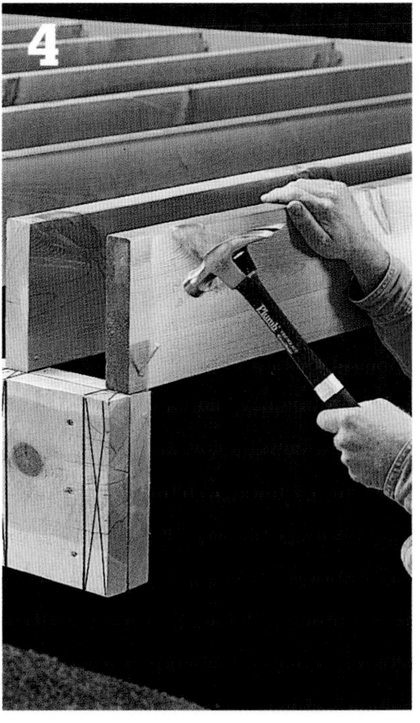

Measure, cut, and install joists for the upper platform, leaving a 1½" setback to allow for the thickness of the rim joist. At the beam, secure the joists by toenailing with 16d galvanized nails.

Attach joist hangers for the lower platform along the face of the beam, using a scrap piece of lumber as a spacer. Cut and install the joists for the lower platform.

Cut rim joists for both the upper and lower platforms, and attach them to the ends of the joists by endnailing with 16d nails. Complete the deck, using standard deck-building techniques.

How to Install a Deck Support Wall

Lay out and install the ledger and all posts and footings, then frame the lower platform, using standard deck-building techniques.

Use a straight 2 × 4 and a level to establish a reference point level with the bottom of the ledger, then find the total height for the support wall by measuring the vertical distance to the top of the lower platform. Cut the wall studs 3" less than this total height, to allow for the thickness of the top and bottom plates.

Cut 2 × 4 top and bottom plates to cover the full width of the upper platform, then lay out the stud locations on the plates, 16" on center. Cut studs to length, then assemble the support wall by endnailing the plates to the studs, using galvanized 16d nails.

Set a long "sway" brace diagonally across the stud wall, and nail it near one corner only. Square the wall by measuring the diagonals and adjusting until both diagonal measurements are the same. When the wall is square, nail the brace at the other corner, and to each stud. Cut off the ends of the brace flush with the plates.

Raise the support wall into position, aligning it with the edge of the beam and the end of the deck. Nail the sole plate to the beam with 16d galvanized nails driven on both sides of each stud.

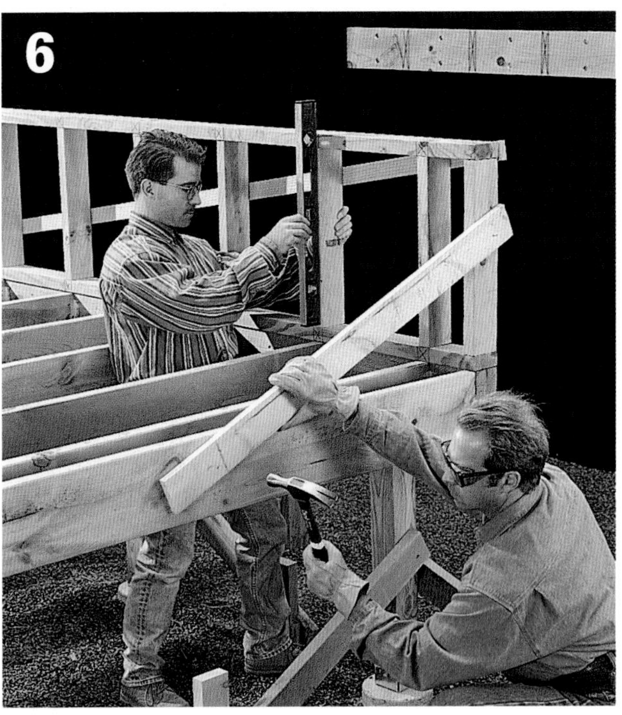

Adjust the wall so it is plumb, then brace it in position by nailing a 1 × 4 across the end stud and outside joist.

Lay out joist locations for the upper platform, and install joist hangers on the ledger. Cut joists so they are 1½" shorter than the distance from the ledger to the front edge of the wall. Install the joists by toenailing them to the top plate with 16d nails. Remove the braces.

Measure and cut a rim joist, and attach it to the ends of the joists by endnailing with 16d nails. Also toenail the rim joist to the top plate of the support wall. Complete the deck, using standard deck-building techniques.

Framing Decks on Steep Slopes

Constructing a deck on a steep slope can be a complicated job if you use standard deck-building techniques. Establishing a layout for posts and footings is difficult on steeply pitched terrain, and construction can be demanding when one end of the deck is far above your head.

Professional deck contractors adapt to steep slope situations by using a temporary post-and-beam support structure, and by slightly altering the construction sequence. Rather than beginning with post-footing layout, experienced builders begin by constructing the outer frame and raising it onto a temporary support structure. Once the elevated frame is in position, the locations of the permanent posts and footings can be determined.

In most instances, you will need helpers when building a deck on a steep slope. To raise and position the deck frame on temporary supports, for example, you will need the help of three or four other people. *Note: The steep slope deck construction shown on the following pages was built using primarily 4 × 4" posts. Recent changes to many building codes require 6 × 6" posts. Always check with your local building department to learn applicable codes for your deck.*

Another important consideration when building a deck on a steep slope is the composition of the soil. The slope needs to be stable and suitable for anchoring deep footings. If the earth is loose, rocky or prone to erosion, have it inspected by a landscape architect or civil engineer first to make sure it will safely support a deck. The slope may need to be stabilized in other ways before construction begins.

If building the deck will require working at heights, use temporary support ledgers and bracing to prevent falls from ladders. Consider installing scaffolding, which may be a better solution than ladders if several people will be assisting you with the project. Scaffolding is available at many large rental centers for reasonable weekly and monthly rates.

The directions on the following pages show the construction of a deck featuring a corner-post design, but the technique can easily be adapted to cantilevered decks.

Positioning and measuring posts on a steep slope is much easier if the deck frame is already in position, resting on temporary supports.

Building Decks on Slopes

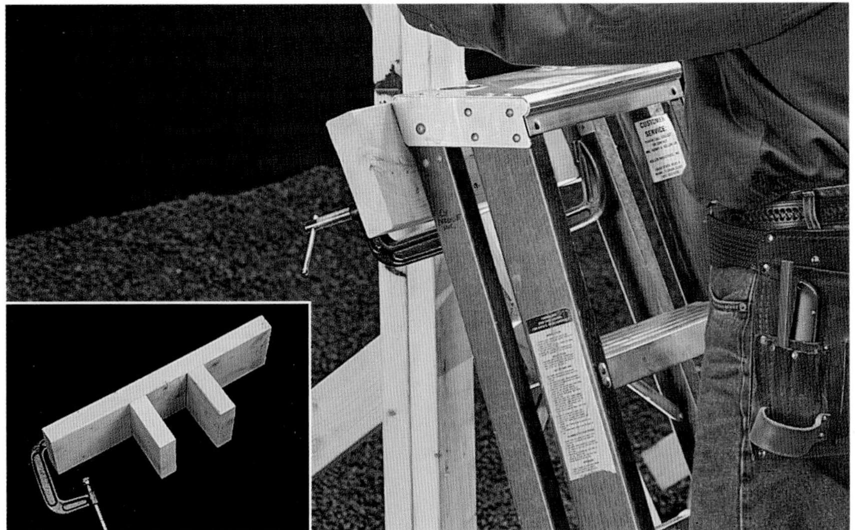

Stepladders should be used in the open position only if the ground is level. On uneven ground you can use a closed stepladder by building a support ledger from 2 × 6 scraps (inset) and clamping it to a post. Lean the closed ladder against the ledger, and level the base of the ladder, if necessary (below). Never climb onto the top step of the ladder.

Extension ladders should be leveled and braced. Install sturdy blocking under ladder legs if the ground is uneven or soft, and drive a stake behind each ladder foot to keep it from slipping. Never exceed the weight limit printed on the ladder.

Scaffolding can be rented from rental centers or paint supply stores. When working at heights, scaffolding offers a safer, more stable working surface. Place blocking under the legs of the scaffolding, and level it by screwing the threaded legs in or out.

How to Build a Deck on a Steep Slope

After installing the ledger, use spray paint or stakes to mark the approximate locations for the post footings, according to your deck plans. Lay two 2 × 12 scraps on the ground to support temporary posts. Level the scraps, and anchor them with stakes. The bases for the temporary posts should be at least 2 ft. away from post-footing locations.

Construct two temporary posts by facenailing pairs of long 2 × 4s together. Erect each post by positioning it on the base and attaching a diagonal 2 × 4 brace. Toenail the post to the base.

Attach a second diagonal brace to each post, running at right angles to the first brace. Adjust the posts until they are plumb, then secure them in place by driving stakes into the ground and screwing the diagonal braces to the stakes.

Mark a cutoff line on each post by holding a long, straight 2 × 4 against the bottom of the ledger and the face of the post, then marking the post along the bottom edge of the 2 × 4. Cut off the posts at this height, using a reciprocating saw.

Construct a temporary support beam at least 2 ft. longer than the width of your deck by facenailing a pair of 2 × 4s together. Center the beam on top of the posts, and toenail it in place.

Build the outer frame of your deck according to your construction plans, and attach joist hangers to the inside of the frame, spaced 16" on center. With several helpers, lift the frame onto the temporary supports and carefully move it into position against the ledger. *Note: On very large or high decks, you may need to build the frame piece-by-piece on top of the temporary supports.*

(continued)

Endnail the side joists to the ends of the ledger, then reinforce the joint by installing angle brackets in the inside corners of the frame.

Check to make sure the frame is square by measuring diagonally. If the measurements are not the same, adjust the frame on the temporary beam until it is square. Also check the frame to make sure it is level; if necessary, shim between the temporary beam and the side joists to level the frame. Toenail the frame to the temporary beam.

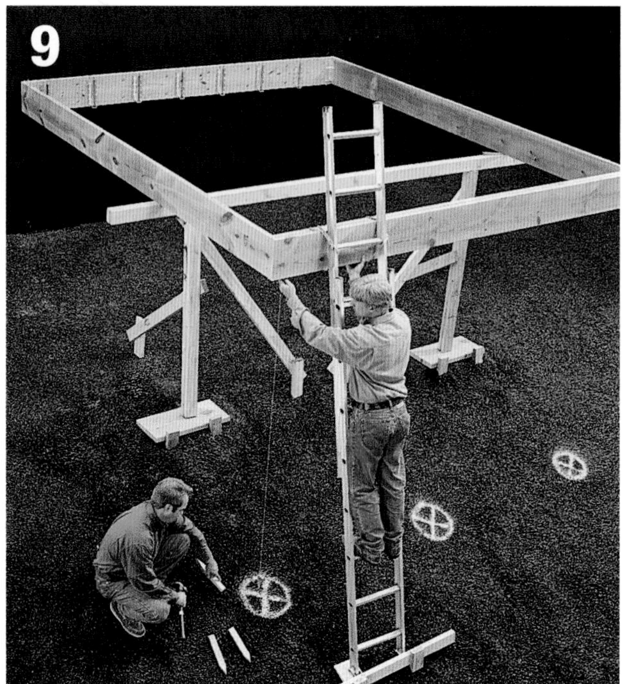

Use a plumb bob suspended from the deck frame to stake the exact locations for post footings on the ground. *Note: Make sure the footing stakes correspond to the exact center of the posts, as indicated by your deck plans.*

Dig and pour footings for each post. While the concrete is still wet, insert J-bolts for post anchors, using a plumb bob to ensure that the bolts are at the exact center of the post locations. Let the concrete dry completely before continuing.

Check once more to make sure the deck frame is square and level, and adjust if necessary. Attach post anchors to the footings, then measure from the anchors to the bottom edge of the deck beam to determine the length for each post. *Note: If your deck uses a cantilever design, make sure to allow for the height of the beam when cutting the posts.*

Cut posts and attach them to the beam and footing with post-beam caps and post anchors. Brace the posts by attaching 2 × 4 boards diagonally from the bottom of the post to the inside surface of the deck frame. Remove the temporary supports, then complete the project using standard deck-building techniques.

Working with Angles

Decks with geometric shapes and angled sides have much more visual interest than basic square or rectangular decks. Most homes and yards are configured with predictable 90° angles and straight sides, so an angled deck offers a pleasing visual surprise.

Contrary to popular belief, elaborate angled decks are relatively easy to plan and build, if you follow the lead of professional designers. As professionals know, most polygon-shaped decks are nothing more than basic square or rectangular shapes with one or more corners removed. An octagonal island deck, for example, is simply a square with all four corners omitted.

Seen in this light, complicated multi-level decks with many sides become easier to visualize and design.

For visual balance and ease of construction, use 45° angles when designing an angled, geometric deck. In this way, the joinery requires only common cutting angles (90°, 45°, or 22½°), and you can use skewed 45° joist hangers, readily available at home centers. *Note: The angled deck construction shown on the following pages was built using primarily 4 × 4" posts. Recent changes to many building codes require 6 × 6" posts. Always check with your local building department to learn applicable codes for your deck.*

Joists on a cantilevered deck can be easily marked for angled cuts by snapping a chalk line between two points on adjacent sides of the deck corner. Marking and cutting joists in this fashion is easier than measuring and cutting the joists individually. To help hold the joists in place while marking, tack a brace across the ends. Mark joist locations on the brace for reference.

Design Options for Angled Decks

Cantilever design is the easiest and least expensive to build, since it requires the fewest posts. But the length of the angled side is limited by code regulations that restrict the amount of joist overhang. And since the joists rest on top of the beam, cantilever designs are not suited for a deck with a very low profile. On cantilever designs, the joists along the angled side are beveled at 45° at the ends, and are attached to the rim joist by endnailing.

Corner-post design is a good choice for large decks with long angled sides. It also works well for low-profile decks, since the joists are mounted to the inside faces of the beams. Many builders use a single beveled post to support the angled corners on this type of deck, but our method calls for two posts and footings at each of these corners, making the design easier to construct and more versatile. On a corner-post deck, the joists on the angled side are square-cut, and are attached to the beam with skewed 45° joist hangers (see page 115).

Multi-level design features an upper platform built using the corner-post method (above), but adds a lower platform. The lower level is supported by a second angled beam, created by sandwiching timbers around the same posts that support the upper platform. On the lower platform, the joists rest on top of the beam and are beveled on the back ends so they are flush with the edge of the beam. Check with your local building department to make sure this design strategy is allowed by your local building codes.

How to Build Support for an Angled Deck

Lay out and begin construction, using standard deck-building techniques. After installing the joists, mark cutting lines on the angled side by snapping a chalk line across the tops of the joists. Make sure the chalk line is angled 45° to the edge of the deck.

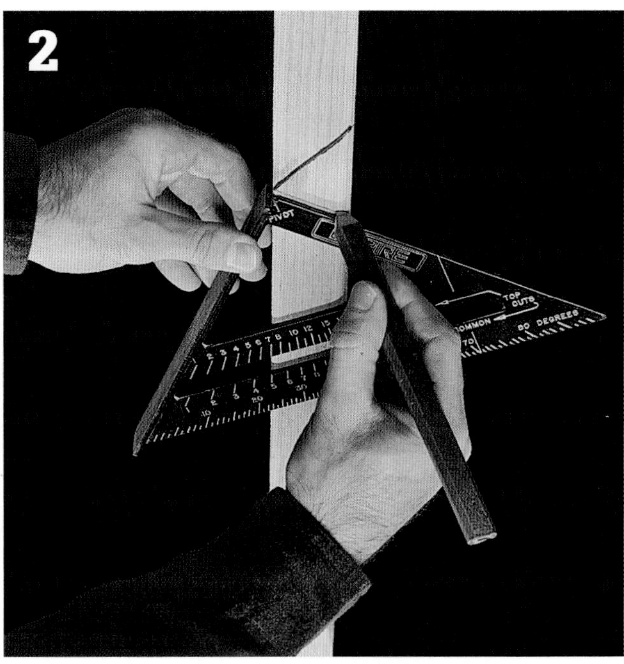

At the outside joists, use a speed square to change the 45° chalk line to a line angled at 22½° in the opposite direction. When joined to a rim joist that is also cut to 22½°, the corner will form the correct angle.

Use a combination square to extend the angle marks down the faces of the joists. Bevel-cut the deck joists with a circular saw, using a clamped board as a guide for the saw foot. Interior joists should be beveled to 45°; outside joists to 22½°.

Cut and install the rim joists. At the angled corners, bevel-cut the ends of the rim joists at 22½°. Endnail the rim joists in place, and reinforce the inside corners with adjustable angle brackets attached with joist-hanger nails. Finish the deck, using standard deck-building techniques.

How to Build an Angled Deck Using the Corner-post Design

Use boards to create a rectangular template of the deck. To ensure that the template is square, use the 3-4-5 triangle method: From the corner directly below the ledger, measure 3 ft. along the foundation, and mark a point. Measure out along the template board 4 ft., and mark a second point. Measure diagonally between the two points. This measurement should be 5 ft.; if not, adjust the template to square it.

Indicate each angled edge by positioning a board diagonally across the corner of the template. To ensure that the angles measure 45°, make sure the perpendicular legs of the triangle have exactly the same measurement. Nail the boards together where they overlap.

Mark locations for post footings with stakes or spray paint. At each 45° corner, mark locations for two posts, positioned about 1 ft. on each side of the corner. Temporarily move the board template, then dig and pour concrete footings.

While the concrete is still wet, reposition the template and check to make sure it is square to the ledger. Use a nail to scratch a reference line across the concrete next to the template boards, then insert J-bolts in the wet concrete. Let the concrete dry completely.

(continued)

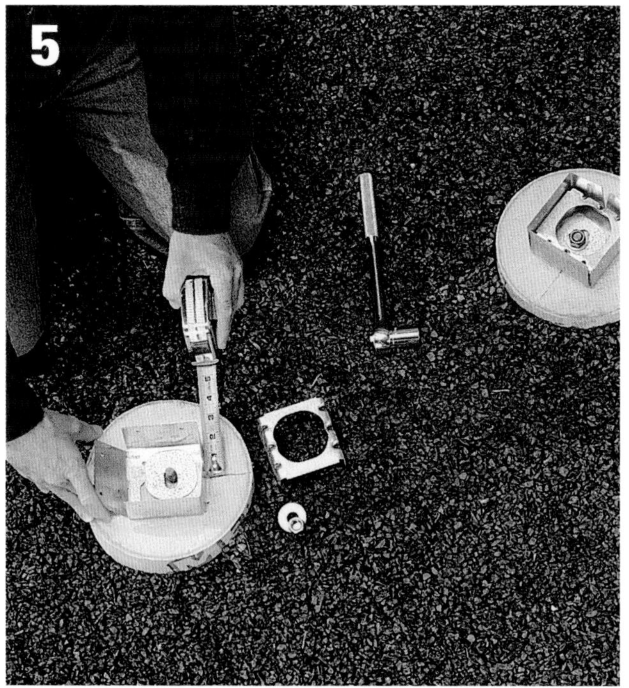

Attach metal post anchors to the J-bolts, centering them on the reference lines scratched in the concrete. The front and back edges of the anchors should be parallel to the reference line.

Measure and cut beam timbers to size. On ends that will form angled corners, use a speed square to mark 22½° angles on the tops of the timbers, then use a combination square to extend cutting lines down the face of the boards. Use a circular saw set for a 22½° bevel to cut off the timbers, then join them together with 16d nails.

Set posts into the post anchors, then use a mason's string and line level to mark cutoff lines on the posts at a point level with the bottom of the ledger. Cut off the posts, using a circular saw. Attach post-beam caps to the posts, then set the beams into place. Secure beam corners together with adjustable angle brackets attached to the inside of each corner with joist-hanger nails.

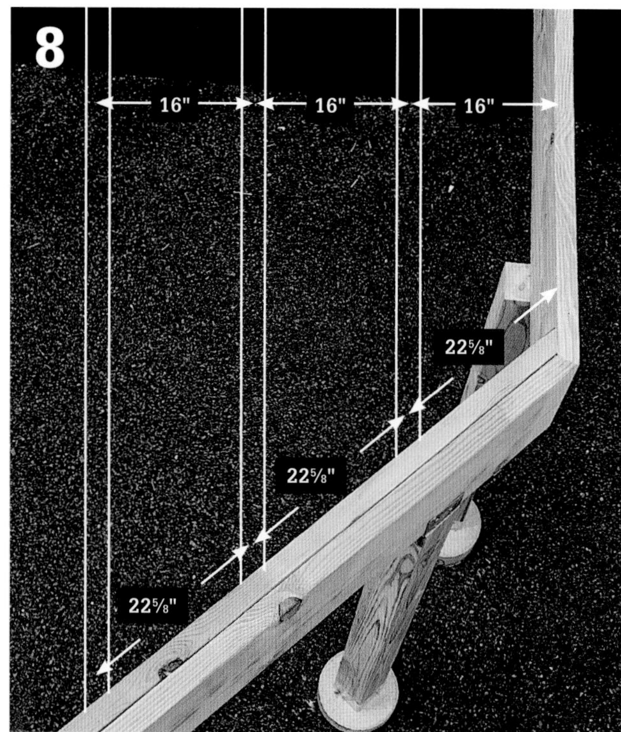

Measure and mark joist locations on the ledger and beams. If your joists are spaced 16" on center along the ledger, they will be spaced 22⅝" apart measured along the angled beam. If they are spaced 24" on center at the ledger, the joists will be spaced 33$\frac{5}{16}$" apart along the angled beam.

Attach joist hangers at the layout marks on the ledger and beam. Use skewed 45° joist hangers on the angled beam.

Cut and install joists, securing them with joist-hanger nails. Joists installed in skewed 45° joist hangers can be square-cut; they need not be beveled to match the angle of the beam. Complete the deck, using standard deck-building techniques.

Creating Curves

By their nature, curved shapes lend a feeling of tranquility to a landscape. A deck with curved sides tends to encourage quiet relaxation. A curved deck can also provide an effective visual transition between the sharp architectural angles of the house and the more sweeping natural lines of the surrounding landscape.

Curved decks nearly always use a cantilevered design, in which the curved portion of the deck overhangs a beam that is set back from the edge of the deck. This setback distance generally should be no more than one-third of the total length of the deck joists, but longer cantilevers are possible if you use a combination of thicker joists, closer joist spacing, and stronger wood species, such as southern yellow pine.

Note: The curved deck shown on the following pages was built using primarily 4 × 4" posts. Recent changes to many building codes require 6 × 6" posts. Always check with your local building department to learn applicable codes for your deck.

If your curved deck will be high enough to require a railing, we recommend a design that incorporates a circular curve rather than an elliptical or irregular curve. Adding a curved railing (pages 178 to 181) is much easier if the deck curve is based on a circular shape.

A curved deck is created by cutting joists to match the curved profile, then attaching a curved rim joist, which can be shaped in one of two ways (page opposite). Braces attached to the tops of the joists hold them in place as the rim joist is installed.

Curves and Deck Design ▸

Adding curves to your deck is not something you should do on the spur of the moment. Consider the pros and cons carefully before you commit to curves. Here are some to think about:

Pros:

- Curves can add visual appeal and uniqueness to your deck.
- Curves soften the overall feeling.
- Used wisely, curves have a natural, organic visual quality.
- A curve can be used to work around an obstacle in a pleasing way.
- A curved corner can preserve space below the deck.

Cons:

- Decks that incorporate curves almost always require more posts and beams, and they make less efficient use of building materials.
- A deck with curves takes at least twice as long to build as a square or rectangular one.
- Curved railings are tricky to make.
- Impact is lessened if curves are overused.
- Curves reduce and constrict deck floorspace.

Design Options for Curved Decks

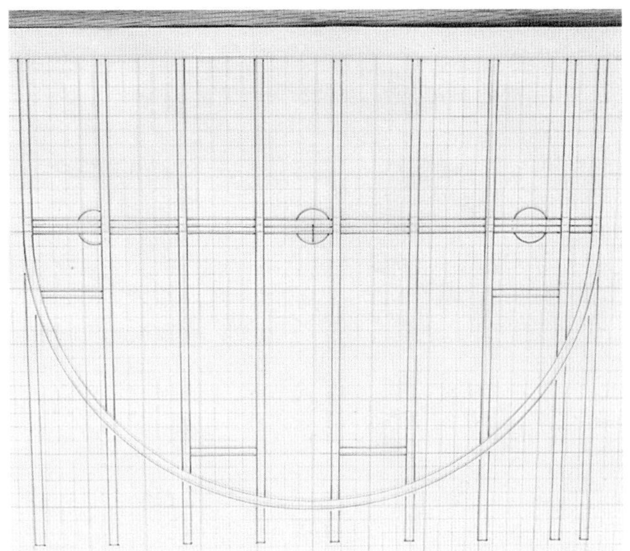

Circular designs are the best choice for curved decks that require railings. However, circular curves require a fairly long cantilever, a limitation that may limit the overall size of your deck. Circular decks are laid out using simple geometry and a long compass tool, called a trammel, which you can make yourself.

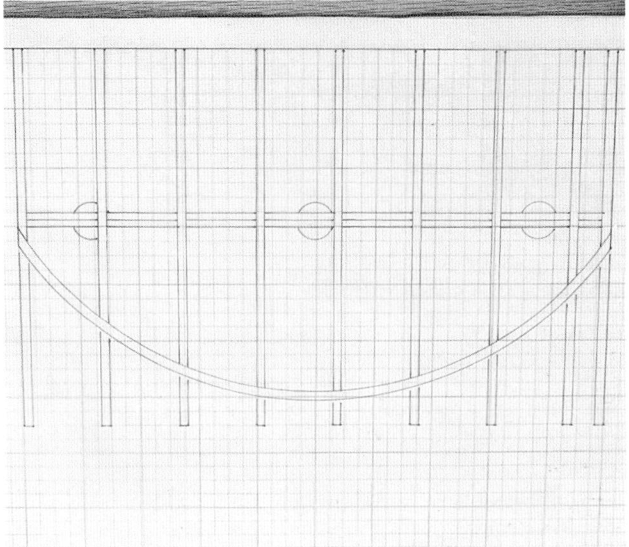

Irregular or elliptical curves should be used only on relatively low decks, since railings are quite difficult to construct for this kind of curve. These designs also work well for large decks, since the amount of overhang on the cantilever is relatively short compared to that for a circular curve.

Construction Options

A kerfed rim joist is formed by making a series of thin vertical cuts (kerfs) across the inside face of the board, making it flexible enough to wrap around the curve. A kerfed rim joist made from 2"-thick dimension lumber is sufficiently strong, but if you are kerfing a 1"-thick redwood or cedar fascia board, it should be backed with a laminated rim joist (photo, right).

Laminated rim joist is made by bending several layers of flexible ¼"- or ⅜"-thick exterior-grade plywood around the curve, joining each layer to the preceding layer with glue and screws. A laminated rim joist can stand alone, or it can provide backing for a more decorative fascia, such as a kerfed redwood or cedar board.

How to Lay Out a Curved Deck

Install posts and beam for a cantilevered deck. Cut joists slightly longer than their final length, and attach them to the ledger and the beam. Add cross-blocking between the two outside joists to ensure that they remain plumb.

Mark the joist spacing on a 1 × 4 brace, and tack it across the tops of the joists at the point where the deck curve will begin. Measure the distance between the inside edges of the outer joists at each end of the beam, then divide this measurement in half to determine the radius of the circular curve. Mark the 1 × 4 brace to indicate the midpoint of the curve.

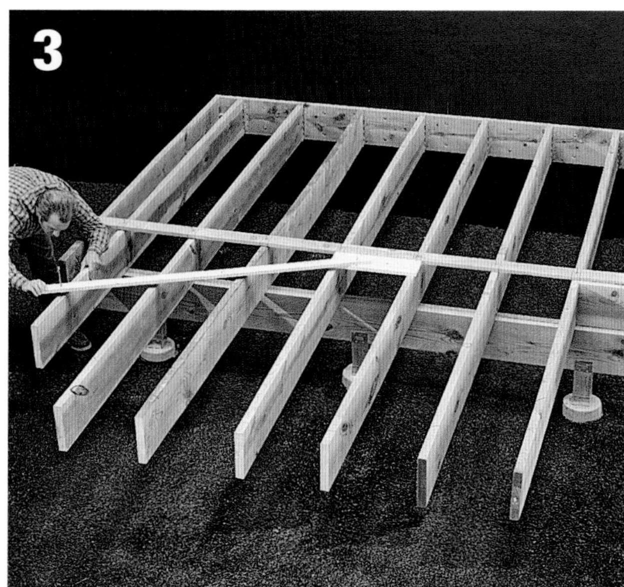

Build a trammel by anchoring one end of a long, straight 1 × 2 to the centerpoint of the curve, using a nail. (If the centerpoint lies between joists, attach a 1 × 4 brace across the joists to provide an anchor.) Measure out along the arm of the trammel a distance equal to the curve radius, and drill a hole. Insert a pencil in the hole, and pivot the trammel around the centerpoint, marking the joists for angled cuts.

Variation: For elliptical or irregular curves, temporarily nail vertical anchor boards to the outside joists at the start of the curve. Position a long strip of flexible material, such as hardboard or paneling, inside the anchor boards, then push the strip to create the desired bow. Drive nails into the joists to hold the bow in position, then scribe cutting lines on the tops of the joists.

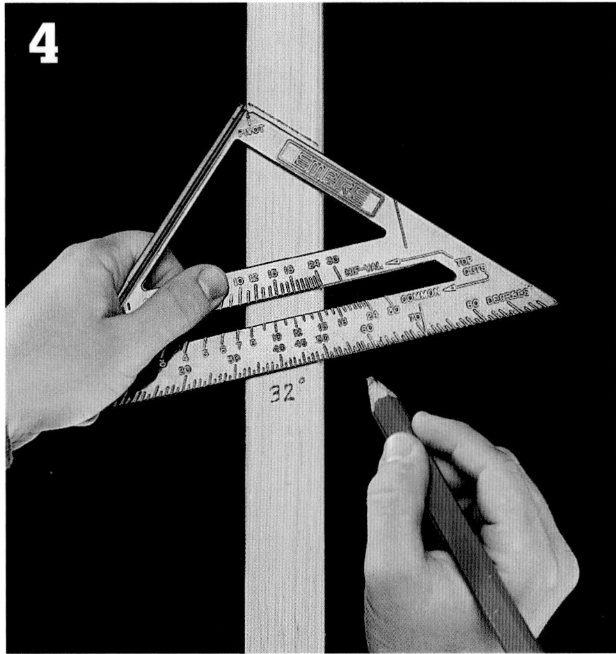

Use a speed square or protractor to determine the bevel angles you will use to cut the joists. Position the square so the top is aligned with the layout mark on the joist, then find the degree measurement by following the edge of the joist down from the pivot point and reading where it intersects the degree scale on the square.

Use a combination square to extend the cutting lines down the front and back faces of the joists. At the outside joists where the curve begins, mark square cutting lines at the point where the circular curve touches the inside edge of the joists.

Cut off each joist with a circular saw set to the proper bevel. Clamp a straightedge to the joist to provide a guide for the foot of the saw. On the outside joists where the curve begins, make 90° cuts.

Where the bevel angle is beyond the range of your circular saw, use a reciprocating saw to cut off the joists.

How to Construct a Kerfed Rim Joist for a Curved Deck

Mark the inside face of the rim joist lumber with a series of parallel lines, 1" apart. Using a circular saw or radial-arm saw set to a blade depth equal to ¾ of the rim joist thickness (1⅛" for 1½"-thick lumber), make crosscut kerfs at each line. Soak the rim joist in hot water for about 2 hours to make it easier to bend.

Install a cross block between the first two joists on each side of the curve, positioned so half the block is covered by the square-cut outside joist (inset). While it is still damp, attach the rim joist by butting it against the end joist and attaching it to the cross block with 3" deck screws. Bend the rim joist so it is flush against the ends of the joists, and attach with two or three 3" deck screws driven at each joist.

Where butt joints are necessary, mark and cut the rim joist so the joint will fall at the center of a joist. To avoid chipping, cut off the rim joist at one of the saw kerfs.

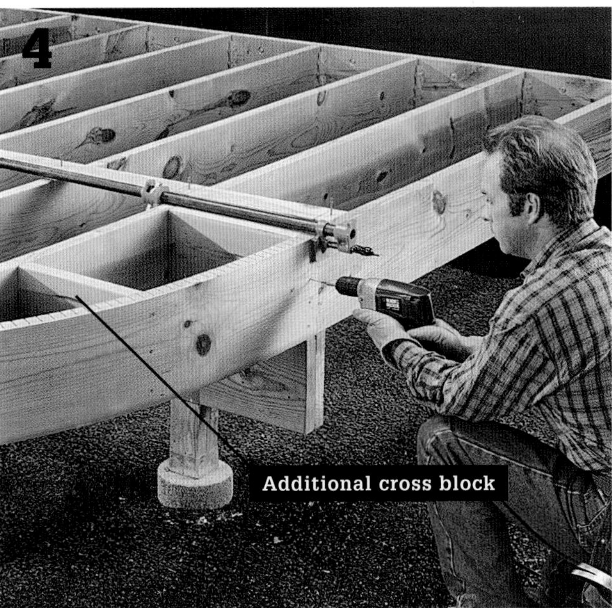

Complete the installation by butting the end of the rim joist against the outside joist and attaching it to the cross block. Use bar clamps to hold the rim joist in position as you screw it to the blocking. *Note: If the rim joist flattens near the sides of the deck, install additional cross-blocking, cut to the contour of the curve, to hold the rim joist in proper position.*

How to Construct a Curved Rim Joist with Laminated Plywood

Install blocking between the first two joists on each side of the deck (step 2, previous page). Cut four strips of ¼"-thick exterior plywood the same width as the joists. Butt the first strip against the outside joist and attach it to the blocking with 1⅝" deck screws. Bend the strip around the joists and attach with deck screws. If necessary, install additional blocking to keep the plywood in the proper curve. If butt joints are necessary, make sure they fall at the centers of joists.

Attach the remaining strips of plywood one at a time, attaching them to previous layers with 1" deck screws and exterior wood glue. Make sure butt joints are staggered so they do not overlap previous joints. For the last layer, use a finish strip of ⅜" cedar plywood. Where the finish strip butts against the outside joists, bevel-cut the ends at 10° to ensure a tight fit.

How to Install Decking on a Curved Deck

Install decking for the square portion of the deck, then test-fit decking boards on the curved portion. If necessary, you can make minor adjustments in the spacing to avoid cutting very narrow decking boards at the end of the curve. When satisfied with the layout, scribe cutting lines on the underside of the decking boards, following the edge of the rim joist.

Remove the scribed decking boards, and cut along the cutting lines with a jig saw. Install the decking boards with deck screws, and smooth the cut edges of the decking boards with a belt sander or random-orbit sander, if necessary.

Framing for Insets

If your planned deck site has a tree, boulder, or other large obstacle, you may be better off building around it rather than removing it. Although framing around a landscape feature makes construction more difficult, the benefits usually make the effort worthwhile. A deck with an attractive tree set into it, for example, is much more appealing than a stark, exposed deck built on a site that has been leveled by a bulldozer.

The same methods used to frame around a preexisting obstacle also can be used to create a decorative or functional inset feature, such as a planter box, child's sandbox, or brick barbecue. On a larger scale, the same framing techniques can be used to enclose a hot tub or above-ground pool.

A framed opening can also provide access to a utility fixture, such as a water faucet, electrical outlet, or central air-conditioning compressor. Covering a framed opening with a removable hatch (page 266) preserves the smooth, finished look of your deck.

Large insets that interrupt joists can compromise the strength of your deck. For this reason, inset openings require modified framing to ensure adequate strength. Double joists on either side of the opening bear the weight of double headers, which in turn support the interrupted joists. Always consult your building inspector for specifics when constructing a deck with a large inset.

Inset framing makes it possible to save mature trees when building a deck. Keeping trees and other landscape features intact helps preserve the value and appearance of your property. Check with a tree nursery for an adequate opening size for any tree you want to contain within an inset.

How to Frame for an Inset

Modify your deck plan, if necessary, to provide the proper support for the interrupted joists in the inset opening. If the inset will interrupt one or two joists, frame both sides of the opening with double joists. If the opening is larger, you may need to install additional beams and posts around the opening to provide adequate support. Consult your building inspector for specific requirements for your situation.

Rough-frame the opening by using double joist hangers to install double joists on each side of the inset, and double headers between these joists. Install the interrupted joists between the double headers and the rim joist and ledger.

Where needed, cut and install angled nailing blocks between the joists and headers to provide additional support for the decking boards. When trimmed, decking boards may overhang support members by as much as 4" around an inset opening.

Inset box shown cutaway for clarity.

Variation: An inset box can be used as a planter for flowers or herbs. Build the box from ¾"-thick exterior-grade plywood, and attach it to the framing members with deck screws. A deep box can be supported by landscape timbers. Line the inside of the box with layers of building paper, then drill ½"-wide holes in the bottom of the box to provide drainage. To keep soil from washing out through drainage holes, line the box with landscape fabric.

Decking

The decking material you choose, and the method in which you install it, will impact your deck in several important ways. All decking must provide a comfortable surface on which to walk. The decking must be strong and durable, slip resistant, and uniformly sized. Although wood has been, and remains, the most popular decking material, several other viable materials are available. You can select from aluminum, recycled plastic, or other types of products in manufactured decking, or opt for the material that is challenging wood's predominance: composite decking. The rapidly growing popularity of composite is due to the more modest maintenance requirements of the material, ease of installation, and an ever-increasing selection of colors and surface treatments, many of which convincingly mimic wood grain, color, and texture. High-end composites are extremely durable once installed, but they are more expensive than most types of wood.

Regardless of the material you choose, you can create greater aesthetic appeal by laying the decking in unusual patterns. Diagonals, herringbones, and other patterns are all more visually interesting than a simple rectilinear style. These types of patterns will, however, entail more effort and greater expense.

You'll find a comprehensive overview of deck materials and pattern options in this chapter. You will also find information on decking fastener styles, which include a growing number of "invisible" fasteners that hold decking in place without marking the surface of your beautiful outdoor structure.

In this chapter:

Decking Patterns

Decking boards are the most visible element of your deck, and there are a number of ways to install them. You can use different board widths and lay the boards in any of a number of patterns to increase visual interest. The pattern you choose will affect joist spacing and layout. For instance, a straight decking pattern usually requires joists spaced 16" on-center. Diagonal decking generally requires joist spacing of 12" on-center. Parquet and other intricate patterns may require extra support, such as double joists or additional blocking. For sturdy wood decking, always use at least 5/4 lumber. Thinner boards are more likely to twist or cup.

Diagonal decking is one of the simplest alternatives to straight runs, and can be an interesting look—especially if you run the diagonals in different directions on different platforms or levels of the deck. However, diagonal patterns often require joists spaced closer than a straight pattern.

Parquet patterns are visually stunning and best suited to more formal decks, and those that don't include bi- or multicolored design features. These patterns require double joists and blocking to provide adequate support surface for attaching the butted ends of boards.

Even a straight pattern can be interesting when interrupted with built-in shapes. A framed opening for a tree or large rock requires extra blocking between joists. Short joists are attached to blocking with joist hangers.

Border patterns with mitered corners provide an elegant finished look to any deck. They are especially effective when used around the inside deck edge bordering a swimming pool. Install trim joists to support the border decking.

Laying Decking

Buy decking boards that are long enough to span the width of the deck, if possible. If you have to use more than one, butt the boards end-to-end over a joist. Stagger butted joints so that they do not overlap row to row.

Install decking so that there is a gap approximately ⅛" between boards to provide drainage. You can use a nail as a spacer between rows. Some wood boards naturally "cup" as they age. Lay the boards with the bark side facing down (see page 39), so that any cupping occurs on the bottom side, and to prevent the board holding water on the top.

The common installation method for wood decking is shown here. We've limited the discussion to face-screwing boards to joists, but you can nail the boards down as well. However, nailing is rarely used on modern decking because it requires as much work, and nails inevitably pop down the road. Screws are just more efficient. If you do decide to nail boards down, use 10d galvanized common nails, angling the nails toward each other to improve holding power. Composite and plastic deck boards are never nailed down. For a much sleeker appearance, you can choose from the large number of "invisible" fasteners on the market. The technology for these has come a long way and, whether you're using wood, composite, or another type of deck boards, hidden fasteners are an easy, quick, and just slightly more expensive option than screwing the boards down. In any case, always follow the installation instructions and methods recommended by the manufacturer of the product you select.

Tools & Materials ▸

- Tape measure
- Circular saw
- Screwgun
- Hammer
- Drill
- ⅛" twist bit
- Pry bar
- Chalk line
- Jigsaw or handsaw
- Decking boards
- 2½" corrosion-resistant deck screws
- Galvanized common nails (8d, 10d)
- Redwood or cedar facing boards

How to Lay Decking

Position the first row of decking flush against the house. The first decking board should be perfectly straight, and should be precut to proper length. Attach the first decking board by driving a pair of 2½" corrosion-resistant deck screws into each joist.

Position remaining decking boards so that ends overhang outside joists. Space boards about ⅛" apart. Attach boards to each joist with a pair of 2½" deck screws driven into each joist.

If the boards are bowed, use a pry bar to maneuver them into position while fastening. You can also use a specialized tool (see page 55) to align the a warped board.

Drill ⅛" pilot holes in the ends of boards before attaching them to the outside joists. Pilot holes prevent screws from splitting decking boards at ends.

After every few rows of decking are installed, measure from the edge of the decking board to the edge of header joist. If the measurements show that the last board will not fit flush against the edge of the deck, adjust board spacing.

Adjust board spacing by changing the gaps between boards by a small amount over three or four rows of boards. Very small spacing changes will not be obvious to the eye.

(continued)

Use a chalk line to mark the edge of the decking flush with the outside of deck. Cut off decking, using a circular saw. Set the saw blade ⅛" deeper than the thickness of the decking so that saw will not cut the side of the deck. At areas where the circular saw cannot reach, finish the cutoff with a jigsaw or handsaw.

For a more attractive appearance, face the deck with redwood or cedar facing boards. Miter cut corners, and attach boards with deck screws or 8d galvanized nails.

Alternate facing technique: Attach facing boards so that the edges of the end decking boards overhang the facing.

Composite Decking

Lay composite decking as you would wood decking (pages 128 to 130). Position with the factory crown up so water will run off, and space rows ⅛" to ¼" apart for drainage.

Predrill pilot holes at ¾ the diameter of the fasteners, but do not countersink. Composite materials allow fasteners to set themselves. Use spiral shank nails, hot-dipped galvanized ceramic coated screws, or stainless steel nails or deck screws.

Alternate method: Attach composite decking with self-tapping composite screws. These specially designed screws require no pilot holes. If the decking "mushrooms" over the screw head, use a hammer to tap back in place.

Lay remaining decking. For boards 16-ft. or shorter, leave a gap at deck ends and any butt joints, $\frac{1}{16}$" for every 20°F difference between the temperature at the time of installation and the expected high temperature for the year.

Tongue-and-groove Decking

Position the starter strip at the far end of the deck. Make sure it is straight and properly aligned. Attach it with 2½" galvanized deck screws driven into the lower runner found under the lip of the starter strip.

Fit the tongue of a deck board into the groove of the starter strip. There will be approximately a ¼" gap between the deck board and the starter strip. Fasten the deck board to the joists with 2½" galvanized deck screws, working from the middle out to the sides of the deck.

Continue to add decking. To lay deck boards end-to-end, leave a ⅛" gap between them, and make sure any butt joints are centered over a joist.

Place the final deck board and attach it with 2½" galvanized deck screws driven through the top of the deck board into the joist. If necessary, rip the final board to size, then support the board with a length of 1 × 1 and attach both to the joist. Attach facing boards to conceal exposed ends (photo 4, next page).

T-clip Decking

Insert 2" galvanized deck screws into T-clips. Loosely attach one T-clip to the ledger at each joist location.

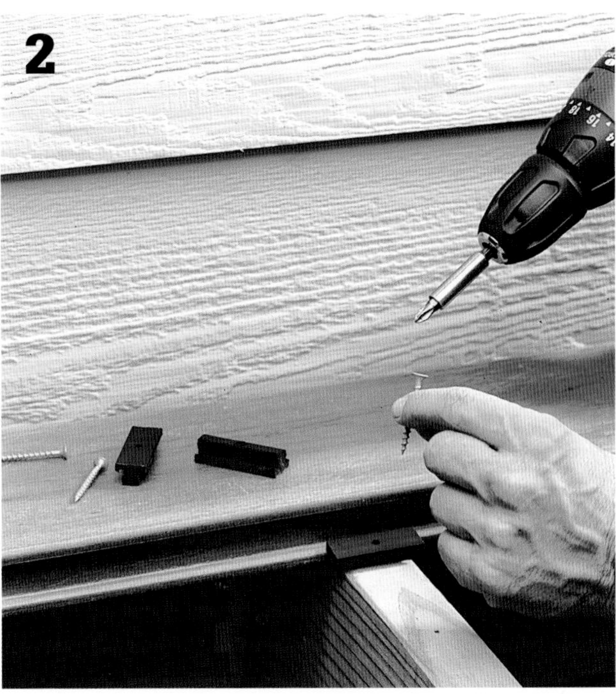

Position a deck board tight against the T-clips. Loosely attach T-clips against bottom lip on front side of deck board, just tight enough to keep the board in place. Fully tighten T-clips at the back of the board, against the house.

Push another deck board tightly against the front T-clips, attach T-clips at the front of the new board, then fully tighten the previous set of T-clips. Add another deck board and repeat the process, to the end of the deck.

Cover exposed deck board ends. Miter cut corners of the facing, and drill pilot holes ¾ the diameter of the screws. Attach with 3" galvanized deck screws.

Fiberglass Deck Systems

Place a length of retaining clips on top of the first joist. Center it on the joist and fasten with 2" galvanized deck screws. Attach lengths of retaining clips to the subsequent joists, so that the clips are perfectly aligned with the first length of clips, creating straight rows.

Place the open face of a decking board perpendicular to the joists, resting on top of a row of clips. Apply firm pressure to the top of the deck board until the decking snaps into place over the retaining clips. Work along the row, snapping the deck board in place. Attach the remaining deck boards in place, snapping each onto a row of retaining clips.

Cut the overhanging ends of the decking boards flush with the outside joists, using a circular saw with a fresh carbide-tipped blade or a masonry cut-off disc.

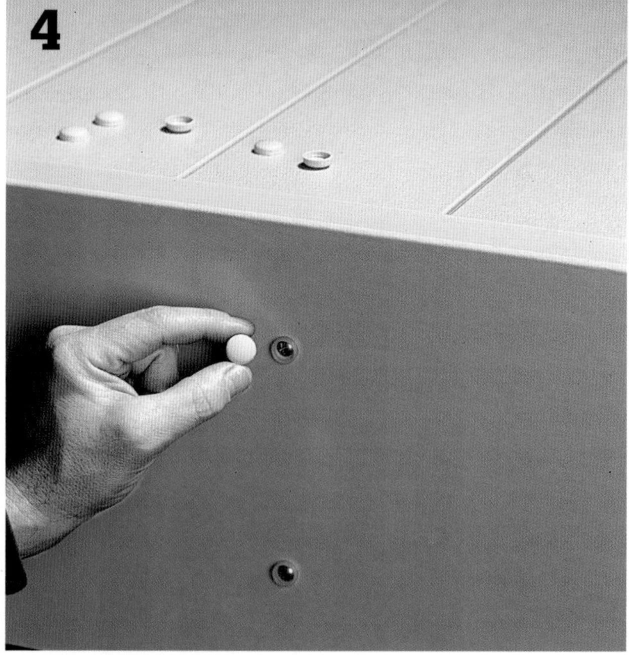

Use 2" galvanized deck screws to attach the pre-fabricated facing, covering the exposed hollow ends and creating a decorative trim. Cover the screw heads with the screw caps.

Use a Template ▸

Lay the decking boards so the ends overhang the rough opening. Make a cardboard template to draw a cutting line on the deck boards. (When framing for a tree, check with a tree nursery for adequate opening size to provide space for growth.) Cut the decking boards along the marked line, using a jigsaw. Unattached deckboards can also be cut to curved profiles with a jigsaw (inset).

How to Install Decking with Spiked Clips

Drive a spiked clip into the edge of wood decking at joist locations. Use the included fastening block to prevent damage to the spikes.

Drive a deck screw through the hole in the clip and down at an angle through the deck board and into the joist. One screw secures two deck boards at each joist location.

Set the adjacent deck board into place. Tap it against the clips to seat the spikes, using a scrap block and hand maul or sledge hammer.

How to Install Decking with Biscuit-style Clips

Cut a #20 biscuit slot into the edge of deck boards at each joist location using a biscuit joiner (plate joiner). Set the slot height so the bottom edge of the biscuit clip will touch the joist edge.

Insert the biscuit clip into the slot. Drive a deck screw through the hole in the clip and down at an angle through the deck board and into the joist. One screw secures two deck boards at this joist location.

Lay a bead of construction adhesive along the edge of the joist to keep it from squeaking later. Cut slots in the adjacent deck board and fit it over the clips of the previous board.

The Case for Hidden Fasteners ▸

The hidden fastener options shown here are only a few of the excellent alternatives to conventional face-nailing or screwing methods. The biggest advantage is aesthetic: no screwheads or nail heads mar the surface of your deck. But there are other benefits to hidden fasteners as well. Face-screwed wood decking is more prone to rotting, because water can collect in the screw head pockets. If you nail the decking down, the nail heads are bound to eventually pop up as the decking dries, contracts, or moves under use and wear. Hidden fasteners eliminate both of these problems. If you use spike- or biscuit-style clip systems, be aware that you may need to remove large sections of deck boards in order to replace a damaged or defective board in the future, because the fasteners lock adjacent boards together and hide access to the fasteners. The same is true of many other hidden-fastener systems.

How to Install Decking with Undermount Deck Brackets

Install the deck brackets along the top edge of each joist, alternating brackets from one side of the joist to the other in a continuous series. Secure the brackets with screws driven into the side of the joist.

Secure the deck boards by driving screws up through the bracket holes and into the joists. Depending on space constraints, these screws can be driven from above if necessary.

Continue installing all of the deck boards from below. When you reach the last board, you may need to install it from above for access reasons. Drive deck screws through the deck board and into the joists below. To maintain the hidden fastener appearance, counterbore the pilot holes for the screws and fill the counterbore with a plug cut from a piece of scrap decking.

How to Install Decking with Undermount Clips

Set a deck board into place on the joists, and slide a clip against it so the spacer tab touches the edge of the deck board. Drive a screw through the center hole of the clip and into the joist.

Drive a deck screw up through the plastic clip and into the deck board to secure it.

Position the next deck board against the clip's spacer tab, and drive a deck screw up through the clip to fasten it in place. One clip secures two deck boards at each joist location.

Stairs

Nearly every deck, including most low-profile styles, requires at least one step to reach the deck platform. For complex, multi-level decks or decks built on steep slopes, you may need to build several runs of stairs and possibly a landing. Given the potential risks when using deck stairs, the International Building Code is very specific regarding the size and spacing of treads and risers, the minimum stair width, and the structural sizes for stringers. Here's where your local building official can help you steer clear of potential code violations so you can build a safe stair system that will pass inspection.

Because the vertical drop of every deck varies, you'll need to make several calculations to figure out exactly what the layout of your stairs will be. This chapter will show you how. You'll also learn basic stair construction, how to build a longer flight of stairs with a landing, and even how to build a simple box-frame or suspended step when your deck is close to the ground.

In this chapter:

Building Stairs

How you build stairs and railings for your deck is perhaps the most tightly regulated portion of the building code related to decks. Whenever you are in doubt about measurements for deck stairs—or wondering if you even need to install stairs in the first place—consult the local building codes or local building inspector. Basically, designing deck stairs involves four calculations:

The number of stairs depends on the vertical drop of the deck—the distance from the deck surface to the nearest ground level.

Rise is the vertical space between treads. The proper rise prevents stumbling on the stairs. Most codes call for a maximum rise of 7¾"; a lower rise generally makes it easier to ascend or descend the stairs. The thickness of one tread is added to the space between steps to determine actual rise.

Run is the depth of the treads, and is usually a minimum of 10", although the deeper the tread, the more comfortable the stairs will be. Stair step thickness is also dictated by code and is usually a minimum of 1", although most builders use 2× lumber for stair steps. A convenient way to build step treads is by using two 2 × 6s.

Span is calculated by multiplying the run by the number of treads. The span helps you locate the end of the stairway so that you can properly position the posts.

Specifications for other elements such as the stringers and the method of attachment used to connect stairs to decking are also usually mandated in local codes. For instance, stringers normally have to be at least 1½" thick.

Although there are different ways to construct stairs, the same basic code requirements apply to any staircase used with a deck.

Tools & Materials ▸

Tape measure
Pencil
Framing square
Level
Plumb bob
Clamshell posthole digger
Wheelbarrow
Hoe
Circular saw
Hammer
Drill
⅛" twist bit
1⅜" spade bit
Ratchet wrench
Caulk gun
Sand
Portland cement
Gravel
J-bolts
Metal post anchors
2 × 12 lumber
Metal cleats
¼" × 1¼" lag screws
Joist angle brackets
10d joist hanger nails
½ × 4" lag screws and 1⅜" washers
2 × 6 lumber
16d galvanized common nails
Silicone caulk
Long, straight 2 × 4
Pointed stakes
Masking tape

Materials for Deck Stairs ▸

Most local building codes require that you use pressure-treated lumber for stairway posts and stringers. Install stair treads and risers cut from material that matches the surface decking. If possible, create treads that use the same board pattern as the decking. You may cover visible pressure-treated portions of the stairway with material matching the decking, too, or stain them to match the decking as closely as possible. Local codes may require handrails on stairways with three or more treads. Many codes also require a separate grippable handrail attached inside stair railings (on one side) in certain circumstances.

Platform steps feature wide treads. Each step is built on a framework of posts and joists.

Stairway Styles

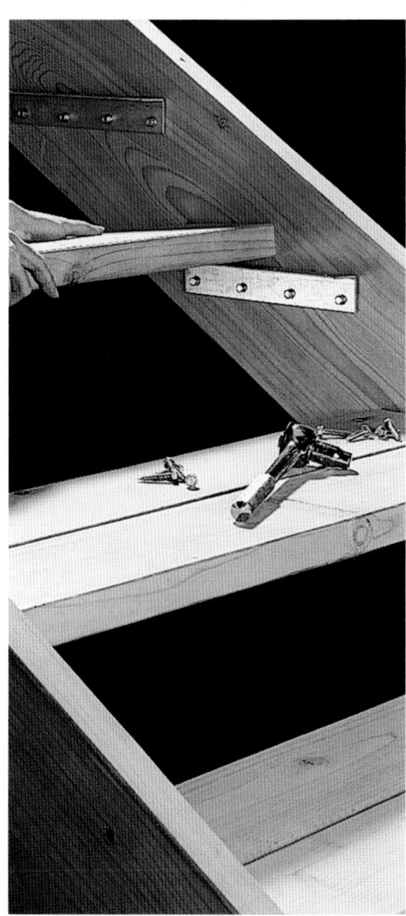

Open steps have metal cleats that hold the treads between the stringers. The treads on this stairway are built with 2 × 6s to match the surface decking.

Boxed steps, built with notched stringers and solid risers, give a finished look to a deck stairway. Predrill the ends of treads to prevent splitting.

Long stairways sometimes require landings. A landing is a small platform to which both flights of stairs are attached (see pages 150 to 159).

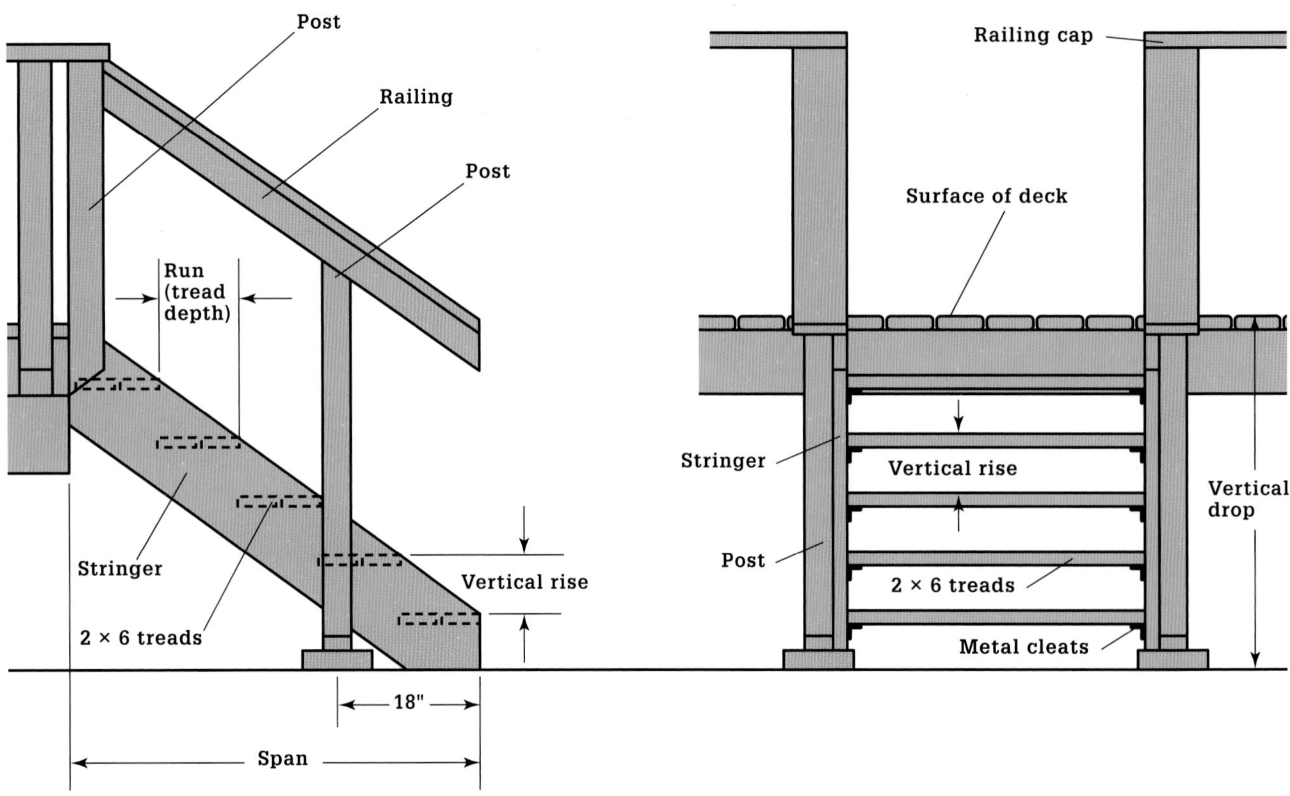

A common deck stairway is made from two 2 × 12 stringers and pairs of 2 × 6 treads attached with metal cleats. Posts set 18" back from the end of the stairway help to anchor the stringers and the railings. Calculations needed to build stairs include the number of steps, the rise of each step, the run of each step, and the stairway span.

How to Find Measurements for Stairway Layout ▸

				EXAMPLE (39" High Deck)
1.	Find the number of steps: Measure vertical drop from deck surface to ground. Divide by 7. Round off to nearest whole number.	Vertical drop:		39"
		÷ 7 =		÷ 5.57"
		Number of steps: =		= 6
2.	Find step rise: Divide the vertical drop by the number of steps.	Vertical drop: =		39"
		Number of steps: ÷		÷ 6
		Rise: =		= 6.5"
3.	Find step run: Typical treads made from two 2 × 6s have a run of 11¼". If your design is different, find run by measuring depth of tread, including any space between boards.	Run:		11¼"
4.	Find stairway span: Multiply the run by the number of treads. (Number of treads is always one less than number of steps.)	Run:		11¼"
		Number of treads:		× 5
		Span: =		= 56¼"

Simple Stairs: How to Build a Box-frame Step

Construct a rectangular frame for the step using dimension lumber (2 × 6 lumber is standard). Join the pieces with deck screws. The step must be at least 36" wide and 10" deep. Cut cross blocks and install them inside the frame, spaced every 16".

Dig a flat-bottomed trench, about 4" deep, where the step will rest. Fill the trench with compactible gravel, and pack with a tamper. Set the step in position, then measure and attach deck boards to form the tread of the step.

Simple Stairs: How to Build a Suspended Step

Screw 2 × 4 furring strips against one side of the deck joists where the step joists will be installed. These strips provide an offset so the step joists will not conflict with the joist hangers attached to the beam. Use a reciprocating saw and chisel to make 1½"-wide notches in the rim joist adjacent to the furring strips. *Note: To maintain adequate structural strength, notches in the joists should be no more than 1½" deep.*

Measure and cut step joists, allowing about 3 ft. of nailing surface inside the deck frame, and 10" or more of exposed tread. Make sure the step joists are level with one another, then attach them to the deck joists, using deck screws. Cut and attach deck boards to the tread area of the step.

How to Build Basic Deck Stairs

Use the stairway elevation drawings to find measurements for stair stringers and posts. Use a pencil and framing square to outline where stair stringers will be attached to the side of the deck.

Locate the post footings so they are 18" back from the end of the stairway span. Lay a straight 2 × 4 on the deck so that it is level and square to the side of the deck. Use a plumb bob or level to mark the ground at footing centerpoints.

Dig holes and pour the footings for posts. Attach metal post anchors to the footings and install the posts. Check with your building department to find out if 6 × 6 posts are now required.

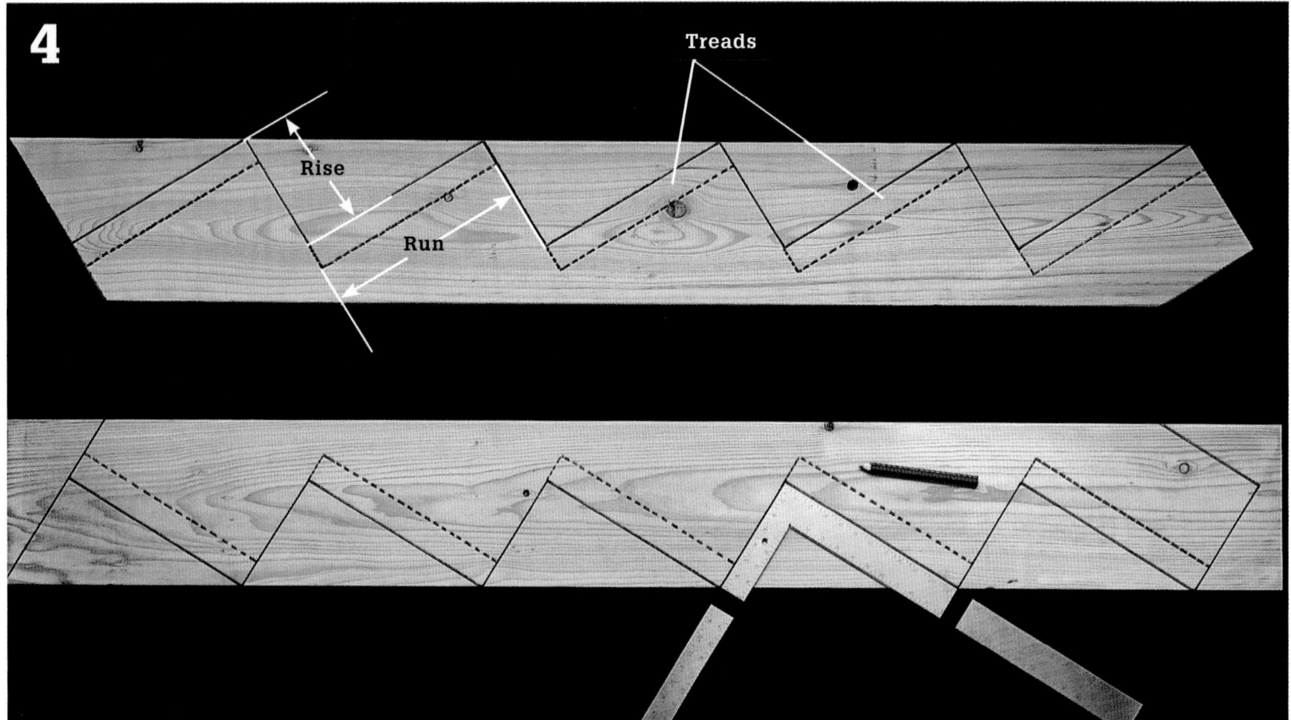

Lay out the stair stringers. Use tape to mark the rise measurement on one leg of a framing square, and the run measurement on the other leg. Beginning at one end of the stringer, position the square with tape marks flush to edge of the board, and outline the rise and run for each step. Then draw in the tread outline against the bottom of each run line. Use a circular saw to trim the ends of the stringers as shown. (When cutting the stringers for stairs without metal cleats, just cut on the solid lines.)

Attach metal tread cleats flush with the bottom of each tread outline, using ¼" × 1¼" lag screws. Drill ⅛" pilot holes to prevent the screws from splitting the wood.

Attach angle brackets to the upper ends of the stringers, using 10d joist hanger nails. Brackets should be flush with the cut ends of the stringers.

(continued)

Position the stair stringers against the side of the deck, over the stringer outlines. Align the top point of the stringer flush with the surface of the deck. Attach the stringers by nailing the angle brackets to the deck with joist hanger nails.

Drill two ¼" pilot holes through each stringer and into each adjacent post. Counterbore each hole to a depth of ½", using a 1⅜" spade bit. Attach the stringers to the posts with ½ × 4" lag screws and washers, using a ratchet wrench or impact driver. Seal screw heads with silicone caulk.

Measure the width of the stair treads. Cut two 2 × 6s for each tread, using a circular saw.

For each step, position the front 2 × 6 on the tread cleat, so that the front edge is flush with the tread outline on the stringers.

Drill ⅛" pilot holes, then attach the front 2 × 6 to the cleats with ¼ × 1¼" lag screws.

Position the rear 2 × 6 on the cleats, allowing a small space between boards. Use a 16d nail as a spacing guide. Drill ⅛" pilot holes, and attach the 2 × 6 to the cleats with ¼ × 1¼" lag screws. Repeat for the remaining steps.

Stairbuilding Option

Notched stringers precut from pressure-treated wood are available at building centers. Edges of cutout areas should be coated with sealer-preservative to prevent rot.

Building Stairs with Landings

Designing and building a stairway with a landing can be one of the most challenging elements of a deck project. Precision is crucial, since building codes have very exact standards for stairway construction. To ensure that the steps for both the top and bottom staircases have the same vertical rise and tread depth, the landing must be set at the right position and height.

Even for professional builders, designing a stairway layout is a process of trial and revision. Begin by creating a preliminary layout that fits your situation, but as you plan and diagram the project, be prepared to revise the layout to satisfy code requirements and the demands of your building site. Measure your site carefully, and work out all the details on paper before you begin any work. Accuracy and meticulous planning will help ensure that your steps are level and uniform in size.

Remember that local building codes may require handrails for any stairway with three or more risers.

A landing functions essentially as a large step that interrupts a tall stairway. For the builder, the landing provides a convenient spot from which to change the direction of the stairway. For the homeowner, the landing provides a spot to catch your breath momentarily while climbing.

Stairway Basics

The goal of any stairway is to allow people to move easily and safely from one level to another. When designing a deck stairway, the builder must consider the vertical drop—the vertical distance from the surface of the deck to the ending point; and the span—the horizontal distance from the starting point to the end of the stairway.

During the planning stage, the vertical drop is divided into a series of equal-size steps, called rises. Similarly, the horizontal span is divided into a series of equal-size runs. On a stairway with a landing, there are two span measurements to consider: the distance from the deck to the edge of the landing, and from the landing to the end point on the ground. In general, the combined horizontal span of the staircases, not counting the landing, should be 40% to 60% more than the total vertical drop.

For safety and comfort, the components of a stairway must be built according to clearly prescribed guidelines, as listed on page 142.

Anatomy of a Stair with Landing

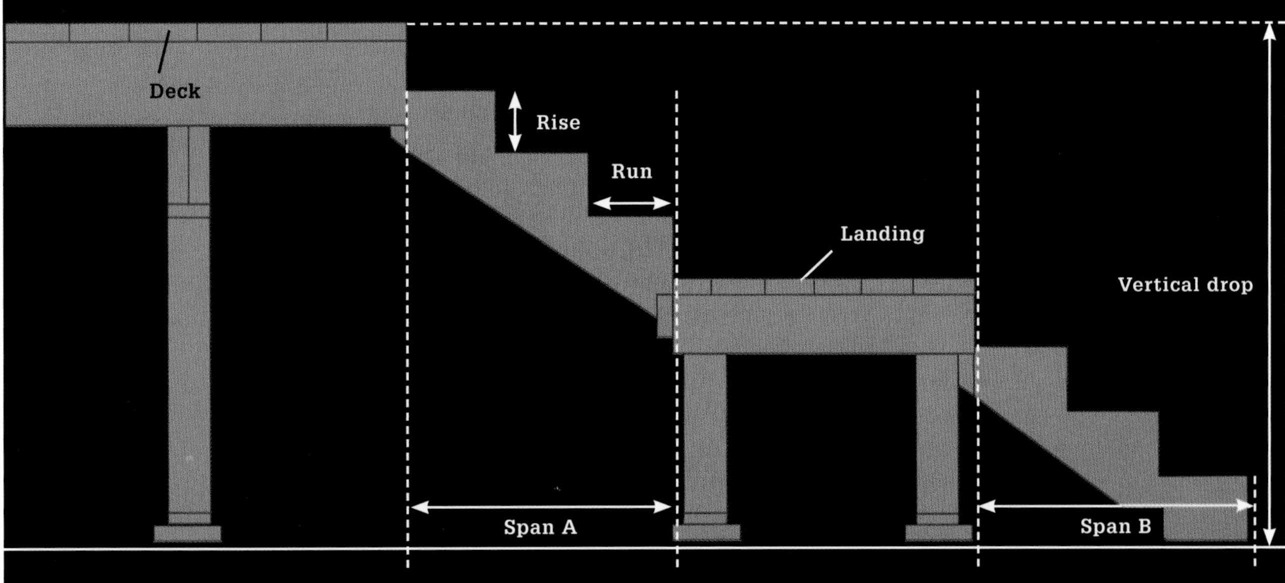

The challenge when planning a stairway is adjusting the preliminary layout and the step dimensions as needed to ensure that the stairway fits the building site and is comfortable to use.

Rises must be no less than 4" and no more than 7¾" high.

Runs, the horizontal depth of each step, must be at least 10". The number of runs in a staircase is always one less than the number of rises.

Combined sum of the step rise and run should be about 18" to 20". Steps built to this guideline are the most comfortable to use.

Variation between the largest and smallest rise or run measurement can be no more than ⅜".

Stair width must be at least 36", so two people can comfortably pass one another.

Stringers should be spaced no more than 36" apart. For added support, a center stringer is recommended for any staircase with more than three steps.

Landings serve as oversized steps; their height must be set as precisely as the risers for the other steps in the stairway. Landings should be at least 36" square, or as wide as the staircase itself. U-shaped stairways should have oversized landings, at least 1 ft. wider than the combined width of the two staircases. Landings very often require reinforcement with diagonal cross braces between the support posts.

Concrete footings should support all stringers resting on the ground.

Code Update: Stair Pads ▸

Some local building codes now prohibit the use of a concrete stair pad to support the bottom run of stair stringers. The "floating" nature of a slab like this allows it to move up and down as the ground freezes and thaws, and that causes the stairs to shift as well. Use full-depth concrete footings instead of a pad to support your deck stairs (see page 158).

Construction Details

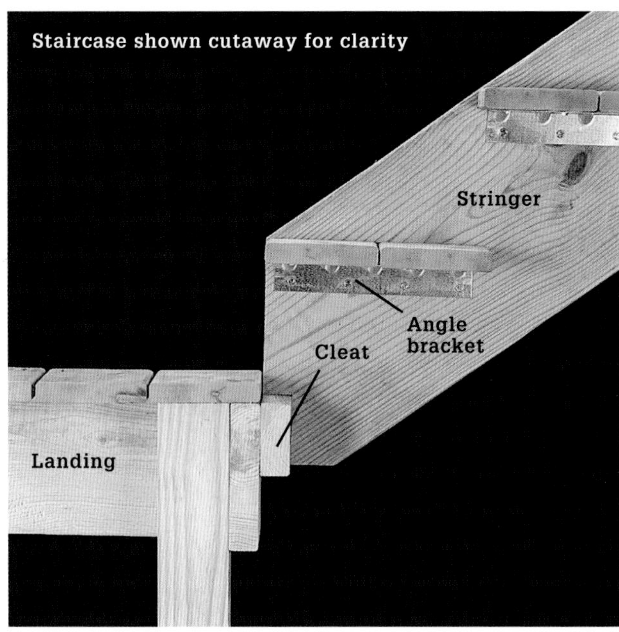

Stringers for the top staircase rest on a 2 × 4 cleat attached to the side of the landing. The stringers are notched to sit on top of the cleat. On the outside stringers, angle brackets support the treads.

Steps may be boxed in the riser boards, and may have treads that overhang the front edge of the step for a more finished look. Treads should overhang the riser boards by no more than 1".

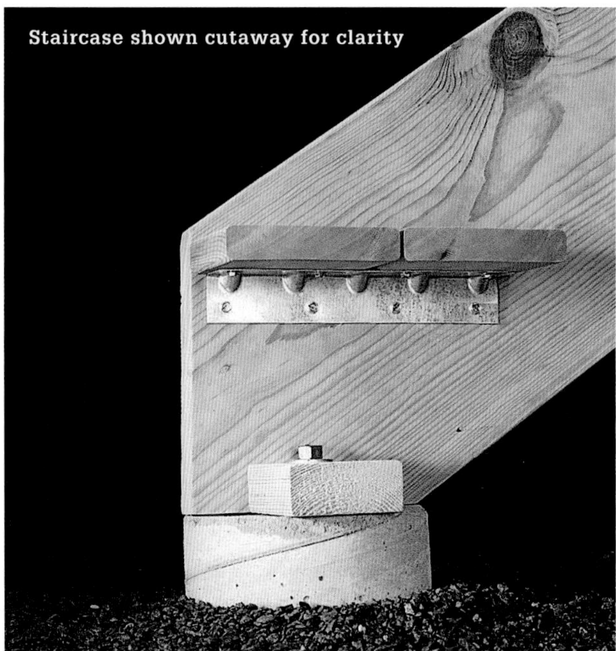

Concrete footings support the stringers for the lower staircase. J-bolts are inserted into the footings while the concrete is still wet. After the footings dry, wooden cleats are attached to the bolts to create surfaces for anchoring the stringers. After the staircase is positioned, the stringers are nailed or screwed to the cleats.

Center stringers are recommended for any staircase that has more than 3 steps or is more than 36" wide. Center stringers are supported by a 2 × 6 nailer attached with metal straps to the bottom of the rim joist. The bottom edge of the nailer can be beveled to match the angle of the stringers. The center stringer is attached by driving deck screws through the back of the nailer and into the stringer.

How to Create a Preliminary Layout

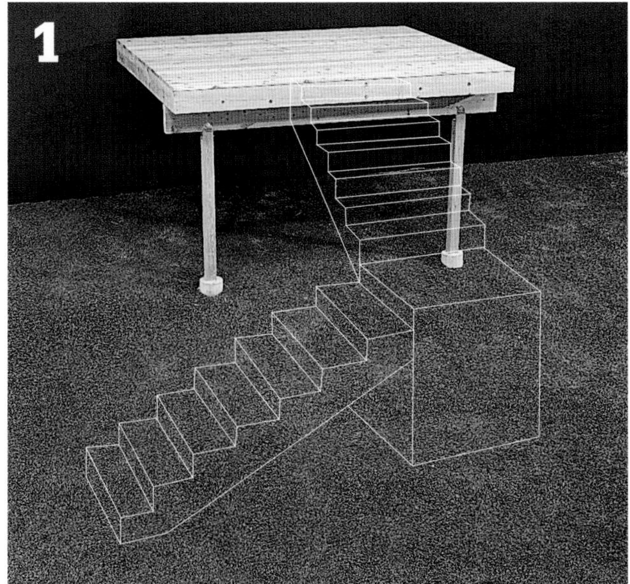

Evaluate your building site and try to visualize which stairway design best fits your needs. When creating a preliminary layout, it is generally best to position the landing so the upper and lower staircases will be of equal length. Select a general design idea.

Establish a rough starting point for the stairway on the deck, and an ending point on the ground that conforms with your design. Mark the starting point on the rim joist, and mark the ending point with two stakes, spaced to equal the planned width of your stairway. This is a rough layout only; later calculations will give you the precise measurements.

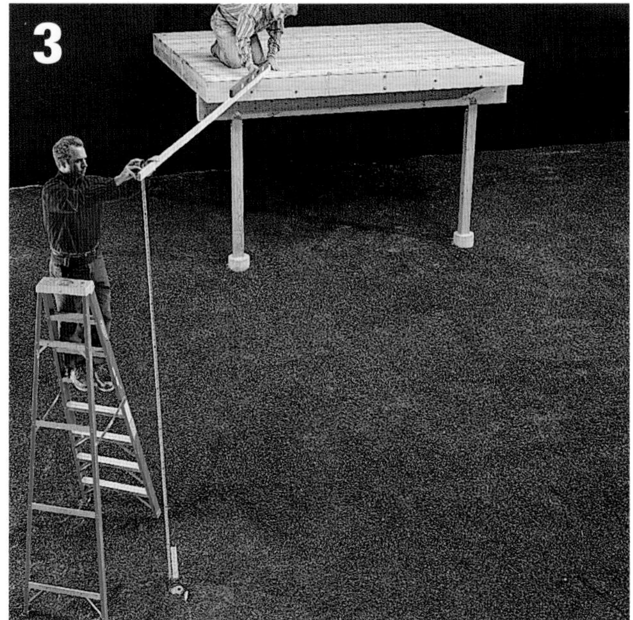

To determine the vertical drop of the stairway, extend a straight 2 × 4 from the starting point on the deck to a spot level with the deck directly over the ending point on the ground. Measure the distance to the ground; this measurement is the total vertical drop. *Note: If the ending point is more than 10 ft. from the starting point, use a mason's string and line level to establish a reference point from which to measure.*

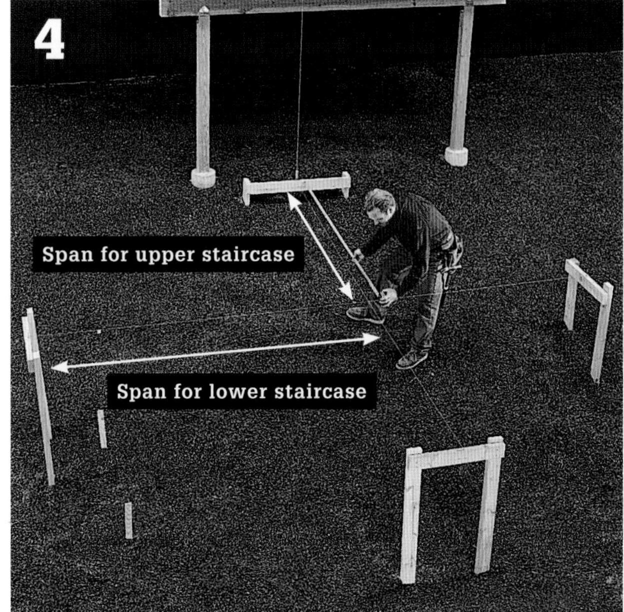

Measure the horizontal span for each staircase. First, use batterboards to establish level layout strings representing the edges of the staircases. Find the span for the upper staircase by measuring from a point directly below the edge of the deck out to the edge of the landing. Measure the span for the lower staircase from the landing to the endpoint.

Create Final Stair Landing Layouts ▸

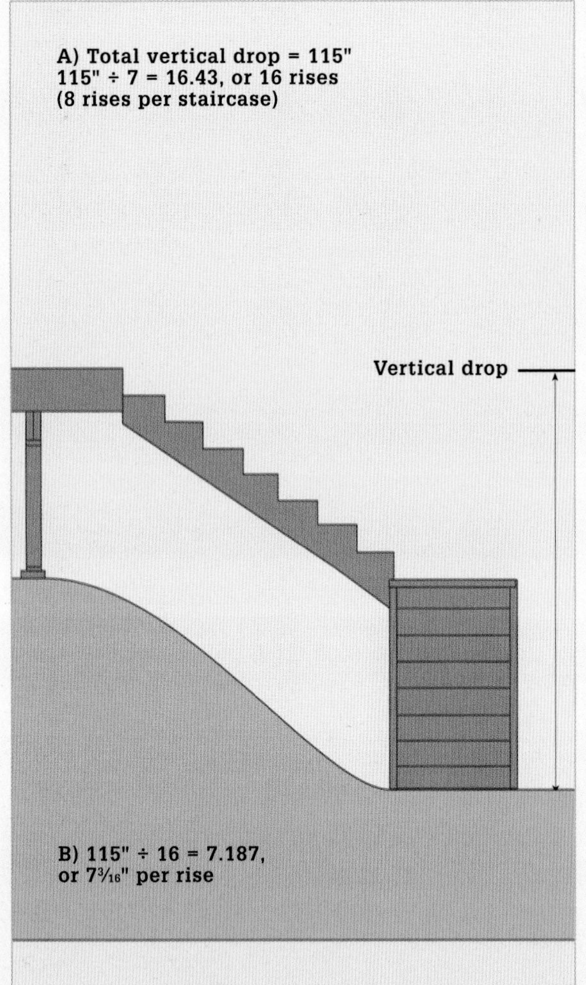

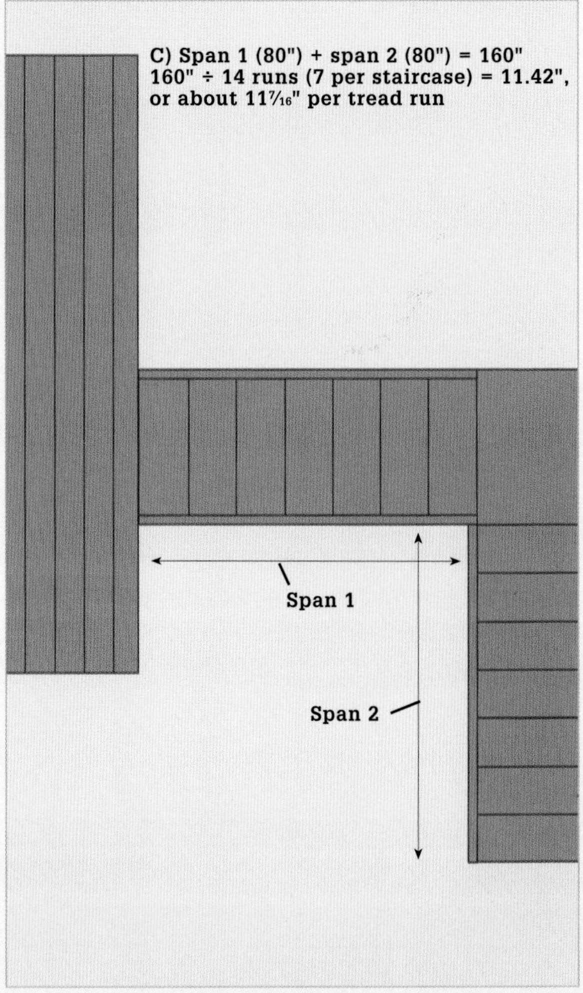

ILLUSTRATIONS ABOVE:

Find the total number of step rises you will need by dividing the vertical drop by 7, rounding off fractions. (A, example above). Next, determine the exact height for each step rise by dividing the vertical drop by the number of rises (B).

Find the horizontal run for each step by adding the spans of both staircases (not including the landing), then dividing by the number of runs (C). Remember that the number of runs in a staircase is always one less than the number of rises.

If the layout does not conform with the guidelines on page 142, adjust the stairway starting point, ending point, or landing, then recalculate the measurements. After finding all dimensions, return to your building site and adjust the layout according to your final plan.

ILLUSTRATIONS NEXT PAGE:

Lay out stringers on 2 × 12 lumber using a carpenter's square. Trim off the waste sections with a circular saw, finishing the notched cuts with a handsaw. In the illustrations on page 155, the waste sections are left unshaded. In standard deck construction, the outside stringers are fitted with metal tread supports that are attached to the inside faces of the stringers. The middle stringer in each flight of stairs is notched to create surfaces that support the stair treads—when cut, these surfaces must align with the tops of the metal tread supports. For the upper staircase stringers, notches are cut at the bottom front edges to fit over a 2 × 4 cleat that is attached to the landing (see page 158). The top of each notch should lie below the nose of the bottom tread by a distance equal to one rise plus the thickness of a decking board (see next page).

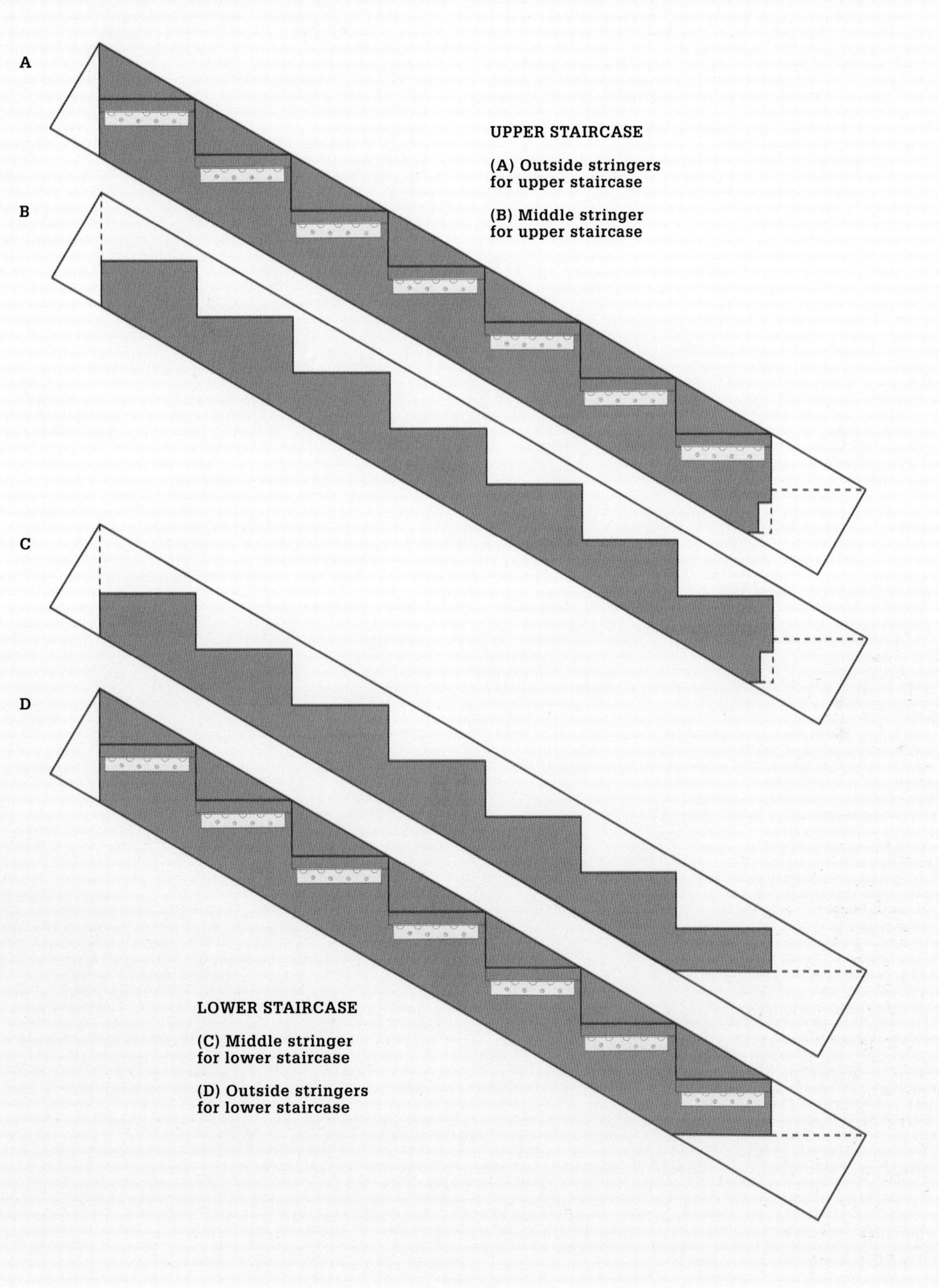
A
B
C
D
UPPER STAIRCASE
(A) Outside stringers for upper staircase
(B) Middle stringer for upper staircase
LOWER STAIRCASE
(C) Middle stringer for lower staircase
(D) Outside stringers for lower staircase

How to Build Stairs with a Landing

Begin construction by building the landing. On a flat surface, build the landing frame from 2 × 6 lumber. Join the corners with 3" deck screws, then check for square by measuring diagonals. Adjust the frame until the diagonals are equal, then tack braces across the corners to hold the frame square.

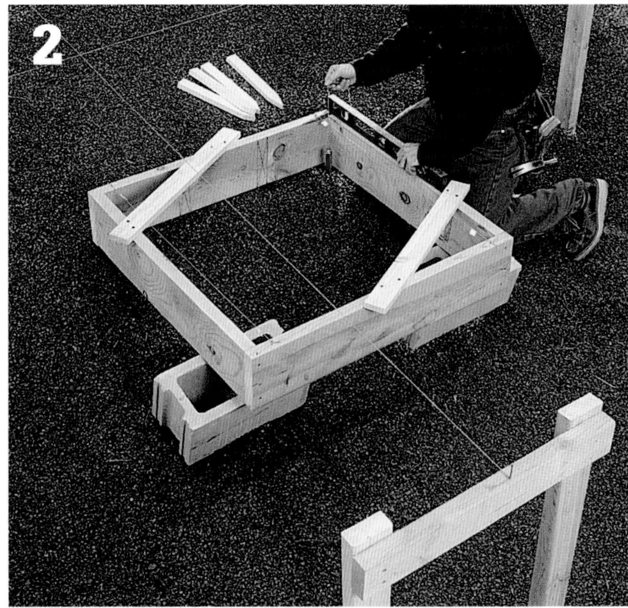

Using your plan drawing, find the exact position of the landing on the ground, then set the frame in position and adjust it for level. Drive stakes to mark locations for the landing posts, using a plumb bob as a guide. Install the footings and posts for the landing.

From the top of the deck, measure down a distance equal to the vertical drop for the upper staircase. Attach a 2 × 4 reference board across the deck posts at this height. Position a straightedge on the reference board and against the landing posts so it is level, and mark the posts at this height. Measure down a distance equal to the thickness of the decking boards, and mark reference lines to indicate where the top of the landing frame will rest.

Attach the landing frame to the posts at the reference lines. Make sure the landing is level, then secure it with joist ties attached to the posts with ⅝ × 3" lag screws. Cut off the posts flush with the top of the landing frame using a reciprocating saw.

Remove the diagonal braces from the top of the landing frame, then cut and install joists. (For a diagonal decking pattern, space the joists every 12" on-center.) Attach the decking boards, and trim them to the edge of the frame.

For extra support and to help prevent sway, create permanent cross braces by attaching 2 × 4 boards diagonally from the bottoms of the posts to the inside of the landing frame. Brace at least two sides of the landing. Remove the temporary braces and stakes holding the posts.

Lay out and cut all stringers for both the upper and lower staircases (page 155). For the center stringers only, cut notches where the treads will rest. Start the notches with a circular saw, then finish the cuts with a handsaw. Measure and cut all tread boards.

Use ¾"-long lag screws to attach angle brackets to the stringers where the treads will rest, then turn the stringers upside down and attach the treads with lag screws. Gaps between tread boards should be no more than ⅜".

(continued)

Dig and pour a concrete footing to support each stringer for the lower staircase. Make sure the footings are level and are the proper height in relation to the landing. Install a metal J-bolt in each footing while the concrete is wet, positioning the bolts so they will be offset about 2" from the stringers. After the concrete dries, cut 2 × 4 footing cleats, drill holes in them, and attach them to the J-bolts using nuts.

Attach a 2 × 6 nailer to the landing to support the center stringer (page 152), then set the staircase in place, making sure the outside stringers are flush with the top of the decking. Use corner brackets and joist-hanger nails to anchor the stringers to the rim joist and nailer. Attach the bottoms of the stringers by nailing them to the footing cleats.

Measure and cut a 2 × 4 cleat to match the width of the upper staircase, including the stringers. Use lag screws to attach the cleat to the rim joist on the landing, flush with the tops of the joists. Notch the bottoms of all stringers to fit around the cleat (page 155), and attach angle brackets on the stringers to support the treads.

To support the center stringer at the top of the staircase, measure and cut a 2 × 6 nailer equal to the width of the staircase. Attach the nailer to the rim joist with metal straps and screws.

Position the stringers so they rest on the landing cleat. Make sure the stringers are level and properly spaced, then toenail the bottoms of the stringers into the cleat, using galvanized 16d nails. At the top of the staircase, use angle brackets to attach the outside stringers to the rim joist and the middle stringer to the nailer.

Measure, cut, and position tread boards over the angle brackets, then attach them from below, using ¾"-long lag screws. The gap between tread boards should be no more than ⅜". After completing the stairway, install railings (pages 160 to 191).

BLACK&
DECKER
BLACK&DECKER 12V

Deck Railings

Decks that are built 30 inches above the ground or higher must have a system of railings installed around their perimeter. Building codes dictate the important spacing and height requirements for railings, but what you may not know is that wood isn't the only option from which to build them. Granted, traditional wooden railings are quick to build and relatively affordable, but there are other exciting and attractive alternatives. This chapter will show you a variety of different railing systems, including those made with prefabricated composite parts, steel cable, clear glass panels, and copper tubing. With a measure of creativity on your part, railings can be a showcase design feature of your new deck and not just a means of preventing injuries.

This chapter will also teach you how to outfit your deck stairs with handrails and balusters and even shape a curved railing using several challenging woodworking techniques.

In this chapter:

Deck Railing Basics

Railings must be sturdy and firmly attached to the framing members of the deck. Never attach railing posts to the surface decking. Check local building codes for guidelines regarding railing construction. Most codes require that railings be at least 36" above decking. Vertical balusters should be spaced no more than 4" apart. In some areas, a grippable handrail may be required for any stairway over four treads. Check with your local building inspector for the building codes in your area.

Tools & Materials ▸

- Tape measure
- Pencil
- Power miter saw
- Drill
- Twist bits (⅛", ⅜")
- 1⅜" spade bit
- Combination square
- Awl
- Ratchet wrench
- Caulk gun
- Reciprocating saw
- Circular saw
- Jigsaw with wood-cutting blade
- Miter saw
- Level
- Railing lumber (4 × 4s, 2 × 6s, 2 × 4s, 2 × 2s)
- Clear sealer-preservative
- ½ × 4½" lag screws and 1⅜" washers
- Silicone caulk
- 2½" corrosion-resistant deck screws
- 10d galvanized common nails

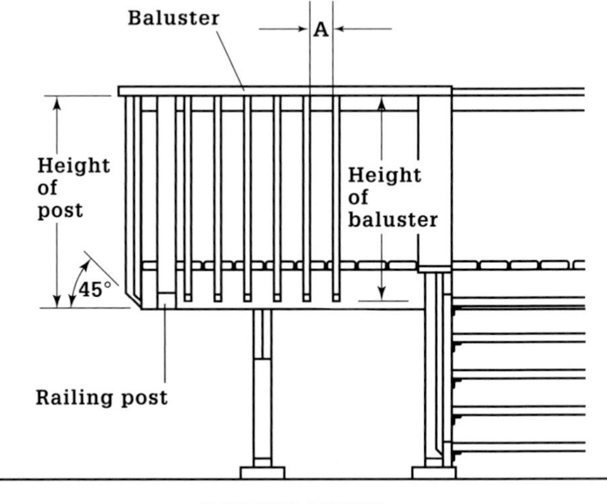

Refer to your deck design plan for spacing (A) and length of railing posts and balusters. Posts should be spaced no more than 6 ft. apart.

Railings are mandatory safety features for any deck that's more than 30 in. above grade. There are numerous code issues and stipulations that will dictate how you build your deck railings. Consult with your local building inspector for any code clarification you may need.

Types of Railings

Vertical balusters with posts and rails are a good choice for houses with strong vertical lines. A vertical baluster railing like the one shown above is a good choice where children will be present.

Horizontal railings are often used on low, ranch-style homes. Horizontal railings are made of vertical posts, two or more wide horizontal rails, and a railing cap.

Lattice panels add a decorative touch to a deck. They also provide extra privacy.

Railing Codes ▸

Railings usually are required by building codes on any deck that is more than 30" above existing grade. Select a railing design that fits the style of your home.

For example, on a low, ranch-style house, choose a deck railing with wide, horizontal rails. On a Tudor-style home with a steep roof, choose a railing with closely spaced, vertical balusters. See pages 174 to 191 for information on how to build other railing styles, including a curved railing.

Codes may require easily gripped hand rails for stairways with 4 risers or more (page 177). Check with your building inspector.

Preshaped products let you easily build decorative deck railings. Railing products include shaped handrails, balusters, and posts.

How to Install a Wood Deck Railing

Measure and cut 4 × 4 posts, using a power miter saw or circular saw. Cut the tops of the posts square, and cut the bottoms at a 45° angle. Seal cut ends of lumber with clear sealer-preservative.

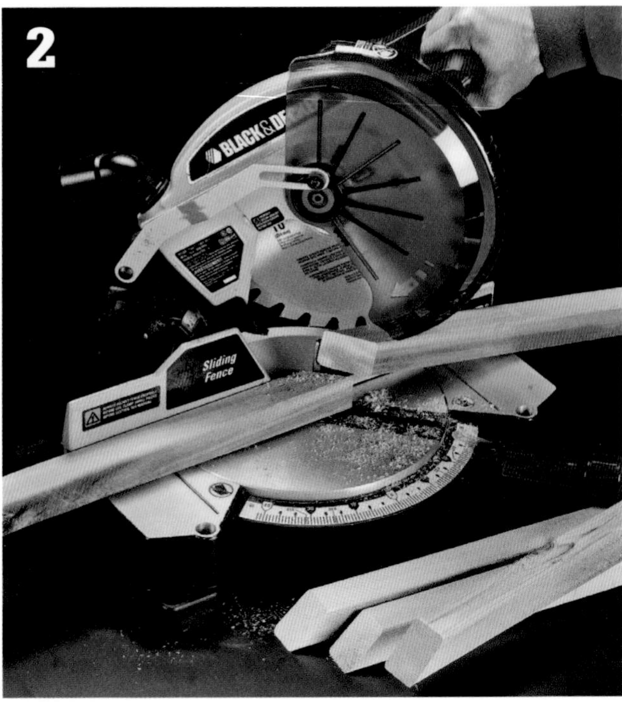

Measure and cut the balusters for the main deck railing, using a power miter saw or circular saw. Cut the tops of the balusters square, and cut the bottoms at a 45° angle. Seal cut ends of lumber with clear sealer-preservative.

Drill two ⅜" pilot holes spaced 2" apart through the bottom end of each post. Counterbore each pilot hole to ½" depth, using a 1⅜" spade bit.

Drill two ⅛" pilot holes spaced 4" apart near the bottom end of each baluster. Drill two ⅛" pilot holes at the top of each baluster, spaced 1½" apart.

Measure and mark the position of posts around the outside of the deck, using a combination square as a guide. Plan to install a post on the outside edge of each stair stringer.

Position each post with the beveled end flush with the bottom of the deck. Plumb the post with a level. Insert a screwdriver or the ⅜" drill bit into the pilot holes and mark the side of the deck.

Remove the post and drill ⅜" holes into the side of the deck.

Attach railing posts to the side of the deck with ⅜ × 4½" lag screws and washers, using a ratchet wrench or impact driver. Seal the screw heads with silicone caulk.

Measure and cut 2 × 4 side rails. Position the rails with their edges flush to the tops of posts, and attach to posts with 2½" corrosion-resistant deck screws.

(continued)

Join 2 × 4s for long rails by cutting the ends at 45° angles. Drill ⅛" pilot holes to prevent nails from splitting the end grain, and attach the rails with 10d galvanized nails. (Screws may split mitered ends.)

Attach the ends of rails to the stairway posts, flush with the edges of the posts, as shown. Drill ⅛" pilot holes, and attach the rails with 2½" deck screws.

At a stairway, measure from the surface of the decking to the top of the upper stairway post (A).

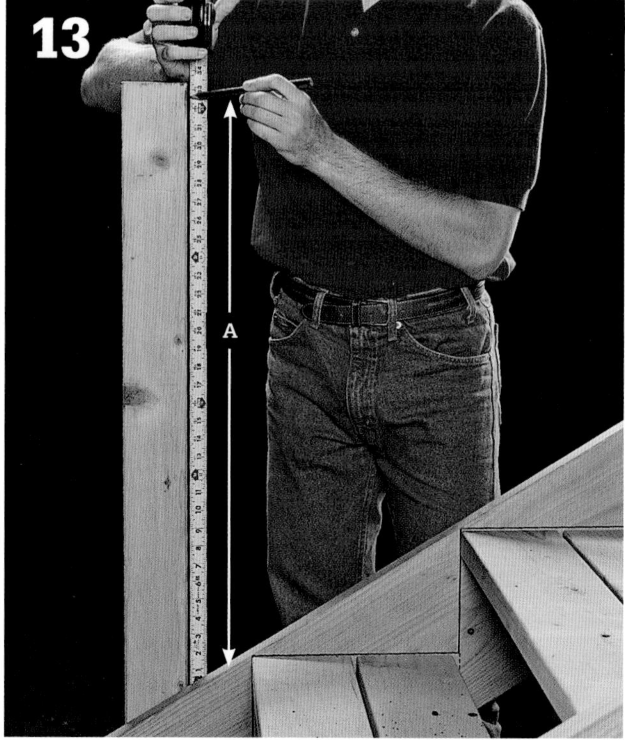

Transfer measurement A to the lower stairway post, measuring from the edge of the stair stringer.

Position a 2 × 4 rail against the inside of the stairway posts. Align the rail with the top rear corner of the top post and with the pencil mark on the lower post. Have a helper attach the rail temporarily with 2½" deck screws.

Mark the outline of the post and the deck rail on the back side of the stairway rail.

Mark the outline of the stairway rail on the lower stairway post.

Use a level to mark a plumb cutoff line at the bottom end of the stairway rail. Remove the rail.

(continued)

Extend the pencil lines across both sides of the stairway post, using a combination square as a guide.

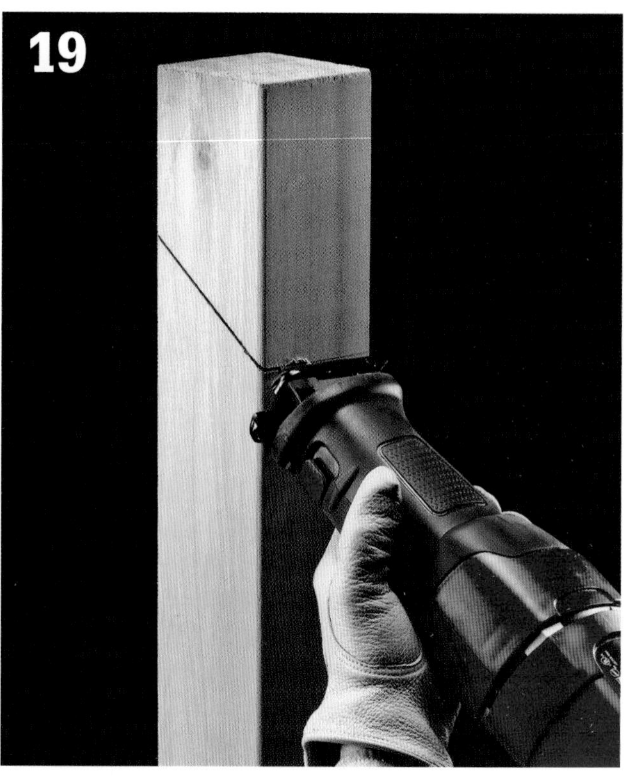

Cut off the lower stairway post along the diagonal cutoff line, using a reciprocating saw or circular saw.

Use a jigsaw or miter saw to cut the stairway rail along the marked outlines.

Position the stairway rail flush against the top edge of the posts. Drill ⅛" pilot holes, then attach the rail to the posts with 2½" deck screws.

Use a spacer block to ensure equal spacing between balusters. Beginning next to a plumb railing post, position each baluster tight against the spacer block, with the top of the baluster flush to the top of rail. Attach each baluster with 2½" deck screws.

For the stairway, position the baluster against the stringer and rail, and adjust for plumb. Draw a diagonal cutoff line on top of the baluster, using the top of the stair rail as a guide. Cut the baluster on the marked line, using a power miter saw. Seal the ends with clear sealer-preservative.

Beginning next to the upper stairway post, position each baluster tight against the spacer block, with the top flush to the top of the stair rail. Predrill and attach the baluster with 2½" deck screws.

Position the 2 × 6 cap so that the edge is flush with the rail's inside edge. Drill ⅛" pilot holes and attach the cap to the rail with 2½" deck screws every 12". Drive screws into each post and into every third baluster. For long caps, bevel the ends at 45°. Drill 1⁄16" pilot holes and nail to the post with 10d nails.

(continued)

At the corners, miter the ends of the railing cap at 45°. Drill ⅛" pilot holes, and attach the cap to the post with 2½" deck screws.

At the top of the stairs, cut the cap so that it is flush with the stairway rail. Drill ⅛" pilot holes and attach the cap with 2½" deck screws.

Measure and cut the cap for the stairway rail. Mark the outline of the post on the side of the cap, and bevel cut the ends of the cap. Position the cap over the stairway rail and balusters so that the edge of the cap is flush with the inside edge of the rail.

Drill ⅛" pilot holes and attach the cap to the rail with 2½" deck screws driven every 12". Also drive screws through the cap into the stair post and into every third baluster.

Wood Railing Style Variations

Vertical baluster railings are a popular style because they complement most house styles. To improve the strength and appearance of the railing, the advanced variation shown here uses a "false mortise" design. The 2 × 2 balusters are mounted on 2 × 2 horizontal rails that slide into mortises notched into the posts (see page 172).

Horizontal railing visually complements modern ranch-style houses with predominantly horizontal lines. For improved strength and a more attractive appearance, the style shown here features 1 × 4 rails set on edge into dadoes cut in the faces of the posts. A cap rail running over all posts and top rails helps unify and strengthen the railing (see page 173).

Wall-style railing is framed with short 2 × 4 stud walls attached flush with the edges of the deck. The stud walls and rim joists are then covered with siding materials, usually chosen to match the siding on the house. A wall-style railing creates a more private space and visually draws the deck into the home, providing a unified appearance (see pages 174 to 175).

Stairway railings are required for any stairway with more than three steps. They are usually designed to match the style used on the deck railing (see pages 176 to 177).

How to Build a Vertical Baluster Railing

Cut 4 × 4 railing posts to size (at least 36", plus the height of the deck rim joists). Lay out and mark partial dadoes 1½" wide and 2½" long where the horizontal 2 × 2 rails will fit. Use a circular saw set to ½" blade depth to make a series of cuts from the edge of the post to the end of layout marks, then use a chisel to clean out the dadoes and square them off. On corner posts, cut dadoes on adjoining sides of the post.

Attach the posts inside the rim joists. To find the length for the rails, measure between the bases of the posts, then add 1" for the ½" dadoes on each post. Measure and cut all balusters. Install the surface boards before continuing with railing construction.

Assemble the rails and balusters on a flat surface. Position the balusters at regular intervals (no more than 4" apart), and secure them by driving 2½" deck screws through the rails. A spacing block cut to match the desired gap can make this easier.

Slide the assembled railings into the post dadoes, and toenail them in position with galvanized casing nails. Cut plugs to fit the exposed dadoes, and glue them in place. The resulting joint should resemble a mortise-and-tenon.

Measure and cut the 2 × 6 cap rails, then secure them by driving 2" deck screws up through the top rail. At corners, miter-cut the cap rails to form miter joints.

How to Build a Notched Deck Railing

Cut all 4 × 4 posts to length, then clamp them together to lay out 3½"-wide × ¾"-deep dadoes for the horizontal rails. For corner posts, cut dadoes on adjacent faces of the post. Cut the dadoes by making a series of parallel cuts, about ¼" apart, between the layout marks.

Knock out the waste wood between the layout marks, using a hammer, then use a chisel to smooth the bottom of each dado. Attach the posts inside the rim joists. Install the decking before continuing with the railing construction.

Determine the length of the 1 × 4 rails by measuring between the bases of the posts. Cut rails to length, then nail them in place using 8d splitless cedar siding nails. At the corners, bevel-cut the ends of the rails to form miter joints. If the rails butt together, the joint should fall at the center of a post.

Measure and cut 2 × 2 cleats and attach them between the posts, flush with the top rail, using galvanized casing nails. Then, measure and cut cap rails, and position and attach them by driving 2" deck screws up through the cleats. At corners, miter-cut the ends of the cap rails.

How to Build a Sided Railing

Cut the posts to length, using a circular saw or miter saw. If your saw does not have enough cutting capacity, make the cut in two passes. *Note: Many codes no longer permit notched handrail posts. Check with your local building department.*

Attach the posts inside the rim joists with lag screws or through bolts, then add blocking between joists to reinforce the posts. Install decking before continuing with railing construction.

Build a 2 x 4 stud wall to match the planned height of your railing. Space studs 16" on center, and attach them by driving deck screws through the top plate and sole plate.

Position the stud wall on the deck, flush with the edges of the rim joists, then anchor it by driving 3" deck screws down through the sole plate. At corners, screw the studs of adjoining walls together. At open ends, screw the end studs to posts.

At corners, attach 2 × 4 nailers flush with the inside and outside edges of the top plate and sole plate to provide a nailing surface for attaching trim boards and siding materials.

On inside corners, attach a 2 × 2 trim strip, using 10d splitless cedar siding nails. Siding materials will be butted against this trim strip.

On outside corners, attach a 1 × 3, then overlap it with a 1 × 4 so the sides look equal. The trim boards should extend down over the rim joist. Also attach trim boards around posts.

Cut and position cap rails on the top rail, then secure them with 2" deck screws driven up through the rail. Railing caps should be mitered at the corners.

Attach siding materials to the inside and outside faces of the wall, using splitless cedar siding nails. Snap level chalk lines for reference, and try to match the reveal used on your house siding; the first course should overhang the rim joist slightly. Where joints are necessary, stagger them from course to course so they do not fall on the same studs.

How to Build an Angled Stair Railing

Use a combination square to mark the face of the top stairway post, where the railings will fit. For most horizontal stairway designs, the top stairway rail should start level with the second deck rail. Mark the other stairway posts at the same level.

Position a rail board against the faces of the posts, with the bottom edge against the stringer, then scribe angled cutting lines across the rail along the inside edges of the posts. Cut the rail at these lines, then cut the remaining rails to match.

Secure the rails to the posts with galvanized metal L-brackets attached to the insides of the rails.

Measure and cut a 2 × 2 cleat, and attach it flush with the top inside edge of the top rail, using 2" deck screws. Anchor the cleat to the posts by toenailing with galvanized casing nails.

Measure and cut the cap rail to fit over the top rail and cleat. At the bottom of the railing, cut the post at an angle and attach the cap rail so it overhangs the post slightly. Secure the cap rail by driving 2" deck screws up through the cleat.

Measure and cut a grippable handrail, attaching it to the posts with mounting brackets. Miter cut the ends, and create a return back to the post by cutting another mitered section of handrail and nailing it in place between the handrail and post (right).

Grippable Handrails ▸

Grippable handrails are required for stairways with 4 risers or more. The handrail should be shaped so the grippable portion is between 1¼" and 2" in diameter, and should be angled into posts at the ends. The top of the handrail should be 34" to 38" above the stair treads, measured from the nose of a step.

Curved Railings

Laying out and constructing a curved railing requires a basic understanding of geometry and the ability to make detailed drawings using a compass, protractor, and a special measuring tool called a scale ruler. It is a fairly advanced technique, but the results are worth the effort. Making the top rail involves bending and gluing thinner strips of wood together around the deck's curved rim joist, which acts like a bending form. You'll need lots of medium-sized clamps on hand to hold the railing in the proper shape while it dries. The cap rail is formed by joining several mitered pieces of lumber together, end to end, to form an oversized blank, then cutting out the curved shape.

The method for constructing a curved cap rail shown on the following pages works only for symmetrical curves—quarter circles, half circles, or full circles. If your deck has irregular or elliptical curves, creating a cap rail is very difficult. For these curves, it is best to limit the railing design to include only balusters and a laminated top rail. Lastly, if this seems too complicated for your skills, you can opt for a composite curved railing, which can be made to order.

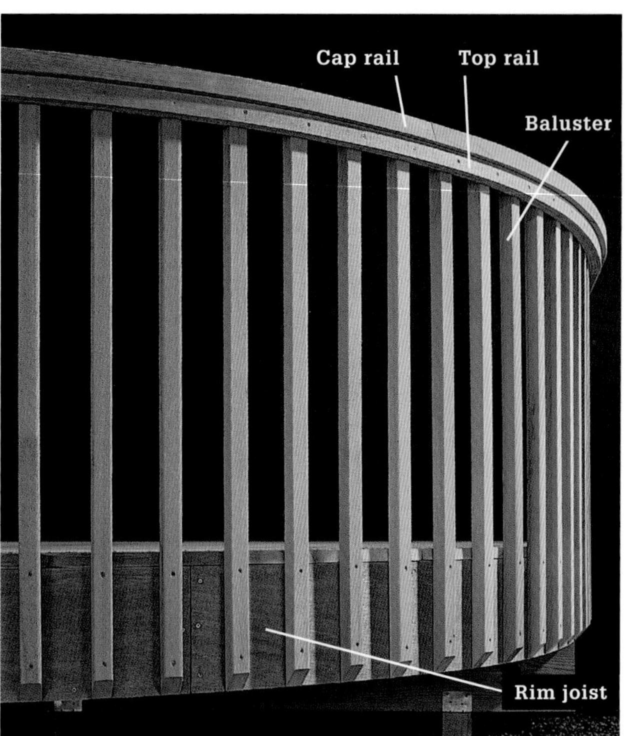

Components of a curved railing include: vertical balusters attached to the curved rim joist, a top rail built from laminated layers of plywood, and a curved cap rail. The cap rail is constructed by laying out mitered sections of 2 × 12 lumber, marking a curved shape, and cutting it out with a jigsaw.

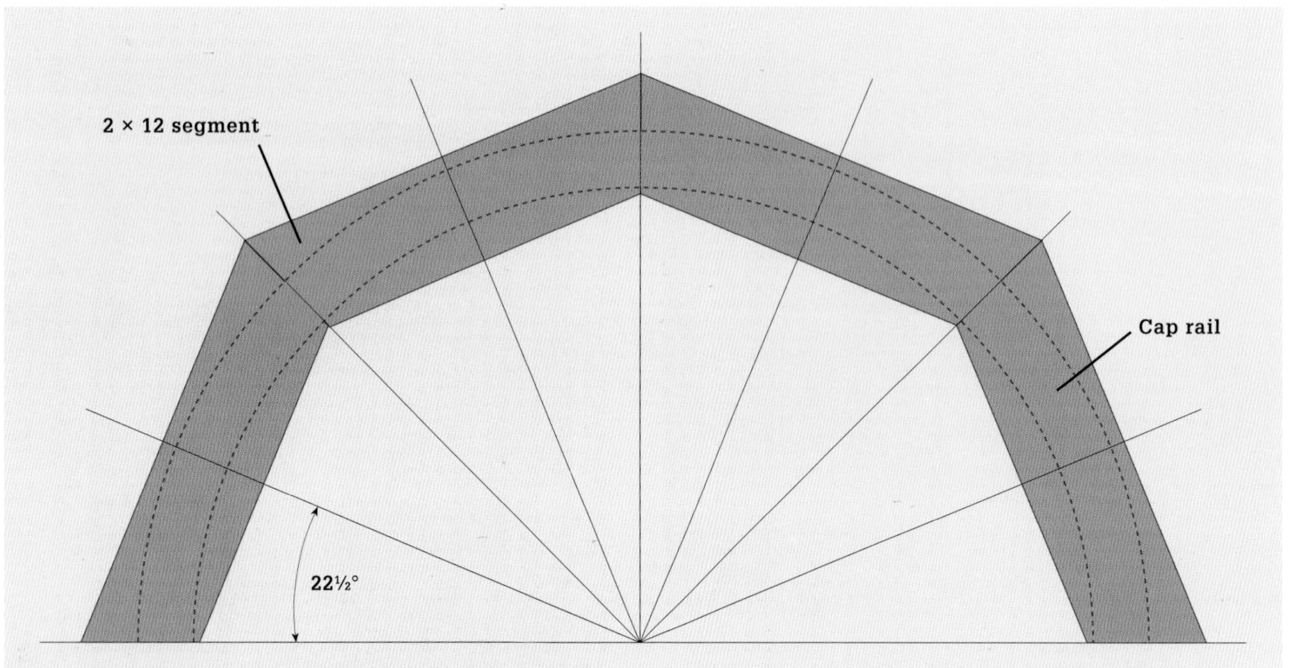

A curved cap rail is created from mitered segments of 2 × 12 lumber. After positioning the 2 × 12 segments end to end, the shape of the 6"-wide cap rail is outlined on the pieces. For a semicircle with a radius of up to 7 ft., four 2 × 12 segments will be needed, with ends mitered at 22½°. For a semicircle with a larger radius, you will need eight segments, with ends mitered at 11¼°.

How to Build a Curved Railing

To create a curved top rail, use exterior glue to laminate four 1½"-wide strips of ⅜"-thick cedar plywood together, using the curved rim joist of the deck as a bending form. First, cover the rim joist with kraft paper for protection. Then, begin wrapping strips of plywood around the rim joist. Clamp each strip in position, starting at one end of the curve. The strips should differ in length to ensure that butt joints will be staggered from layer to layer.

Continue working your way around the rim joist, toward the other end. Make sure to apply clamps on both sides of the butt joints where plywood strips meet. Cut the last strips slightly long, then trim the laminated rail to the correct length after the glue has set. For extra strength, drive 1" deck screws through the rail at 12" intervals after all strips are glued together. Unclamp the rail, and sand the top and bottom edges smooth.

Install posts at the square corners of the deck. Then, cut 2 × 2 balusters to length, beveling the bottom ends at 45°. Attach the balusters to the rim joist with 2½" deck screws, using a spacer to maintain even intervals. Clamp the curved top rail to the tops of the balusters and posts, then attach it with deck screws.

After the top rail and balusters are in place, attach 2 × 2 top rails to the balusters in the straight sections of the deck. The ends of the straight top rails should be flush against the ends of the curved top rail. Now, measure the distance between the inside faces of the balusters at each end of the curve. Divide this distance in half to find the required radius for the curved cap rail.

(continued)

Using a scale of 1" to 1 ft., make a diagram of the deck. (A scale ruler makes this job easier.) First, draw the arc of the deck with a compass, using the radius measurement found in step 4. Divide the curved portion of the deck into an even number of equal sections by using a protractor to draw radius lines from the center of the curve. For a semicircular curve, it is usually sufficient to draw eight radius lines, angled at 22½° to one another. (For a deck with a radius of more than 7 ft., you may need to divide the semicircle into 16 portions, with radius lines angled at 11¼°.)

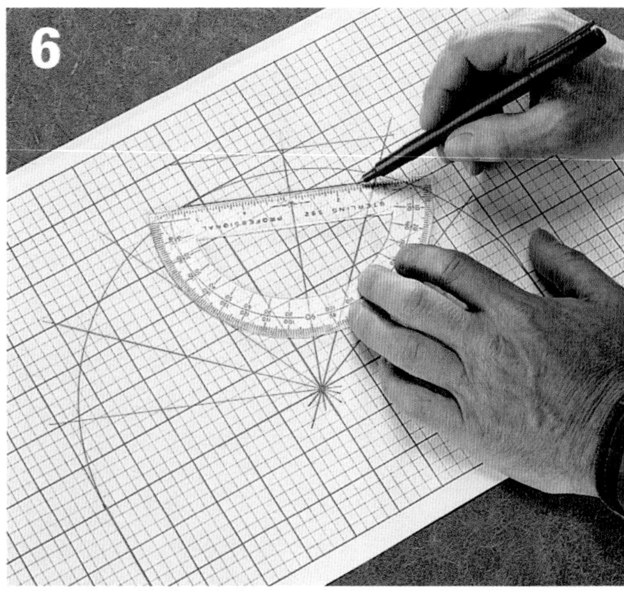

From the point where one of the radius lines intersects the curved outline of the deck, use the scale ruler to mark points 5½" above and 5½" below the intersection. From these points, use a protractor to draw perpendicular lines to the adjoining radius lines. The polygon outlined by the perpendicular lines and the adjoining radius lines represents the shape and size for all of the 2 × 12 segments that will be used to construct the cap rail.

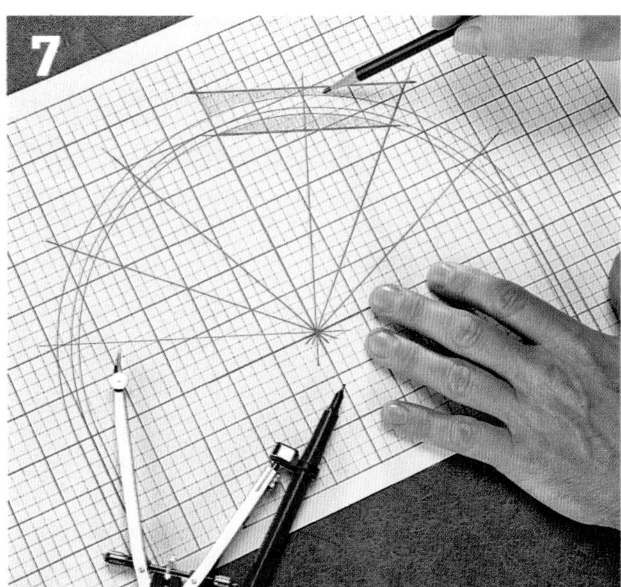

Draw a pair of parallel arcs 5½" apart, representing the curved cap railing, inside the outline for the 2 × 12 segments. Shade the portion of the drawing that lies between the straight parallel lines and the two adjacent radius lines. This area represents the shape and size for each of the angled 2 × 12 segments. Measure the angle of the miter at the ends of the board; in this example, the segments are mitered at 22½°.

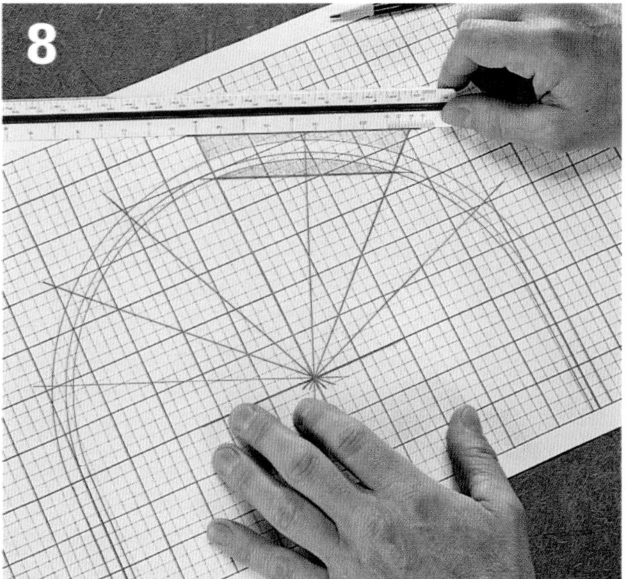

Measure the length of the long edge; this number is the overall length for each of the 2 × 12 segments you will be cutting. Using this highlighted area, determine how many segments you will need to complete the curve. For a semicircular curve with a radius of up to 7 ft., four segments are required, with ends mitered at 22½°. For curves with a larger radius, you need eight segments, with ends mitered at 11¼°.

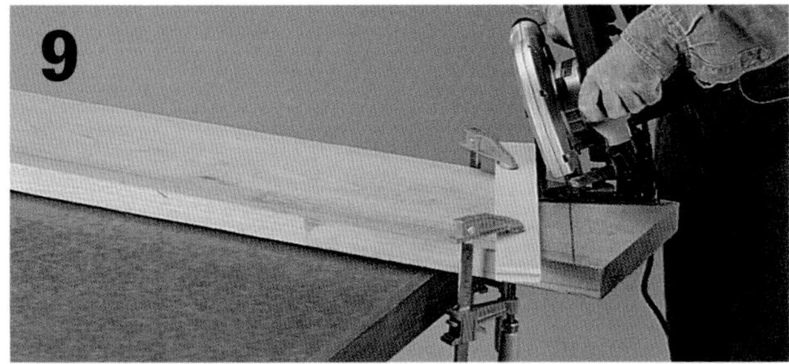

Measure and mark 2 × 12 lumber for the cap rail segments, with ends angled inward at 22½° from perpendicular. Set the blade on your circular saw or tablesaw to a 15° bevel, then make compound miter cuts along the marked lines. When cut to compound miters, the segments will form overlapping scarf joints that are less likely to reveal gaps between the boards.

Arrange the cap rail segments over the curved deck railing, and adjust the pieces, if necessary, so they are centered over the top rail. When you are satisfied with the layout, temporarily attach the segments in place by driving 2" deck screws up through the curved top rail. Measure and install the 2 × 6 cap railing for the straight portion of the railing.

Temporarily nail or clamp a long sturdy board between the sides at the start of the curve. Build a long compass, called a *trammel*, by nailing one end of a long 1 × 2 to a 1 ft.-long piece of 1 × 4. Measure from the nail out along the arm of the trammel, and drill holes at the desired radius measurements; for our application, there will be two holes, 5½" apart, representing the width of the finished cap rail. Attach the 1 × 4 base of the trammel to the temporary board so the nail point is at the centerpoint of the deck rail curve, then insert a pencil through one of the holes in the trammel arm. Pivot the arm of the trammel around the cap rail, scribing a cutting line. Move the pencil to the other hole, and scribe a second line.

Remove the trammel, and unscrew the cap rail segments. Use a jigsaw to cut along the scribed lines, then reposition the curved cap rail pieces over the top rail. Secure the cap rail by applying exterior adhesive to the joints and driving 2½" deck screws up through the top rail. Use a belt sander to remove saw marks.

Decorative Railing Options ▸

Even if you are committed to using wood posts and railings for your deck, there are numerous ways to customize your railing system to make it look fresh and different from other decks. One dramatic step you can take is to choose an unusual material option for the balusters. Balusters are available in various metals, including aluminum, stainless or powder-coated steel, copper, and iron. Metal balusters are fabricated in straight or contoured styles as well as turned and architectural profiles. They install into holes in wooden top and bottom rails or attach with screws. Strips of tempered glass are another baluster option, and they fasten in place with screws or slip into grooves in the rails. Or, fill the spaces between posts and rails with brightly colored outdoor fabric. It can be ordered with metal grommets installed so you tie it in place with weather-resistant rope.

If you use metal balusters, consider adding a centerpiece baluster between them. These unique balusters are made in various fleur de lis, classic, and nouveau patterns. They'll add shape and distinctiveness to your baluster pattern.

Wooden posts need not be drab, either. One option is to cover them with composite or vinyl sleeves in various colors or outfit them with a sleeve that looks like stacked stone. Instead of running hand rails over the top of your deck posts, let them extend above the railings and install post caps or decorative wood finials. Caps and finials simply fit over the tops of posts and nail or screw in place. Caps are widely available from home centers in copper or stainless steel. You can also order them made from stained glass or as low-voltage solar lights. Then, add a little flair to the bottoms of your posts with one-piece, composite trim skirts in decorative profiles.

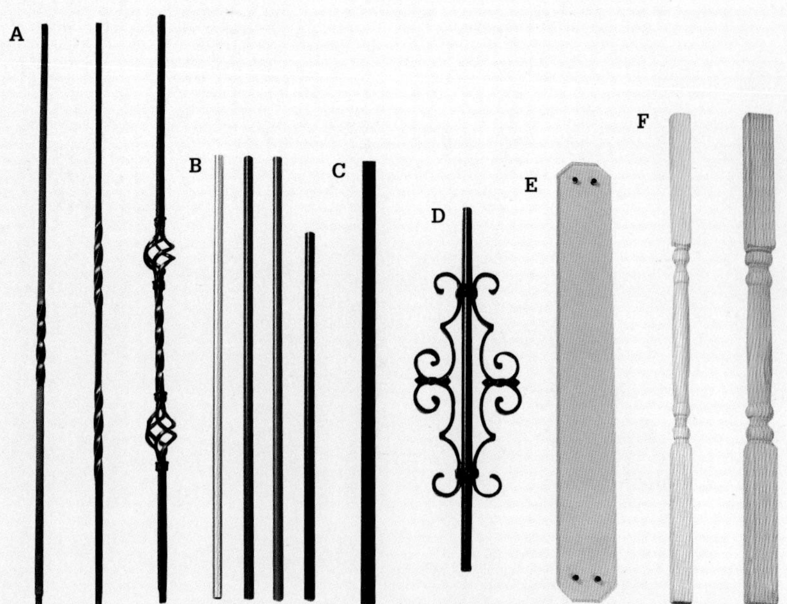

Balusters are available in a variety of styles and material options. Metal balusters are fabricated into many contoured profiles (A). You can also buy tubular styles (B) made of aluminum, stainless steel, and copper, or with a painted finish. Flat-bar balusters (C) or decorative centerpiece balusters (D) are other options, as well as strips of tempered glass (E). Wood balusters (F) are more economical than other styles, but they still lend a nicely crafted touch.

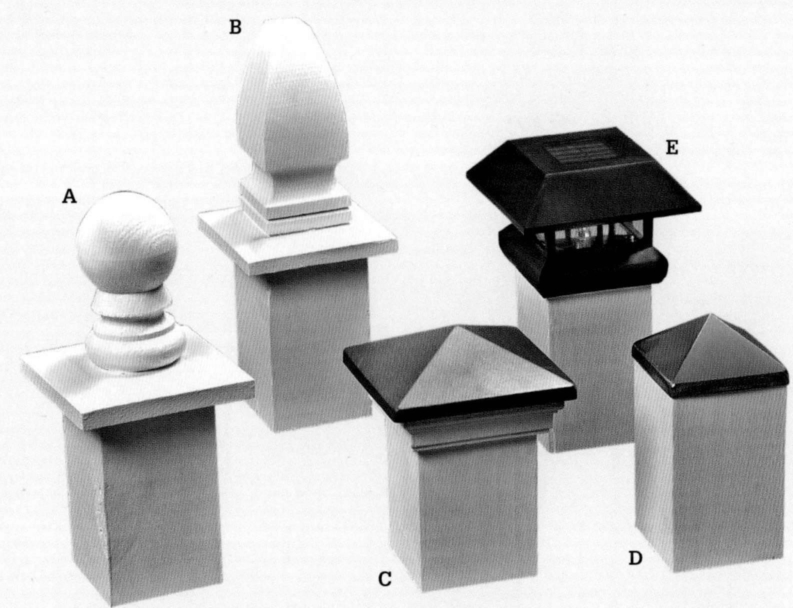

Dress up your deck railing posts with decorative top caps. You'll find them in various ball (A) and finial (B) shapes. Consider topping off your posts with paint (C) or copper (D), or maybe low-voltage or solar powered cap lights (E). Top caps will also help your wooden posts last longer by preventing water from wicking down into the end grain, leading to rot.

Post caps are available in a variety of styles made of metal, composites, or wood. Aside from adding a decorative touch, they also extend the life of the posts by keeping the end grain of the posts dry.

If you'd prefer not to build your railing from scratch, you can buy PVC or other composite railing systems that are long lasting and simple to install. Another advantage is you'll never need to stain or paint them.

Tempered glass or Plexiglas railings are an excellent choice if your deck offers an impressive view. There are no balusters or handrails to peek through or over—just clear "windows" to the world beyond.

Contoured metal balusters will give your deck a fresh, contemporary twist. They attach with screws, just like wooden balusters.

Spindle-style, turned balusters are available in various metal tones and colors. They can lend a tailored effect to wooden railings.

Ordinary wooden deck railings can make you feel like you're "behind bars," but they're not the only option anymore. Today's tempered glass railing systems offer the same safety as wood balusters but with the added advantage of a virtually unobstructed view.

Composite Railing Systems

Most large composite decking manufacturers also offer complete railing systems to match the deck. You can use composite railings with a composite deck for a unified look, or use them with your wood deck as an easier, low-maintenance alternative to wood railings. Composite railings are sold both as complete sections and by the part, which allows you to customize the railings to suit your deck. Modern composite railings are offered in a wide range of styles, colors, and even textures, such as simulated wood grain. Balusters are just as diverse, ranging from simple composite posts, to tubes, to transparent acrylic panels. The diversity of looks, ease of installation, and the fact that material requires little if any care after installation all account for the quickly growing popularity of this railing material (see Resources, p. 347).

Tools & Materials ▸

- Tape measure
- Level
- Ratchet and sockets or impact driver
- Miter saw
- Drill/driver
- 16-gauge pneumatic nailer
- Bracket tool
- Lag screws
- Posts
- Balusters
- Rail cap
- Stringers

Composite deck railing systems are very durable and require only minimal maintenance.

How to Install a Composite Railing

Fasten composite railing posts to the deck rim joists with pairs of ½-in.-diameter countersunk bolts, washers, and nuts. Position the posts 72" on center. Do not notch the posts.

Install railing support brackets, if applicable, to the posts using corrosion-resistant deck screws. For the railing system shown here, an assembly bracket tool sets the placement of the brackets on the posts without measuring.

Assemble the railing sections on a flat surface. Again, the assembly tool shown here sets the spacing of the balusters. Fasten the bottom and top rails—in that order—to balusters with 16-gauge pneumatic nails or screws, according to the manufacturer's instructions.

Place the assembled railing section onto the railing support brackets and check it for level. Drive pairs of deck screws up though the support bracket holes and into the handrail. Toenail the bottom rail to the post with 16-gauge pneumatic nails.

Glass-panel Railings

For the ultimate in unobstructed viewing, you can install a glass-panel railing system on your deck and avoid balusters altogether. The system shown here (see Resources, page 347) is quite manageable to install without special tools. It consists of a framework of aluminum posts, and top and bottom rails that fasten together with screws. Extruded vinyl liner inserts that fit inside the top and bottom rails hold the glass without fasteners. Tempered glass panels that are at least ¼-in. thick will meet building codes, provided the railing posts are spaced 5 ft. on center. Some manufacturers offer poly-carbonate panels that are easier to work with and satisfy most building codes, although it can be scratched and may cloud over time. With a system such as the one shown here, you assemble the railing framework first, then measure and order the glass panels to fit the rail openings.

Tools & Materials ▸

Tape measure
Level
Ratchet and sockets or impact driver
Drill/driver
Posts
Post brackets
Tempered glass panels
Fasteners
Railings
Stringers

Tempered glass panels are both do-it-yourself friendly and code approved, provided you install them according to manufacturers' guidelines.

How to Install a Glass-panel Railing

Once you've determined the layout of the deck posts, fasten the post brackets to the deck with lag screws. Install all the posts before proceeding.

Insert the top post sleeves into the post ends, then measure and cut the top rails to length. Assemble the rails and sleeves, fastening the parts with screws. Check each post for plumb with a level before driving the attachment screws, and adjust if necessary.

Measure the length of the top rail inner channels, and cut glass insert strips to fit. Fasten the glass rail brackets to the posts with screws.

Measure the distance between the glass insert strips and add ¾" to this length to determine the height of the glass panels. Measure the distance between posts and subtract 3 to 6" from this measurement to find the glass panel width, less air gaps. Order your glass. Install the bottom rails on the brackets.

Slip each glass panel into the top insert, swing it into place over the bottom insert and lower it into the bottom channel to rest on the rubber setting blocks. No further attachment is required.

Steel Cable Railings

Another railing option that can open up the view from a deck—not to mention give the deck some distinctive style—is to use braided steel cables run horizontally between posts. Lengths of cables are run continuously through holes in the posts and tension is created with special threaded fittings on the ends of the cable runs. Cables are spaced 3" apart or less, with railing posts spaced 3 ft. on center. Most people purchase complete railing systems with prefabricated metal posts as shown here, although you can make your own wood posts. In any case, the posts need to be securely fastened to the decking to resist the tension in the cables. A sturdy top rail is used with special fasteners to stabilize the railing and provide additional lateral reinforcement. Because of the tension inherent in cable railings, always follow the manufacturer's instructions to the letter.

Your Cable System ▸

There are many ways to create a cabled railing. The complete system shown here (see Resources) is one of the easiest; the manufacturer supplies all the parts you need with complete, code-compliant instructions. Installation is easy, even for someone with modest skills. However, the cost of a system like this can become prohibitive if your deck is large. Other systems involve cables run between turnbuckles bolted or screwed to the posts. These require more work, and you have to be careful to install a sturdy top plate between posts to oppose the tension of the cables. The simplest system involves eyehooks screwed into the posts, and cables threaded through the eyehooks. Whichever you choose, it is extremely important when thinking about cabled railings to check with the local building inspector. Some localities prohibit horizontal cables—and horizontal balusters of any kind—because they can be climbed.

Tools & Materials ▸

- Measuring tape
- Level
- Drill/driver
- Hacksaw
- Cable cutters
- Self-locking pliers
- Wrenches
- Electric grinder
- Cable-lacing needle

A series of braided steel cables can replace ordinary wood balusters and give your deck a clean, contemporary look. Posts must be spaced closely together to handle the cable tension and ensure safety.

How to Install Cable Railings

If you install flanged metal posts, secure them to the deck's framing with stainless steel lag screws and washers.

Drill holes through the railing posts to fit the cables, threaded end fittings, and quick connect locking fittings. Pass the terminal threaded ends of the cables through one railing end post and install washer nuts about ¼" onto the threads.

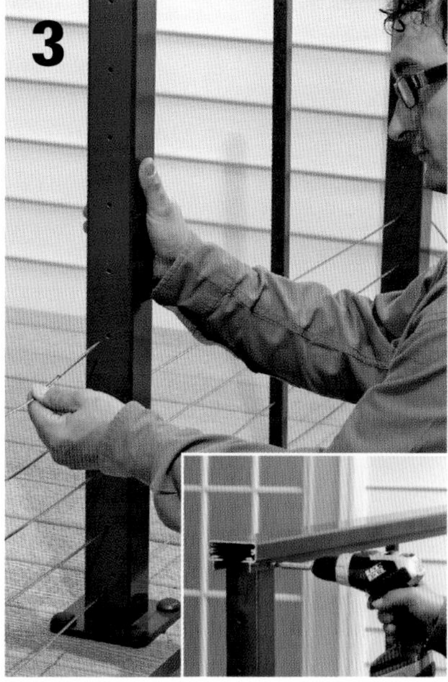

Feed the cables through the intermediate posts and the opposite end post. Work systematically to prevent tangling the cables. A cable-lacing needle will make it easier to pass cables through each post without snagging it. Attach cap rails (inset).

Slip a self-locking fitting over the end of each cable and seat the fitting in the cable hole in the post. You may need to counterbore this hole first to accommodate the fitting. Pull the cable tight. Jaws inside the fitting will prevent the cable from becoming slack again.

Tighten each cable nut with a wrench, starting from the center cable and working outward. A locking pliers will keep the cable from twisting as you tighten the nut. Tighten the nut until you cannot flex the cables more than 4" apart.

Cut off the excess cable at the quick-connect fitting end with a cable cutter or hacksaw. Grind the end of the cable flush with the fitting, and cover it with a snap-on end cap.

Copper Tube Railings

Use ¾" copper tubing available in the plumbing section of building centers for decorative balusters in a railing. Over time, the copper will oxidize and develop an attractive green patina. Metal balusters coated in colors are also available from some manufacturers. If you can't find them at your local building center, manufacturers and suppliers can be found on the Internet. In some areas, notching 4 × 4 posts to attach them to your deck (as shown here) may not be allowed by local codes. Inquire at your local building department for the restrictions in your area.

How to Build Copper Tube Railings

Lay out and attach railing posts as you would for traditional railings. Measure and cut pairs of 2 × 4 rails to fit between post faces or in notches cut in the post faces.

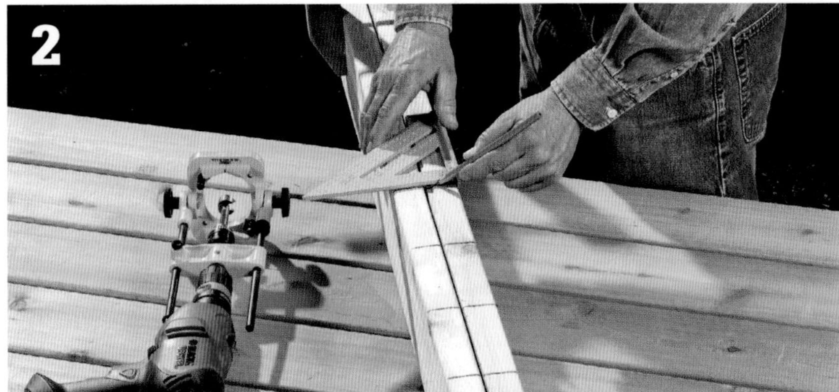

On one edge of an 8-ft. 2 × 4, lay out and mark hole locations every 4½", beginning at the centerpoint and working towards the ends. Use this board as a story pole to create consistent spacing between balusters. Clamp the story pole to each rail pair, aligning the centerpoint of the rails with that of the story pole. If the hole locations fall within 1½" of the ends, adjust the rails, as necessary. Transfer marks to the rails using a speed square.

Drill a ¾"-diameter hole ¾" deep at each location using a portable drill guide and Forstner bit.

Apply a small amount of silicone caulk in each hole in the bottom rail and insert a baluster. The caulk prevents moisture penetration.

Lay a 1 × 4 under the baluster ends to hold them up uniformly. Brace the bottom end so it won't move, then fit the top rail over the baluster ends. A helper will make this much easier. Set the assembly upright, and hammer against a scrap block placed on the top rail to fully seat the balusters in both rails.

For stair rails, mark hole locations that are 5½" apart on center. Turn the top rail 180° and flip it upside down before clamping the rails together. Begin marking at the centerpoint of the rails. Drill holes for the balusters with the clamped rail pair resting on the stair treads. Use a level to set the proper angle for the drill guide if necessary.

Install each rail assembly between the appropriate posts, using 2½" deck screws. Attach cap rails following the methods shown on pages 164 to 170.

Deck Accessories

The addition of one or more built-in features not only adds to the potential uses of the deck, the features can also add immeasurably to the look of the structure. Regardless of whether you choose a bench, a planter, a pergola, or other structure, you can customize the look to blend in or stand out.

Take benches, for instance. A built-in deck bench can be plain or sophisticated, sleek or boxy. In any case, they add useful extra seating to the deck, and a high back on a deck bench can serve in place of railings.

But the choices hardly stop with benches. Add planters to your deck to bring a touch of the garden to the area. Privacy screens—like so many other built-in features—serve both practical and aesthetic purposes, blocking the view from neighbors' yards or nearby streets.

Of course, individual add-ons are only the beginning. You can mix and match for a truly one-of-a-kind look. Build a bench with two planters on either end, or join a privacy screen and pergola to create a show-stopping deck focal point.

Whatever feature or features you choose, keep in mind that many of these must adhere to the same code requirements imposed on the deck structure itself. Whenever you're planning on building anything that will be attached to the deck—and certainly something as significant as a privacy fence or bench—your first stop should be the local building department.

In this chapter:

Choosing the Perfect Accessories

Although you can add built-in features even after you've built your deck, it's always wiser to include deck extras as part of your initial planning. That way you can buy the necessary materials all at once and, in the case of a larger structure such as a screened gazebo, you'll have a chance to adjust the actual layout of your deck to accommodate the feature. Planning ahead also allows you to budget for the additional features. Depending on how intricate or extensive the feature is, it may add a considerable amount to the cost of a small- or medium-sized deck.

When deciding on extras for your particular deck, start with how you'll be using the platform. Which feature will best suit the activities you had in mind when you first decided to build your outdoor getaway? Some features, such as benches, are practical and functional no matter how you intend to enjoy your deck. Other features, such as privacy screens, are additions that serve a specific, easily identifiable need. Ask yourself how often you'll have big groups of people over for outdoor parties, how private you want the space to be, and how unique and special you want to make your deck.

The bigger your deck is, the more options you have. A larger deck is also often a great opportunity to combine features to get the most bang for your money and effort. Planters and benches are natural partners on the surface of a deck. You can build them as separate units, or choose a plan in which the planters are used as the supports for the bench seat itself. Either way, it's always more pleasurable to sit surrounded by flowers and plant life.

Many built-in features are combined with, or run into, the railing. For instance, benches are often built in lieu of a railing on a lower deck for which code requires no railing, and with a back on higher decks that serves in place of a railing. Privacy screens and fences are often linked to railings as well, and can be visually blended with the railing by accenting them with similar finials, materials, and detailing to make them seem like an extension of the railings. For practical purposes—and to meet code requirements—railings are often built right into the supporting members of larger structures such as pergolas, arbors, and especially gazebos.

A house-mounted pergola can be both a stunning deck addition and a handy shade structure. Use shade sails between the rafters, as this homeowner has done, to create a completely shaded alcove.

Deck Accessories and Codes

As with most elements of deck construction, built-in features are regulated by local codes and zoning requirements. Taller, more substantial structures such as fences, privacy screens, and gazebos must be positioned so that they don't impede egress or stand too close to windows or property line setbacks.

Edge-mounted structures, such as benches and some planters, generally have to conform to the same code requirements that regulate deck railing construction. For instance, many codes no longer allow for notched railing posts mounted over the edge of the deck and bolted into the rim joist. The same is true for bench posts, screens, and fences mounted in this fashion. In the case of fences or privacy screens, the code requirements may actually be more rigid than with railings because of the added stress of wind loads.

All this means that adding built-in features to your deck merits a trip to the building department to determine which, if any, codes bear directly on the construction of the feature.

More involved built-in features, such as complete outdoor kitchens, are almost as big a project as the deck itself. These require enormous planning and often involve running electric, gas, and other connections. That means multiple codes and much more involved construction. These sorts of extensive deck additions are discussed in more detail on page 234 to 240.

A screened gazebo serves as a fabulous outdoor room that is at once a beautiful part of the deck and a separate area entirely. Check with your local building department because an elevated gazebo such as this may be regulated by additional codes.

Deck Planters

What better way to truly integrate a deck with your landscaping than to introduce plants right on top of the surface? Supplement your deck design with one or more planters and you have the opportunity to grow just about any vegetation that catches your fancy.

The easiest planters to build are simple squares or rectangles like the one featured here. However, you shouldn't feel confined to those basic shapes; most planter plans can easily be adapted to just about any shape. That adaptability can come in handy when you need to tuck the planter into the odd corner of an unusual deck design.

Regardless of what shape you choose, it's always helpful to have some idea of what you want to plant in the planter. Different plants can require radically different types of soil and space for roots. A tree will require a much different planter than a small display of blooming annuals. In any case, it's wise to attach the planter to the deck to prevent it from falling over due to high winds or rambunctious party guests.

Tools & Materials ▸

Circular saw	1 × 4 lumber
Miter saw	3" galvanized deck screws
Power drill & bits	2½" galvanized deck screws
Measuring tape	¾" exterior grade plywood
4 × 4 lumber	Nail set
1 × 3 lumber	Pond liner or 6-mil poly
1 × 1 nailing strips	

A planter like this is relatively easy to construct and adds immeasurably to the look of the deck, not only with its design, but also by hosting attractive plant life.

How to Build a Deck Planter

Use a miter saw or circular saw to cut all the framing members. Mark and cut four 4 × 4 legs and twenty 1 × 4 side panels, all 18" long. Cut four 1 × 2 rails 21" long, and four 14" long. Cut eight 1 × 1 nailing strips 14" long.

Assemble the end panels by laying four 1 × 4s side by side, aligning them perfectly. Lay a short 1 × 2 rail across one end, running it perpendicular to the boards. Drill pilot holes, and screw the rail to each of the panel boards.

Position the nailing strips along the outside edges of the panel and drill pilot holes. Screw the nailing strips in place, and then screw the bottom rail in place as you did with the top rail. Butt it up against the bottom of the nailing strips (there should be a gap between the bottom edge of the rail and the bottom edges of the panel boards). Repeat the process using six 1 × 4s to construct the side panels.

Set a leg on the worktable and align a panel with the leg. Drill pilot holes through the nailing strip on the back of the panel, into the leg, and screw the panel to the leg using a screw every 2". Continue attaching the legs in the same manner until the box of the planter is complete.

(continued)

Cut a rectangle of exterior-grade ¾" plywood, 26½" × 19½". Notch the corners by cutting in 2¾" from each edge.

Turn the planter box upside down and screw the plywood bottom into place, drilling pilot holes at the edges into the bottom rails, and then screwing the bottom to the rails. Use a ¼" bit to drill holes in the center of the plywood to allow for drainage.

Cut the 1 × 4s for the plinth and top frame. Cut four 28" long, and four 21" long. Miter the ends of all pieces 45°.

Attach the planter box to the deck by measuring and setting it into position. Drive 2½" decking screws down through the plywood bottom and into the deck. Use one screw at each corner, located as close to the outer panel as possible.

Screw the plinth pieces in place around the base of the planter by driving 2" deck screws from the inside of the box, through the bottom rail and into the plinth piece. Use three screws per side.

Staple the planter box liner all around, attaching it over the top rail, but not so that it overlaps onto the outside of the side panels. Cut some holes in the bottom for drainage.

Drill pilot holes through the outside edges of the top frame pieces through the miters. Position the frame in place on the planter and drill pilot holes down through the frame and into the legs. Nail the frame in place with galvanized finish nails, and use a nailset to sink the nails.

Sand and finish the box if desired. Add a few inches of gravel at the bottom, then soil and plants. Water thoroughly.

Privacy Screen

Today's deck has the potential to be much, much more than just a simple step-out platform. You can design your deck to be an outdoor dining room with a secluded nook for quiet, intimate meals, a discrete sunbathing platform, or a sanctuary to read the paper in peace and get away from it all. But for all of these, privacy is key. A romantic brunch is no fun when it's in direct view of a neighbor's yard or kitchen window. And that's where a privacy screen can come in mighty handy.

Deck-mounted privacy screens have to conform to the same codes—or in some cases, more stringent versions—that the deck railings do. You have to be very careful that the placement of a screen does not impede on an egress opening, and that the clearance around windows and vents is adequately maintained. If you live in an area subject to strong winds, code issues will be even more of a concern and the screen may require special reinforcement so that it can withstand added wind load. Ultimately, you may also have to install blocking between the joists running to where the screen is mounted, to help combat the stress from the wind load.

As important as code issues are, don't lose sight of the fact that a privacy screen is a substantial deck feature. Take the time to make sure the design adds to the look, as well as the function, of your deck.

Tools & Materials ▸

- Measuring tape
- Power drill and bits
- Miter saw
- Jigsaw or circular saw
- 1⅜" spade bit
- 5 × ½" lag screws and washers
- 3" deck screws
- 2½" deck screws
- 1½" 4d galvanized finish nails
- 4 × 4 lumber
- 1 × 2 lumber
- 2 × 4 lumber
- Exterior grade ¾" lattice
- Pyramid or other post finial

A lattice privacy screen allows for airflow and some light to filter through, and offers privacy from other yards.

How to Build a Privacy Screen

Measure and cut the 4 × 4 posts for the screen. Each post should be 6'5" long. Miter the bottom ends of the posts to a 22½° angle. Seal the cut ends with a sealant/preservative, even if you're using pressure treated wood.

Measure and mark 2" up from the bottom of the backside of the posts, and 2" above that mark. Drill ½" deep holes at these marks, using a 1⅜" spade bit. Drill ⅜" pilot holes in the center of the larger holes, all the way through the post.

Mark the locations of the top and bottom plates on the inside faces of the posts. Mark the post positions on the side of the deck and double check your measurements (the posts should be exactly 46" apart on center). Hold the posts in position and mark through the pilot holes for the joist holes.

Attach the privacy screen posts to the edge of the deck with the aid of a helper. Hold each post in place, checking plumb with a level, and use 5 × ½" lag screws and washers to connect the post to the deck.

(continued)

Position the bottom plate between the two posts, using spacers to hold the plate in place. Screw the plate to the posts from the top, in toenail fashion, using two 3" deck screws on both sides.

Cut the screen frame pieces from 1 × 2 stock: 2 side pieces 5 ft. long, and top and bottom pieces 43" long. Miter the ends of the framing pieces to 45°. Mark a 4 × 8 sheet of lattice and use a jigsaw or circular saw to cut the sheet down to 4 × 5.

Drill countersunk pilot holes in the edges of all the screen framing pieces for the 3" deck screws that will secure the frame to the posts and plates. Space the holes about 10" apart.

Assemble the front frame by clamping pieces at the mitered joints, drilling pilot holes for 2" deck screws. Measure diagonally after the frame is finished to ensure square. Assemble the rest of the frame in the same way, and repeat to construct the back frame.

Add the outside frame. Drill pilot holes into the post and attach with 3" deck screws.

Place the lattice in position and install the inner frame. Predrill and nail the inner to the outer frame through a lattice strip every 8" with 4d galvanized nails.

Screw the top plate into place, and screw the top frame pieces to the top plate and to each other. Finish the screen by covering the post tops with finials. The finials used here are glued to the post top with construction adhesive.

Add additional segments by repeating these steps and adding a 2 × 6 cap mitered at 22½° at the mated ends. This plate will replace the finials.

Deck Benches

A well-designed deck bench can often serve double duty. Installed along the perimeter of a low-lying deck, a long bench adds visual interest to what is often a fairly uninteresting uniform shape. Benches with built-in backs can stand in for railings on higher decks, ensuring the safety, as well as comfort, of everyone.

You can build fully enclosed deck benches to create useful additional storage—a handy way to hide sporting goods and cookout gear when they are not in use. Benches are also the perfect partner to planters, visually linking one or more independent mini-gardens.

Of course, the most important role any deck bench fulfills is that of accessible, durable, and comfortable seating on the deck. If you can measure accurately and operate a miter saw precisely, you can complete this bench in a weekend. It's a good idea to drive screws up through the underside of the deck into the legs so that the screws are completely invisible.

Tools & Materials ▸

Tape measure	3 prefab braces and hardware
Circular saw	1" spade bit
Miter saw	⅜" drill bit
Power drill	Pressure treated 2 × 4s
4 × 4 lumber	3" galvanized deck screws
1 × 4 lumber	2½" decking screws
2 × 4 lumber	5 × ⅜" lag screws
2 × 6 lumber	Bar clamps

Improve the look and comfort of a deck with a built-in bench. Building one is fairly easy, whether you're retrofitting an existing deck or adding one as part of a brand-new platform.

How to Build a Deck-mounted Bench

Cut six 15"-long legs from 4 × 4s. Cut 3 bases from the same material as the legs. Each base should be 4" long.

Place a leg on the worktable with a scrap piece underneath. Mark and drill a 1" hole, ½" deep, 1½" up from the bottom of the leg on the outside face (use a depth gauge on a spade bit). Change to a ⅜" bit to complete the pilot hole, drilling a hole in the center of the larger hole, and through the other side of the leg.

Drill identical base holes on all the other legs. Place a base in position against the inside edges of two legs, aligned with the bottom of the legs. Stick a long thin spike, awl, or other marking device through the hole to mark the location of the pilot holes on each end of the base.

Remove the base and drill ¼" pilot holes into the ends at the marks. Repeat with all the bases and mark each base for the legs it goes with.

(continued)

Measure and cut the leg top plates. These can be pressure-treated 2 × 4s because they won't be visible once the bench is assembled. Cut three plates 16½" long. Make marks on the long edges of the plates 2¾" from each end.

Complete the leg assemblies by aligning the edge marks on each top plate with the outside edges of the legs, and drilling two pilot holes through the top of the plate into each leg. Attach the plates to the legs with 3" screws.

Cut three 2 × 6s, each exactly 6 ft. long, for the seat. Lay them side by side, clamped together with the ends aligned. Mark the leg positions across the boards. The end leg units should be 2" from each end. The center leg unit should be centered along the span. *Note: Make attaching the legs to the decking easier and more secure by determining leg position along the deck before attaching them to the seat. Center each leg board on top of a decking board so that you can screw into the center of the board to secure the legs.*

Set the leg assemblies in place, upside down on the 2 × 6s, using the marks for reference. Screw through the bottom of the top plates into the seat boards. Use two 2½" decking screws per 2 × 6, for each leg unit.

Cut two 2 × 4 side frame pieces 6'3" long, and two end pieces 19½" long. Miter each edge 45° and dry fit the frame around the outside of the bench seat.

Assemble the frame by attaching the end pieces to the ends of the 2 × 6s, and the side pieces to the pressure-treated top plates. Use 3" deck screws to secure the frame pieces in place. Drill pilot holes through the miters and screw the frame pieces to each other.

Position the bench on the deck. Mark the leg base locations. Remove the bench and drill pilot holes for each base, down through the base and deck board. Use a spade bit to countersink the holes. Drive ⅜" lag screws down through the bases into the deck boards. Put the bench into position and secure it to the bases using ⅜" lag bolts and washers.

For a more finished look, cut plugs from the same wood as the legs, and glue them into place to cover the lag bolt heads in the sides of the legs. Sand as necessary, and finish the bench with whatever finish you prefer.

VARIATION: How to Build an Edge-mounted Bench

This project is an edge-mounted bench built by using prefab braces (See Resources, page 347) that make constructing the bench much easier. It has a canted back that allows a person to lean back and relax, and is mounted right to the band joist. We've built this as a double bench, with mitered boards on one side so that the benches look like a continuous unit.

Tools & Materials ▸

- Power drill & bits
- Miter saw
- Tape measure
- 2½" deck screws
- Prefab deck braces and hardware
- 2 × 6 Lumber
- 2 × 4 Lumber

Attach the first bracket centered along the band joist 6" from where the bench will end. Screw it to the decking and band joist using the 1½" screws and washers provided, screwing through the holes in the bracket.

Attach the second bracket on the band joist, no more than 24" away from the first bracket. Screw two brackets to the adjacent band joist in exactly the same pattern.

Measure and mark six 2 × 6s for the seats and top caps of the benches. The boards should be same width on the inside edge as the band joist, mitered out to the wider back edge 22½°, so that the members of each bench butt flush against each other.

Cut four 2 × 4 back supports 41" long. Miter the top ends 12°. Position each back support in a bracket, mark the 2 × 4 through the holes in the brackets, and drill for the mounting bolts. Attach the back supports with the 2½" bolts supplied, using washers on both sides.

Position the top cap on top of the back supports, leaving a ¾" overhang in the back. Drill pilot holes and screw the top caps to the back supports with 2½" deck screws, with the mitered edges meeting on the inside corner between the two bench segments. Screw the seat boards into position the same way, driving the supplied 1" screws up through the bottom of the leg brackets, into the 2 × 6 seat boards.

Measure and miter twelve 2 × 4 back and leg boards in the same way as you did the seat and top cap boards, but with the boards on edge. Butt the top back board up underneath the top cap, so that the mitered end is positioned on the inside corner between the two bench segments. Screw it into the back supports using 2½" deck screws.

Attach the two remaining back boards in the same way, leaving a 2" gap between the boards. Position the seat skirt on the front of the bench seat in the same way you positioned the seat boards. Mark and drill pilot holes, and screw the skirt to the front 2 × 6 using 2½" deck screws.

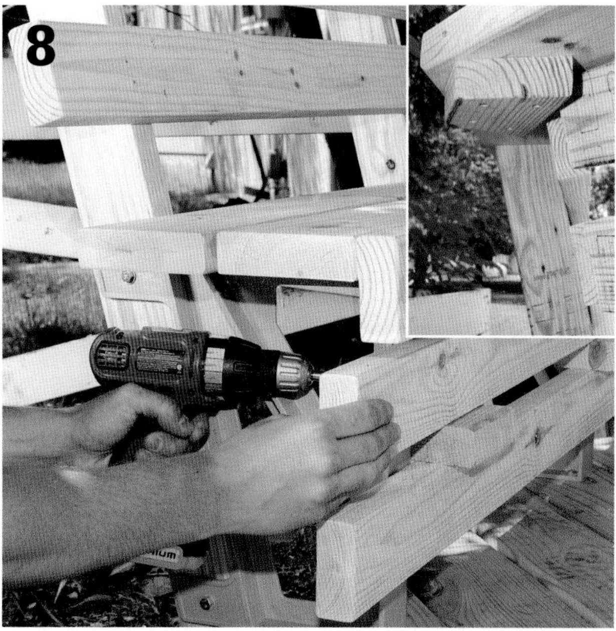

Screw the leg boards into position, using 1" screws driven through the holes in the brackets and scrap 2 × 4 blocks on the flat as spacers. Attach the back, seat, and leg boards on the adjacent bench section in the same way, making sure that the mitered edges leave a 1" gap between the two bench sections. *Inset: Install added support behind the back boards where the adjacent benches meet using scrap blocking and deck screws.*

Deck Skirting

Elevated decks are often the best solution for a sloped yard or a multi-story house. A deck on high can also take advantage of spectacular views. But the aesthetic drawback to many elevated decks is the view from other parts of the yard. The supporting structure can seem naked and unattractive.

The solution is to install deck skirting. Skirting is essentially a framed screen attached to support posts. Skirting effectively creates a visual base on an elevated deck and adds a more finished look to the entire structure. It looks attractive on just about any deck.

There are many different types of skirting. The project here uses lattice skirting, perhaps the most common and easiest to install. But you can opt for solid walls of boards run vertically or horizontally, depending on the look you're after and how much time and money you're willing to spend. However, keep in mind that lattice allows for air circulation underneath the deck. If you install solid skirting, you may need to add vents to prevent rot or other moisture related conditions under the deck. Codes also require that you allow access to egress windows, electrical panels, and other utilities under the deck, which may involve adding a gate or other structure to the skirting.

Regardless of the design, the basic idea behind building skirting is to create a supporting framework that runs between posts, with the skirting surface attached to the framework. Obviously, this provides the opportunity to add a lot of style to an elevated deck. The lattice skirting shown here is fairly easy on the eyes. If you choose to use boards instead, you can arrange them in intriguing patterns, just as you would design a showcase fence for your property. You can use wood skirting of the same species as the decking, or vary the material to create a more captivating look. You can even build in a storage space underneath the deck—a perfect location for lawnmowers, leaf blowers, and other yard equipment.

Tools & Materials ▸

- Measuring tape
- Speed square
- Circular saw
- Miter saw
- Power drill & bits
- ¾" exterior grade lattice panel
- 1 × 4 pressure treated lumber
- 2" galvanized finish nails
- 3" deck screws
- Angle and T braces

How To Install Deck Skirting

Determine the length of the skirting sections by measuring the space between posts. Measure on center and mark the posts. At corners, measure from the outer edge of the corner post to the center of the next post in line. Determine the height of the skirting by measuring from the top of a post to grade leaving at least 1" between the skirt bottom and ground.

Cut the top and side frame sections for the skirting from 1 × 4 pressure treated lumber. You can also use cedar or other rot- and insect-resistant material. Snap a chalk line 1" above the bottom of the post, and use a speed square to find the angle of the slope.

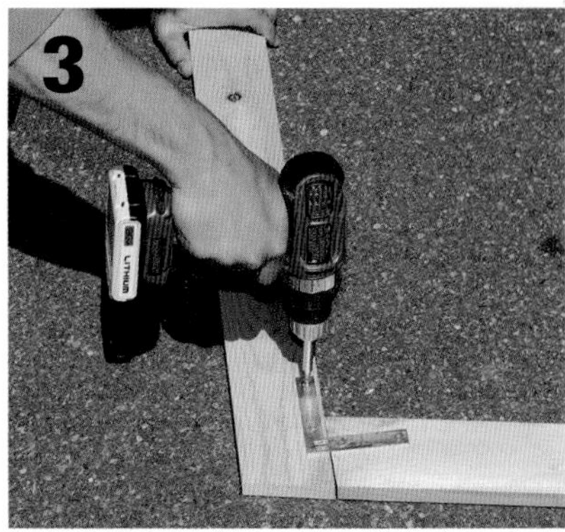

Cut the ends of the frame pieces to fit. Assemble the 1 × 4 frame using galvanized angle brackets.

Cut the ¾" lattice to dimensions of the frame, using a circular saw or jigsaw. Align the lattice on the back of the 1 × 4 frame, and screw the lattice to the frame about every 10".

Install each finished lattice skirting section as soon as it is assembled. Align the edges of the frame with the marks you've made on the posts and drill pilot holes through the front of the frame and lattice into the post. Screw the section to the post with 3" galvanized deck screws, using a screw at the top, bottom, and middle of the frame.

Optional: If the length between posts is greater than 8 ft., add stiles in the frame to support extra lattice panels. Cut 1 × 4 stiles to length so that they fit between the top and bottom rails. Screw it in place by using a 4" or larger T brace on the back of the frame. Then nail the lattice in place.

Once the skirting is in place, finish it to match the deck or your house. If you have access to spray equipment, you'll find that lattice can be painted much faster with it than with a brush or roller.

Gazebos & Pergolas ▸

Deck shade structures—specifically gazebos and pergolas—are always decorative to one degree or another. But they are also quite useful, especially where direct sun beats down on the deck throughout the day. But whether you're choosing a pergola or a gazebo, the structure is bound to have a big impact on the look of the deck. Picking a shade structure is all about understanding the sun exposure and choosing a design that fits the look and style of your particular deck and home.

Pergolas break up direct sun with an overhead series of rafters and crosspieces that create a gridwork roof. The shade cast by pergolas is not complete, and they are generally used where total shade isn't the goal. Pergolas can be self-supporting with posts on all sides, or they can be attached to the house on one side by way of a ledger with flashing.

Either type requires a great deal of planning because a completed pergola is generally heavy and prone to tipping if not correctly supported. Pergolas are often built on the extended beams used for the structure of the deck itself. This is usually the best way to craft a deck pergola, because retrofitting an older deck with a new pergola structure means properly supporting it—something that may require an engineer's input depending on the age of the deck.

Smaller decorative versions are often built into a run of railing just as privacy screen would be. A single beam is mounted across two deck-mounted posts, and topped with perpendicular rafters. Larger pergolas inevitably incorporate lath or lumber pieces running perpendicular to the rafters, providing even more fractured shade and a more detailed design.

Doorway pergolas are also popular, attached on the house side to a ledger, with the rafters supported on a post-and-beam structure on the opposite side. This type of pergola design can create a very tangible visual connection linking the deck to the house, and can help shade the doorway through the hottest part of a day.

Pergolas are often dressed up by using columns instead of bare posts, capitals and feet at the top and bottom of the supports, and decorative beam and rafter end cuts that range from simple bevels to more intricate patterns cut with a jigsaw.

A pergola mounted over a doorway adds impressive elegance to both the deck and home.

Build a screened gazebo for an outdoor room that provides an insect-free place to dine or relax on the deck.

Gazebos are significant deck additions that are rarely retrofitted because of the structural support the construction requires. They are usually planned as an original part of the deck, and range in complexity from a simple peaked roof supported on posts, to a nearly complete outdoor room, fully framed and ventilated, with a working door and windows.

The gazebo design you choose should depend on how you are going to use the structure. If you just need a shaded place for swimmers to rest when they come out of the pool on a hot day, a simple structure will suffice. If you envision an outdoor dining space with protection from insects, consider a gazebo with walls and screening—and possibly a door.

Gazebos, like pergolas, can be styled to suit any type of deck. Not only can the roof be shingled in a number of different materials, you can also add another tier for a more elaborate look. The ends of the roof rafters can be cut to decorative patterns, and railing styles can be replicated to serve as half-height walls around the perimeter of the gazebo. Gazebos are also commonly painted to match or complement the siding on the house.

Like pergolas, gazebos can be embellished with plants trained up the posts and other decorative items. The gazebo itself can be wired for lights, to provide a wonderful nook for enjoying the deck at night.

Several companies offer complete gazebo and pergola kits, with pieces manufactured to your specifications. These not only simplify the prep work you need to do in building the structure, they also come with detailed assembly instructions and tech support to ensure that construction does not become a DIY nightmare.

Whether you're building a modest pergola or constructing a full-scale walled gazebo, you'll need to consult closely with your local building department. Gazebos especially can be regulated not only by the codes that govern decks, but may also be subject to codes regarding independent structures.

BLACK & DECKER
BEHR
TRANSPARENT
Waterproofing
Wood Finish

Finishing & Maintaining Your Deck

As outdoor structures, decks are constantly subjected to the elements, the wear and tear of foot traffic and use, and in some cases, damage from insects. To ensure that your deck lasts as long as possible, take steps to protect the surface and maintain the structural integrity. Wood decks should be treated with a protective finish every few years, which will keep the wood attractive and slow the damaging effects of the elements. Composite, metal, and plastic decking should be regularly and thoroughly cleaned.

Eventually, you may need to make more drastic structural repairs as your deck ages or structural issues arise. If you are diligent on the necessary upkeep and maintenance, your deck will last for decades.

This chapter will introduce you to the common cleaning and finishing products that are available for preserving wood decks. You'll learn how to apply finish to new wood and clean weathered or previously finished wood in preparation for refinishing. We'll show you how to inspect your deck for rotten wood, and walk you through the step-by-step process for replacing decking, joists, and rotten posts. We'll also outline how to clean composite and other non-wood materials, and we'll discuss how to ensure that the basic structure of your deck is supporting the deck as well as it should be.

In this chapter:

Cleaning, Sealing & Coloring a Wood Deck

Whenever you finish or refinish your wood deck, there are three objectives: Cleaning the wood, protecting it, and creating the color you want. First, you need to clean the wood or remove the previous finish to prepare for applying new finish. Otherwise, the stain or sealer may not penetrate and bond properly. Second, a protective topcoat of stain or a sealer/preservative weatherizes the wood, limiting its ability to absorb water. Water absorption leads to rot and invites mildew and algae growth that can prematurely damage the finish. The topcoat also helps to block out ultraviolet sunlight, which will fade wood's natural color, age the finish, and dry out the wood until it cracks or splits. The third goal of finishing is the most obvious: staining allows you to change the wood color and either hide the wood grain or enhance it, depending on the product you choose.

If you think of finishing products in terms of cleaning, weatherizing, and coloring, you'll have an easier time choosing the right products for your wood deck-finishing project. Here is an overview of each category of finishing product.

Deck Cleaner

If your deck's current finish has faded or the wood has algae or mildew growth, use a deck cleaner to remove the stubborn stains. Deck cleaner will restore gray, weathered wood back to its original color. It will remove general dirt and grime as well as grease spots left by grilling. If the deck is just dirty but not weathered, try using a dilute solution of ordinary dish soap, followed by a good scrubbing. Soap may be all the cleaning agent your deck really needs.

Waterproofing Sealer

Oil-based waterproofing sealers and wood finishes penetrate the wood, carrying silicone or wax additives that keep wood from absorbing water. Most sealers contain mildewcides and UV inhibitors for added protection. Use a waterproofing sealer when you want to preserve the natural color and grain of the wood. Some products will impart a bit of tinting and color, but generally a sealer will leave the wood looking natural when it dries. Unlike stains, sealers have little or no pigment to ward off fading from sunlight. You'll need to reapply a sealer every year or two to maintain UV protection.

Semi-transparent Stain

Semi-transparent stains offer protective qualities similar to waterproofing sealer, but with more pigment added to help the wood resist fading. The more obvious purpose of the pigment, however, is to color the wood or blend different wood tones without obscuring the grain pattern. These stains are oil-based and penetrating, but they do not form a film on the wood's surface. They're a better choice for decking, benches, and horizontal surfaces than solid-color stains, because they won't peel. Plan to reapply every two to four years.

Solid-color Stain

Solid-color stain contains much more pigment than semi-transparent stain, and the formulation is closer to thinned paint than to stain. If you want to completely hide wood grain, a solid-color stain is the right choice for the job. It's a blend of oil and latex or latex only, so the stain forms a film on the wood surface instead of penetrating it. As long as the film doesn't peel or crack, it provides superior protection against both water and UV degradation. However, it doesn't stand up to foot traffic as well as oil-based stain. Solid-color stains can be blended in thousands of paint colors. The finish can last five years or more, but generally it will need to be stripped or sanded first before recoating. Avoid using solid-color stain on redwood or cedar. These woods contain tannins and resins than can bleed through the stain and leave spots.

Finishing a New Wood Deck

Finish a new deck with clear sealer-preservative or staining sealer. Sealer-preservatives protect wood from water and rot, and are often used on cedar or redwood because they preserve the original color of the wood. If you want the wood to look weathered, wait several months before applying sealer-preservative.

Staining sealers, sometimes called toners, are often applied to pressure-treated lumber to give it the look of redwood or cedar. Staining sealers are available in a variety of colors.

For best protection, use finishing products with an alkyd base. Apply fresh finish each year.

Tools & Materials ▸

- Orbital sander
- Sandpaper
- Shop vacuum
- Pressure sprayer
- Eye protection
- Paint brush
- Clear sealer-preservative or staining sealer

Preparing the Deck ▸

Use an orbital sander to smooth out any rough areas before applying finish to decking boards, railings, or stair treads.

A hand-pump style sprayer is inexpensive and speeds up the finish application process.

How to Finish a Redwood or Cedar Deck

Test wood surface by sprinkling water on it. If wood absorbs water quickly, it is ready to be sealed. If wood does not absorb water, let it dry for several weeks before sealing.

Sand rough areas and vacuum the deck. Apply clear sealer to all wood surfaces, using a pressure sprayer. If possible, apply sealer to the underside of decking and to joists, beams, and posts.

Use a paint brush to work sealer into cracks and narrow areas that could trap water.

How to Finish a Pressure-treated Deck

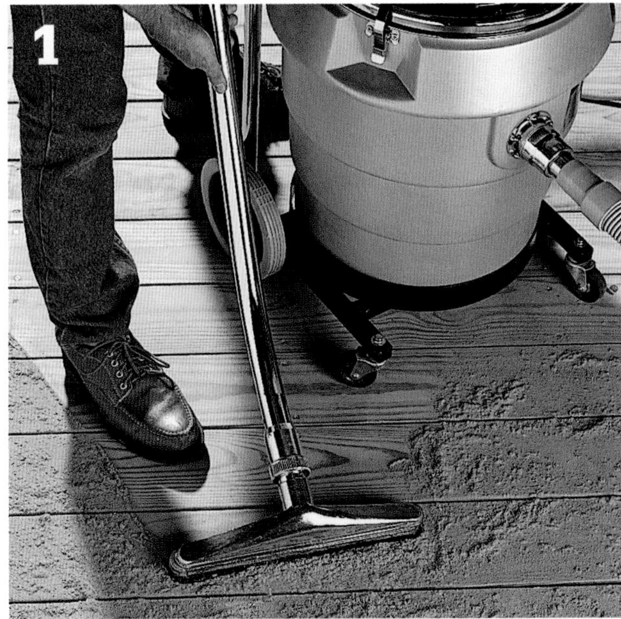

Sand rough areas and vacuum the deck. Apply a staining sealer (toner) to all deck wood using a pressure sprayer. *Note: Sanding older pressure-treated wood is not advisable because of the toxic chemicals in the wood. Any time you cut or sand pressure-treated wood, wear a respirator.*

Use a paint brush to smooth out drips and runs. Porous wood may require a second coat of staining sealer for even coverage.

Maintaining a Deck

Inspect your deck at least once a year, more often if the weather over any given season is especially severe. Replace loose or rusting hardware or fasteners as soon as you detect them to prevent future problems. Apply a new coat of sealant as necessary, according to the requirements of the type of wood or other material used in your deck.

Carefully inspect the deck surface, railings, and structure for signs of damage. Replace or reinforce damaged wood as soon as possible. Replace damaged composite decking if it is split or otherwise compromised.

Restore an older, weathered deck to its original wood color and luster with a deck-brightening product. Brighteners are available at most hardware stores and home centers.

Tools & Materials ▸

- Flashlight
- Awl or screwdriver
- Screwgun
- Putty knife
- Scrub brush
- Rubber gloves
- Eye protection
- Pressure sprayer
- 2½" deck screws
- Deck brightener

Inspect the entire deck, including underneath. Look for signs of rot, damage, or wear. Apply a sealant or new finish regularly, as required for the wood in your deck.

Maintaining an Older Deck

Use an awl or screwdriver to check deck for soft, rotted wood. Replace or reinforce damaged wood.

Clean debris from cracks between decking boards with a putty knife. Debris traps moisture and can cause wood to rot.

Drive new fasteners to secure loose decking to joists. If using the old nail or screw holes, new fasteners should be slightly longer than the originals.

How to Renew a Deck

Mix deck cleaning solution as directed by the manufacturer. Apply the solution with a pressure sprayer and let it set for 10 minutes.

Scrub the deck thoroughly with a stiff scrub brush. Wear rubber gloves and eye protection.

Rinse the deck with clear water. If necessary, apply a second coat of cleaner to extremely dirty or stained areas. Rinse and let dry. Apply a fresh coat of sealer or stain.

Power Washing ▸

An alternative to hand scrubbing a deck, power washing can be an economical way to clean and prepare even a large deck for sealant in the space of a few hours. Inexpensive home power washers don't always have enough power to completely strip the accumulated coating of dirt and debris off a deck. Instead, rent a gas-powered unit from a local rental center. Use a medium number 2 or 3 nozzle and hold the jet of water about 4 to 6 inches off the surface of the wood. You can easily clean to the bare wood with one slow pass. Apply a sealant/protectant as soon as the wood dries.

Repairing a Deck

Replace or reinforce damaged deck wood as soon as possible. Wood rot can spread and weaken solid wood.

After replacing or reinforcing the rotted wood, clean the entire deck and apply a fresh coat of clear sealer-preservative or staining sealer. Apply a fresh coat of finish each year to prevent future water damage. If you need to repair more than a few small areas, it is probably time to replace the entire deck.

Tools & Materials ▸

Cat's paw
Flat pry bar
Screwgun
Awl or screwdriver
Hammer
Chisel
Eye protection
Pressure-sprayer
Circular saw
Scrub brush
Paint brush
Hydraulic jack
Drill or hammer drill
⅝" masonry bit
Level
Ratchet wrench
Sealer-preservative or staining sealer
Galvanized nails (6d, 10d)
Deck lumber
Baking soda
Corrosion-resistant deck screws
⅝" masonry anchor
⅜" lag screw
Rubber gloves
Bucket
Concrete block
Scrap plywood

How to Repair Damaged Decking & Joists

Remove nails or screws from the damaged decking board using a cat's paw. Remove the damaged board.

Inspect the underlying joists for signs of rotted wood. Joists with discolored, soft areas should be repaired and reinforced.

Use a hammer and chisel to remove any rotted portions of the joist.

Apply a thick coat of sealer-preservative to the damaged joist. Let it dry, then apply a second coat of sealer. Cut a reinforcing joist (sister joist) from pressure-treated lumber.

Coat the sister joist with clear sealer-preservative and let it dry. Position the sister joist tightly against the damaged joist, and fasten it in place with 10d nails or screws driven every 2 ft.

Attach the sister joist to the ledger and the header joist by toenailing with 10d nails. Cut replacement decking boards from matching lumber using a circular saw.

If the existing decking is gray, "weather" the new decking by scrubbing it with a solution made from 1 cup baking soda and 1 gallon of warm water. Rinse and let dry.

(continued)

Apply a coat of sealer-preservative or staining sealer to all sides of the new decking boards.

Position the new boards and fasten them to the joists with galvanized deck screws. Make sure the space between boards matches that of the existing decking.

How to Replace a Post

Build a support using plywood scraps, a concrete block and a hydraulic jack. Place a 1½" layer of plywood between the head of the jack and the beam. Apply just enough pressure to lift the beam slightly. *Note: Because of recent code revisions you may be required to replace old posts with larger lumber. Check with your local building department.*

Remove the nails or lag screws holding the damaged post to the anchor pad and to the beam. Remove the damaged post and the wood anchor pad, if any, on the concrete pier.

Drill a hole in the middle of the concrete pier, using a hammer drill and a ⅝" masonry bit. Insert a ⅝" masonry anchor into the hole.

Position a galvanized post anchor on the pier block, and thread a ⅜" lag screw with washer through the hole in the anchor and into the masonry anchor. Tighten the screw with a ratchet wrench.

Cut a new post from pressure-treated lumber, and treat the cut ends with sealer-preservative. Position the post and make sure it is plumb.

Attach the bottom of the post to the post anchor using 10d joist hanger nails. Attach the post to the beam by redriving the lag screws, using a ratchet wrench. Release the pressure on the jack and remove the support.

How to Repair Popped Decking Nails

The cure for most popped nails is simply to remove the nail. Use a nail extractor, cat's paw, or a claw hammer, using a scrap of wood or other protective surface to limit damage to the deck surface. Once the nail is removed, drive a 3" galvanized deck screw down through the nail hole.

Where a nail has come loose from the joist below, but the head is still securely buried in the board, digging the popped nail out would damage the board. Instead, drive a 3" galvanized deck screw right next to the nail, so that the screw head overlaps the nail head.

How to Reface a Rotted Deck Edge

Measure the deck overhang from the joist outward. Decide how far back you want to cut the edge of the deck (usually about ½" to ¾" less than the measurement from the joist).

Transfer that measurement to the two end boards on the deck. Drive nails into the boards and snap a chalk line between them to create the cut line.

Use a circular saw to cut along the chalk line. Depending on how much you've cut off and what type of material the decking is, you may need to seal the ends with a waterproof protectant/sealant.

Cut a cedar, redwood, or pressure treated 1 × 2 to length to cover the edges. Scarf any joints that are necessary along the edging. Use 2½" galvanized deck screws to fasten the 2 × 2 in place. As an alternative, you can stain the 2 × 2 edging in a contrasting shade from the deck, and seal it before fastening to the edge.

Cleaning Vinyl & Composite Decking

Vinyl, recycled plastic, aluminum, and composite decking may be easier to maintain and is often more durable than solid wood, but these materials aren't completely exempt from a bit of cosmetic cleanup now and again. Non-wood decking will get dirty and stained in the course of normal use, and you'll need to use different cleaning products, depending on the type of stain. Although it may be tempting to pull out the pressure washer and give your deck a good going over, pressure washers can harm some types of synthetic decking and may even void your deck warranty (check with the manufacturer of your particular decking). A little elbow grease and the right cleaners are often a better approach. Here are suggestions for cleaning various types of stains and marks from vinyl, plastic, or composite decking. Be sure to wear safety glasses and protective gloves when working with strong chemicals.

Dirt & Tree Sap: Remove ordinary residue from foot traffic, bird droppings, or tree sap with household dish soap diluted with water. Mix a strong concentration in a bucket, scrub the stains, and rinse with clean water.

Fastener, Leaf, or Tannin: Steel fasteners, tree leaves, or resin stains from cedar or redwood can leave dark tannin stains on composite decking. To remove these, spray on a deck brightener/cleaner product that contains oxalic or phosphoric acid, then flush the surface with lots of fresh water.

Oil & Grease: Oil and grease spots from barbecuing or tanning lotions should be cleaned immediately, before they dry. Use a household degreaser (such as an orange citrus cleaner), Simple Green, or ammonia and a scrub brush to remove the stain. Follow with soapy water and thorough rinsing.

Mold & Mildew: Use a diluted solution of household bleach and water or a deck cleaner with mildew and stain remover to kill off mold and mildew growth. A good preventive measure is to scrub and wash your deck at least once a season, especially in shady or damp areas where mold and mildew are likely to grow.

Berry & Wine: Use a dilute solution of household bleach and water to spot-clean wine or berry stains from decking. Depending on the depth of the stain, you may not be able to remove it entirely, but generally these stains will fade over time.

Crayon & Marker: If you have young kids, sooner or later crayon or marker stains are inevitable. The trick to removing them is using the correct solvent. Mineral spirits will remove crayon wax, and soapy water cleans up water-based marker stains. Use denatured alcohol (available at home centers) to remove dye-based, permanent markers.

How to Stop Deck Sway

Measure 24" down from where the post meets the beam. Clearly mark that point on the post.

Measure 24" from one edge of the post out along the beam. Mark that point on the beam. Repeat on the other side of the beam. Measure from the mark on the beam to the mark on the post. Add 4" for the total length of the brace.

Hold the brace in place between the mark on the post and the mark on the beam, so that the marks intersect the brace on center. Mark the brace for the angled end cuts, using the underside of the beam and edge of the post as straightedges.

Top: Use a miter saw to make the angled end cuts. Place the brace in position and drill top and bottom pilot holes (two at each location), and then screw the brace to the post and beam using 6" lag screws. **Bottom:** Fasten the brace to the underlying deck joists by drilling pilot holes through the post and into the brace and securing again with carriage bolts.

How to Stiffen a Spongy Deck

Measure the space between joists. Use this measurement to cut blocking from pressure treated lumber the same size as the joists. Snap a chalkline down the center of the joists' span.

Tap the blocking in place, positioning blocks in an alternating pattern with one block to the left and one to the right of the chalk line.

Screw through the joists into the end of the blocks on each side using 3" galvanized decking screws.

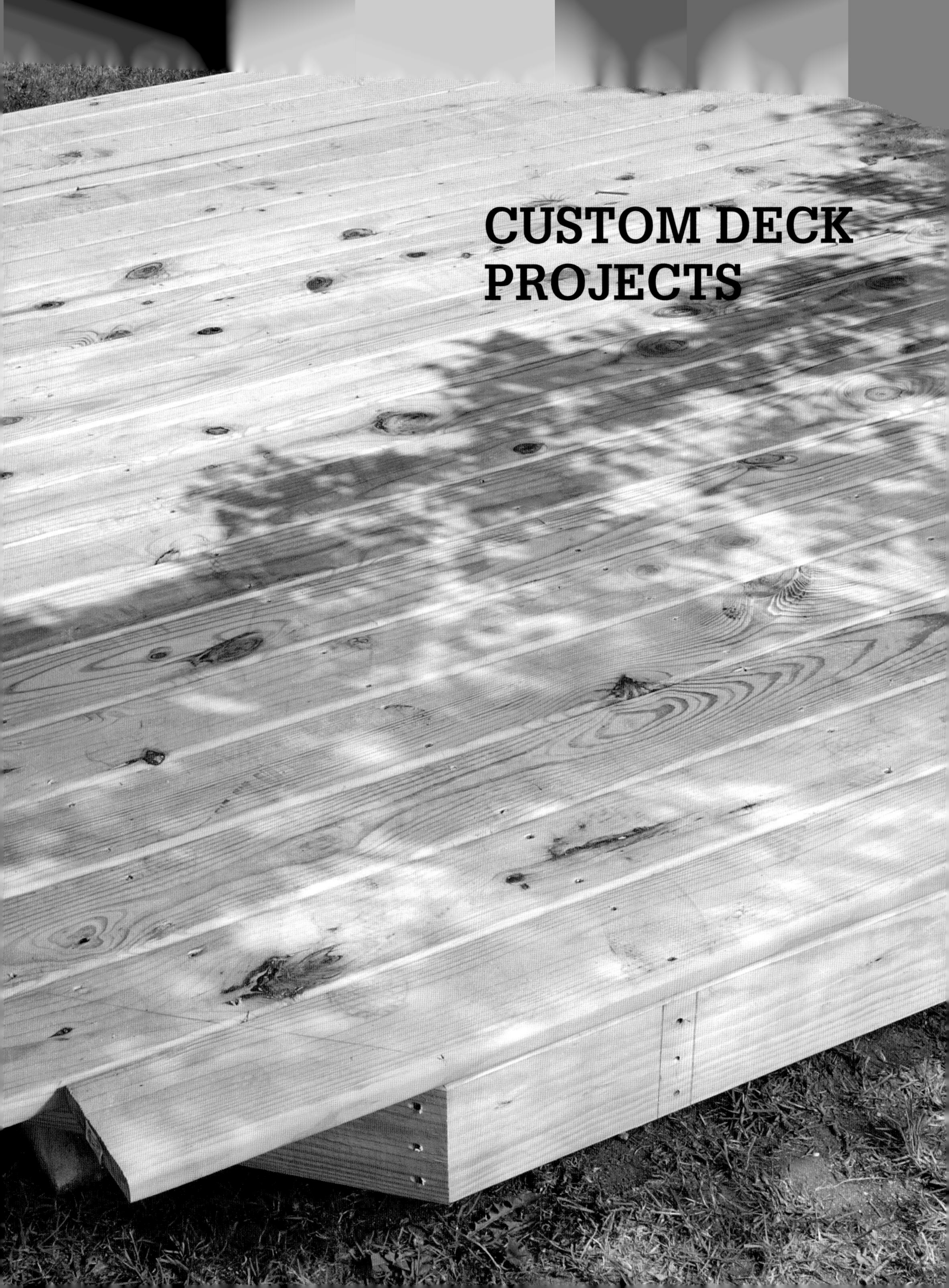

CUSTOM DECK PROJECTS

A Deck for Entertaining

Outdoor entertaining on a deck often involves preparing a meal. If the menu is just burgers and hot dogs, most of that food prep takes place at the grill. But even the simplest fare still involves those inevitable trips back and forth to the kitchen to toss a salad, warm up a side dish, or replenish the cold drinks. More complex meals will keep the chef in the kitchen even longer—and that means less time spent out on the deck with family and friends. Wouldn't it be great if you could bring the kitchen to the deck to take care of more—or even all—of those food prep tasks?

At one time, outdoor kitchens were still more fantasy than reality, but that's no longer the case. Today, Americans are increasingly seeing their decks as important outdoor entertainment areas, and not just places to park the patio table and grill. An assortment of custom grills, outdoor appliances, and storage cabinets can help you transform your deck into a fully functional kitchen. These appliances are UL-listed, so your kitchen doesn't have to be located in a covered porch or tucked under a roof. You can cook and prepare right where you serve. Outdoor appliances are generally more expensive than their indoor cousins, but if outdoor entertaining is an important part of your lifestyle, you can now enjoy it more fully than ever before and without compromise.

Imagine the dinner parties you could host if your deck had a fully functional outdoor kitchen! It's a trend in outdoor entertaining that continues to grow in popularity. These days, there are outdoor appliances to suit most kitchen tasks.

Whether you use your deck for intimate outdoor dining, boisterous parties, or quiet conversation, decks provide an ideal way to extend your home's dining space into the outdoors.

A sturdy outdoor patio table and chairs, made of suitable exterior-rated wood or metal, is a beneficial improvement to any deck. Tables that accept large shade umbrellas are even more practical, especially if your deck is located in a sunny spot.

A high-end outdoor kitchen with stainless steel appliances and solid wood cabinetry leaves no question that this deck owner is serious about food.

Outdoor Appliances

For years, better quality grills have included a sideburner and second grate to keep food warm. Now, you can purchase expansive grilling stations that may include dedicated infrared warming drawers, storage cabinets and drawers, insulated cubbies for ice, and extended serving counters. They're a relatively affordable way to take your grilling and food preparation tasks to the next level, and you can buy these units at most home centers.

Self-contained grilling stations are just one of many appliance options to choose from. For more culinary convenience, you can also buy outdoor-rated ovens, multi-burner rangetops and refrigerators, ice makers, and beverage coolers from a number of reputable manufacturers. Ovens and rangetops are heated by either propane or natural gas, depending on the model. They're designed as modular components that fit into a bank of cabinets or a custom-built kitchen island. Outdoor refrigerators are relatively compact and nest under a countertop where they can be at least partially sheltered from the elements. They range in capacity from around 3 to 6 cubic feet. Outdoor sinks, wet bars, and dedicated food prep stations are other options you might consider adding to your deck kitchen.

A variety of outdoor kitchen appliances, such as refrigerators, ice makers, and wine coolers, can help keep food and drinks cold no matter how hot the day may be.

Custom barbecue islands can be configured in lots of different ways to suit your space and food prep needs. The primary appliance is generally a gas grill with a cabinet underneath for storing the LP tank. A bank of drawers provides handy places to keep grilling tools and other cooking utensils or spices.

A warming drawer outfitted in your barbecue island can help you stage various dinner items while you grill the main course. Some prefabricated barbecue islands include a warming drawer.

This self-contained beer keg cooler will keep your favorite brew cold on the hottest summer day and for as long as the party lasts. All it takes is an electrical outlet.

Consider adding a plumbed sink to your outdoor kitchen. It will make food prep and clean-up much easier. Be sure to check with local building codes concerning running hot and cold supply lines or installing an appropriate drain.

If your barbecue grill isn't equipped with a side burner, it's an essential feature you'll want to add to your outdoor kitchen. Side burners are available as independent accessories that can be built into a kitchen island or bank of cabinets.

Cabinets & Countertops

Once you step beyond a one-piece grilling station, you'll need to store a stove, refrigerator, or other appliances in a system of cabinets or an island base of some kind. This could be as simple as an enclosed framework with a countertop, or it can be as elaborate as you like. Chances are, you'll want to include a few storage cabinets and drawers to keep utensils, cookware, and other supplies close at hand. Some cabinet manufacturers offer weather-resistant cabinets made from teak, cypress, mahogany, or other exterior woods. They're available as modular components that can be mixed and matched like other cabinetry. Polyethylene, marine-grade polymer, or stainless steel cabinets are more options to consider: they're corrosion-resistant, waterproof, and hypoallergenic. It's a good idea to buy your appliances first, then design an island or bank of cabinets that will fit what you own.

A variety of countertop materials could make a durable and attractive serving surface for your kitchen. Porcelain tile is weather-resistant and affordable, and it's manufactured in virtually any style and color you can dream of. You could choose a fabricated countertop made of stainless steel, soapstone, granite, or marble. Or, build your counter from a piece of tempered glass. If your deck kitchen will be sheltered under an awning or roof, solid-surface material is also good choice. However, the polymer blends that make up solid-surface materials aren't formulated to be UV stable, and they could deteriorate over time.

If you build your own countertop, be sure to start with a substrate layer of cement backer board if you use grouted tile or other permeable material. It will prevent water from seeping through to appliances or into storage cabinets.

If you're a competent woodworker, consider building custom cabinets to outfit your deck kitchen rather than buying them. Make them from the same wood as your other patio furniture or decking so they blend into your deck scheme perfectly.

Building an Island Base

For handy do-it-yourselfers, designing a weatherproof kitchen island can offer a hearty challenge and an excellent chance to explore some new building materials. Start with a framework of pressure-treated or cedar lumber, and sheathe it with waterproof cement backer board. Then, cover the exposed surfaces with patio tile, stucco, veneered stone or brick. Or, use exterior plywood as the substrate for your island framework, then follow with vinyl, fiber cement, or cedar lap siding to match the siding of your house. You could even use composite decking to sheathe your kitchen island or grilling station so it visually ties in with your deck's design. Or, wrap the outside in sheets of stainless steel or aluminum for a sleek, modern look.

You'll want to expand the storage capabilities of your deck kitchen by including a variety of cabinets. Exterior-grade cabinets are made with durable polymers, rot-resistant woods, or stainless steel, and they are available in a range of sizes and styles to suit your needs.

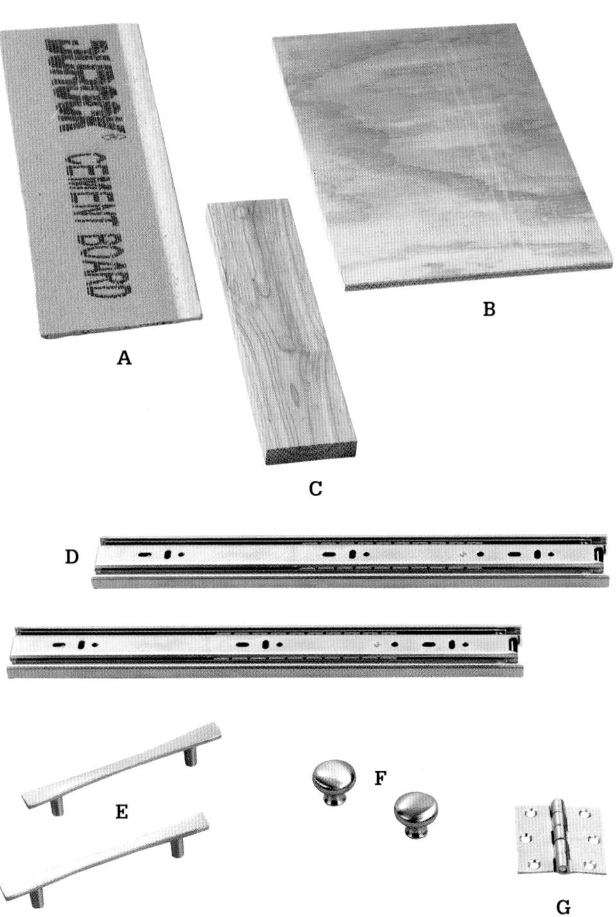

Choose water-resistant building materials for the structural and sheathing components of your island. Cement board (A), outdoor woods like cedar or redwood (B), and exterior-rated plywood (C) are all suitable home-center options. For cabinets, choose corrosion-resistant drawer slides (D), drawer hardware (E, F), and hinges (G).

Build or Hire?

Depending on where you live, you might be able to hire a contractor to design and build the countertop, base, and cabinets for your deck appliances. However, given that deck kitchens are still a relatively new concept, you may need to carry out these projects on your own. Companies that sell outdoor appliances and cabinetry may be able to help you design your outdoor deck kitchen. You can also find grilling station and island project designs in outdoor kitchen design books.

Keep in mind that you may need to run a natural gas line and several ground-fault protected outlets to the kitchen. If you decide to include a functional sink in your design, you'll need at least one potable water line and possibly a sanitary drain that empties into a dry well or your home's plumbing system. Be sure to install these utilities so that they conform to the building codes in your area. The proper course of action is to apply for the appropriate utility permits and have the work inspected. If you are in doubt of your skills with running gas lines or wiring electrical receptacles, have this work performed by a licensed plumber and electrician.

Soapstone is a moderately hard, natural material that works well for exterior countertop applications. The stone is semi-porous, so it should be periodically sealed if it's exposed to the elements. Sealing helps maintain water resistance.

Granite is an excellent countertop material. It's much harder than soapstone and available in many natural colors and surface textures. Common varieties of granite are in the same price range as soapstone.

Concrete is more affordable than natural stone, and it can be tinted in a wide range of colors or mixed with other aggregates to add texture and visual interest. Another benefit to concrete is that it can be poured to suit any shape of countertop you may need.

Grouted patio tile will also work well for an outdoor kitchen countertop. It's inexpensive, easy to install without special skills, and comes in many sizes, colors, and styles. You'll need to seal the grout periodically if the countertop is exposed to the elements or has a sink.

Is Your Deck Well Suited for a Kitchen? ▸

A deck kitchen may sound like an intriguing notion, but think carefully about the ramifications of dedicating part of your deck to this purpose. You'll need a certain amount of counter space for preparing food and staging it for cooking or storing it while you cook. Do you want to reserve a portion of the counter area for dining, or will that take place at a separate patio table? Are your home's utilities close enough to the deck to make gas lines or plumbing convenient to run? Will a kitchen island, patio table, and other deck furniture all fit comfortably on your deck without making the space feel crowded? As you begin to plan your outdoor kitchen, it may help to use masking tape, pieces of plywood, or cardboard boxes to lay out a space for your kitchen. This will help you visualize how the size of the kitchen would impact the rest of your deck. Ultimately, an outdoor kitchen should enhance your outdoor entertaining options and make your deck more useful, not overwhelm it.

A Deck for Livability

Decks are significant investments, so you should try to use yours as much as possible. Don't let those dog days of summer, a chilly fall afternoon, or sundown cut your deck enjoyment short. A few carefully chosen accessories can improve creature comforts and get you back out on the deck earlier each spring or extend your entertaining later into the year. If you are a serious audiophile or sports fan, an outdoor sound system or television might be just what you need to spend more time outdoors and on the deck. Manufacturers of lighting and deck accessories are continually expanding their product lines. Visit their websites or attend a home and garden show to get a better taste of what's new and exciting in deck accessories. The selection of products on display at your local home center are just the tip of the iceberg.

The following pages cover a variety of deck accessories that will make your deck a more practical and vital part of your leisure lifestyle.

The "livability" of your deck is a somewhat intangible quality rooted in form, function, and the natural conditions that impact it. Shade and sunlight, location and furniture, amenities like hot tubs or kitchens, provisions for privacy, and the way in which the desk's space is laid out all influence how often and well you'll use it.

An outdoor kitchen with ample counterspace for food preparation and serving, as well as seating for casual dining, will help to make it a hard-working feature of your deck.

If your deck will receive lots of sunshine or you are located in a southern climate, consider adding a retractable sunshade for those really hot days. Or, cover a portion of your deck with a fixed awning.

Deck living can extend well into the fall or even the winter if you include a heat source on your deck. A permanent outdoor fireplace like the one shown here is only one option. You can also buy free-standing or fixed radiant heaters that burn propane or natural gas. Or, use a chiminea or a raised firepit to keep folks warm when there's a chill.

Broad, sturdy benches will invite relaxation, especially if they're located on a portion of your deck that receives some shade. Depending on the height of your deck, fixed benches could even take the place of railings.

Recessed stair lighting clearly serves a safety function, but it also offers a cheery welcome for evening visitors. It should be combined with other light sources to create a pleasant, well-lit area.

Railing posts are another good spot for adding accent lighting. You can buy low-voltage post cap lights in various styles to take your deck lighting "to the next level," so to speak. It's a custom touch that will impress.

There are lots of options for deck lighting fixtures. These low-standing, pier-styled lights suggest a nautical theme and would be ideal for a deck located near a lake or other water feature.

An arbor provides a pleasant filter of sun and shade. It's also a great place to plant vining leafy plants, which will eventually cover the top and contribute even more natural shade. Wooden arbors make great DIY projects, whether you install one when your deck first goes up or any time you want to add a custom touch.

Your deck will be a more inviting place to gather and spend time if you break up the space with lots of interesting details. Raised planters, benches, and a unique railing style all contribute a sense of craftsmanship and purpose to a well-planned deck.

Exterior-rated audio systems and even waterproof televisions can help transform your deck into an outdoor living room. Add a few comfy patio chairs and occasional tables, and you may be surprised how much more time you spend on the deck than in the living room!

These white lattice railings and attached arbor give this deck a bright, friendly atmosphere. Thanks to ample shading, a long, cushioned bench certainly makes a perfect spot for reading or even an afternoon nap on a lazy day.

A Deck with Power

The wiring installation shown on the following pages provides step-by-step instructions for installing light fixtures and power receptacles on a deck. These instructions are based on the National Electrical Code (NEC), which stipulates minimum standards for outdoor wiring materials. But because climate and soil conditions vary from region to region, always check with your local building and electrical codes for additional restrictions in your area. For example, some codes require that all underground cables be protected with conduit, even though the NEC allows UF cable to be buried without protection at the proper depths.

Note: This project requires general knowledge of electrical materials and techniques beyond the specific instructions shown here. Make certain you know how to do this work before attempting this project.

Check for underground utilities when planning trenches for underground cable runs. Avoid lawn sprinkler pipes, and call 811 or consult your electric utility office, phone company, gas and water department, and cable television vendor for the exact locations of underground utility lines. Utility companies send field representatives to accurately locate dangerous underground hazards.

Running underground cable to supply power to your deck is a relatively simple wiring job that offers high payback in deck enjoyment for your family.

How to Wire a Deck

PLAN THE CIRCUIT

Visit your electrical inspector to check local code requirements for outdoor wiring and to obtain a permit for your project. Because outdoor wiring is exposed to the elements, it requires the use of special weatherproof materials, including UF cable, rigid metal or schedule 40 PVC plastic conduit, and weatherproof electrical boxes and fittings. Some local codes allow either rigid metal or PVC plastic, while others allow only metal.

For most homes, an outdoor circuit for a deck is a modest power user. Adding a new 15-amp, 120-volt circuit provides enough power for most needs. However, if your circuit will include more than three large light fixtures (each rated for 30 watts or more) or more than four receptacles, plan to install a 20-amp, 120-volt circuit.

Consider the circuit length when choosing cable sizes for the deck circuit. In very long circuits, normal wire resistance leads to a substantial drop in voltage. If your circuit extends more than 50 feet, use cable wire that is one gauge larger to reduce the voltage drop. For example, a 15-amp circuit that extends more than 50 feet should be wired with 12-gauge wire instead of the usual 14-gauge.

Plan to bury UF cables 12" deep if the wires are protected by a GFCI and the circuit is no larger than 20 amps. Use metal conduit or bury cable at least 24" deep if the circuit is larger than 20 amps **(photo 1)**.

Prevent shock by making sure all outdoor receptacles are GFCI protected. A single GFCI receptacle can be wired to protect other fixtures on the circuit. Outdoor receptacles should be at least 12" above ground level and enclosed in weatherproof electrical boxes with watertight covers **(photo 2)**.

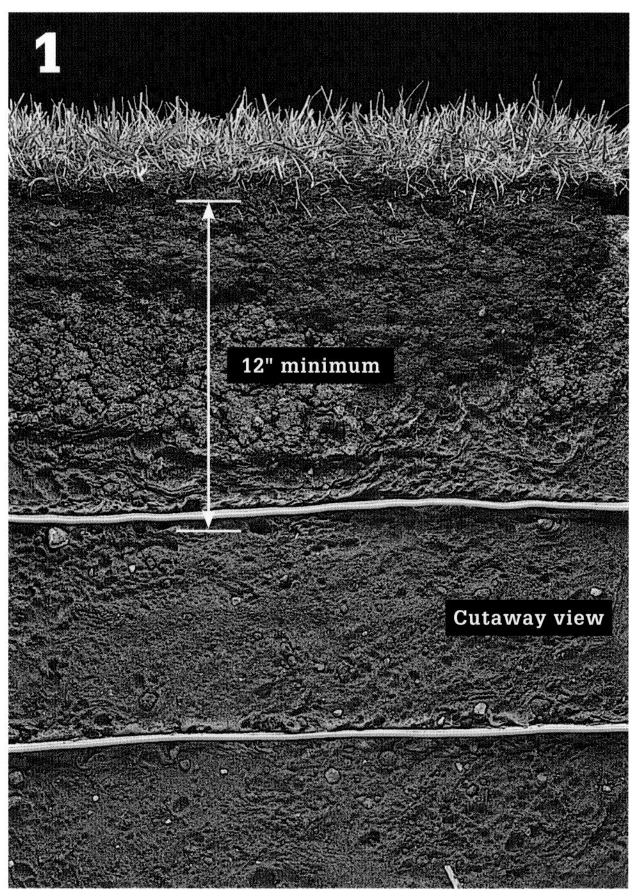

Bury UF cables 12" deep if the wires are protected by a GFCI and the circuit is no larger than 20 amps. Bury cable at least 24" deep if it is larger than 20 amps.

Install GFCI receptacles in weatherproof electrical boxes at least 1 ft.—and no more than 6½ ft.—above ground level.

DIG TRENCHES

When laying underground cables, save time and minimize lawn damage by digging trenches as narrow as possible. Plan the circuit to reduce the length of cable runs. If your soil is sandy, or very hard and dry, water the ground thoroughly before you begin digging.

Mark the outline of the trenches with wooden stakes and string.

Cut two 18"-wide strips of plastic, and place one strip on each side of the trench outline.

Remove blocks of sod from the trench outline, using a shovel. Cut sod 2" to 3" deep to keep roots intact. Place the sod on one of the plastic strips and keep it moist but not wet. It should be replaced within two or three days, otherwise the grass underneath the plastic may die.

Dig the trenches to the depth required by your local code. Heap the dirt onto the second strip of plastic **(photo 3)**.

To run cable under a sidewalk, cut a length of metal conduit about 12" longer than the width of sidewalk, then flatten one end of the conduit to form a sharp tip. Drive the conduit through the soil under the sidewalk using a ball-peen or masonry hammer and a wood block to prevent damage to the pipe **(photo 4)**. Cut off the ends of the conduit with a hacksaw, leaving about 2" of exposed conduit on each side. Attach a compression fitting and plastic bushing to each end of the conduit. The plastic fittings will prevent the sharp edges of the conduit from damaging the cable sheathing.

If the trenches must be left unattended during the project, temporarily cover them with scrap plywood to prevent accidents.

INSTALL BOXES & CONDUIT

Outline the GFCI receptacle box on the exterior wall of the house. First drill pilot holes at the corners of the box outline, then use a piece of stiff wire to probe the wall for electrical wires or plumbing pipes. Complete the cutout with a jigsaw or reciprocating saw. *Masonry variation:* To make cutouts in masonry, drill a line of holes inside the box outline using a masonry bit, then remove the waste material with a masonry chisel and ball-peen hammer.

Install NM cable from the circuit breaker panel to the GFCI cutout. Allow an extra 24" of cable at the panel end and an extra 12" at the GFCI end. Attach the cable to framing members with cable staples. Strip 10" of outer sheathing from the GFCI end of the cable and ¾" of insulation from each wire.

Outline trench locations with stakes and string, then dig the trenches to the depths required by your local code.

Drive conduit beneath sidewalks and other obstacles, using a block of wood and a hammer.

Route cables into the GFCI box, push the box into the cutout, then tighten the mounting screws until the box is secure.

Open one knockout for each cable that will enter the GFCI box. Insert the cables so at least ¼" of sheathing reaches into the box. Push the box into the cutout and tighten the mounting screw until the bracket draws the plaster ears tight against the wall **(photo 5)**.

Position a foam gasket over the GFCI box, then attach an extension ring to the box, using the mounting screws included with the extension ring. Seal any gaps around the extension ring with silicone caulk.

Measure and cut a length of IMC conduit (steel conduit) to reach from the bottom of the extension ring to a point about 4" from the bottom of the trench. Attach the conduit to the extension ring using a compression fitting **(photo 6)**. Anchor the conduit to the wall with a pipe strap and masonry screws. Or use masonry anchors and pan-head screws. Drill pilot holes for the anchors using a masonry drill bit.

Attach compression fittings to the ends of the metal sweep fitting, then attach the sweep fitting to the end of the conduit. Screw a plastic bushing onto the exposed fitting end of the sweep to keep the metal edges from damaging the cable.

At the deck, attach mounting ears to the back of a weatherproof receptacle box, then attach the box to the deck frame by driving galvanized screws through the ears and into the post.

Measure and cut a length of IMC conduit to reach from the bottom of the receptacle box to a point about 4" from the bottom of the trench. Attach the conduit to the box with a compression fitting. Attach a sweep fitting and plastic bushing to the bottom of the conduit using compression fittings **(photo 7)**.

Cut a length of IMC conduit to reach from the top of the receptacle box to the switch box location. Attach the conduit to the receptacle box with a compression fitting. Anchor the conduit to the deck frame with pipe straps.

Attach mounting ears to the back of the switch box, then loosely attach the box to the conduit with a compression fitting. Anchor the box to the deck frame by driving galvanized screws through the ears and into the wood. Tighten the compression fitting with a wrench. Measure and cut a short length of IMC conduit to reach from the top of the switch box to the deck light location. Attach the conduit with a compression fitting **(photo 8)**.

At the house, install conduit so it extends from the bottom of the extension ring to 4" from the bottom of the trench.

At the deck, attach conduit to the receptacle box so it extends from the bottom of the box to 4" from the bottom of the trench.

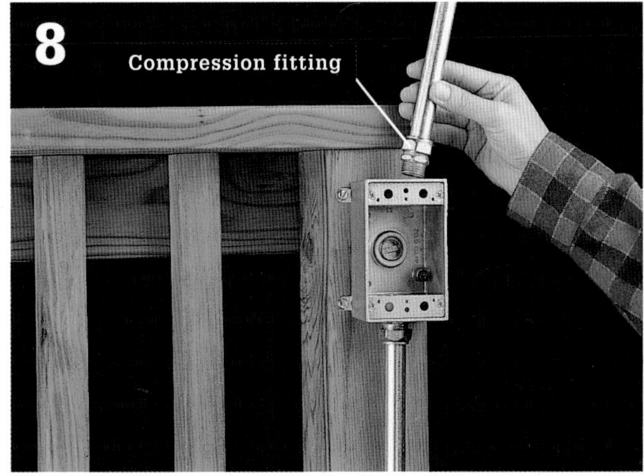

Attach conduit to the switch box so it extends from the box to the deck light location, using a compression fitting.

INSTALL THE CABLE

Measure and cut all UF cables, allowing an extra 12" at each box. At each end of the cable, use a utility knife to pare away about 3" of outer sheathing, leaving the inner wires exposed.

Feed a fish tape down through the conduit from the GFCI box. Hook the wires at one end of the cable through the loop in the fish tape, then wrap electrical tape around the wires up to the sheathing. Carefully pull the cable through the conduit **(photo 9)**.

Lay the cable along the bottom of the trench, making sure it is not twisted. Where cable runs under a sidewalk, use the fish tape to pull it through the conduit.

Use the fish tape to pull the end of the cable up through the conduit to the deck receptacle box at the opposite end of the trench **(photo 10)**. Remove the cable from the fish tape.

Cut away the electrical tape at each end of the cable, then clip away the bent wires. Bend back one of the wires in the cable, and grip it with needlenose pliers. Grip the cable with another pliers, then pull back on the wire, splitting the sheathing and exposing about 10" of wire. Repeat with the remaining wires, then cut off excess sheathing with a utility knife. Strip ¾" of insulation from the end of each wire using a combination tool.

Measure, cut, and install a cable from the deck receptacle box to the outdoor switch box, using the fish tape. Strip 10" of sheathing from each end of the cable, then strip ¾" of insulation from the end of each wire using a combination tool.

Attach a grounding pigtail to the back of each metal box and extension ring. Join all grounding wires with a wire connector. Tuck the wires inside the boxes, and temporarily attach the weatherproof coverplates until the inspector arrives for the rough-in inspection **(photo 11)**.

CONNECT THE RECEPTACLES

At the GFCI receptacle, connect the black feed wire from the power source to the brass terminal marked "line." Connect the white feed wire from the power source to the silver screw terminal marked "line."

Attach the short white pigtail wire to the silver screw terminal marked "load," and attach a short black pigtail wire to the brass screw terminal marked "load."

Connect the black pigtail wire to all the remaining black circuit wires using a wire connector. Connect the white pigtail wire to the remaining white circuit wires.

At the house, use fish tape to pull cable through the conduit and into the GFCI box.

At the deck, use the fish tape to pull cable through the conduit and into the receptacle box and switch box.

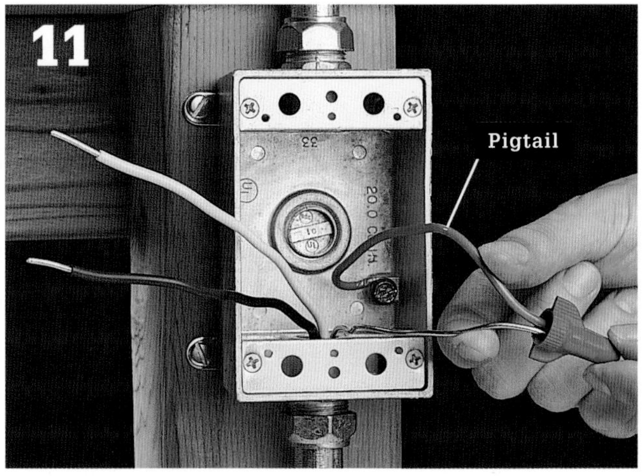

Connect a grounding pigtail to each metal box and extension ring and join all grounding wires with the pigtail. Install the coverplates for the rough-in inspection.

Attach a grounding pigtail to the grounding screw on the GFCI. Join the grounding pigtail to the bare copper grounding wires using a wire connector **(photo 12)**.

Carefully tuck the wires into the box. Mount the GFCI, then fit a foam gasket over the box and attach the weatherproof coverplate.

At each remaining receptacle in your deck circuit, connect the black circuit wires to the brass screw terminals on the receptacle. Connect the white circuit wires to the silver screw terminals on the receptacle. Attach a grounding pigtail to the grounding screw on the receptacle, then join all grounding wires with a wire connector.

Carefully tuck all wires into the box, and attach the receptacle to the box using the mounting screws. Fit a foam gasket over the box, and attach the weatherproof coverplate.

CONNECT THE DECORATIVE LIGHT FIXTURES

Thread the wire leads of the light fixture through a threaded compression fitting. Screw the union onto the base of the light fixture **(photo 13)**.

Feed the wire leads through the conduit and into the switch box. Slide the light fixture onto the conduit, and tighten the compression fitting.

CONNECT THE SWITCH

Switches for outdoor use have weatherproof coverplates with built-in toggle levers. The lever operates a single-pole switch mounted to the inside of the coverplate.

Connect the black circuit wire to one of the screw terminals on the switch, and connect the black wire lead from the light fixture to the other screw terminal.

Connect the white wire lead to the white circuit wire with a wire connector **(photo 14)**. Use a wire connector to join the grounding wires.

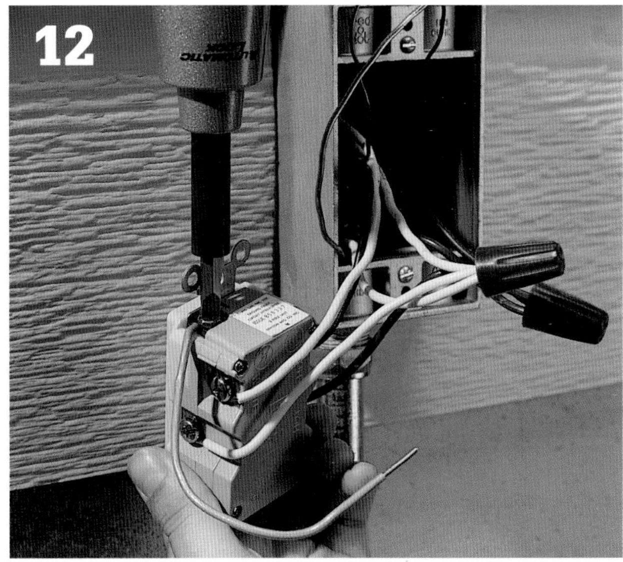

To install a GFCI receptacle, connect the black feed wire from the power source to the brass screw terminal (line), and the white feed wire to the silver screw terminal (line). Use pigtails and wire connectors to connect the remaining black circuit wires to the brass screw terminal (load), the white circuit wires to the silver screw terminal (load), and the green or copper wires to the grounding screw.

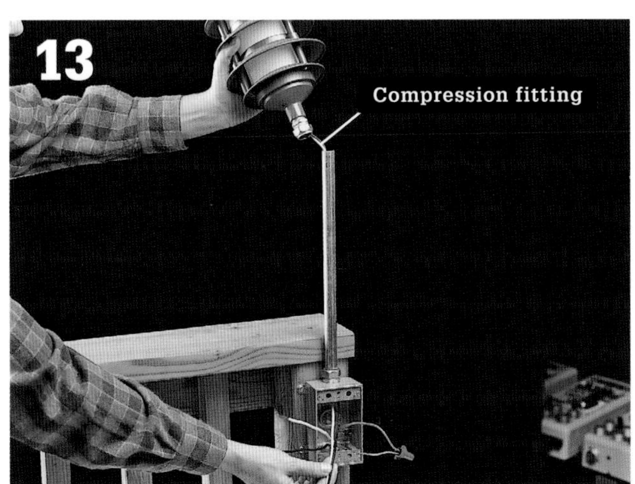

Feed the wire leads through the conduit into the switch box, then attach the light fixture using a compression fitting.

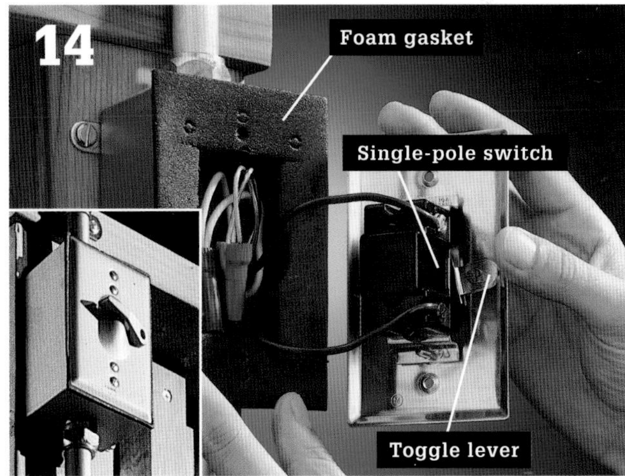

To install a weatherproof switch, connect the black circuit wire to one of the screw terminals on the switch, and the black wire lead from the fixture to the other screw terminal. Use wire connectors to join the white circuit wires and the grounding wires.

How to Install Low-voltage Step Lights

Low-voltage recessed lights are great for decks. Installed inconspicuously in the deck boards, they provide accent lighting for plant boxes or pathway lighting for stairs.

CUT THE HOLES FOR THE FIXTURES

Use the template or trace the bottom of the fixture onto the treads to mark a hole for each light. Center the fixture on the tread, 1 to 2" from the edge (the hole will center on the gap between the 2 × 6s on most deck stairs).

Drill holes at the corners, then cut the holes with a jigsaw **(photo 1)**.

Test the fixtures to be sure they will fit (they should fit snugly), and adjust the holes as necessary.

RUN CABLE FOR THE FIXTURES

Run cable to the stairs from an existing low-voltage system or from a new transformer. Drill a hole in the bottom riser if necessary, and snake the cable under the stairs along the inside edge.

Pull a loop of cable through each of the holes for the fixtures and temporarily secure it to the tread with tape **(photo 2)**.

WIRE THE FIXTURE

At the middle of the first loop of cable in the series, separate 3 to 4" of the two conductors in the cable by slicing down the center.

Strip about 2" of insulation off of each wire. Cut the wire in the center of the stripped section, and twist the two ends and the end of one of the fixture wires into an outdoor wire connector **(photo 3)**. Secure the connection with electrical tape.

Repeat with the other fixture wire and the other circuit wire.

Tuck the wires back into the hole, and place the fixture into the hole.

Test each fixture before installing the next one.

Mark the fixture location, drill pilot holes at the corner of the cutout, then cut the holes using a jigsaw.

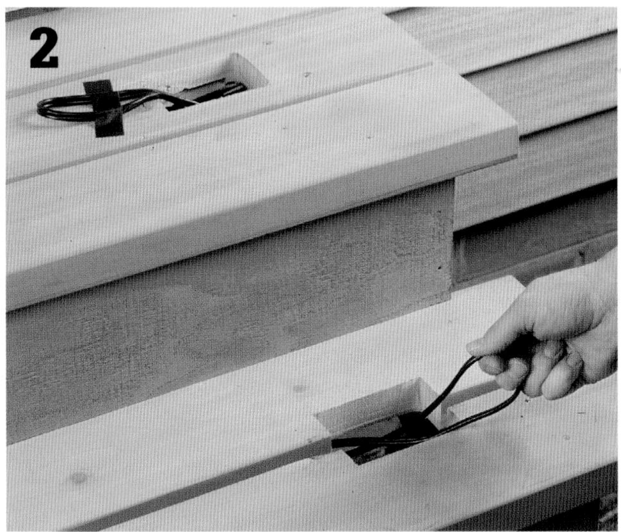

Run the cable from an existing low-voltage system or from a new transformer to the stair location.

Join the lead wires of the fixture with the wires of the low-voltage cable using outdoor wire connectors.

How to Install Low-voltage Railing Lights

Rope light is thin, flexible, clear tubing with tiny light bulbs embedded every few inches along its length. Most rope lights are meant to plug into a receptacle and use household current. While this is all right for indoor decorating, it limits their use outdoors. Low-voltage versions, however, are powered by transformers and can be connected inconspicuously to a low-voltage landscape lighting circuit. They are available from specialty lighting stores and catalogs.

ROUTE THE CABLE

Run a cable from a transformer or from a nearby low-voltage circuit using a T-connector.

Route the cable up a post at the end of the rail, and secure it with cable staples. Leave enough length at the end of the cable to connect it to the rope light **(photo 1)**.

SECURE THE ROPE LIGHT

Secure the rope light to the underside of the railing with U-channel. Cut the channel to length, and nail it to the bottom of the railing.

Press the rope into the channel **(photo 2)**.

WIRE THE ROPE LIGHT

Connect the fixture cord to the end of the rope with the twist-on fitting.

Connect the rope wires to the branch cable with a cable connector designed for low-voltage outdoor cable **(photo 3)**.

Cap the end of the rope with a plastic cap.

Run low-voltage cable from a transformer or low-voltage circuit to the end of the railing and secure with cable staples.

Fasten U channel to the bottom of the railing, then press the rope light in the channel securely.

Connect the rope wires to the branch cable with a cable connector designed for outdoor cable.

Under-deck Enclosure

Second-story walkout decks can be a mixed blessing. On top, you have an open, sun-filled perch with a commanding view of the landscape. The space below the deck, however, is all too often a dark and chilly nook that is functionally unprotected from water runoff. As a result, an under-deck area often ends up as wasted space or becomes a holding area for seasonal storage items or the less desirable outdoor furniture.

But there's an easy way to reclaim all that convenient outdoor space—by installing a weatherizing ceiling system that captures runoff water from the deck above, leaving the area below dry enough to convert into a versatile outdoor room. You can even enclose the space to create a screened-in patio room.

The under-deck system featured in this project (see Resources) is designed for do-it-yourself installation. Its components are made to fit almost any standard deck and come in three sizes to accommodate different deck-joist spacing (for 12", 16", and 24" on-center spacing). Once the system is in place, the under-deck area is effectively "dried in," and you can begin adding amenities like overhead lighting, ceiling fans, and speakers to complete the outdoor room environment.

The system works by capturing water that falls through the decking above and channeling it to the outside edge of the deck. Depending on your plans, you can let the water fall from the ceiling panels along the deck's edge, or you can install a standard rain gutter and downspout to direct the water to a single exit point on the ground or a rain barrel. Steps for adding a gutter system are given on pages 261 to 263.

Tools & Materials ▸

- 4-ft. level
- Chalk line
- Caulking gun
- Drill
- Aviation snips
- Hacksaw (for optional rain gutter)
- Under-deck ceiling system
- Waterproof acrylic caulk
- 1" stainless steel screws
- Rain gutter system (optional)

Made of weather-resistant vinyl, this under-deck system creates an attractive, maintenance-free ceiling that keeps the space below dry throughout the seasons.

Design Tips

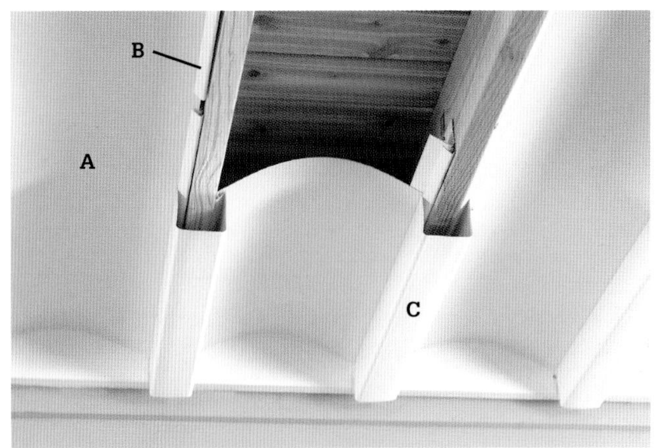

This under-deck system (see Resources, page 347) consists of four main parts: The joist rails mount to the deck joists and help secure the other components. The collector panels (A) span the joist cavity to capture water falling through the deck above. Water flows to the sides of the panels where it falls through gaps in the joist rails (B) and into the joist gutters (C) (for interior joists) and boundary gutters (for outer joists). The gutters carry the water to the outside edge of the deck.

For a finished look, paint the decking lumber that will be exposed after the system is installed. Typically, the lower portion of the ledger board (attached to the house) and the outer rim joist (at the outer edge of the deck) remain exposed.

Consider surrounding architectural elements when you select a system for sealing off the area below your deck. Here, the under-deck system is integrated with the deck and deck stairs both visually and functionally.

How to Install an Under-deck System

Check the undersides of several deck joists to make sure the structure is level. This is important for establishing the proper slope for effective water flow.

If your deck is not level, you must compensate for this when setting the ceiling slope. To determine the amount of correction that's needed, hold one end of the level against a joist and tilt the level until it reads perfectly level. Measure the distance from the joist to the free end of the level. Then, divide this measurement by the length of the level. For example, if the distance is ¼" and the level is 4 ft. long, the deck is out of level by 1⁄16" per foot.

To establish the slope for the ceiling system, mark the ends of the joists closest to the house: Measure up from the bottom 1" for every 10 ft. of joist length (or approximately ⅛" per ft.) and make a mark. Mark both sides of each intermediate joist and the inside faces of the outer joists.

Create each slope reference line using a chalk line: Hold one end of the chalk line at the mark made in Step 3, and hold the other end at the bottom edge of the joist where it meets the rim joist at the outside edge of the deck. Snap a reference line on all of the joists.

Install vinyl flashing along the ledger board in the joist cavities. Attach the flashing with 1" stainless steel screws. Caulk along the top edges of the flashing where it meets the ledger and both joists, using quality, waterproof acrylic caulk. Also caulk the underside of the flashing for an extra layer of protection.

Begin installing the joist rails, starting 1" away from the ledger. Position each rail with its bottom edge on the chalk line and fasten it to the joist at both ends with 1" stainless steel screws, then add one or two screws in between. Avoid over-driving the screws and deforming the rail; leaving a little room for movement is best.

Install the remaining rails on each joist face, leaving a 1½" (minimum) to 2" (maximum) gap between rails. Install rails along both sides of each interior joist and along the insides of each outside joist. Trim the final rail in each row as needed, using aviation snips.

Measure the full length of each joist cavity, and cut a collector panel ¼" shorter than the cavity. This allows room for expansion of the panels. For narrower joist cavities, trim the panel to width following the manufacturer's sizing recommendations.

(continued)

Scribe and trim collector panels for a tight fit against the ledger board. Hold a carpenter's pencil flat against the ledger, and move the pencil along the board to transfer its contours to the panel. Trim the panel along the scribed line.

Trim the corners of collector panels as needed to accommodate joist hangers and other hardware. This may be necessary only at the house side of the joist cavity; at the outer end, the ¼" expansion gap should clear any hardware.

Install the collector panels, starting at the house. With the textured side of the panel facing down, insert one side edge into the joist rails, and then push up gently on the opposite side until it fits into the opposing rails. When fully installed, the panels should be tight against the ledger and have a ¼" gap at the rim joist.

Prepare each joist gutter by cutting it ¼" shorter than the joist it will attach to. If the joists rest on a structural beam, see Working Around Beams, on page 260. On the house end of each gutter, trim the corners of the flanges at 45°. This helps the gutter fit tightly to the ledger.

Cut four or five ⅛" tabs into the bottom surface at the outside ends of the gutters. This helps promote the drainage of water over the edge of the gutter.

Attach self-adhesive foam weatherstrip (available from the manufacturer) at the home-end of each joist gutter. Run a bead of caulk along the foam strip to water-seal it to the gutter. The weatherstrip serves as a water dam.

Install each joist gutter by spreading its sides open slightly while pushing the gutter up onto the joist rails until it snaps into place. The gutter should fit snugly against the collector panels. The gutter's home-end should be tight against the ledger, with the ¼" expansion gap at the rim joist.

Prepare the boundary gutters following the same steps used for the joist gutters. Install each boundary gutter by slipping its long, outside flange behind the joist rails and pushing up until the gutter snaps into place. Install the boundary gutters working from the house side to the outer edge of the deck.

(continued)

Run a bead of color-matched caulk along the joint where the collector panels meet the ledger board. This is for decorative purposes only and is not required to prevent water intrusion.

If collector panels are misshapen because the joist spacing is too tight, free the panel within the problem area, then trim about ⅛" from the side edge of the panel. Reset the panel in the rails. If necessary, trim the panel edge again in slight increments until the panel fits properly.

Working Around Beams ▸

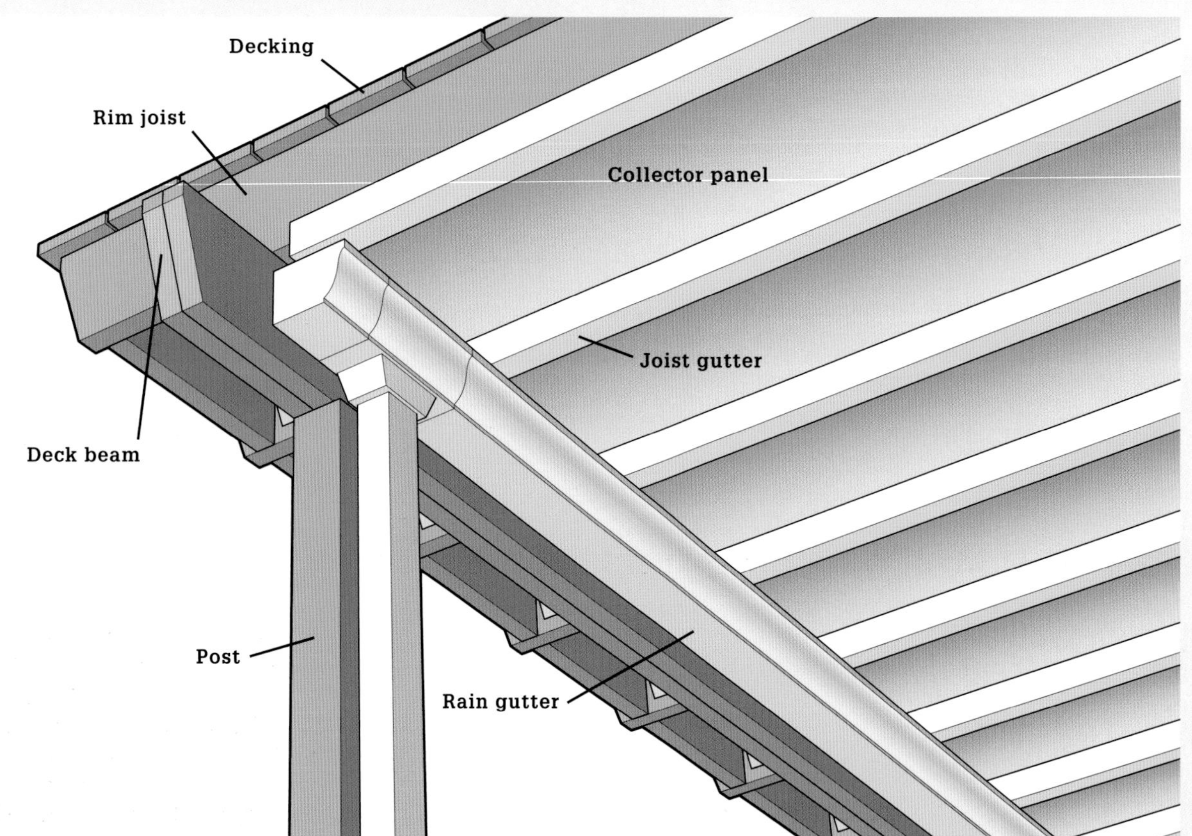

For decks that have joists resting on top of a structural beam, stop the joist gutters and boundary gutters 1½" short of the beam. Install a standard rain gutter along the house-side of the beam to catch the water as it exits the system gutters (see pages 261 to 263). (On the opposite side of the beam, begin new runs of joist gutters that are tight against the beam and stop ¼" short of the rim joist. The joist rails and collector panels should clear the beam and can be installed as usual.) Or, you can simply leave the overhang area alone if you do not need water runoff protection below it.

Runoff Gutters

A basic gutter system for a square or rectangular deck includes a straight run of gutter channel with a downspout at one end. Prefabricated vinyl or aluminum gutter parts are ideal for this application. Gutter channels are commonly available in 10-ft. and 20-ft. lengths, so you might be able to use a single channel without seams. Otherwise, you can join sections of channel with special connectors. Shop around for the best type of hanger for your situation. If there's limited backing to support the back side of the channel or to fasten into, you may have to use strap-type hangers that can be secured to framing above the gutter.

How to Install an Under-deck Runoff Gutter

Snap a chalk line onto the beam or other supporting surface to establish the slope of the main gutter run. The line will correspond to the top edge of the gutter channel. The ideal slope is $\frac{1}{16}$" per foot. For example, with a 16-ft.-long gutter, the beginning is 1" higher than the end. The downspout should be located just inside the low end of the gutter channel. Mark the beam at both ends to create the desired slope, then snap a chalk line between the marks. The high end of the gutter should be just below the boundary gutter in the ceiling system.

(continued)

Install a downspout outlet near the end of the gutter run so the top of the gutter is flush with the slope line. If you plan to enclose the area under the deck, choose an inconspicuous location for the downspout, away from traffic areas.

Install hanger clips (depending on the type of hangers or support clips you use, it is often best to install them before installing the gutter channel). Attach a hanger every 24" so the top of the gutter will hang flush with slope line.

Gutter Options ▸

Gutters come in several material types, including PVC, enameled steel, and copper. In most cases you should try and match the surrounding trim materials, but using a more decorative material for contrast can be effective.

Cut sections of gutter channel to size using a hacksaw. Attach an end cap to the beginning of the main run, then fit the channel into the downspout outlet (allowing for expansion, if necessary) and secure the gutter in place.

Join sections of channel together, if necessary, using connectors. Install a short section of channel with an end cap on the opposite side of the downspout outlet. Paint the area where the downspout will be installed if it is unpainted.

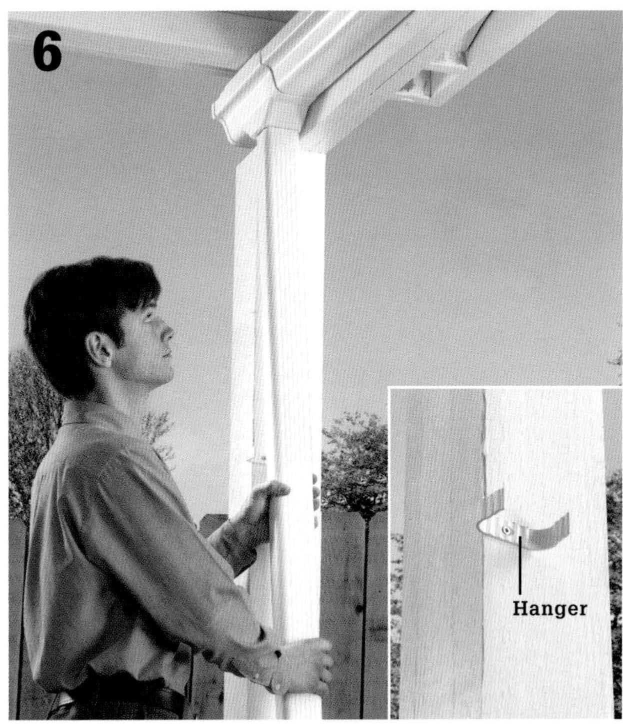

Cut the downspout piping to length and fasten an elbow fitting to its bottom end. Attach the downspout to the downspout outlet, then secure the downspout to a post or other vertical support using hangers (inset).

Cut a drain pipe to run from the downspout elbow to a convenient drainage point. Position the pipe so it directs water away from the house and any traffic areas. Attach the pipe to the downspout elbow. Add a splash block, if desired.

Rerouting Downspouts ▸

You may have to get a little creative when routing the downspout drain in an enclosed porch or patio. Shown here, two elbows allow for a 90° turn of the drainpipe.

Spa Tub Deck

Building a spa tub into a deck is usually done in one of two ways. If you design your deck at exactly the right height, you can create a full inset by resting the tub on a concrete pad and building the deck around it.

But on a low-profile deck, or a tall deck, the most practical solution is to mount the tub on the surface of the deck and build a secondary platform around it, creating a partial inset. As shown on the following pages, the structural design of the deck must be modified to ensure that it can support the added weight of a spa tub filled with water. Make sure your deck plans are approved by the building inspector before you begin work.

Installing a spa tub usually requires the installation of new plumbing and electrical lines. When planning the installation, make sure to consider the location of plumbing pipes, electrical cables, switches, and access panels. For convenience, arrange to have the rough-in work for these utilities done before you install the decking boards.

Whether the tub is inset into the deck or rests on top, adding a spa tub is a very popular deck improvement project.

Gallery of Spa Tub Decks

Hot tubs aren't limited to ground-level decks. However, you'll need to plan for additional framing and footings to support the tub safely, whatever the height of your deck may be. Here's another important reason why your deck plans should be reviewed by a building inspector before you build.

When planning for a spa tub, consider locating it in a space that's adjacent to your primary deck. That way, the tub won't interfere with traffic patterns or block larger spaces you may need for tables, other patio furniture, or groups of people.

If your yard doesn't offer much privacy for a tub, it's easy to create some by building a privacy wall onto your deck. A colored fabric wind shade could serve the same purpose. Now, you'll be able to enjoy your soaks or tanning time with a greater sense of peace.

Planning for Spa Tubs

An access hatch made from decking can hide a utility feature, such as a water faucet or air-conditioner compressor. Install cleats along the inside of the framed opening to support the hatch. Construct the hatch from decking boards mounted on a 2 × 4 frame. Finger holes drilled in the hatch make removal easier.

Plan posts and beams to support the maximum anticipated load, including the weight of the spa tub filled with water. In most cases, this means altering your deck plan to include extra beams and posts directly under the tub.

How to Build a Spa Tub Deck

Lay out and install the ledger, footings, posts, and support beams, according to your deck plans. Lay out joist locations on the ledger and beams, and install the joists, following local code requirements. Many building codes require joists spaced no more than 12" on center if the deck will support a spa tub. If your spa tub requires new plumbing or electrical lines, have the preliminary rough-in work done before continuing with deck construction.

Install the decking boards, then snap chalk lines to outline the position of the tub and the raised platform that will enclose the tub.

Lay out and cut 2 × 4 sole plates and top plates for the stud walls on the raised platform.

Mark stud locations on the top and bottom plates. Studs should be positioned every 16" (measured on center), and at the ends of each plate.

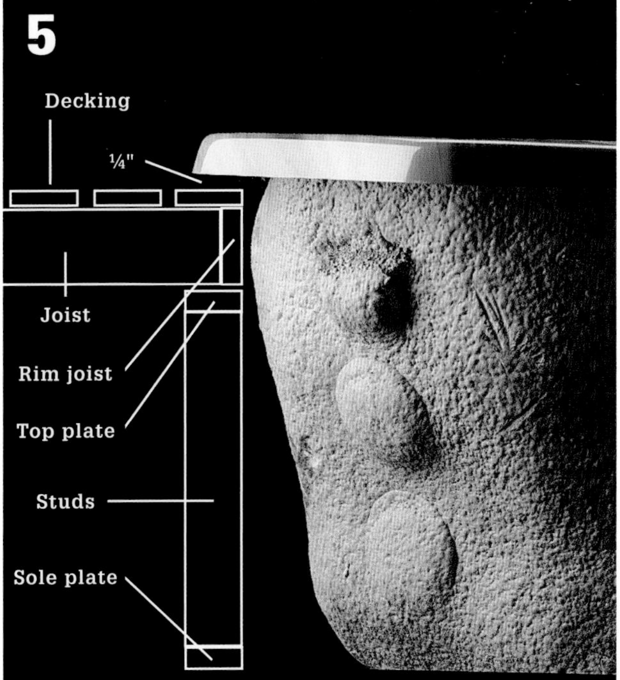

Measure the height of the spa tub to determine the required height of the studs in the platform walls. Remember to include the thickness of both wall plates, the joists that will rest on the walls, and the decking material on the platform. The surface of the finished platform should be ¼" below the lip of the spa tub.

(continued)

Construct the stud walls by screwing the plates to the studs. Position the walls upright on the deck over the outline marks, and anchor them to the deck with 2½" deck screws.

At the corners, fasten the studs together with 3" deck screws. Check the walls for plumb, and brace them in position.

Toenail a 2 × 6 rim joist along the back edge of the platform, then cut and install 2 × 6 joists across the top of the stud walls at 16" intervals, toenailing them to the top plates. The ends of the joists should be set back 1½" from the edges of the top plates to allow for the rim joist.

Cut 2 × 6 rim joists to length, and endnail them to the joists with 16d nails. At angled wall segments, cut diagonal blocking and attach it between the rim joist and adjoining joists with deck screws.

Cut decking boards, and attach them to the platform joists with 2½" deck screws. If your spa tub requires cutouts for plumbing or electrical lines, do this work now.

Set the tub in place so it rests on the deck—the rim should not bear weight. Build 2 × 2 stud walls around the exposed sides of the tub. Measure, cut, and install siding materials on the exposed walls.

Build platform steps to provide access to the platform using siding materials to box in the risers. Where required by code, install railings around the elevated platform.

Boardwalk Deck on a Slab

There's no need to let a cracked, aging concrete patio ruin the look and enjoyment of your backyard. You can build a very simple deck platform right over the failing slab with very little effort or expense. Make no mistake though, the result will be a beautiful new outdoor platform that improves the look of the home and the yard.

This is an independent deck; the structure is not attached to the house, but is instead laid atop the slab and allowed to move with any shifting in the concrete. It's constructed on a simple frame base laid level with sleepers over the concrete itself. This means that the deck will be very close to the ground and subject to a great deal of moisture. Only certain types of decking will tolerate those conditions. We've used pressure-treated pine deckboards.

The design of the deck is a plain rectangle and can easily be constructed over a weekend. We've spruced up the look a bit by laying the decking in a standard "Boardwalk" pattern. More complex patterns would make the deck surface look even more impressive—just remember to do yourself a favor and work the patterns out on graph paper before cutting any decking. Proper planning will inevitably save a lot of waste.

Turn a boring or failing concrete slab into an attractive walkout or entertainment space with a short utility or "Boardwalk" deck installed on top of it.

Cutaway View

Supplies

Galvanized metal corner brackets (16)
2½" galvanized deck screws
2" composite shims
Circular saw
Miter saw
Power drill and bits
Treated lumber (2 × 4 and 2 × 2)

Cutting List

KEY	QTY	SIZE	PART	MATERIAL
A	3	1½ x 3½ x 128"	Frame side	PT pine
B	2	1½ x 1½ x 128"	Nailer	PT pine
C	2	1½ x 3½ x 76"	Frame end	PT pine
D	60	1½ x 3½ x (cut to fit)	Decking	PT pine

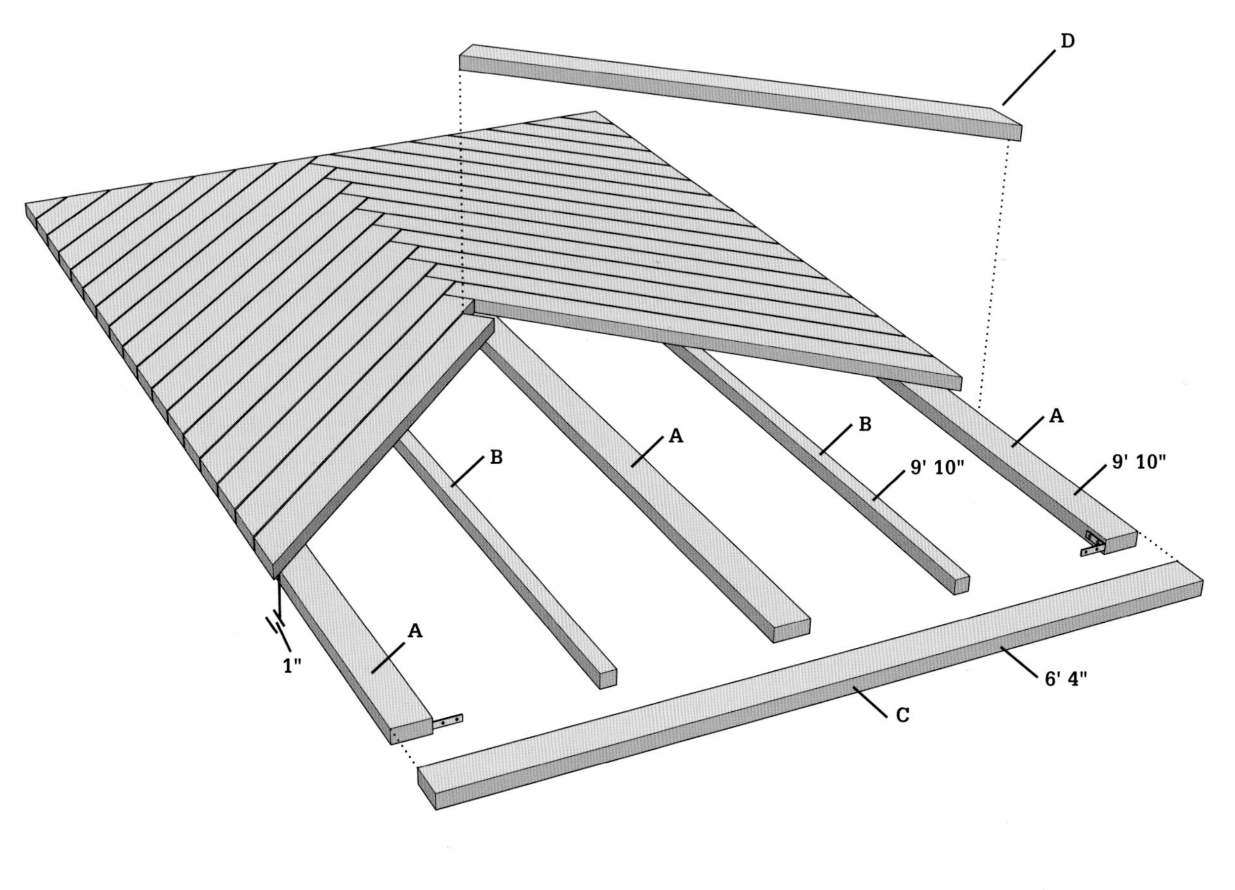

How to Build a Boardwalk Deck

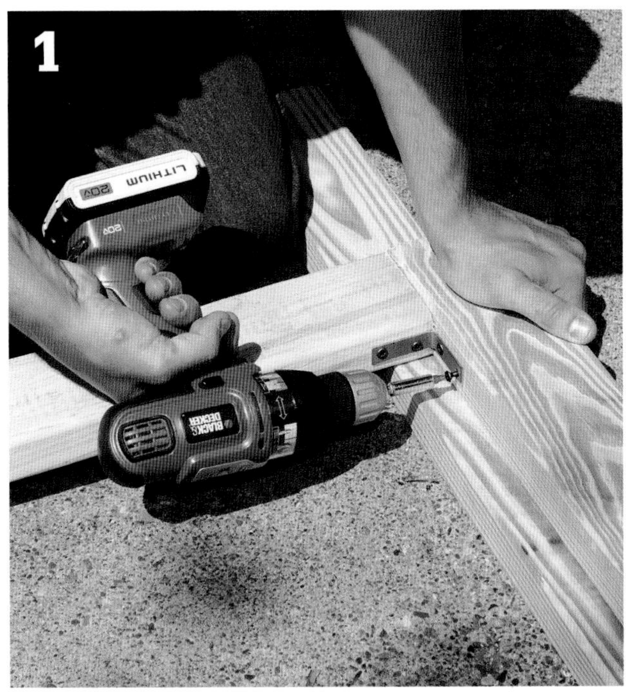

Build and assemble the frame offsite by cutting and measuring 10-ft. 2 × 4s to length and securing them together with galvanized metal corner brackets.

Install the nailer joists by measuring and cutting parallel boards to the length of the frame. Use 2" deck screws and galvanized metal corner brackets to secure the nailer joists to the frame.

Clear away any dust and debris from the concrete slab. Set the frame atop the slab and use 8" plastic shims to level it. Glue shims in place and cut off excess so shims are flush with the frame.

Use a level as you work with the shims to ensure an even plane on which to build the deck.

Remove the frame from the slab before installing the decking. Stagger the 2 × 4s in a crosshatch pattern in opposing 45° angles from the center nailing joist. Attach the boardwalk pattern to the frame using 3" deck screws. Boards should abut one another the length of the joist and allow for at least 1" of overhang from the frame.

Mark 1" overhang on all sides of the frame using a chalk-line, and cut off excess decking using a circular saw equipped with a carbide blade.

Use a helper to install the decking atop the concrete slab, checking for level and using shims to adjust as necessary.

Clear away dust and debris and stain the decking as desired.

Floating Octagon Island Deck

Sometimes all you need is a simple, easy-to-build platform to complete an otherwise perfect backyard. The project shown here is an "island deck," detached from the house and requiring no ledger attachment.

That means it has the simplest of foundations; a set of pre-cast concrete pier blocks that are simply set in place, making them far easier to work with than poured footings. The piers are cast to a standardized shape and size: 10" square and 10" high, with slots in the top to accommodate joists and posts. Because the pier blocks are not secured in the ground, the deck "floats." This allows for movement in response to settling and the freeze-thaw cycle of the soil. Floating pier decks meet most local codes—but check yours just to be sure.

This deck is also low enough to the ground that it won't require a handrail (unless, in your particular case, the yard slopes severely off to one side).

Design Tips ▸

We've installed a three-sided privacy screen (see pages 200 to 203) that serves as a wind barrier for easy grilling. We've also added double benches (see pages 204 to 209) along the side opposite the privacy screen, so you'll have ample seating for guests to relax while their steaks are cooking. The only way for this deck to be more convenient is if the steaks grilled themselves!

(25) — see Resources, page 347

	PART	MATERIAL
9¾"	Joist	PT pine
cut to fit)	Post	PT pine
3½"	Spreader	PT pine
cut to fit)	Decking	PT pine

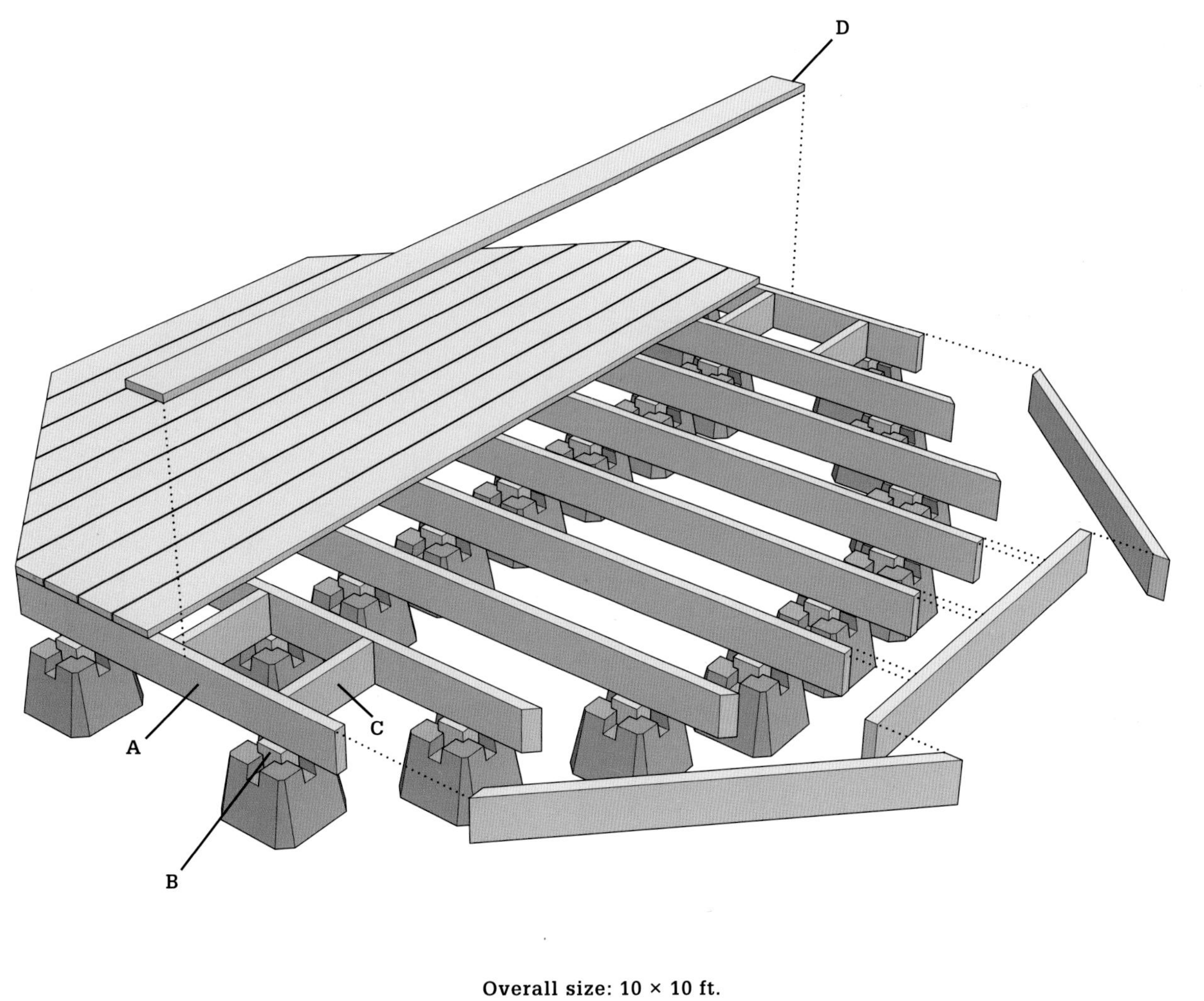

Overall size: 10 × 10 ft.

Framing Plan

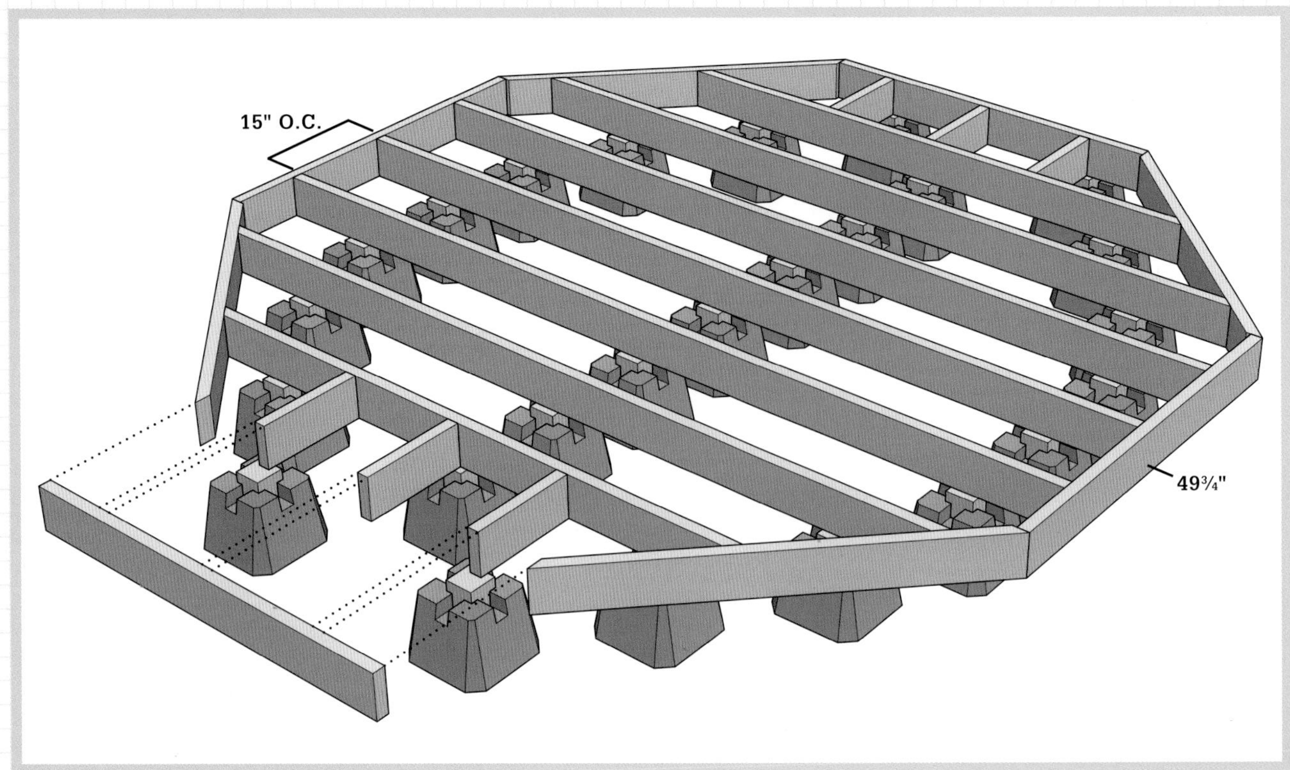

Decking Detail

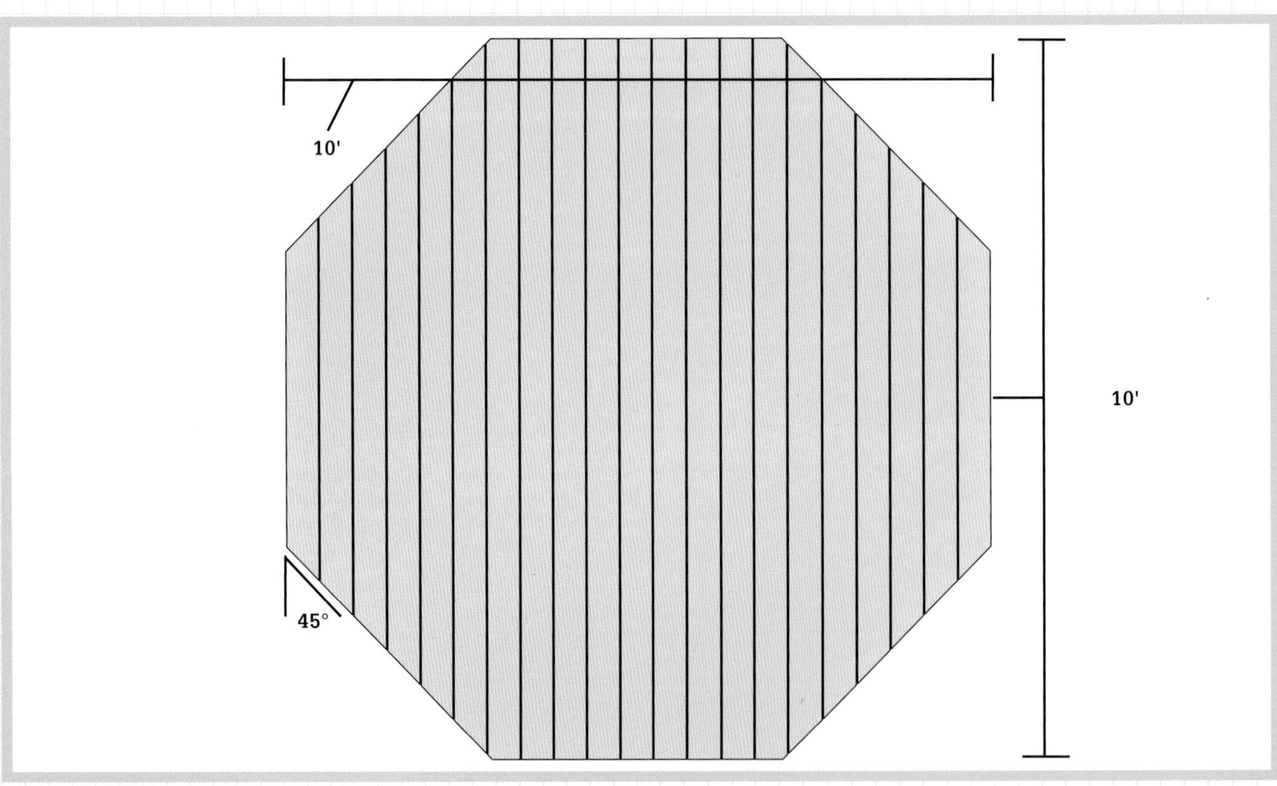

How to Build a Floating Octagon Deck

POSITION THE PIERS

Clear any large rocks or debris from the area over which the deck will be positioned. Measure and mark the locations for the pier blocks. Set out the pier blocks for the center of the deck; you'll start by building the center "box" rectangle off of which all the other joists will be leveled.

Position three rows of three blocks each. The rows for this deck were placed 46½" OC row to row, with 1½" OC between the pier blocks in each row. Check that each pier block is level, adding or removing dirt underneath to level it as necessary.

BUILD THE CENTER BOX

Set a 10-ft. long 2 × 6 joist on edge in the slots of the three pier blocks along one end of each row. Hold a carpenter's level along the top of the joist as a helper raises or lowers the lowest end of the joist.

Position the piers accurately to ensure a stable deck. They need to be the proper distance from each other and level side to side.

Leveling a joist is a job that calls for a helper. You'll need to focus on the precise measurements for the posts, if any.

Once the posts are cut, it's important to check the joists for level in place. Only screw the joists down when the preliminary "box" for the frame is complete.

The first two opposite band joists complete the box.

With the helper holding the joist level, measure any gaps between the bottom of the joist and the pier block sockets.

Cut 4 × 4 posts to match the gap measurements, and place the posts in the pier block sockets. Set the 2 × 6 joist on top of the posts, if any, and check for level again. Adjust as necessary.

Repeat the process with a joist set in the sockets of the outside blocks on the other end of each row. Position the joist as before, and check level with the aid of a helper. Once you've established level along the length of the second joist, make sure the joists are level side to side.

Now cut 2 × 6 band joists for the ends of the floor joists. The band joists will be 49¾" long. Measure and mark the band joist so that it will extend equal lengths from both sides of where it is screwed to the floor joists.

Check diagonal measurements of the foundation center box. This must be square because the rest of the deck is built off the box. If the diagonal measurements are off at all, adjust the "box" until they match.

Complete the center of the deck frame by screwing the center joist into place, attaching it to the band joists on either end.

Use 3" deck screws to screw the band joists to each end of the floor joists to create the center box of the deck floor frame.

Ensure this box is square by measuring diagonally both ways. If the frame is square, the diagonal measurements should be exactly the same.

Position the center joist in this box, cutting 4 × 4 posts as necessary to keep the joist level along its length and in relation to the two outside joists. Screw the band joist into the end of the center floor joist, completing the frame center box. Screw the joists to their 4 × 4 posts in toenail fashion.

COMPLETE THE FRAME

Measure and set the remaining pier blocks in place on both sides of the center frame box. There should be a row of three piers and a row of two piers on each side of the center box, as shown in the Framing Plan (page 277).

Cut and position the outer floor joists in the octagon, leveling them in place as before.

Install the blocking to support the side piers. Once level, screw the outside joist to the 4 × 4 posts (if any) with the joist positioned so that the overhang on both sides is equal.

Drive 3" screws through the mitered ends to secure the band joists to one another. Use three screws per connection. Complete the outside frame by screwing diagonal band joists onto the mitered ends of the middle floor joists, and to the band joists.

Install the decking boards, allowing for overhang that will be trimmed at the end of construction.

Cut the shorter outside floor joists to length. Set them in place in the outside piers, and measure and level as before. Cut 4 × 4s as necessary, and set the outside joists in position. Miter the two outside joist ends 22½°. Screw all joists to the posts in toenail fashion.

Complete the outside frame by cutting the remaining six band joists. Miter the ends of the four diagonal band joists 22½° before installing them. Drill pilot holes and screw the band joists to the spacer blocks using 3" deck screws. Install the remaining joists. At each end, the band joists will extend beyond the outside row of pier blocks so no blocks will be visibly exposed at the edge of the deck.

INSTALL THE DECKING

Begin laying the decking at one edge of the octagon, so that the decking lays perpendicular to the floor joists. Place the first deck board into position with its edge aligned with the edge of the band joist. Screw down each decking board using two 3" deck screws per joist.

Continue laying the decking, allowing the boards to overhang the edges of the band joists. Maintain a ⅛" gap between boards.

When all the decking boards have been screwed down, snap a chalk line along the edges over which the deck boards hang; use a circular saw equipped with a carbide blade to cut the deck board ends so that the decking is flush with the band joists.

Stain, paint, or finish the deck as you prefer, including the rim joists. Add other built-on structures to suit your needs.

Lay the rest of the decking boards by screwing them down to the joists, maintaining a ⅛" spacing between boards.

Use a circular saw equipped with a carbide blade to make quick work of trimming the ends of the deck boards, leaving a clean edge.

Ground Level Walkout Deck

Sometimes less really is more. This modest deck has a pleasing shape and is perched high enough to provide a clear view of the yard. Even better, the deck is a study in simplicity and it won't cost you a lot in either time or money. The framing and decking plans are straightforward and uncomplicated. You can likely build the entire structure over the course of two or three weekends, even if you have limited carpentry and building experience. That means that before a month is out, you'll have access to a convenient outdoor platform that can be used for a relaxing meal surrounded by nature, a place to read the paper, or to just sit and recharge your batteries after a long day at work.

This basic rectangular platform is as plainly handsome as it is useful and easy to build.

Cutaway View

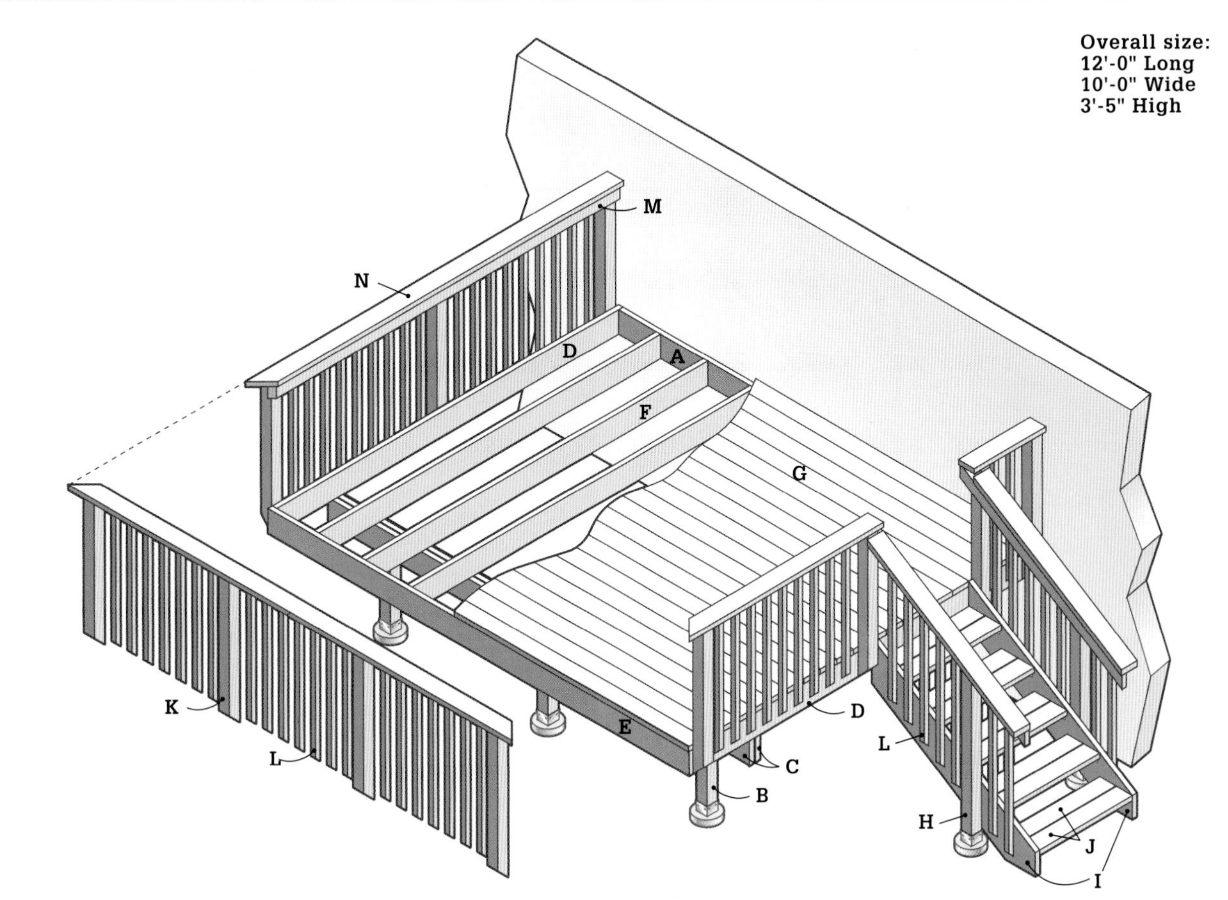

Supplies

10"-diameter footing forms (3)
8"-diameter footing forms (2)
J-bolts (5)
6 × 6" metal post anchors (3)
4 × 4" metal post anchors (2)
6 × 6" metal post-beam caps (3)
2 × 8" joist hangers (16)
1½ × 6" angle brackets (6)
1½ × 10" angle brackets (10)
3" galvanized deck screws
16d galvanized nails
2½" galvanized deck screws
⅜ × 4" lag screws and washers (20)
⅜ × 5" lag screws and washers (22)
¼ × 1¼" lag screws and washers (80)
Flashing (12 ft.)
Exterior silicone caulk (3 tubes)
Concrete as needed

Lumber List

QTY.	SIZE	MATERIAL	PART
4	2 × 8" × 12'	Trtd. lumber	Ledger (A), Beam bds (C), Rim joist (E)
1	6 × 6" × 8'	Trtd. lumber	Deck posts (B)
10	2 × 8" × 10'	Trtd. lumber	End joists (D), Joists (F)
25	2 × 6" × 12'	Cedar	Decking (G), Rail cap (N)
7	4 × 4" × 8'	Cedar	Stair posts (H), Rail post (K)
2	2 × 12" × 8'	Cedar	Stringers (I)
5	2 × 6" × 6'	Cedar	Treads (J)
32	2 × 2" × 8'	Cedar	Balusters (L)
2	2 × 4" × 12'	Cedar	Top rail (M)
2	2 × 4" × 10'	Cedar	Top rail (M)

Framing Plan

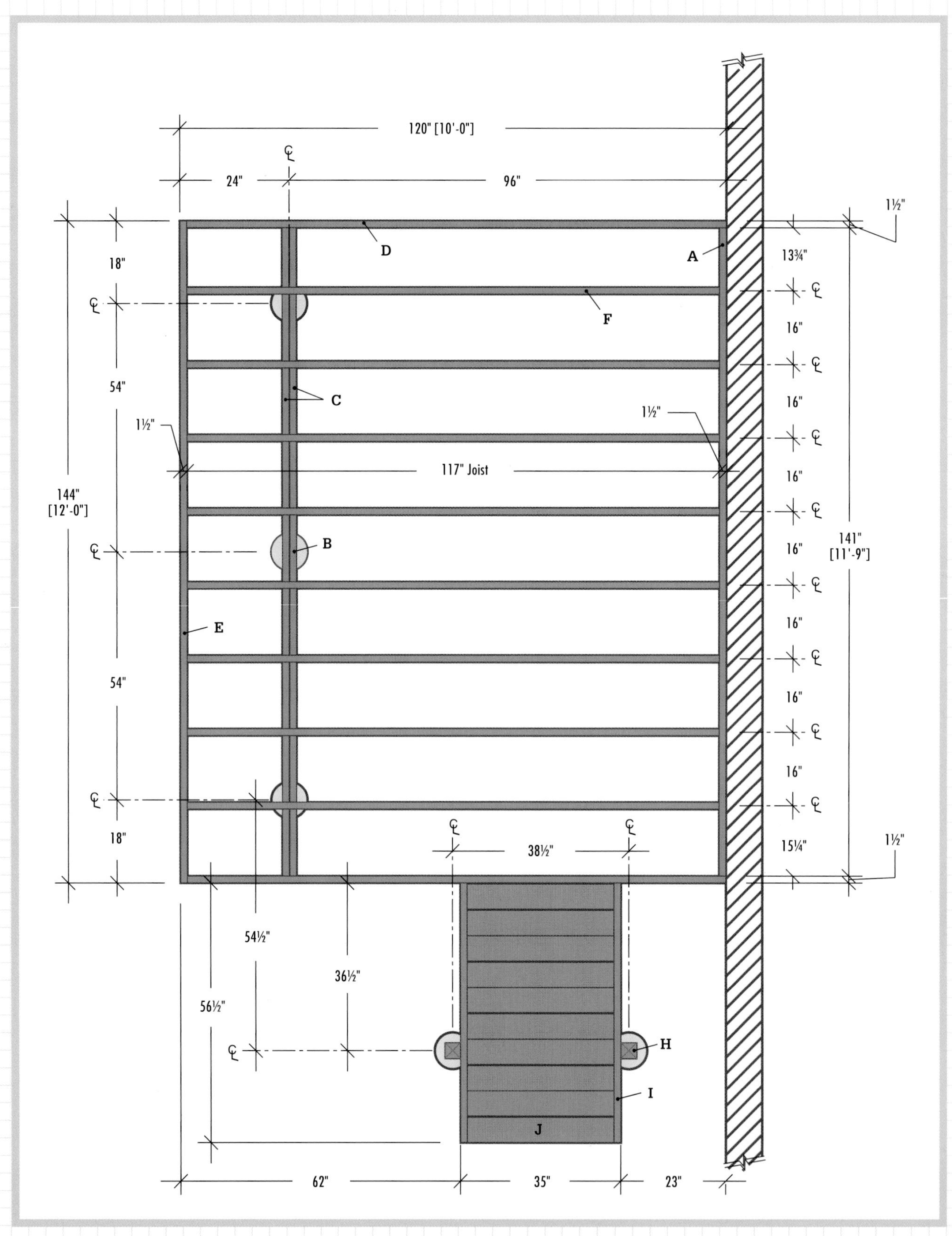

Elevation

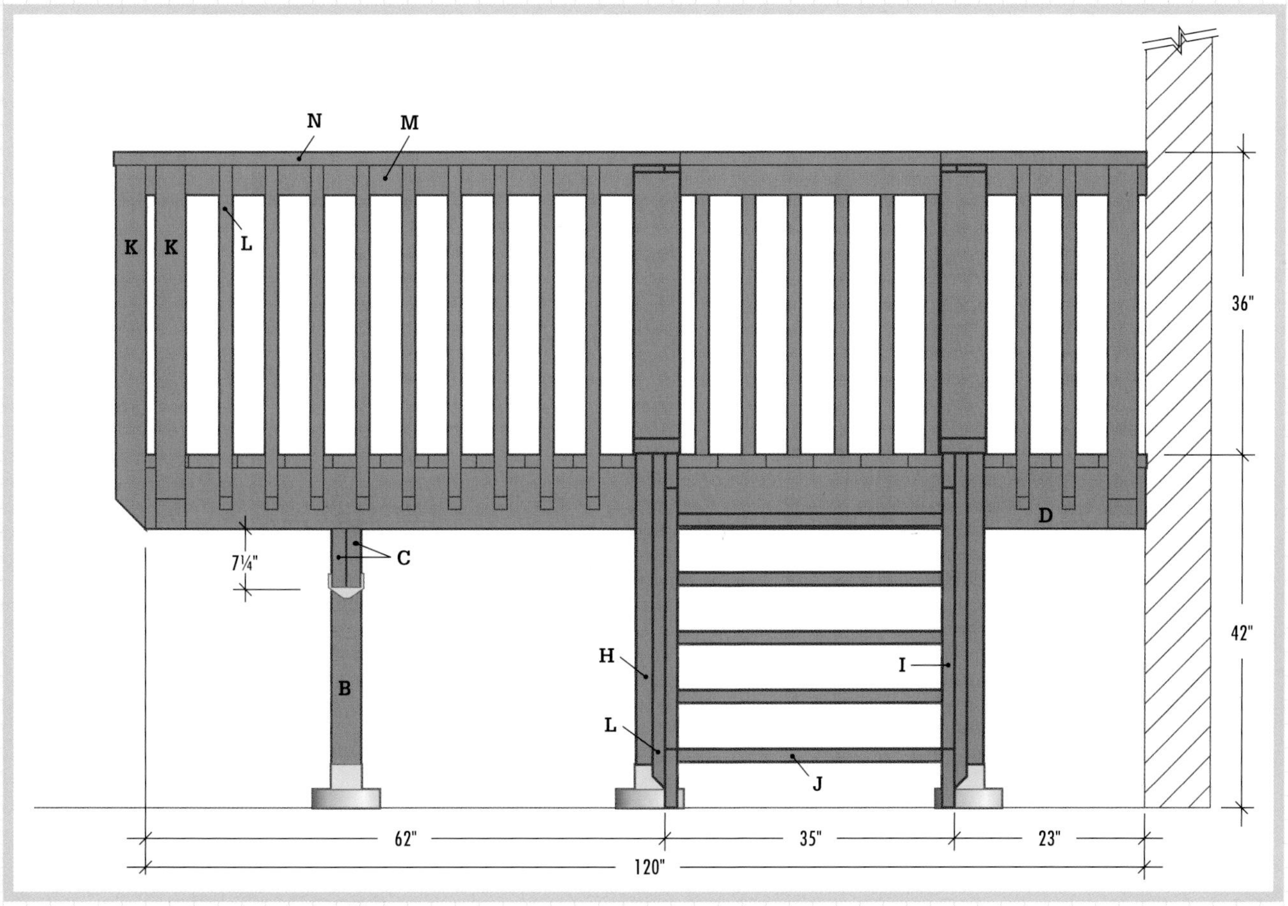

N
M
K
K
L
36"
D
7¼"
C
42"
H
I
B
L
J
62"
35"
23"
120"

62"

Stairway Detail

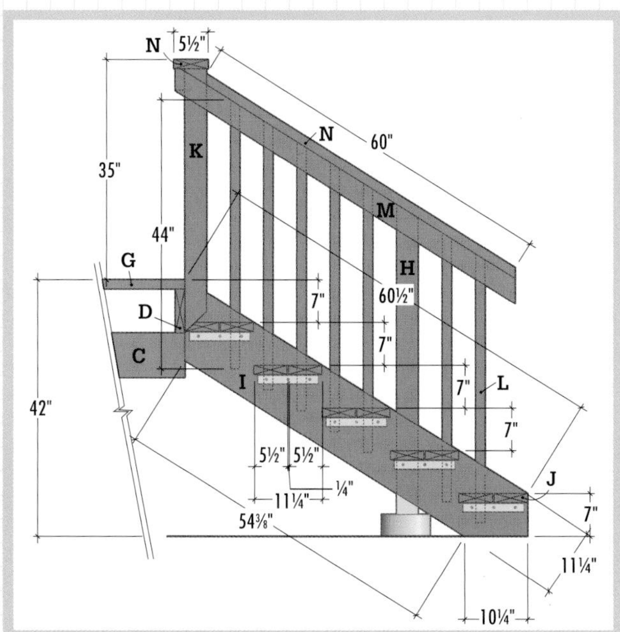

Railing Detail

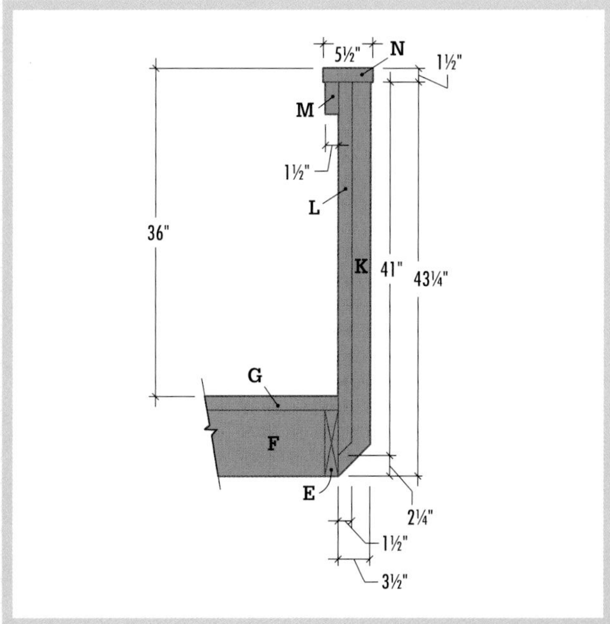

How to Build a Ground-level Walkout Deck

ATTACH THE LEDGER

Draw a level outline on the siding to show where the ledger and the end joists will fit against the house. Install the ledger so that the surface of the decking boards will be 1" below the indoor floor level. This height difference prevents rainwater or melted snow from seeping into the house.

Cut out the siding along the outline with a circular saw. To prevent the blade from cutting the sheathing that lies underneath the siding, set the blade depth to the same thickness as the siding. Finish the cutout with a chisel, holding the beveled side in to ensure a straight cut.

Cut galvanized flashing to the length of the cutout, using metal snips. Slide the flashing up under the siding at the top of the cutout.

Measure and cut the ledger (A) from pressure-treated lumber. Center the ledger end to end in the cutout, with space at each end for the end joist.

Brace the ledger in position under the flashing. Tack the ledger into place with galvanized deck screws.

Drill pairs of 3/8" pilot holes at 16" intervals through the ledger and into the house header joist. Counterbore each pilot hole 1/2", using a 1 3/8" spade bit. Attach the ledger to the wall with 3/8 × 4" lag screws and washers, using a ratchet wrench.

Apply a thick bead of silicone caulk between siding and flashing. Also seal the lag screw heads and the cracks at the ends of the ledger.

POUR THE FOOTINGS

Referring to the measurements shown in the Framing Plan (page 284), mark the centerlines of the two outer footings on the ledger and drive nails at these locations.

Set up temporary batterboards and stretch a mason's string out from the ledger at each location. Make sure the strings are perpendicular to the ledger, and measure along the strings to find the centerpoints of the posts.

Set up additional batterboards and stretch another string parallel to the ledger across the post centerpoints.

Check the mason's strings for square by measuring diagonally from corner to corner and adjusting the strings so that the measurements are equal.

Measure along the cross string and mark the center post location with a piece of tape.

Use a plumb bob to transfer the footing centerpoints to the ground, and drive a stake to mark each point.

Remove the mason's strings and dig the post footings, using a clamshell digger or power auger. Pour 2" to 3" of loose gravel into each hole for drainage. *Note: When measuring the footing size and depth, make sure you comply with your local building code, which may require flaring the base.*

Cut the footing forms to length using a reciprocating saw or handsaw, and insert them into the footing holes, leaving 2" above ground level. Pack soil around the forms for support, and fill the forms with concrete, tamping with a long stick or rod to eliminate any air pockets.

Screed the tops flush with a straight 2 × 4. Insert a J-bolt into each footing, set so 3/4" to 1" of thread is exposed. Retie the mason's strings and position the J-bolts at the exact center of the posts, using a plumb bob as a guide. Clean the bolt threads before concrete sets.

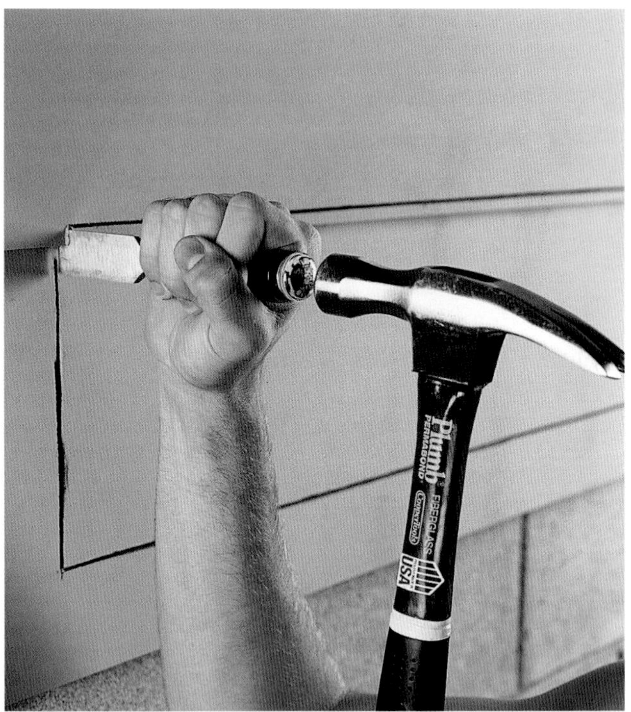

After outlining the position of the ledger and cutting the siding with a circular saw, use a chisel to finish the corners of the cutout.

After the posts have been set in place and braced plumb, use a straight 2 × 4 and a level to mark the top of the beam on each post.

SET THE POSTS

Lay a long, straight 2 × 4 flat across the footings, parallel to the ledger. With one edge tight against the J-bolts, draw a reference line across each footing.

Place a metal post anchor on each footing, centering it over the J-bolt and squaring it with the reference line. Attach the post anchors by threading a nut over each bolt and tightening with a ratchet wrench.

Cut the posts to length, adding approximately 6" for final trimming. Place the posts in the anchors and tack into place with one nail.

With a level as a guide, use braces and stakes to plumb the posts. Finish nailing the posts to the anchors.

Determine the height of the beam by extending a straight 2 × 4 from the top edge of the ledger across the face of a post. Level the 2 × 4, and draw a line on the post along the bottom of the 2 × 4.

From that line, measure 15½" down the post and mark the bottom of the beam. Using a level, transfer this line to the remaining posts.

Use a combination square to extend the level line completely around each post. Cut the posts to this finished height using a circular saw and reciprocating saw.

INSTALL THE BEAM

Cut the beam boards (C) several inches longer than necessary, to allow for final trimming.

Join the beam boards together with 2½" galvanized deck screws. Mark the post locations on the top edges and sides, using a combination square as a guide.

Attach the post-beam caps to the tops of the posts. Position the caps on the post tops, and attach using 10d joist hanger nails.

Lift the beam into the post-beam caps, with the crown up. Align the post reference lines on the beam with the post-beam caps. *Note: You should have at least two helpers when installing boards of this size and length, at this height.*

Fasten the post-beam caps to the beam on both sides using 10d joist hanger nails.

INSTALL THE FRAME

Measure and cut the end joists to length using a circular saw.

Attach end joists to the ends of the ledger with 10d common nails.

Measure and cut the rim joist (E) to length with a circular saw. Fasten to end joists with 16d galvanized nails.

Square up the frame by measuring corner to corner and adjusting until measurements are equal. Toenail the end joists in place on top of the beam, and trim the beam to length.

Reinforce each inside corner of the frame with an angle bracket fastened with 10d joist hanger nails.

Install joists in hangers with crown edge up.

(continued)

To locate the stairway footings, refer to the measurements in the Framing Plan, and extend a straight 2 × 4 perpendicularly from the deck. Use a plumb bob to transfer centerpoints to the ground.

INSTALL THE JOISTS

Mark the outlines of the inner joists (F) on the ledger, beam, and rim joist (see Framing Plan, page 284), using a tape measure and a combination square.

Attach joist hangers to the ledger and rim joist with 10d joist hanger nails, using a scrap 2 × 8 as a spacer to achieve the correct spread for each hanger.

Measure, mark, and cut lumber for inner joists using a circular saw. Place the joists in the hangers with crown side up, and attach at both ends with 10d joist hanger nails. Be sure to use all the holes in the hangers.

Align the joists with the marks on top of the beam, and toenail or strap in place.

LAY THE DECKING

Cut the first decking board (G) to length, position it against the house, and attach by driving a pair of 2½" galvanized deck screws into each joist.

Position the remaining decking boards with the ends overhanging the end joists. Leave a ⅛" gap between boards to provide for drainage, and attach the boards to each joist with a pair of deck screws.

Every few rows of decking, measure from the edge of the decking to the outside edge of the deck. If the measurement can be divided evenly by 5⅝, the last board will fit flush with the outside edge of the deck as intended. If the measurement shows that the last board will not fit flush, adjust the spacing as you install the remaining rows of boards.

If your decking overhangs the end joists, snap a chalk line to mark the outside edge of the deck and cut flush with a circular saw. If needed, finish the cut with a jigsaw or handsaw where a circular saw can't reach.

BUILD THE STAIRWAY

Refer to the Framing Plan (page 284), for the position of the stairway footings.

Locate the footings by extending a 2 × 4 from the deck, dropping a plumb bob, and marking the centerpoints with stakes.

Dig post holes with a clamshell digger or an auger, and pour the stairway footings using the same method as for the deck footings.

Attach metal post anchors to the footings, and install posts (H), leaving them long for final trimming.

Cut the stair stringers (I) to length and use a framing square to mark the rise and run for each step (see Stairway Detail, page 285). Draw the tread outline on each run. Cut the angles at the end of the stringers with a circular saw. (For more information on building stairways, see pages 140 to 159.)

After attaching the stringers to the deck, fasten them to the posts. Drill and counterbore two pilot holes through the stringers into the posts, and attach with lag screws.

Position a 1½ × 10" angle bracket flush with the bottom of each tread line. Attach the brackets with 1¼" lag screws.

Fasten angle brackets to the upper ends of the stringers, using 1¼" lag screws; keep the brackets flush with cut ends on stringers. Position the top ends of the stringers on the side of the deck, making sure the top point of the stringer and the surface of the deck are flush.

Attach the stringers by driving 10d joist hanger nails through the angle brackets into the end joist, and by drilling ¼" pilot holes from inside the rim joist into the stringers and fastening with ⅜ × 4" lag screws.

To connect the stringers to the stair posts, drill two ¼" pilot holes and counterbore the pilot holes ½" deep with a 1" spade bit. Use a ratchet wrench to fasten the stringers to the posts with 4" lag screws and washers.

Measure the length of the stair treads (J) and cut two 2 × 6 boards for each tread. For each tread, position the front board on the angle bracket so the front edge is flush with the tread outline on the stringers. Attach the tread to the brackets with ¼ × 1¼" lag screws.

Place the rear 2 × 6 on each tread bracket, keeping a ⅛" space between the boards. Attach with 1¼" lag screws.

Attach the treads for the lowest step by driving deck screws through the stringers.

INSTALL THE RAILING

Cut posts (K) and balusters (L) to length (see Railing Detail, page 285) with a power miter saw or circular saw. Cut the top ends square, and the bottom ends at a 45° angle.

Mark and drill two ⅜" pilot holes at the bottom end of each post. Holes should be spaced 4" apart and counterbored ½", with a 1" spade bit.

Drill two ⅛" pilot holes, 4" apart, near the bottom of each baluster. At the top of each baluster, drill a pair of ⅛" pilot holes spaced 1½" apart.

Using a combination square, mark the locations of the posts on the outside of the deck. *Note: Position corner posts so there is no more than 4" clearance between them.*

Clamp each post in place. Keep the beveled end flush with the bottom of the deck, and make sure the post is plumb. Use an awl to mark pilot hole locations on the side of the deck. Remove posts and drill ⅜" pilot holes at marks. Attach the railing posts to the side of the deck with ½ × 5" lag screws and washers.

Position the rail cap over the posts and balusters. Make sure mitered corners are tight, and attach with deck screws.

Cut top rails (M) to length, with 45° miters on the ends that meet at the corners. Attach to posts with 2½" deck screws, keeping the top edge of the rail flush with the top of the posts. Join rails by cutting 45° bevels at ends.

Temporarily attach stairway top rails with 3" galvanized screws. Mark the outline of the deck railing post and top rail on the back side of the stairway top rail. Mark the position of the top rail on the stairway post. Use a level to mark a plumb cutoff line at the lower end of the rail. Remove the rail.

Cut the stairway post to finished height along the diagonal mark, and cut the stairway rail along outlines. Reposition the stairway rail and attach with deck screws.

Attach the balusters between the railing posts at equal intervals of 4" or less. Use deck screws, and keep the top ends of balusters flush with the top rail. On the stairway, position the balusters against the stringer and top rail, and check for plumb. Draw a diagonal cut line at top of baluster and trim to final height with a power miter saw.

Confirm measurements, and cut rail cap sections (N) to length. Position sections so that the inside edge overhangs the inside edge of the rail by ¼". Attach the cap to the rail with deck screws. At corners, miter the ends 45° and attach caps to posts.

Cut the cap for stairway rail to length. Mark angle of deck railing post on side of cap and bevel-cut the ends of the cap. Attach cap to top rail and post with deck screws. *Note: Local building codes may require a grippable handrail. Check with your building inspector.*

Second-story Walkout Deck

This simple rectangular deck provides a secure, convenient outdoor living space. The absence of a stairway prevents children from wandering away or unexpected visitors from wandering in. It also makes the deck easier to build.

Imagine how handy it will be to have this additional living area only a step away from your dining room or living room, with no more need to walk downstairs for outdoor entertaining, dining, or relaxing.

And if you'd like to add a stairway, just refer to the chapter on stair-building (see page 140).

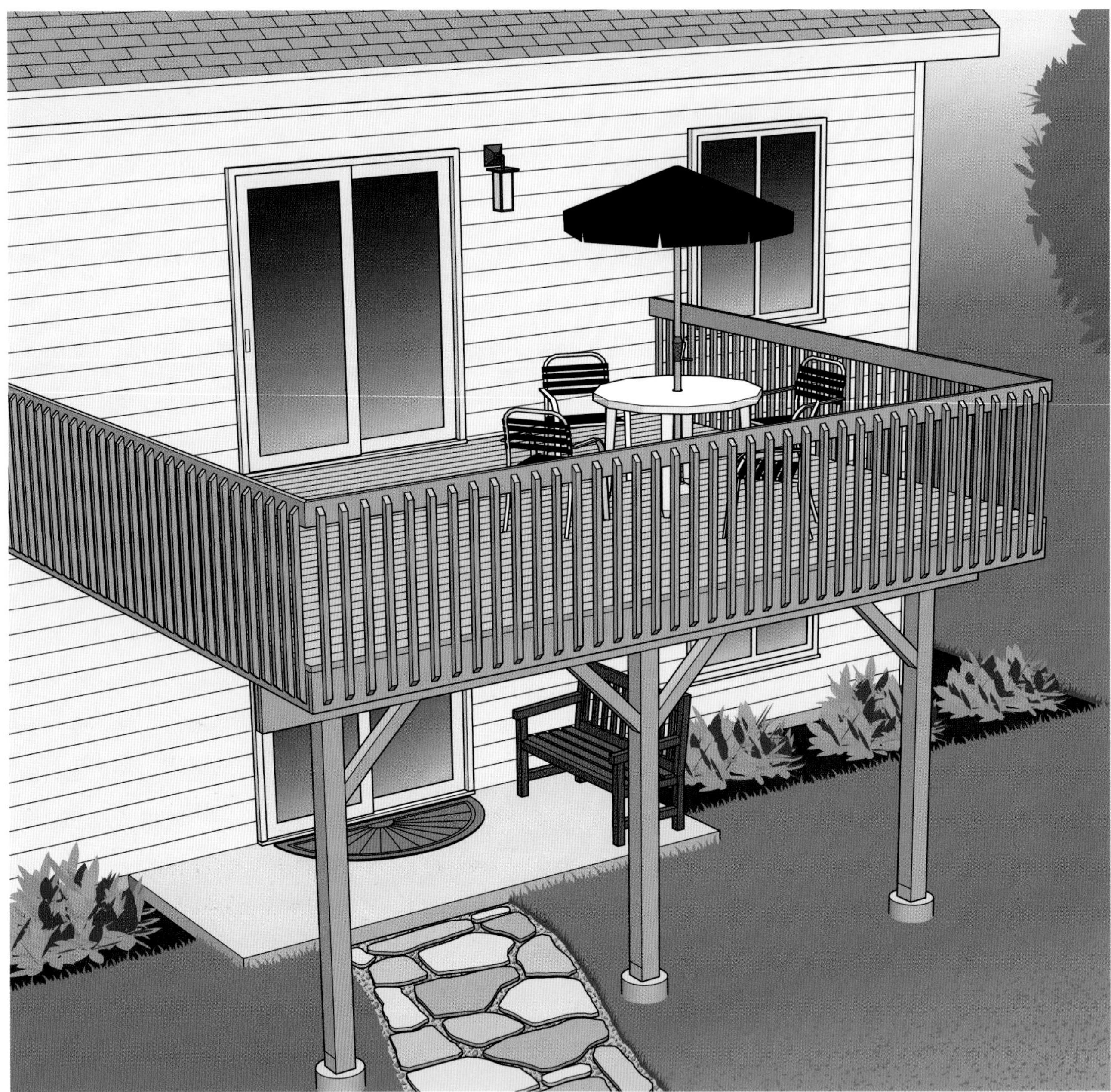

Simplicity, security, and convenience are the hallmarks of this elevated deck.

Cutaway View

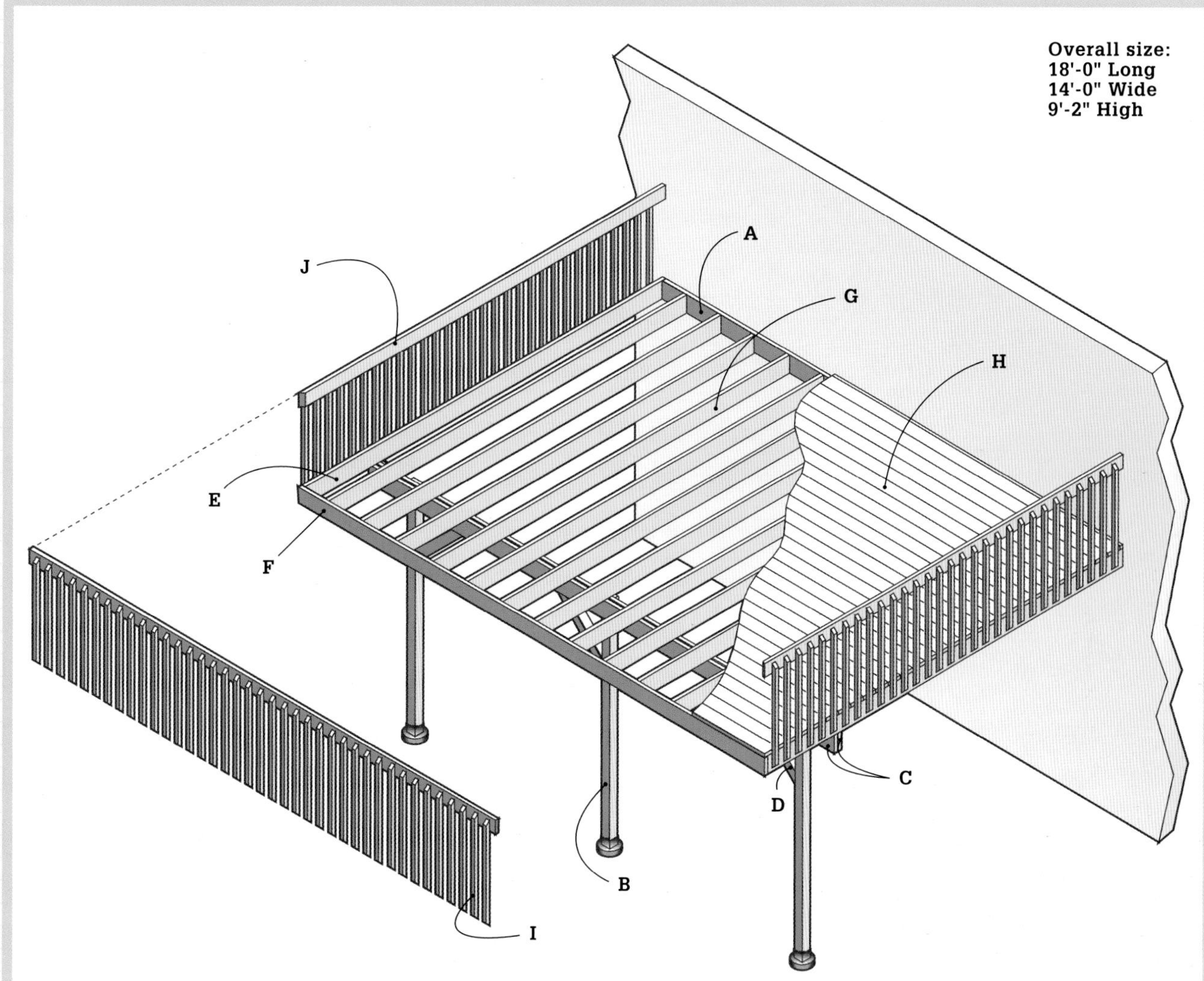

Supplies

12"-diameter footing forms (3)
J-bolts (3)
6 × 6" metal post anchors (3)
2 × 10" joist hangers (26)
Galvanized deck screws (3", 2½", and 1¼")
Joist hanger nails
½ × 4" lag screws and washers (28)
½ × 5" lag screws and washers (16)
½ × 7" carriage bolts, washers, and nuts (6)
16d galvanized nails
Metal flashing (18 ft.)
Silicone caulk (3 tubes)
Concrete as required

Lumber List

QTY.	SIZE	MATERIAL	PART
2	2 × 12" × 20'	Trtd. lumber	Beam boards (C)
2	2 × 10" × 18'	Trtd. lumber	Ledger (A), Rim joist (F)
15	2 × 10" × 14'	Trtd. lumber	Joists (G), End joists (E)
3	6 × 6" × 10'	Trtd. lumber	Deck posts (B)
2	4 × 4" × 8'	Trtd. lumber	Braces (D)
32	2 × 6" × 18'	Cedar	Decking (H), Top rail (J)
2	2 × 6" × 16'	Cedar	Top rail (J)
50	2 × 2" × 8'	Cedar	Balusters (I)

Framing Plan

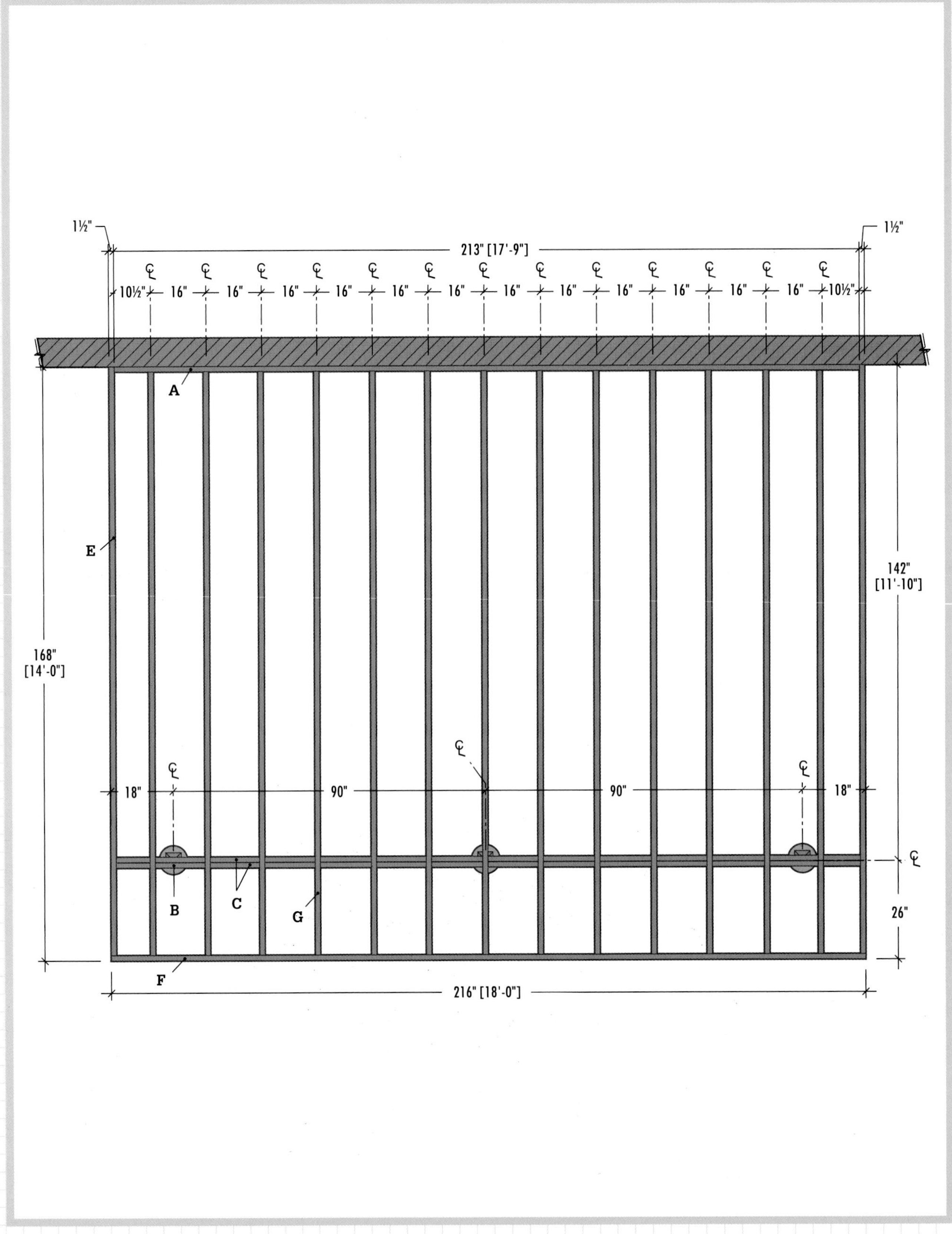

Elevation

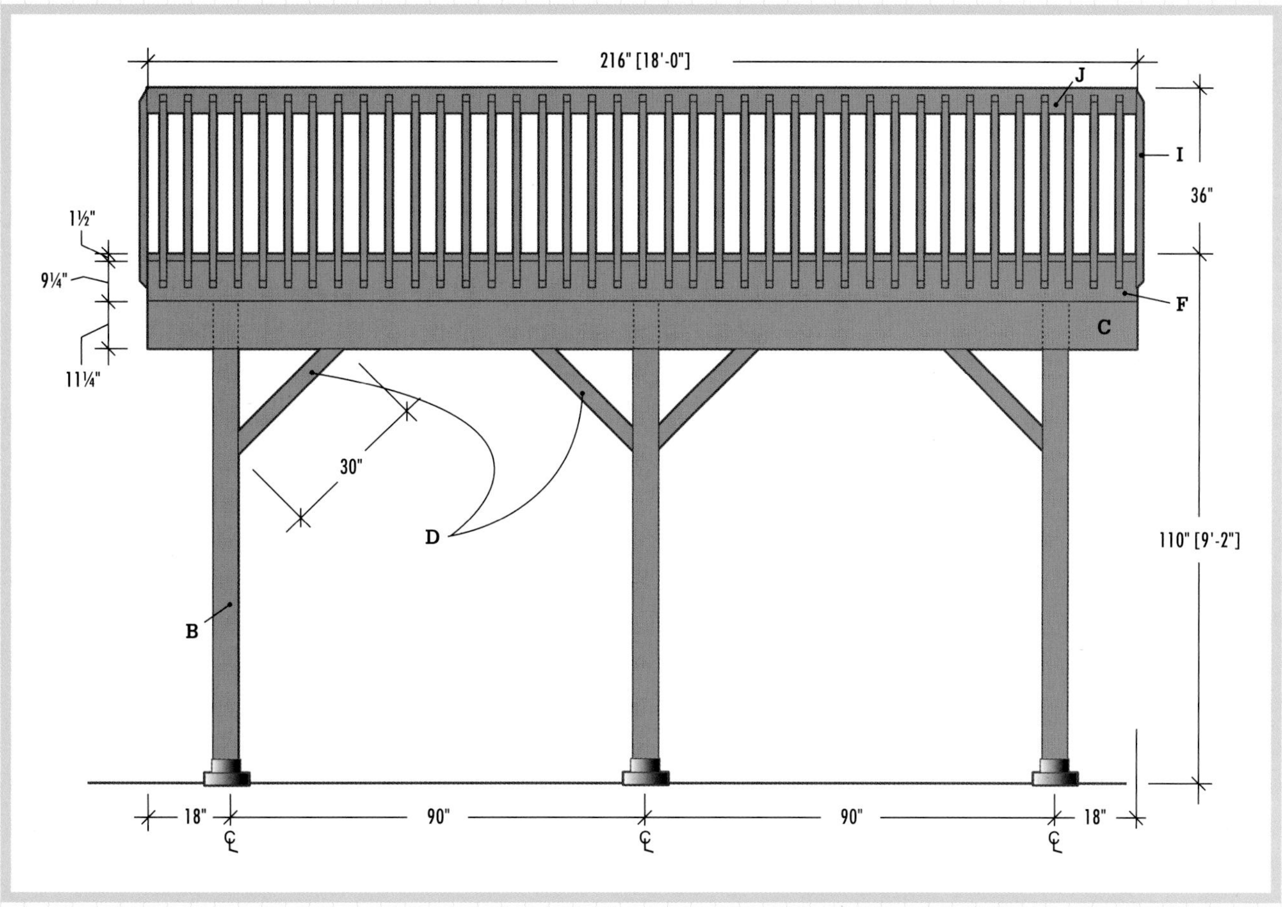

216" [18'-0"]
J
I
36"
1½"
9¼"
11¼"
F
C
30"
D
B
110" [9'-2"]
18"
90"
90"
18"
℄
℄
℄

Railing Detail

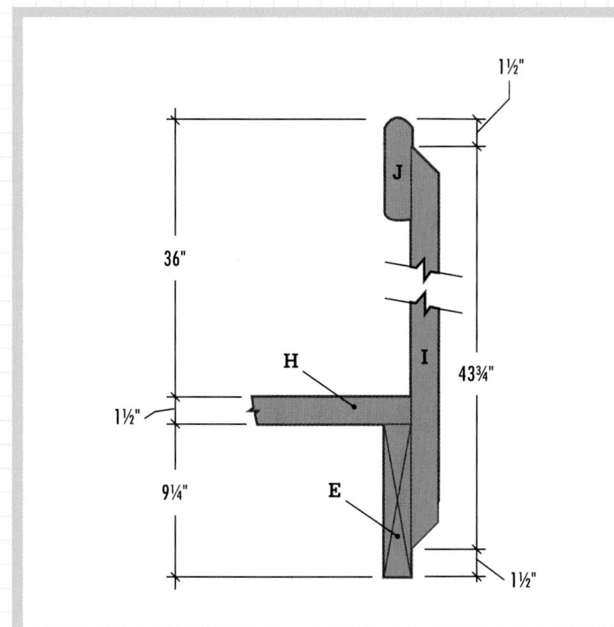

Face Board Detail

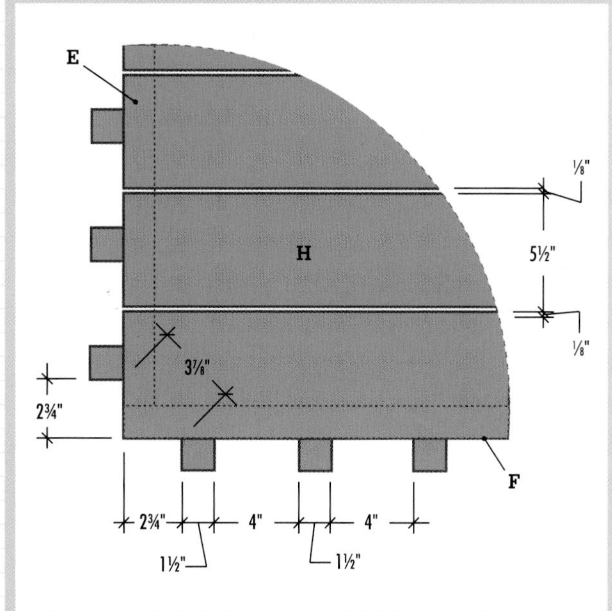

How to Build a Second-story Walkout Deck

ATTACH THE LEDGER

Draw a level outline on the siding to show where the ledger and the end joists will fit against the house. Install the ledger so that the surface of the decking boards will be 1" below the indoor floor level. This height difference prevents rainwater or melted snow from seeping into the house.

Cut out the siding along the outline with a circular saw. To avoid cutting the sheathing that lies underneath the siding, set the blade depth to the same thickness as the siding. Finish the cutout with a chisel, holding the beveled side in to ensure a straight cut.

Cut galvanized flashing to the length of the cutout, using metal snips. Slide the flashing up under the siding at the top of the cutout.

Measure and cut the ledger (A) from pressure-treated lumber. Center the ledger end to end in the cutout, with space at each end for the end joists.

Brace the ledger into position under the flashing. Tack the ledger into place with galvanized nails.

Drill pairs of ⅜" pilot holes at 16" intervals through the ledger and into the house header joist. Counterbore each pilot hole ½", using a 1⅜" spade bit. Attach the ledger with 4" lag screws and washers using a ratchet wrench.

Apply silicone caulk between the siding and flashing. Also seal the lag screw heads and the cracks at the ends of the ledger.

POUR THE FOOTINGS

To establish a reference point for locating the footings, drop a plumb bob from the ends of the ledger down to the ground.

Position a straight 14 ft.-long 2 × 4 perpendicular to the house at the point where the plumb bob meets the ground. *Note: If you are building on a steep slope or uneven ground, the mason's string method of locating footing positions will work better* (see pages 70 to 75).

Check for square, using the 3-4-5 triangle method. From the 2 × 4, measure 3 ft. along the wall and make a mark. Next, measure 4 ft. out from the house and make a mark on the 2 × 4. The diagonal line between the marks will measure 5 ft. when the board is accurately square to the house. Adjust the board as needed, using stakes to hold it in place.

Extend another reference board from the house at the other end of the ledger, following the same procedure.

Measure out along both boards, and mark the centerline of the footings (see Framing Plan, page 292).

Use a template made from 2 × 4s to locate the post footings on the ground, then mark the footings with stakes.

Plumb each post with a level, then use braces and stakes to hold the post in place until the beam and joists are installed.

Lay a straight 2 × 4 between the centerline marks, and drive stakes to mark the footing locations.

Remove the boards and dig the post footings, using a clamshell digger or power auger. Pour 2" to 3" of loose gravel into each hole for drainage. *Note: When measuring the footing size and depth, make sure you comply with local building codes, which may require flaring the base to 18".*

Cut the footing forms to length, using a reciprocating saw or handsaw, and insert them into the footing holes, leaving 2" above ground level. Pack soil around the forms for support, and fill the forms with concrete, tamping with a long stick or rod to eliminate any air gaps.

Screed the tops flush with a straight 2 × 4. Insert a J-bolt into the center of each footing and set with ¾" to 1" of thread exposed. Clean the bolt threads before the concrete sets.

SET THE POSTS

Lay a long, straight 2 × 4 flat across the footings, parallel to the house. With one edge tight against the J-bolts, draw a reference line across the top of each footing to help orient the post anchors.

Place a metal post anchor on each footing, centering it over the J-bolt and squaring it with the reference line. Attach the post anchors by threading a nut over each bolt and tightening with a ratchet wrench.

The tops of the posts (B) will eventually be level with the bottom edge of the ledger, but initially cut the posts several inches longer to allow for final trimming. Position the posts in the anchors and tack into place with one nail each.

With a level as a guide, use braces and stakes to ensure that the posts are plumb.

Determine the height of the beam by using a chalk line and a line level. Extend the chalk line out from the bottom edge of the ledger, make sure that the line is level, and snap a mark across the face of a post. Use the line and level to transfer the mark to the remaining posts.

NOTCH THE POSTS

Remove the posts from the post anchors and cut to the finished height.

Measure and mark a 3 × 11¼" notch at the top of each post, on the outside face. Use a framing square to trace lines on all sides. Rough-cut the notches with a circular saw, then finish with a reciprocating saw or handsaw.

Reattach the posts to the post anchors, with the notch-side facing away from the deck.

INSTALL THE BEAM

Cut the beam boards (C) to length, adding several inches to each end for final trimming after the deck frame is squared up.

Join the beam boards together with 2½" galvanized deck screws. Mark the post locations on the top edges and sides, using a combination square as a guide.

Lift the beam, one end at a time, into the notches with the crown up. Align and clamp the beam to the posts. *Note: Installing boards of this size and length, at this height, requires caution. You should have at least two helpers.*

Thread a carriage bolt into each pilot hole. Add a washer and nut to the end of each bolt and tighten with a ratchet wrench. Seal both ends of the bolts with silicone caulk.

Cut the tops of the posts flush with the top edge of the beam using a circular saw and reciprocating saw.

(continued)

INSTALL THE FRAME

Measure and cut the end joists (E) to length using a circular saw.

Attach the end joists to the ends of the ledger with 16d galvanized nails.

Measure and cut the rim joist (F) to length with a circular saw. Fasten it to the ends of the end joists with 16d nails.

Square up the frame by measuring corner to corner and adjusting until the measurements are equal. When the frame is square, toenail the end joists in place on top of the beam.

Trim the ends of the beam flush with the faces of the end joists using a reciprocating saw or a handsaw.

INSTALL THE BRACES

Cut the braces (D) to length (see Elevation, page 293) with a circular saw or power miter saw. Miter both ends at 45°.

Install the braces by positioning them against the beam boards and against the posts. Make sure the outside faces of the braces are flush with the outside faces of the beam and the posts. Temporarily fasten with deck screws.

Secure the braces to the posts with 5" lag screws. Drill two ⅜" pilot holes through the upper end of each brace into the beam. Counterbore to a ½"-depth using a 1⅜" spade bit, and drive lag screws with a ratchet wrench. Repeat for the lower end of the braces into the posts.

Snap a chalk line flush with the outside edge of the deck, and cut off overhanging deck boards with a circular saw.

After cutting balusters to length, gang them up and drill ⅛" pilot holes through the top and bottom.

INSTALL THE JOISTS

Measure and mark the joist locations (see Framing Plan, page 292) on the ledger, rim joist, and beam. Draw the outline of each joist on the ledger and rim joist, using a combination square.

Install a joist hanger at each joist location. Attach one flange of the hanger to one side of the outline, using joist nails. Use a spacer cut from scrap 2 × 8 lumber to achieve the correct spread for each hanger, then fasten the remaining side flange with joist nails. Remove the spacer and repeat the same procedure for the remaining joist hangers.

Measure, mark, and cut lumber for joists (G) using a circular saw. Place joists in hangers with crown side up and attach with joist hanger nails. Align joists with the outlines on the top of the beam, and toenail in place.

LAY THE DECKING

Measure, mark, and cut the decking boards (H) to length as needed.

Position the first row of decking flush against the house, and attach by driving a pair of galvanized deck screws into each joist.

Position the remaining decking boards, leaving a ⅛" gap between boards to provide for drainage, and attach to each joist with deck screws.

Every few rows of decking, measure from the edge of the decking to the outside edge of the deck. If the measurement can be divided evenly by 5⅝", the last board will fit flush with the outside edge of the deck as intended. If the measurement shows that the last board will not fit flush, adjust the spacing as you install the remaining rows of boards.

If your decking overhangs the end joists, snap a chalk line to mark the outside edge of the deck and cut flush with a circular saw set to a 1½" depth. If needed, finish the cut with a jigsaw or handsaw where a circular saw can't reach.

BUILD THE RAILING

Measure, mark, and cut the balusters (I) to length, with 45° miters at both ends.

Gang the balusters together and drill two ⅛" pilot holes at both ends.

Clamp a 1½" guide strip flush with the bottom edge of the deck platform to establish the baluster height (see Railing Detail, page 293).

To ensure that the balusters are installed at equal intervals, create a spacing jig, less than 4" wide, from two pieces of scrap material.

To make a joint in the top rail, cut the ends at 45° and drill a pair of pilot holes. Then fasten the ends together with deck screws.

Attach the corner balusters first (see Face Board Detail, page 293), using a level to ensure that they are plumb. Then use the spacing jig for positioning, and attach the remaining balusters to the deck platform with 3" deck screws.

Measure, mark, and cut the top rail sections (J) to length. Round over three edges (see Railing Detail, page 293) using a router with a ½" round-over bit. Cut 45° miters on the ends that meet at the corners.

Hold or clamp the top rail in position, and attach with 2½" deck screws driven through the balusters.

If you need to make straight joints in the top rail, cut the ends of the adjoining boards at 45°. Drill angled ⅛" pilot holes and join with deck screws.

Inside Corner Deck

A diamond decking pattern helps make this a stunning deck. The location, tucked inside a corner of the house, creates an accessible area for small get-togethers, large parties, simple outdoor meals, and relaxing. The location offers privacy, shade, and a place out of the wind. Although we've left the posts exposed, you can create an even more integral deck design by adding simple skirting around the base.

The design calls for double joists and blocking for extra strength and stability where decking boards butt together. Joists are spaced 12" on center to support diagonal decking. It takes a little more time to cut the decking boards and match the miter cuts, but the results are spectacular and well worth the effort. The addition of a few low-voltage lights would make this a fabulous nighttime deck as well.

A nested deck is the perfect way to exploit a shaded inside corner, and the position could not be more accessible from the house.

Cutaway View

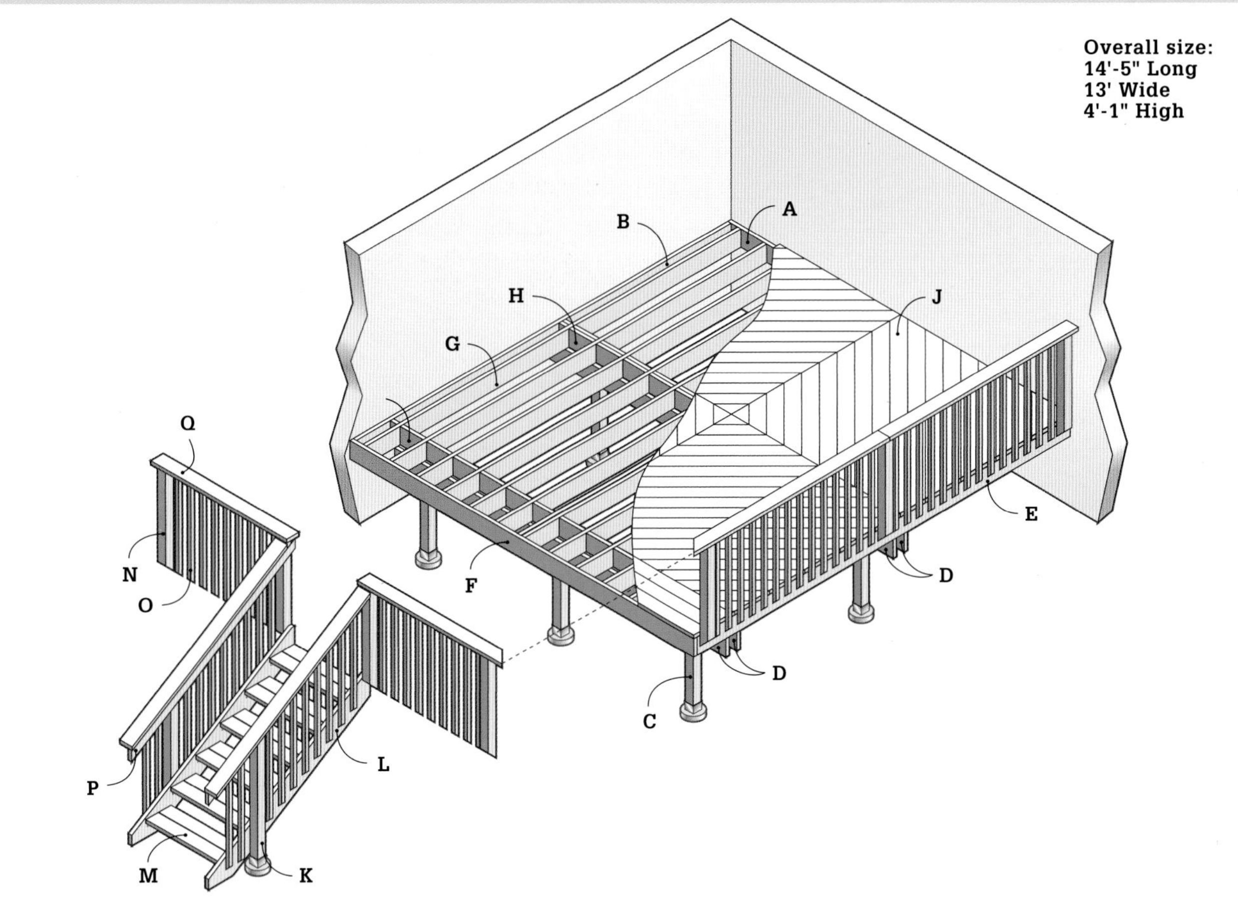

Supplies

10"-diameter footing forms (6)
8"-diameter footing forms (2)
J-bolts (8)
6 × 6" metal post anchors (6)
4 × 4" metal post anchors (2)
2 × 8" single joist hangers (50)
2 × 8" double joist hangers (20)
1½ × 10" angle brackets (12)
3" galvanized deck screws
2½" galvanized deck screws
16d galvanized nails
Joist hanger nails
½ × 4" lag screws and washers (78)
¼ × 1¼" lag screws (96)
½ × 7" carriage bolts, washers, and nuts (12)
Exterior silicone caulk (6 tubes)
Concrete as needed

Lumber List

QTY.	SIZE	MATERIAL	PART
6	2 × 8" × 14'	Trtd. lumber	Short ledger (A), Long ledger (B), Beam boards (D)
14	2 × 8" × 16'	Trtd. lumber	Joists (G), Single blocking (I)
3	2 × 8" × 8'	Trtd. lumber	Double blocking (H)
3	6 × 6" × 8'	Trtd. lumber	Deck posts (C)
1	2 × 8" × 16'	Cedar	End joist (E)
1	2 × 8" × 14'	Cedar	Rim joist (F)
42	2 × 6" × 8'	Cedar	Decking (J), Railing caps (Q)
16	2 × 6" × 14'	Cedar	Decking (J)
1	4 × 4" × 10'	Cedar	Stair posts (K)
6	2 × 6" × 8'	Cedar	Treads (M)
4	4 × 4" × 8'	Cedar	Railing posts (N)
2	2 × 10" × 8'	Cedar	Stringers (L)
33	2 × 2" × 8'	Cedar	Balusters (O)
6	2 × 4" × 8'	Cedar	Top rails (P)

Framing Plan

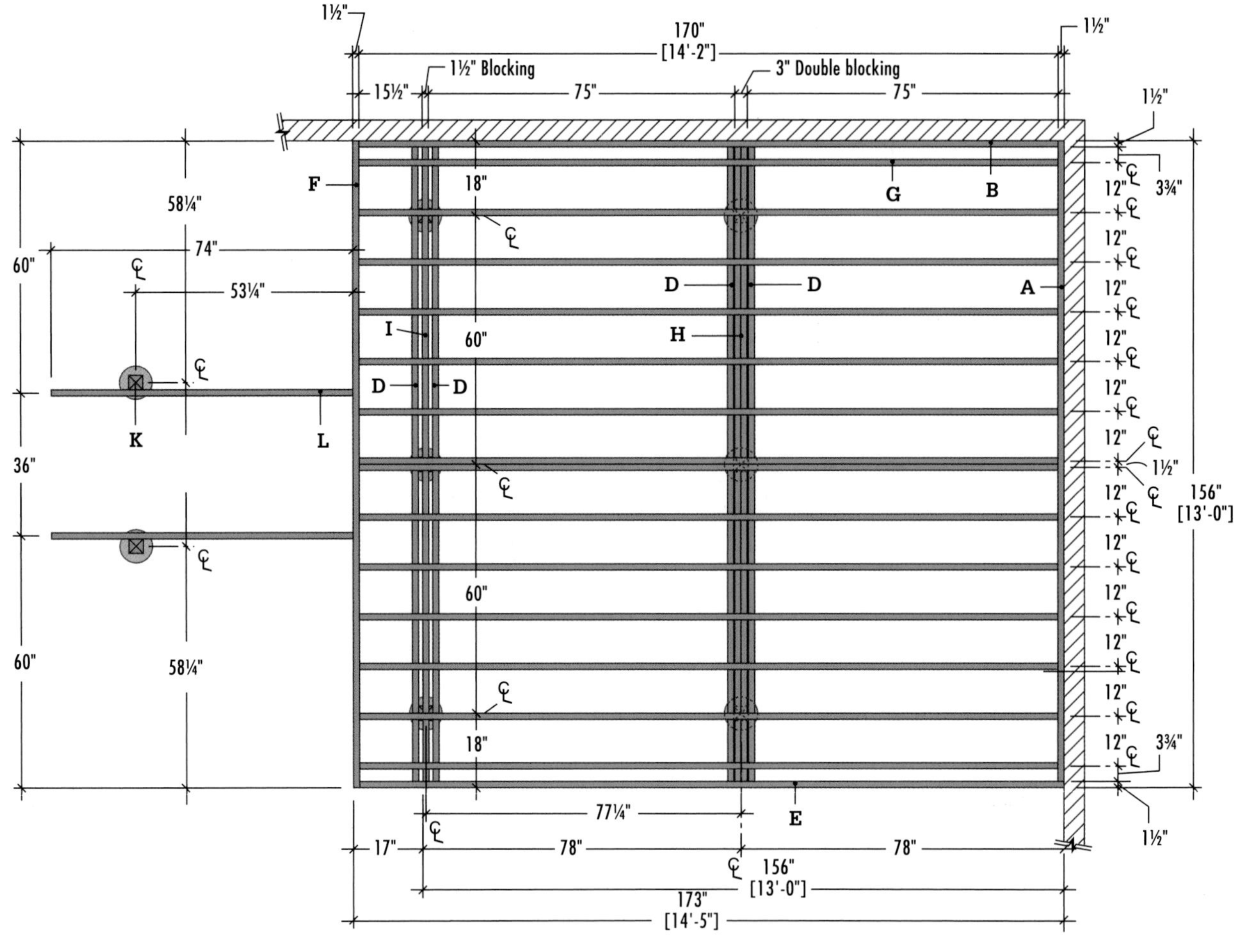

1½"
170" [14'-2"]
1½"
1½" Blocking
3" Double blocking
15½"
75"
75"
1½"
3¾"
58¼"
74"
53¼"
60"
36"
60"
58¼"
18"
60"
60"
18"
F
G
B
A
D
D
I
H
D
D
K
L
E
12"
156" [13'-0"]
3¾"
1½"
77¼"
17"
78"
78"
156" [13'-0"]
173" [14'-5"]

Elevation

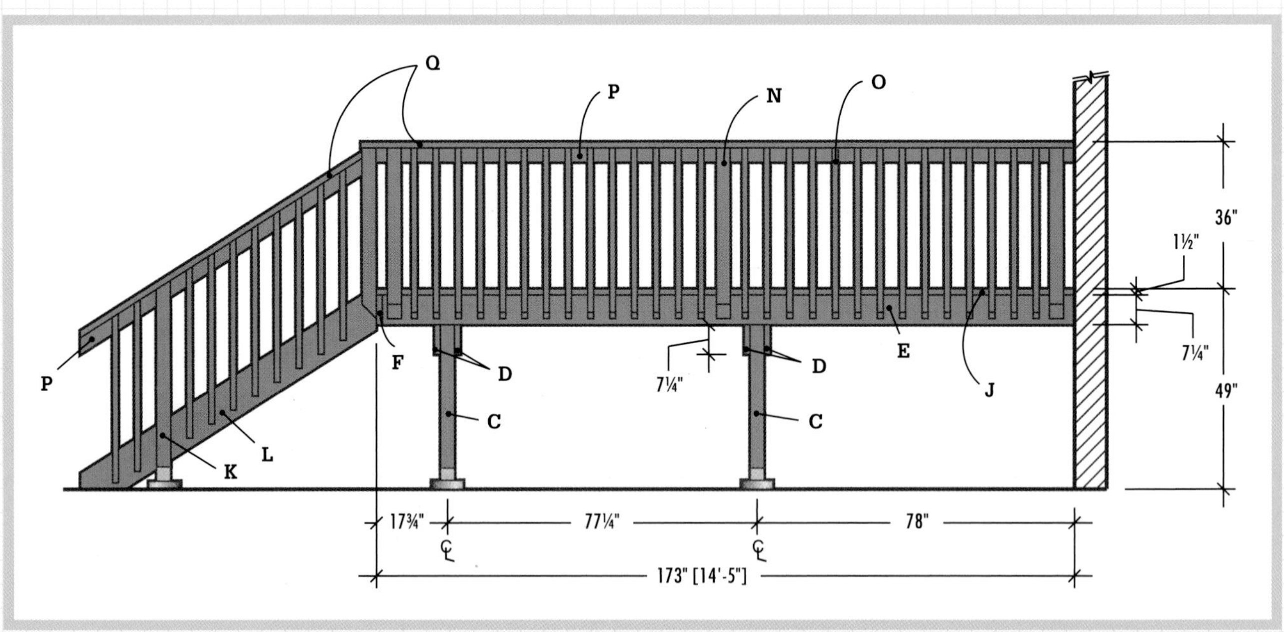

Railing Detail

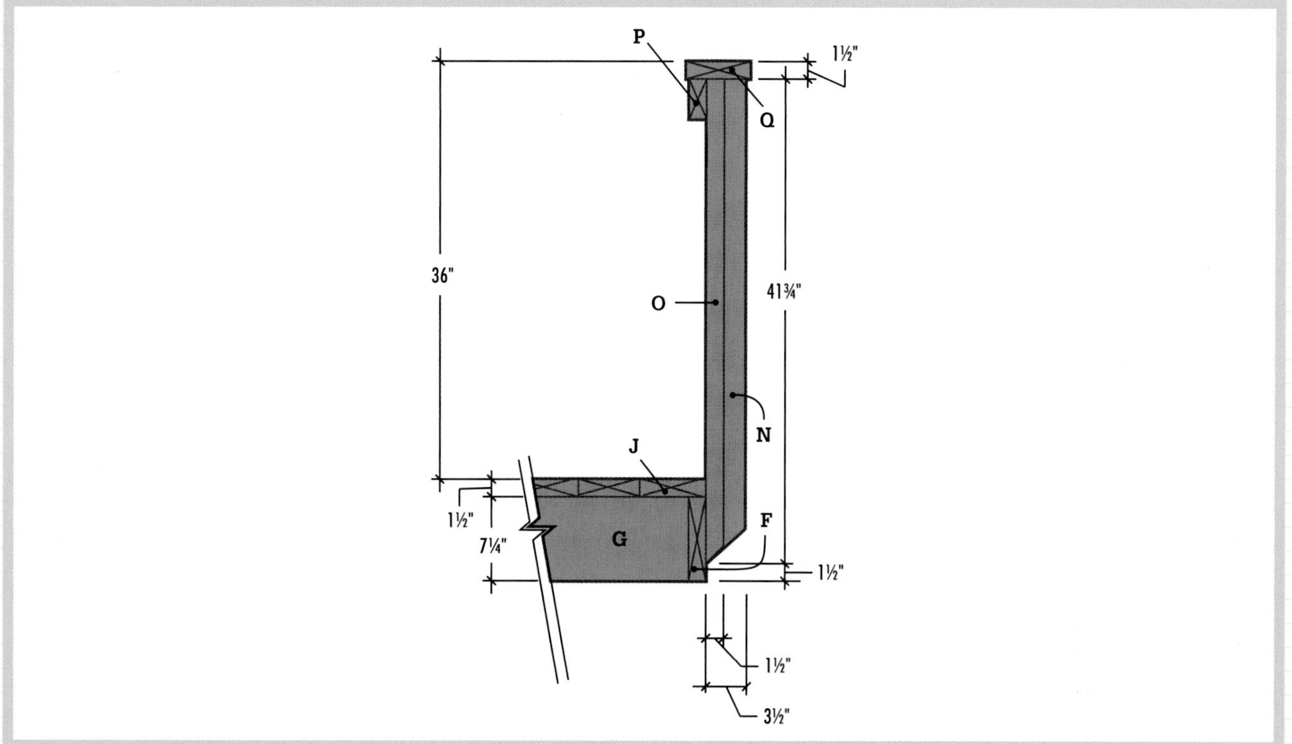

Stairway Detail

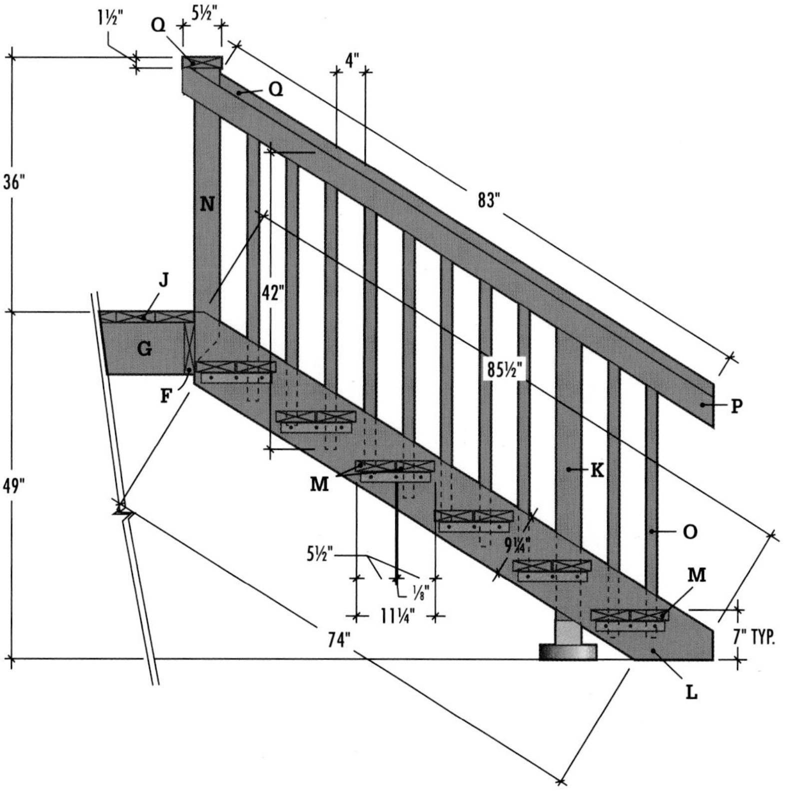

How to Build an Inside Corner Deck

ATTACH THE LEDGERS

The inside angle of the house should form a right angle. If there is a slight deviation, use shims behind the ledger to create a 90° angle in the corner.

To show where the ledgers will be attached to the house, draw outlines on the wall, using a level as a guide. To locate the top of the ledger outline, measure down from the indoor floor surface 1" plus the thickness of the decking boards. This height difference prevents rain and melting snow from seeping into the house.

Measure and cut the ledgers to length. They will be shorter than the outline on the wall to allow for the width of the rim joist and end joist. (See pages 62 to 68 for information about attaching ledgers on different types of siding.)

Drill pairs of ⅜" pilot holes through the ledgers at 16" intervals. Counterbore the pilot holes ½" with a 1⅜" spade bit.

Brace the ledgers in place, and use a ratchet wrench to attach the ledgers to the walls with ½ × 4" lag screws and washers. Seal the screw heads and all cracks between the wall and ledger with silicone caulk.

POUR THE DECK FOOTINGS

To locate the footings, stretch mason's strings between the ledgers and 2 × 4 supports, known as batterboards.

Referring to the measurements shown in the Framing Plan (page 300), mark the centerlines of the footings on the ledgers, and drive a nail into the ledger at each location.

Set up temporary batterboards and stretch a mason's string out from the ledger at each location. Make sure the strings are perpendicular to the ledger.

Check the mason's strings for square, using the 3-4-5 triangle method. From the point where each string meets the ledger, measure 3 ft. along the ledger and make a mark. Next, measure 4 ft. out along the string and mark with tape. The distance between the points on the ledger and the string should be 5 ft. If it's not, adjust the string position on the batterboard accordingly.

Drop a plumb bob to transfer the footing centerpoints to the ground, and drive a stake to mark each point. Remove the strings.

Position the beam against the posts, and attach it temporarily with deck screws. *Note: This method of joinery is no longer allowed in some regions. Consult your building department.*

Dig the post footings using a clamshell digger or power auger. Pour 2" to 3" of loose gravel into each hole for drainage. *Note: Make sure the footing size and depth comply with your local building code, which may require flaring the base.*

Cut the footing forms to length, using a reciprocating saw or handsaw, and insert them into the footing holes so that they extend 2" above grade. Pack soil around the forms for support, and fill the forms with concrete, tamping with a long stick or rod to eliminate any air pockets.

Screed the tops of the footings flush, using a 2 × 4. Insert a J-bolt into the wet concrete of each footing, and set it, with ¾" to 1" of thread exposed. Retie the mason's strings and position each J-bolt at the exact center of the post location, using the plumb bob as a guide. Clean the bolt threads before the concrete sets.

SET THE POSTS

Lay a long, straight 2 × 4 flat across each row of footings, parallel to the short ledger. With one edge tight against the J-bolts, draw a reference line across the top of each footing.

Center a metal post anchor over the J-bolt on each footing, and square it with the reference line. Attach the post anchors by threading a nut over each bolt and tightening with a ratchet wrench.

Working from a plywood platform, install double blocking to support the ends of the deck boards. Attach the blocking by alternating end nailing with using joist hangers.

Cut the posts, leaving an extra 6" for final trimming. Place each post in an anchor and tack it in place with one nail.

With a level as a guide, use braces and stakes to ensure that each post is plumb. Finish nailing the posts to the anchors.

Determine the height of the inside beam by extending a straight 2 × 4 from the bottom edge of the long ledger across the row of posts. Level the 2 × 4, and draw a line on the posts. Use the same method to determine the height of the outer beam. *Note: The sandwich beam construction described here is no longer allowed by most local codes. If sandwich beams are not allowed by your local code, use special hangers or larger posts to support the blocked beam on the top of the posts.*

INSTALL THE BEAMS

Cut the beam boards (D), leaving an extra few inches for final trimming.

Position one beam board, crown up, against the row of posts. Tack the board in place with deck screws.

Attach the remaining beam boards to the posts in the same way.

Drill two ½" holes through the boards and posts at each joint. Secure the beam boards to the posts with carriage bolts, using a ratchet wrench.

Cut the tops of the posts flush with the tops of the beams, using a reciprocating saw or handsaw.

INSTALL THE JOISTS

A double joist at the center of the deck provides extra support for the ends of the decking boards.

Measure, mark, and cut the end joist (E) and the rim joist (F), using a circular saw.

Attach the end joist to the short ledger and the rim joist to the long ledger, using 16d galvanized nails.

Nail the rim joist to the end joist.

Toenail the end joist to the tops of the beams, and cut the ends of the beams flush with the end joist.

Measure, mark, and install the double center joist at the precise center of the deck with double joist hangers.

Measure both ways from the double joist, and mark the centerpoints of the remaining joists at 12" intervals. Using a combination square, mark the outlines of the joists on the ledger, beams, and rim joist.

Nail the joist hangers to the short ledger and rim joist using a scrap 2 × 8 as a spacer to achieve the correct spread for each hanger.

Cut the joists (G) to length. Insert the joists into the hangers with the crown up, and attach them with joist hanger nails. Align the joists with the marks on the beams and toenail them in place.

INSTALL THE BLOCKING

The ends of the decking boards in the diamond pattern are supported by a row of double blocking at the center of the pattern and a row of single blocking at the edge of the pattern.

To locate the rows of blocking, measure from the inside corner of the house along the long ledger (see Framing Plan, page 300). Drive one screw or nail at 78", and another at 156". Make corresponding marks across from the ledger on the end joist.

Snap chalk lines across the joists, between the ledger and the end joist. The line at 78" is the centerline of the double blocking. The line at 156" is the outer edge of the single blocking. Don't be concerned if the blocking is not directly over the beams.

Cut double blocking pieces from 2 × 8s nailed together with 10d galvanized nails.

Install the blocking by alternating end nailing and using galvanized joist hangers.

To achieve the best fit, measure the actual length of the last deck board in each course before cutting.

LAY THE DECKING

Except for the three rows of straight decking at the top of the stairway, the decking is laid in a diamond pattern.

Begin at the center of the diamond pattern, where the double joist and the double blocking intersect. Cut four identical triangles, as large as possible, from 2 × 6" cedar stock.

Drill ⅛" pilot holes in the ends, position the pieces as shown on page 303, and attach with 3" deck screws.

To install the remaining courses, measure, cut, drill, and attach the first three boards in each course. Then, measure the actual length of the last board to achieve the best fit. For best results, install the decking course by course. Maintain a ⅛" gap between courses.

Once the diamond decking pattern is complete, cut and install the three remaining deck boards.

Fasten the stair to the deck with a ratchet wrench, using 4" lag screws.

BUILD THE STAIRS

For the position of the stairway footings, refer to the Framing Plan on page 300. Locate the footings by extending a 2 × 4 from the deck, perpendicular to the rim joist, dropping a plumb bob, and marking the centerpoints on the ground with stakes.

Dig postholes with a clamshell digger or an auger, and pour footings using the same method as for the deck footings. Insert J-bolts, leaving ¾" to 1" of thread exposed. Allow the concrete to set. Attach metal post anchors.

Cut the stairway posts (K) to length, adding approximately 6" for final trimming. Place the posts in the anchors.

Use a level to ensure that the posts are plumb, and attach the posts to the anchors with 16d galvanized nails.

Cut the stringers (L) to length and use a framing square to mark the rise and run for each step (see Stairway Detail, page 301). Draw the tread outline on each run. Cut the angles at the ends of the stringers with a circular saw. (For a more detailed description of stairway construction, see pages 140 to 159.)

Drill pilot holes and then attach the treads to the stringers, using 1¼" lag screws and angle brackets.

Position an angle bracket flush with the bottom of each tread outline. Drill ⅛" pilot holes in the stringers, and attach the angle brackets with 1¼" lag screws.

The treads (M) fit between the stringers, and the stringers fit between the stairway posts. Measure and cut the treads (M) to length, 3" shorter than the distance between the stairway posts.

Assemble the stairway upside down on sawhorses. Mark and drill ⅛" pilot holes at the ends of the treads. Position each front tread with its front edge flush to the tread outline, and attach to the angle brackets with ¼ × 1¼" lag screws.

Attach the rear treads in similar fashion, leaving a ⅛" gap between treads.

Position the stairway in place against the edge of the deck, making sure the top of the stringer is flush with the surface of the deck. From underneath the deck, drill ¼" pilot holes through the rim joist into the stringers. Attach the stringers to the rim joist with 4" lag screws, using a ratchet wrench.

To fasten the stairway to the stair posts, drill two ¼" pilot holes through each stringer into a post. Counterbore the pilot holes ½" deep with a 1⅜" spade bit, and use a ratchet wrench to drive 4" lag screws with washers. Seal the screw heads with silicone caulk.

INSTALL THE DECK RAILING

Cut the railing posts (N) and balusters (O) to length (see Railing Detail, page 301) with a power miter saw or circular saw. Cut the tops square and the bottoms at 45° angles.

Drill two ⅜" pilot holes at the bottom end of each railing post, positioned so the lag screws will attach to the rim joist. Counterbore the holes ½" deep with a 1⅜" spade bit.

Drill two ⅛" pilot holes near the bottom of each baluster, spaced 4" apart. At the top of each baluster, drill a pair of ⅛" pilot holes spaced 1½" apart.

With the help of a combination square, draw the outlines of the railing posts around the perimeter of the deck. The posts at the corner must be spaced so there is less than 4" between them.

Hold each railing post in its position, with the end 1½" above the bottom edge of the deck platform (see Railing Detail, page 301). Make sure the post is plumb, and insert an awl through the counterbored holes to mark pilot hole locations on the deck (or use a longer bit).

Set the post aside and drill ⅜" pilot holes at the marks. Attach the railing posts to the deck with ½ × 4" lag screws and washers. Seal the screw heads with silicone caulk.

Cut the top rails (P) to length with the ends mitered at 45° where they meet in the corner. Attach them to the railing posts with 3" deck screws, keeping the edges of the rails flush with the tops of the posts.

To position the balusters, measure the total distance between two railing posts, and mark the centerpoint on the top rail. The two railing sections on the long side of this deck will have a baluster at the centerpoint; the two railing sections on the stairway side will have a space at the centerpoint. *Note: If the dimensions of your deck vary from the plan, calculate whether you will have a baluster or a space at the center of each section.*

Cut a spacer slightly less than 4" wide. Start at the center of each railing section, and position either a baluster or a space over the line. Measure out from the center both ways, marking the outlines of the balusters on the top rail. The end spaces may be narrow, but they will be symmetrical.

After the top rail and balusters have been installed, install the railing cap with its inside edge overhanging the inside face of the top rail by ¼".

With the stairway top rail cut to size and installed, attach the railing cap with deck screws.

To install the balusters, begin next to a railing post and make sure the first baluster is plumb. Install the remaining balusters, holding each one tight against the spacer and flush with the top rail. Attach the balusters with 2½" deck screws.

Cut the deck railing cap (Q) to length, with the ends mitered at 45° where they meet in the corner. Position the railing cap sections so the inside edge overhangs the inside edge of the top rail by ¼". Attach the cap with 3" deck screws.

INSTALL THE STAIRWAY RAILING

Determine the exact size and shape of the stairway top rail. Tack a cedar 2 × 4 across the faces of the stairway post and deck post with 10d galvanized nails. Make sure the angle of the 2 × 4 is parallel with the angle of the stringer below.

On the back side of the 2 × 4, mark the outline of the deck railing post and the end of the deck top rail. On the stairway post, mark a diagonal cutoff line at the top edge of the 2 × 4. At the lower end of the 2 × 4, use a level to mark a plumb cutoff line directly above the end of the stringer.

Remove the 2 × 4 and make the cuts.

Drill ⅛" pilot holes through the stairway top rail. Place in position and attach with 2½" deck screws.

To trim the top ends of the stairway balusters, hold a baluster against the stairway post and draw a diagonal cut line along the top edge of the rail. Trim the baluster. Using this baluster as a template, mark and cut the remaining stairway balusters.

Install the stairway balusters with 2½" deck screws, using the same procedure as for the deck balusters.

Measure the railing caps for the stairway. Cut the caps to size, with the upper ends beveled to fit against the deck posts, and the lower ends beveled to align with the end of the top rail. Install the caps by drilling ⅛" pilot holes and attaching them with 2½" deck screws.

Wraparound Deck

By wrapping around an outside corner of your house, this versatile deck increases your living space and lets you take advantage of views in several directions. The plan also creates two symmetrical areas for sitting or relaxing, providing space for two distinct activities. Our plan also calls for a front stairway for easy access to your yard or garden. The horizontal rails and notched posts provide striking visual elements that enhance the deck's overall design and add to its intimate nature.

Tools & Materials ▸

- 10"-diameter footing forms (10)
- J-bolts (8)
- 6 × 6" metal post anchors (10)
- Post-beam caps (8)
- 90° 2 × 8" joist hangers (26)
- 45° 2 × 8" joist hangers (3)
- 1½ × 1½" galvanized metal angle brackets (26)
- ½ × 4" lag screws and washers (20)
- ½ × 3" lag screws and washers (32)
- Joist hanger nails
- 5 × 7" mending plate (2)
- Silicone caulk (3 tubes)
- 3" masonry screws
- 3" galvanized deck screws
- 1⅝" galvanized deck screws
- ⅝" galvanized screws
- Concrete as required

The unusual orientation of this deck to the house creates naturally separate areas on the deck, and allows for maximum views out over the landscaping.

Cutaway View

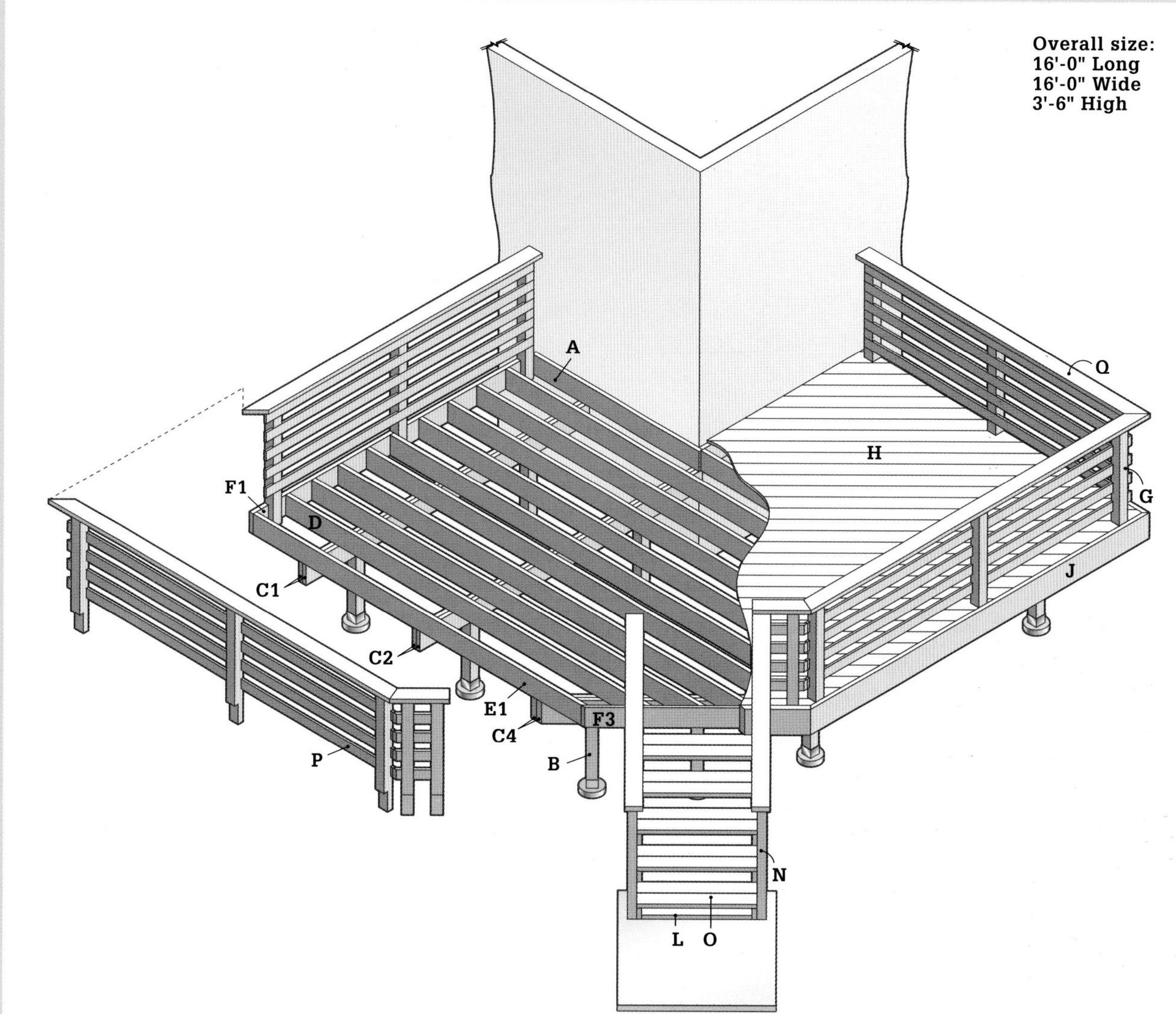

Lumber List

QTY.	SIZE	MATERIAL	PART
9	2 × 8" × 16'	Trtd. Lumber	Joists (D)
6	2 × 8" × 12'	Trtd. Lumber	Ledgers (A), Beam boards (C), End joist (E), Rim joist (F)
13	2 × 8" × 10'	Trtd. Lumber	Beam boards (C), Joists (D), End joist (E), Rim joists (F), Lower gusset (L)
1	2 × 6" × 4'	Trtd. Lumber	Stairway nailer (I)
1	2 × 4" × 4'	Trtd. Lumber	Upper gusset (L)
6	6 × 6" × 8'	Trtd. Lumber	Deck posts (B)
8	4 × 4" × 8'	Cedar	Deck railing posts (G)

QTY.	SIZE	MATERIAL	PART
28	5⁄4 × 6" × 16'	Cedar	Decking (H)
2	2 × 10" × 12'	Cedar	Face boards (J)
2	2 × 10" × 10'	Cedar	Face boards (J)
1	2 × 10" × 6'	Cedar	Face boards (J)
1	2 × 12" × 12'	Cedar	Stringers (K)
5	2 × 6" × 12'	Cedar	Railing cap (Q)
5	2 × 6" × 8'	Cedar	Treads (O)
10	1 × 4" × 12'	Cedar	Rails (P)
11	1 × 4" × 10'	Cedar	Rails (P)
8	1 × 4" × 6'	Cedar	Rails (P)

Framing Plan

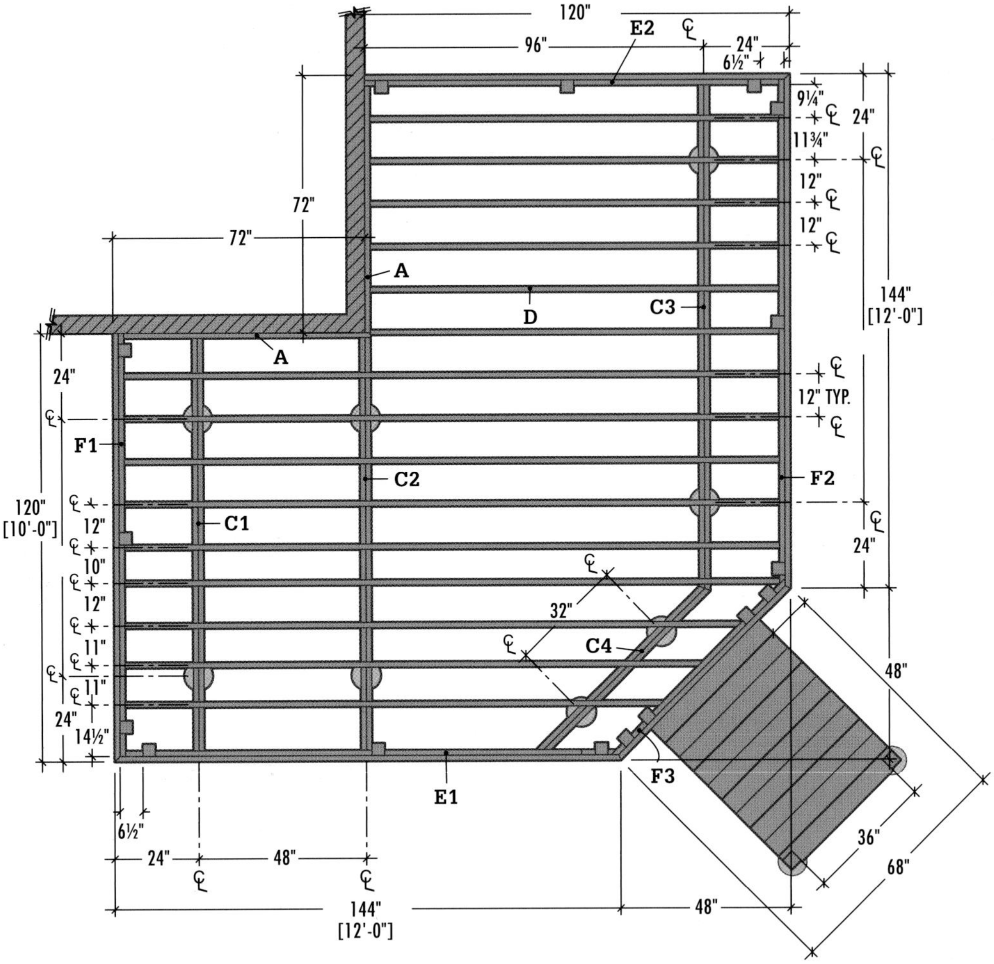

Elevation

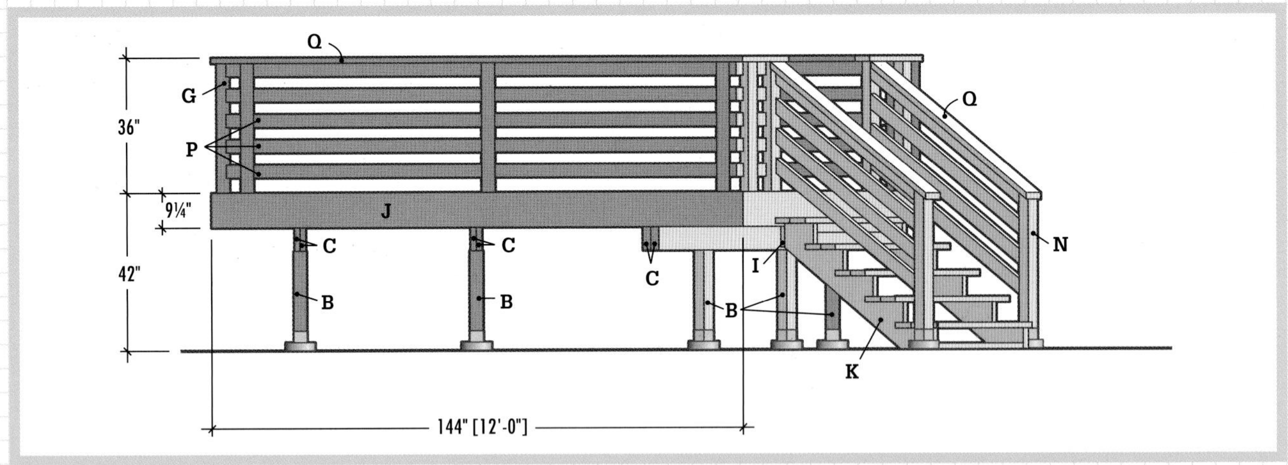

Railing Detail

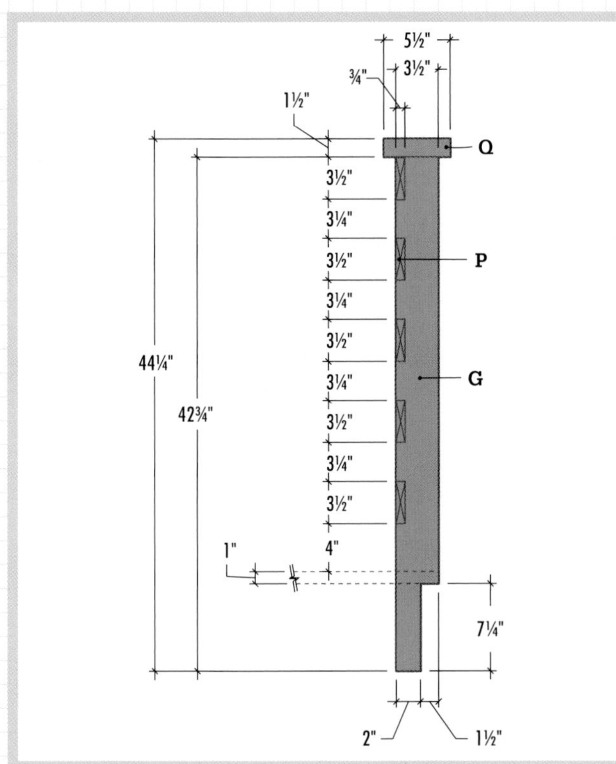

Stairway Detail

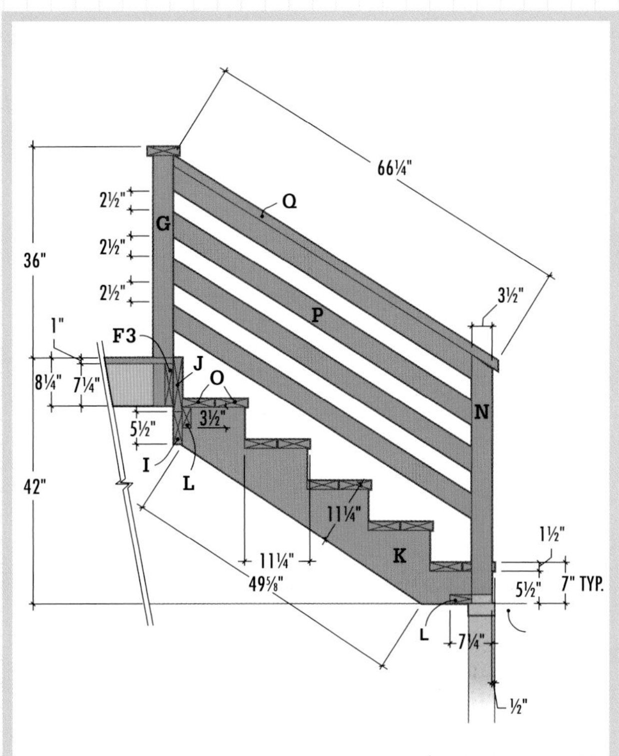

Footing Location Diagram

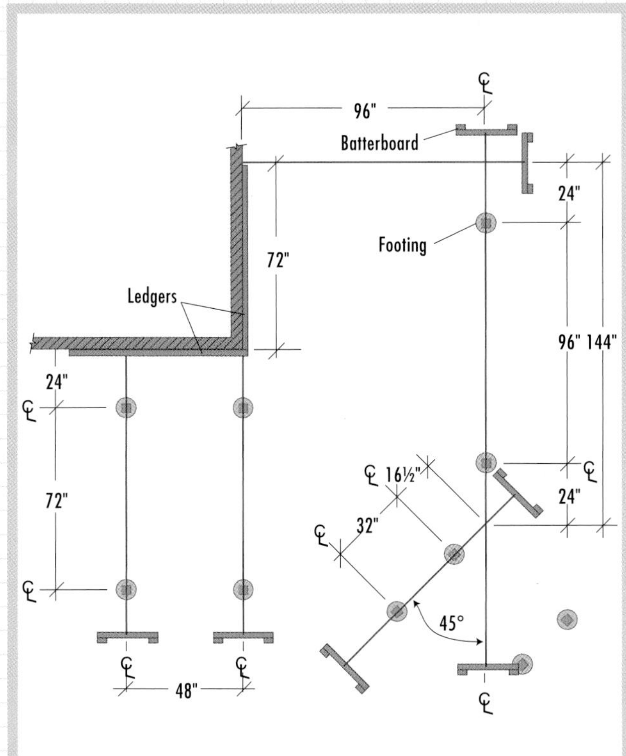

Corner Post Detail

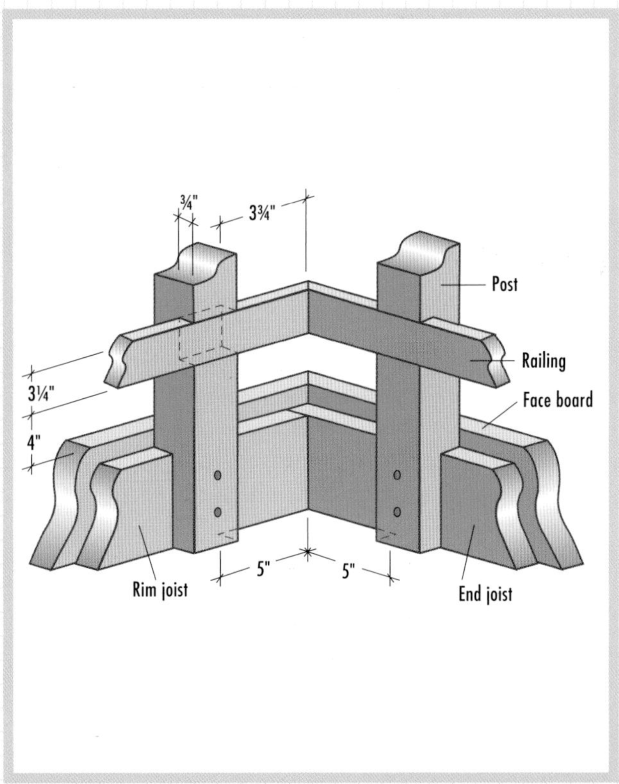

How to Build a Wraparound Deck

ATTACH THE LEDGERS

Draw a level outline on the siding to show where the ledgers and the adjacent end joist and rim joist will fit against the house.

Position the top edge of the ledgers so that the surface of the decking boards will be 1" below the indoor floor level. This height difference prevents rainwater or melted snow from seeping into the house. Draw the outline long enough to accommodate the thickness of rim joist F-1 and end joist E-2.

Cut out the siding along the outline with a circular saw. To keep the blade from cutting the sheathing underneath the siding, set the blade depth to the same thickness as the siding. Finish the corners of the cutout with a chisel, holding the beveled side in to ensure a straight cut. Cut galvanized flashing to the length of the cutout, using metal snips, and slide the flashing up under the siding.

Measure and cut the ledgers (A) to length from pressure-treated lumber, using a circular saw. Remember, the ledger boards should be shorter than the overall length of the cutouts. Position the ledgers in the cutout, underneath the flashing, and brace them in place. Fasten them temporarily with deck screws.

Drill pairs of 3⁄8" pilot holes through the ledger and sheathing and into the house header joist at 2 ft. intervals. Counterbore each pilot hole 1⁄2" deep, using a 1 3⁄8" spade bit. Attach the ledgers to the wall with 1⁄2 × 4" lag screws and washers, using a ratchet wrench.

Apply a thick bead of silicone caulk between the siding and the flashing. Also seal the lag screw heads and any gaps between the wall and the ledger.

POUR THE FOOTINGS

Referring to the Footing Location Diagram (page 309), stretch mason's strings across the site, using 2 × 4 batterboards. Check the mason's strings for square, using the 3-4-5 triangle method. From the point where each string meets the ledger, measure 3 ft. along the ledger and make a mark. Next, measure 4 ft. out along the mason's string and mark with tape. The distance between the points on the ledger and the string should be 5 ft. If not, adjust the mason's strings accordingly. Measure along the strings to locate the centerpoints of the footings. Mark the locations with tape.

Drop a plumb bob at the tape locations, and drive stakes into the ground to mark the centerpoints of the footings. Remove the mason's strings and dig holes for the footings using a clamshell digger or power auger. Pour 2" to 3" of loose gravel into each hole for drainage. Make certain the hole dimensions comply with your local building code, which may require flaring the footings at the base. Cut the footing forms to length using a reciprocating saw or handsaw. Insert the forms into the holes, leaving 2" of each form above grade. Pack soil around the forms.

Use a speed square to mark a 22½° miter cut where the ends of beams C-3 and C-4 fit together.

Fill the forms with concrete and tamp the concrete with a long stick to eliminate any air pockets. Screed the tops flush with a flat 2 × 4. Insert a J-bolt into each footing, leaving 3⁄4" to 1" of thread exposed.

Retie the mason's strings and drop a plumb bob to position each J-bolt at the exact center of the footing. Clean the bolt threads before the concrete sets.

SET THE DECK POSTS

Start by laying a long, straight 2 × 4 flat across each pair of footings. With one edge tight against the J-bolts, draw a reference line across each footing.

Place a metal post anchor on each footing, center it over the J-bolt, and square it with the reference line. Thread a nut over each J-bolt and tighten each of the post anchors in place.

Cut the posts (B) to their approximate length, adding several inches for final trimming. Place the posts in the anchors and tack them into place with one nail each.

With a level as a guide, use braces and stakes to plumb the posts. Once the posts are plumb, finish nailing them to the anchors. To determine the height of the posts (except for the staircase front posts, which should be cut to the length indicated), make a mark on the house 7¼" down from the bottom edge of the ledger.

Use a straight 2 × 4 and a level to extend this line across a post. Transfer this line to the remaining posts. Cut the posts off with a reciprocating saw or a handsaw and attach post-beam caps to the tops using 8d nails. Pour the railing post fittings using the same method.

INSTALL THE BEAMS

Cut the beams from 2 × 10" lumber, adding several inches to each beam for final trimming. Position the beam boards (C) so the crowns face the same direction, and fasten them together with 10d galvanized nails spaced every 16".

Position beams C-1 and C-2 in their post-beam caps and attach them with nails. Mark and cut the angled end of beam C-3 by mitering it at 22½°. Position the beam in the post caps.

Make a 22½° miter cut at one end of beam C-4 to form a 45° corner with beam C-3. Leave the other end long for final trimming. Place beam C-4 in the post-beam caps. Fit the beams tightly together, fasten them with 3" deck screws, and attach them to the post caps with 8d nails.

INSTALL THE JOISTS

Referring to the Framing Plan on page 308, cut rim joist F-1 to final length, and cut end joist E-1 generously long, to allow for final trimming.

Fasten one end of rim joist F-1 to the ledger with 16d galvanized nails. Rest end joist E-1 in place on beams C-1 and C-2. Fasten F-1 and E-1 together with deck screws. Use a framing square to finalize the location of E-1 on the beams. Mark the beams and trim them to length. Toenail E-1 in place on the beams.

Cut end joist E-2 to length. Install it by nailing it to the end of the ledger, checking for square, and toenailing it to the top of beam C-3. Trim the beam to length. Mark the outlines of the inner joists (D) on the ledger, beams, and rim joist F-1 (see Framing Plan, page 308), using a tape measure and a combination square.

Fit beam C-4 tightly against beam C-3 and attach the two beams to each other with deck screws.

Mark the three remaining inside joists for cutting by snapping a chalk line. Brace and miter-cut the three inside joists.

Attach joist hangers to the ledger and rim joist F-1 with 1½" joist hanger nails, using a scrap 2 × 8 as a spacer to achieve the correct spread for each hanger. *Note: Spacing between the joists is irregular to accommodate the installation of railing posts.*

Place the inside joists in the hangers on the ledger and on rim joist F-1, crown up, and attach them with 1½" joist hanger nails. Be sure to use all the nail holes in the hangers. Toenail the joists to the beams and leave the joists long for final trimming.

Mark the final length of the inside joists by making a line across the tops of the joists from the end of end joist E-2. Check for square. Brace the inside joists by tacking a board across their edges for stability. Cut them to length with a circular saw.

Cut rim joist F-2 long to allow for final trimming, and nail into position with 16d galvanized nails.

To mark the remaining joists for trimming at a 45° angle, make a mark 139" from the 90° corner on end joist E-1. Make a second mark 139" from the other 90° corner along rim joist F-2. The distance between these two points should be at least 70". If necessary, move the line back until it measures 70". Regardless of the overall dimensions of your deck, this length will ensure adequate space for mounting the railing posts at the top of the stairway.

Mark the last three joists for cutting by snapping a chalk line between the marked points on end joist E-1 and rim joist F-2. Transfer the cut marks to the faces of the joists with a combination square, and cut the miters with a circular saw.

Measure, cut, and attach rim joist F-3 across the angle with deck screws.

(continued)

Drill pilot holes through the posts and into the rim joists, and attach the posts with lag screws. Note the unnotched stairway post.

INSTALL THE RAILING POSTS

Cut the railing posts (G) to size and notch the lower ends to fit around the rim joists (see Railing Detail, page 309). *Note: Many modern codes prohibit notching railing posts for installation. Check your local code and adjust this design as necessary to attach unnotched posts to the rim joists or beams.*

Clamp all but two of the posts together to lay out and cut ¾ × 3½" notches, or dadoes, for the horizontal rails. *Note: The posts at the stairway are not notched for rails.*

Cut the dadoes by making a series of parallel ¾"-deep cuts within each 3½" space, about ¼" apart, with a circular saw. Knock out the waste wood between the cuts, using a hammer. Then, chisel smooth the bottom of each dado.

To locate the railing posts on the diagonal corner, find the centerline of rim joist F-3 and measure 18" in both directions. These points are the inner faces of the railing posts and the outer faces of the stringers. Drill ¼" pilot holes through the railing posts into the rim joist, and secure the posts with lag screws.

To position the corner railing posts, measure 3" both ways from the outside corners of rim joist F-3. Predrill the posts, and use a ratchet wrench to attach them to the rim joists with lag screws.

Use the Framing Plan (page 308), and the Corner Post Detail (page 309), to locate the remaining railing posts.

INSTALL THE DECKING

If possible, buy decking boards that are long enough to span the deck.

Measure, mark, and cut the decking (H) to size, making notches to fit around the railing posts. Position the first board above the stairway, and attach it by driving a pair of deck screws into each joist.

Position the remaining decking boards so that the ends overhang the deck, leaving a ⅛" gap between the boards to allow for drainage.

Where more than one board is required to span the deck, cut the ends at 45° angles and make the joint at the center of a joist.

Snap a chalk line flush with the edge of the deck, and cut off the overhanging ends of the deck boards with a circular saw set for a 1½"-deep cut.

INSTALL THE NAILER & FACE BOARDS

Measure, mark, and cut the stairway nailer (I) to size and attach it to the rim joist with mending plates and deck screws (see Stairway Detail, page 309).

Measure, mark, and cut the face boards (J) to length, making 45° miter cuts at the right angle corners and 22½° miter cuts at the stairway corners. Attach the face boards to the rim and end joists with pairs of deck screws at 2 ft. intervals.

BUILD THE STAIRWAY

Lay out and cut the stringers (K) to size, according to the Stairway Detail (page 309). Mark the rises and runs with a framing square. Cut the notches with a circular saw, using a reciprocating saw or handsaw to finish the corners.

Measure, mark, and cut the gussets (L) to length. Assemble the stairway framework by nailing the gussets in place between the outer stringers with 16d nails.

Cut the notches for the first decking board and position it above the stairway.

Drill ⅛" pilot holes through the treads to prevent splitting. Then, attach the treads to the stringers with deck screws, using a power driver.

Clamp the long rails, mark the ends, and transfer the lines across the face of the board with a combination square to ensure a tight-fitting 22½° miter with the short rail.

Position the framework against the deck, and attach with deck screws driven through the upper gusset into the face board and nailer. Position the stringers against the bottom stairway posts, drill pilot holes through the stringers into the posts, and attach them to the posts with ½ × 4" lag screws.

Measure, mark, and cut the treads (O) to length. For the bottom treads, use a piece of railing post scrap to trace a line for the notch. Then, cut the notch with a circular saw. Attach the treads to the stringers with deck screws.

BUILD THE RAILING

Measure and cut to length the 10 ft. rails, each with one end mitered at 45°. Install the rails, using 1⅝" deck screws. Miter one end of the long rails at 45°. Leave the other end long for final trimming. Clamp each long rail in place and use a straightedge to mark cut lines at the angled corner. Transfer this line to the face of each rail, using a combination square. Remove the rails and miter-cut the ends for the angled corners at 22½°. Reposition the rails and attach them to the railing posts with 1⅝" deck screws. Measure, mark, and cut the short rails to length with one end mitered at 22½° and the other end cut square.

Fasten the ends of the short rails to the railing posts above the stairway with angle brackets. Use ⅝" galvanized screws to attach the brackets to the rails and 1⅝" deck screws to attach them to the posts. Attach them to the notched post as well, using 1⅝" deck screws.

Measure, mark, and cut the deck railing cap (Q), and install it with 3" deck screws.

Use angle brackets to attach the stairway railing pieces and angled rails. To attach the brackets to the rails, use ⅝" galvanized screws.

BUILD THE STAIRWAY RAILING

Mark and cut the stairway posts to length. Measure, mark, and cut the stairway railing caps (see Stairway Detail, page 309). Place a cedar 2 × 6 on top of the stairway posts, mark the angles for the ends, and cut to length, allowing for a 1" overhang at the end of the stairway.

Install the stairway railing caps with 3" deck screws. To cut the stairway rails, hold each one tight against the bottom of the cap and mark the ends.

Cut the rails to length so that they fit tight between the posts.To install the rails, mark the positions of the rails on the posts and attach them with angle brackets, using ⅝" screws and 1⅝" deck screws.

Angled Deck

Expand your outdoor living space with unusual flair. The design of this attractive deck makes creative use of simple geometry to take advantage of the fact that the eye finds angles and unexpected shapes visually interesting. The look is jazzed up even more with vertical balusters and beefy horizontal rails, topped with interesting decorative finials. It's a winning look all around.

The deck is also convenient. It's been designed with a straight staircase, providing direct and simple access to the backyard. Though designed specifically for construction at medium height on level ground, the deck uses heavy-duty posts, beams, joists, and footings. It's a durable deck that will definitely stand the test of time. It's also an adaptable design that could easily be altered for installation at a higher level, or on a slope.

The view from this deck is arresting, and so is the view toward it.

Cutaway View

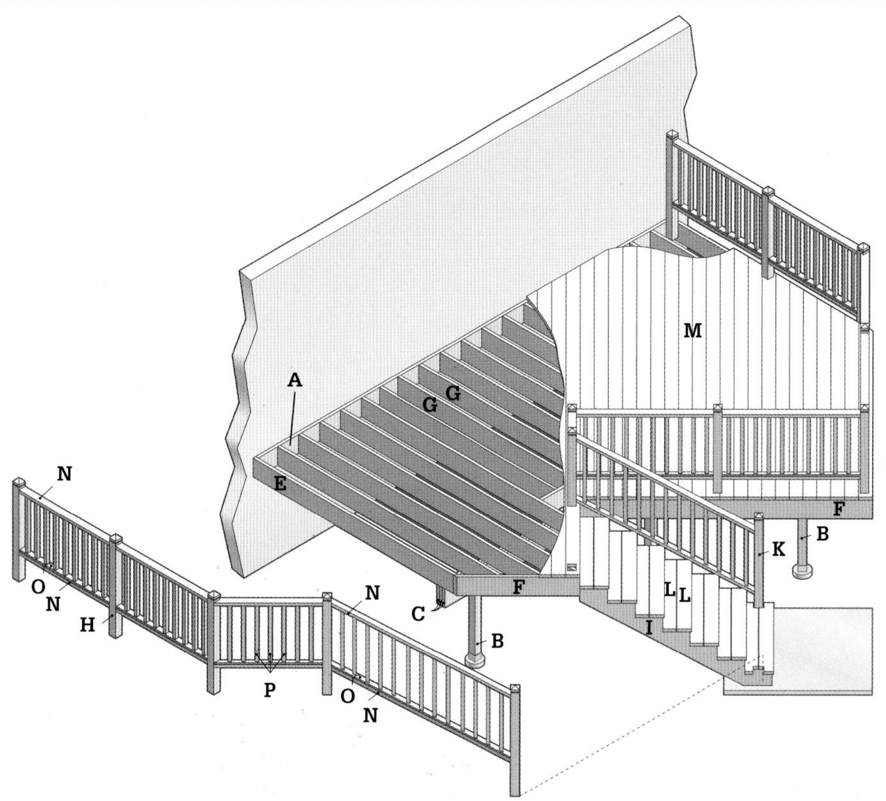

Supplies

12"-diameter footing forms (4)
J-bolts (4)
6 × 6" metal post anchors (4)
90° 2 × 10" joist hangers (22)
45° double 2 × 10" joist hangers (2)
3" galvanized deck screws
1⅝" galvanized deck screws
3" masonry screws (4)
Joist hanger nails
16d galvanized casing nails
½ × 4" lag screws and washers (60)
½ × 5" carriage bolts, washers and nuts (22)
Silicone caulk (3 tubes)
Concrete as required

Lumber List

QTY.	SIZE	MATERIAL	PART
4	2 × 10" × 20'	Trtd. lumber	Ledger (A), Primary beam boards (C)
1	2 × 10" × 18'	Trtd. lumber	Joists (G)
4	2 × 10" × 16'	Trtd. lumber	Joists (G)
5	2 × 10" × 14'	Trtd. lumber	Joists (G)
8	2 × 10" × 12'	Trtd. lumber	Joists (G)
5	2 × 10" × 10'	Trtd. lumber	Joists (G), End joists (E), Rim joists (F)
4	2 × 10" × 8'	Trtd. lumber	Secondary beam boards (D)
2	2 × 10" × 6'	Trtd. lumber	Rim joists (F)
2	6 × 6" × 8'	Trtd. lumber	Deck posts (B)
1	2 × 6" × 8'	Trtd. Lumber	Gussets (J)

QTY.	SIZE	MATERIAL	PART
6	4 × 4" × 8'	Cedar	Railing posts (H)
4	4 × 4" × 10'	Cedar	Stair railing posts (K)
3	2 × 12" × 8'	Cedar	Stringers (I)
7	2 × 6" × 8'	Cedar	Treads (L)
38	2 × 6" × 16'	Cedar	Decking (M)
8	2 × 4" × 10'	Cedar	Top & bottom rails (N)
2	2 × 4" × 8'	Cedar	Top & bottom rails (N)
11	1 × 3" × 10'	Cedar	Top & bottom inner rails (O)
20	2 × 2" × 10'	Cedar	Balusters (P)

Framing Plan

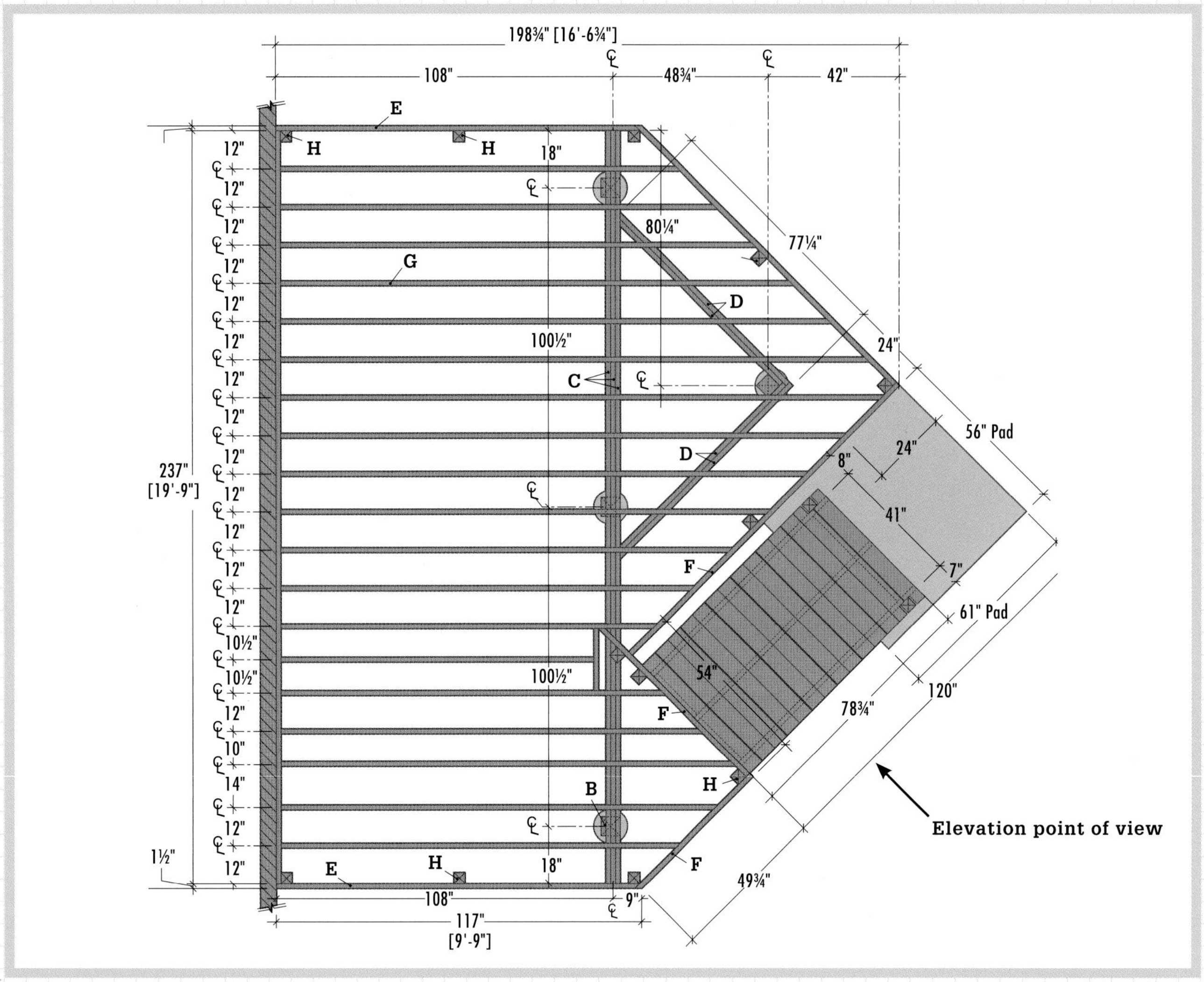

Elevation

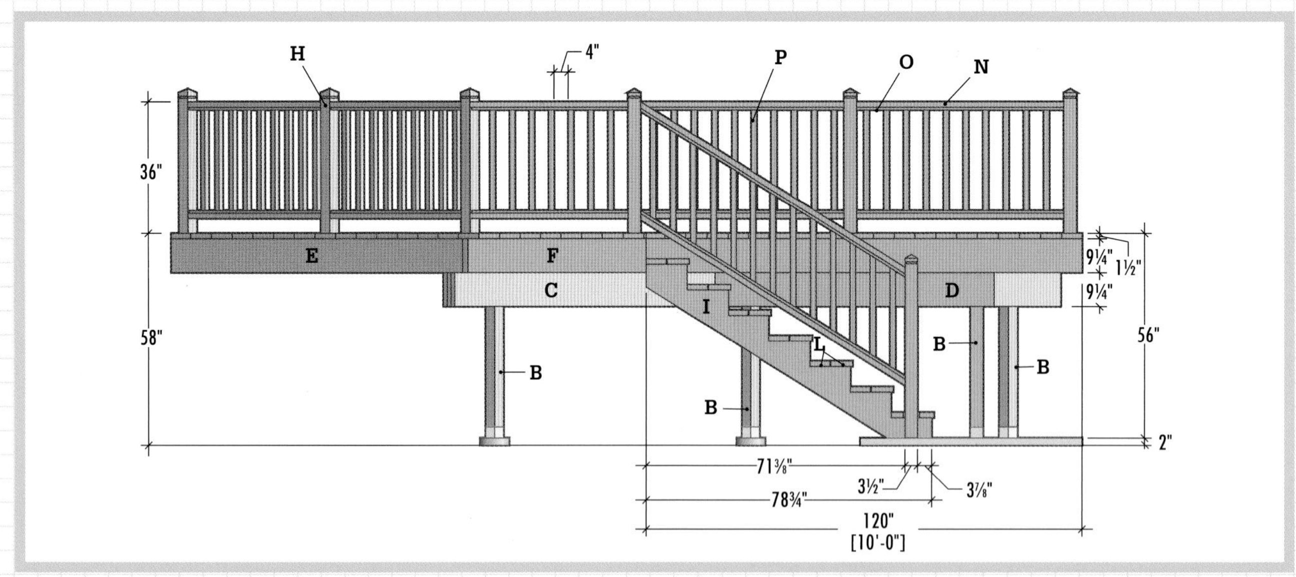

Post Detail

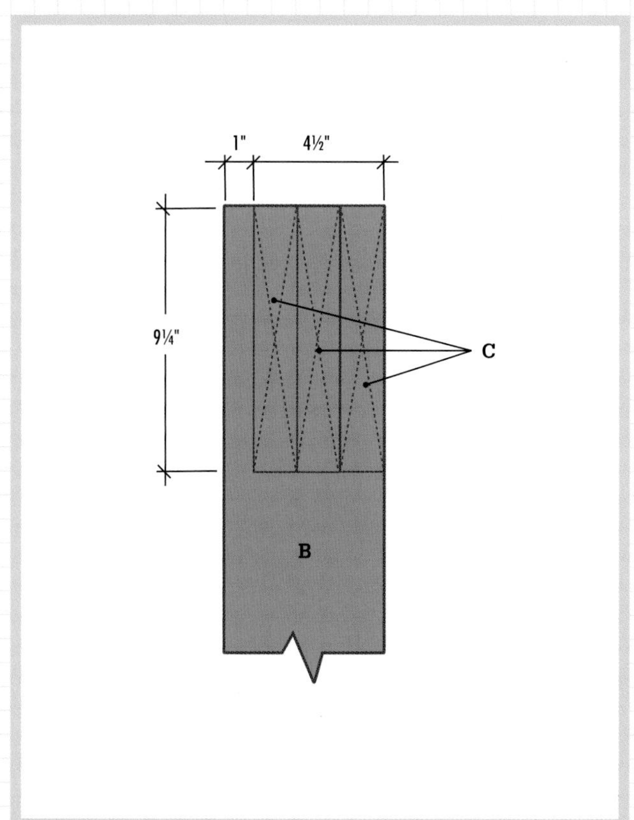

Railing Detail

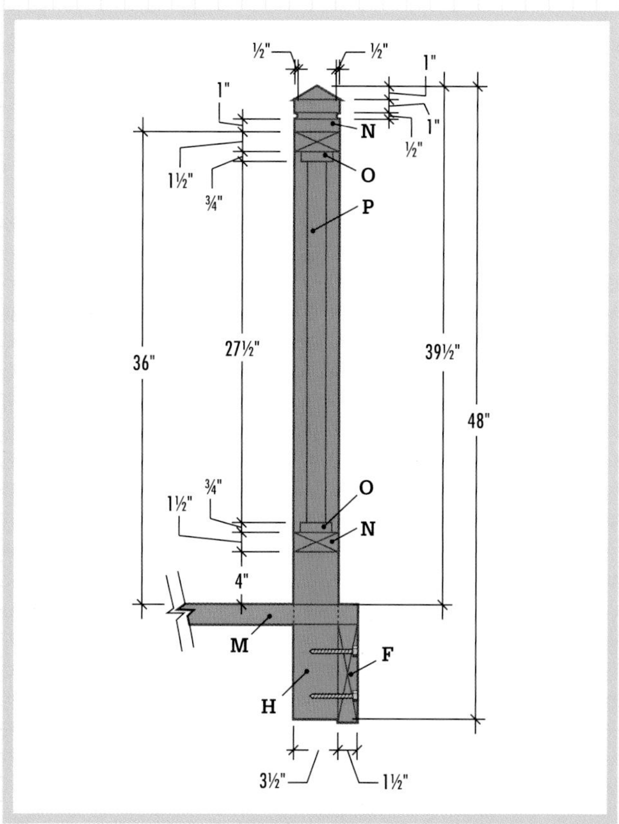

Stairway Detail

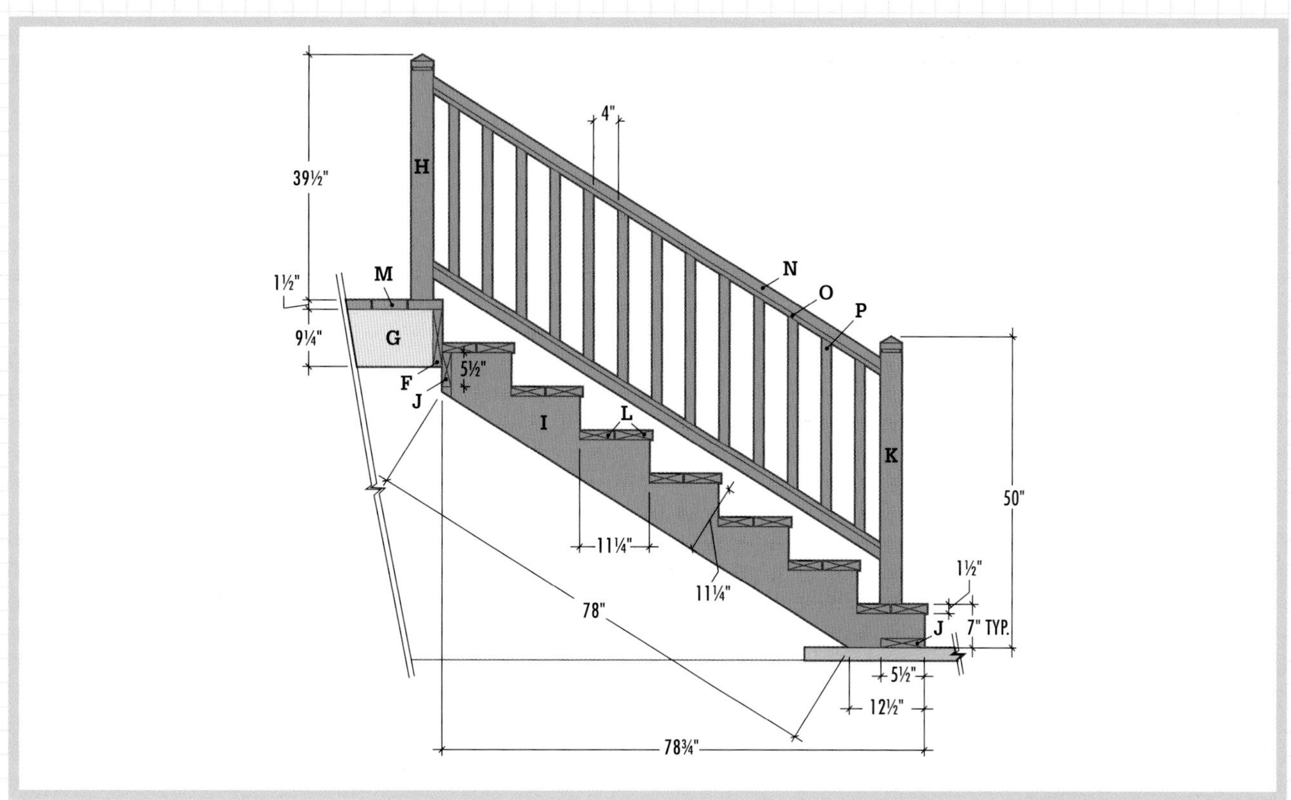

How to Build an Angled Deck

ATTACH THE LEDGER

The ledger anchors the deck and establishes a reference point for building the deck square and level.

Draw a level outline on the siding to show where the ledger and the end joists will fit against the house. Install the ledger so that the surface of the decking boards will be 1" below the indoor floor level. This height difference prevents rainwater or melted snow from seeping into the house.

Cut out the siding along the outline with a circular saw. To prevent the blade from cutting the sheathing that lies underneath the siding, set the blade depth to the same thickness as the siding. Finish the cutout with a chisel, holding the beveled side in to ensure a straight cut.

Cut galvanized flashing to the length of the cutout, using metal snips. Slide the flashing up under the siding at the top of the cutout.

Measure and cut the ledger (A) from pressure-treated lumber. Center the ledger end to end in the cutout, with space at each end for the end joist.

Brace the ledger into position under the flashing. Tack the ledger into place with galvanized nails.

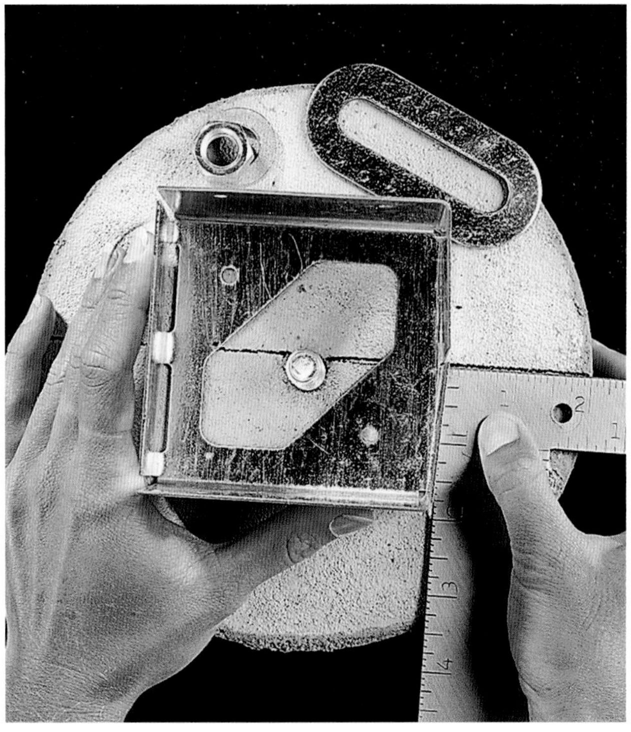

Square the post anchors to the reference lines on the top of each footing to ensure that the posts are aligned with each other.

After attaching the ledger, drop a plumb line to a convenient height and stretch mason's strings. Mark footing locations with tape, and use the 3-4-5 triangle method to verify that the strings are square.

Drill pairs of ⅜" pilot holes at 16" intervals through the ledger and into the house header joist. Counterbore each pilot hole ½", using a 1⅜" spade bit. Attach the ledger with lag screws and washers, using a ratchet wrench.

Apply a thick bead of silicone caulk between siding and flashing. Also seal lag screw heads and the cracks at the ends of the ledger.

POUR THE FOOTINGS

To locate the footings, drop a plumb bob from the end of the ledger down to a level that's comfortable for making measurements and stretching mason's strings.

Measurements for the footing centerpoints are shown on the Framing Plan (page 316). Construct, position, and install temporary 2 × 4 batterboards.

Stretch three strings perpendicular to the house; one at each end of the ledger, and one at the centerline of the footing for the secondary beam, 80¼" from the right end of the ledger.

Make sure that the strings are square to the house by using the 3-4-5 triangle method. Measuring from the point where the string meets the house, make a mark on the house at 3 ft. Then measure out along the string and make a mark at 4 ft. When the string is truly perpendicular, the diagonal line connecting the two marked points will measure 5 ft. Adjust the string on the batterboard as needed.

Stretch the fourth string between batterboards, parallel to the house, at the centerline of the primary beam.

Measure along the parallel string and use tape to mark the three centerpoints of the footings for the primary beam.

To locate the footing for the secondary beam, use tape to mark a point on the middle perpendicular string that is 48¾" out from its intersection with the parallel string.

Transfer the locations to the ground by dropping a plumb bob from each tape mark and driving a stake into the ground at each point.

Remove the mason's strings and dig holes for the footings, using a clamshell digger or power auger. Pour 2" to 3" of loose gravel into each hole for drainage. *Note: When measuring the footing size and depth, make sure you comply with your local building code, which may require flaring the base.*

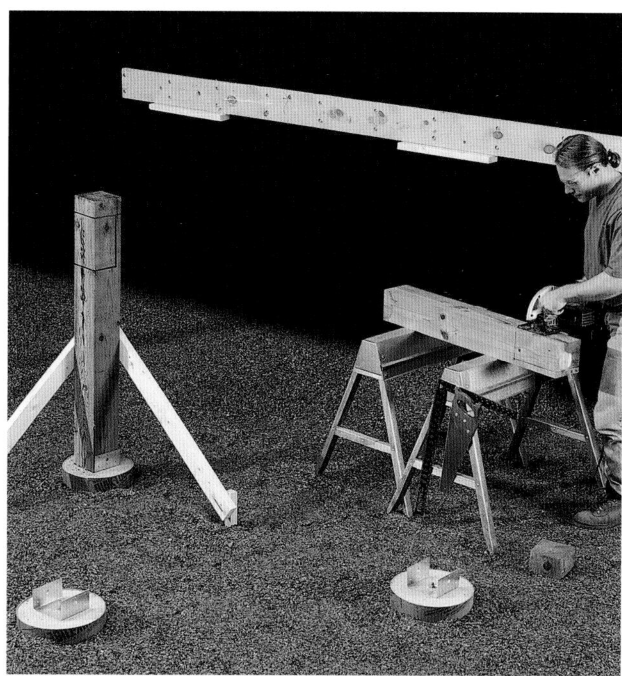

After marking the notches for the primary beam, cut out the tops of the posts with a circular saw and a handsaw.

Determine the finished post height by leveling a straight 2 × 4 from the bottom edge of the ledger.

Cut the footing forms to length using a reciprocating saw or handsaw, and insert them into the footing holes, leaving 2" of tube above ground level. Pack soil around the forms for support, and fill with concrete, tamping with a long stick or rod to eliminate any air gaps.

Screed the tops flush using a straight 2 × 4. Insert a J-bolt into the center of each footing, leaving ¾" to 1" of thread exposed. Retie the mason's strings and use the plumb bob to position the J-bolts at the exact center of each footing. Clean the bolt threads before the concrete sets.

SET THE POSTS

To provide a reference line for orienting the post anchors so the posts will be aligned with each other, lay a long, straight 2 × 4 flat across the primary beam footings, parallel to the ledger. With one edge tight against the J-bolts, draw a line across the top of each footing.

To mark the post anchor position on the footing for the secondary beam, mark a line across the footing at a 45° angle to the primary beam.

Place a metal post anchor on each footing, centering it over the J-bolt and squaring it with the reference line. Thread a nut over each J-bolt and securely tighten the post anchors in place.

(continued)

Use a ratchet wrench to tighten the lag screws that secure the primary beam to the notched posts.

Estimate the height of each post, and cut the posts slightly long to allow for final trimming. Set the posts in the anchors and tack into place with one nail.

With a level as a guide, use braces and stakes to ensure that the posts are plumb.

Determine the top of the posts by extending a straight 2 × 4 from the bottom edge of the ledger and marking a line on the posts level with the bottom of the ledger.

Outline a 4½ × 9¼" notch (see Post Detail, page 317) at the top of each of the primary-beam posts.

Remove the posts from the anchors, cut to finished height, and cut the notches using a circular saw and handsaw.

Reposition the posts with the notches facing away from the house, brace them plumb, and nail them securely to the post anchors.

INSTALL THE BEAMS

We used 20 ft. boards for the primary beam. However, for reasons of cost or availability, you may need to use a smaller size. Check with your local building inspector regarding acceptable joining hardware and techniques.

Construct the primary beam from 2 × 10" boards. Position the primary beam boards (C) so the crowns face the same direction, and fasten together with 16d galvanized nails. Drill pairs of ⅜" holes through the beam at 24" intervals, and secure with carriage bolts, washers, and nuts.

Measure, mark, and cut the beam to length. Position the beam in the post notches, crown side up. Make sure the beam is square to the ledger by measuring the diagonals; adjust the beam position so the diagonal measurements are equal.

Drill two ⅜" pilot holes through each post into the beam. Fasten with lag screws and washers, using a ratchet wrench.

Measure, mark, and cut the post for the secondary beam slightly long to allow for final trimming. Install the post in the post anchor.

Locate and mark the points where the secondary beam butts against the primary beam. Run a straight 2 × 4 across the face of the post to the primary beam in both directions. Outline the ends of the secondary beam on the face of the primary beam, and install 45° 2 × 10 double joist hangers at each point.

Measure, mark, and cut secondary beam boards (D) to length, using a circular saw.

Install the boards one at a time, verifying that they are level and attaching them with deck screws.

Drill pilot holes through the assembled beam and into the post. Counter-bore the holes ½" deep with a 1⅜" spade bit, and secure the secondary beam to the post with lag screws.

Fasten the secondary beam to the joist hangers with 10d galvanized joist hanger nails.

After the secondary beam boards have been cut, assembled, and attached with deck screws, secure the beam to the post with lag screws.

Cut the 45° angles on the ends of the joists with a circular saw.

INSTALL THE JOISTS

Measure and cut the end joists (E), leaving them several inches long for final trimming. Install by nailing into the ends of the ledger with 16d galvanized nails and toenailing to the top of the primary beam.

The joists are not all evenly spaced. Referring to the Framing Plan (page 316) use a combination square and draw the joist outlines on the face of the ledger and the top of the beams.

Install a joist hanger on the ledger at each location. Attach one flange of a hanger to one side of each outline, using joist hanger nails. Use a spacer cut from scrap 2 × 10" lumber to achieve the correct spread for each hanger, then fasten the remaining side flange with joist hanger nails. Remove the spacer and repeat the procedure to install the remaining joist hangers.

Measure, mark, and cut the joists (G), using a circular saw. Be sure to leave the joists long to accommodate final angled trimming. Place joists in hangers with crown side up and attach with nails. Align joists with the outlines on the top of the beam and toenail in place.

Pour the concrete into the staircase pad form, and screed flush, using a straight 2 × 4. *Note: Be aware that most building codes prohibit the securing of deck staircases to a solid concrete pad. You may need to pour individual footings for the staircase bottom posts.*

(continued)

Snap chalk lines along the top edges of the joists (see Framing Plan, page 316) to mark the perimeter of the deck. All the angles are either 45° or 90°. Allow for the 1½" thickness of the rim joists. Extend the cutoff lines to the faces of the joists, and make the cuts using a circular saw.

Referring to the Framing Plan and confirming the actual dimensions of your deck, measure, mark, and cut the rim joists (F) to size and attach them to the joists with deck screws.

INSTALL THE RAILING POSTS

Locate railing posts in the corners of the deck, then center the intermediate posts between them (see Framing Plan, page 316).

Cut railing posts (H) to length (see Railing Detail, page 317). Cut a 60° pyramid on the top of each post, and rout a ½ × ½" groove on all four sides 1" below the pyramid.

To install the railing posts, clamp them one at a time into position, and drill ¼" pilot holes through the rim joist into the post. Counterbore the holes ½" using a 1" spade bit, and secure the posts to the rim joists with lag screws.

Use a nailing block to support the bottom rail, and attach the baluster assembly with nails. Notice the notch where the rails join the post at a 45° angle.

Drill pilot holes through the gusset and into the concrete pad, then attach with masonry screws using a power drill.

POUR THE PAD

Determine the location of the concrete pad. Add 6" in each direction, and excavate approximately 8" deep.

Lay and tamp a 4" base of compactible gravel.

Build a form from 2 × 6 lumber, and align the inside of the form with the outside rim joists as shown in the Framing Plan, page 316. Level the form at 56" below the finished surface of the deck, to accommodate eight 7" stairway rises. Stake the form into place.

Fill the form with concrete, screed with a straight 2 × 4, and let the concrete set up overnight. *Note: Most building codes now prohibit securing a deck staircase to a solid concrete pad. You must check with your local building department to ensure your deck staircase adheres to prevailing standards and codes.*

INSTALL THE STAIRWAY

Lay out the stringers (I), according to the Stairway Detail, page 317. Notch the center stringer at the top and bottom to fit around the gussets. Mark the rises and runs with a framing square. Cut the notches with a circular saw, using a reciprocating saw or handsaw to finish the corners.

Measure, mark, and cut the gussets (J) to length. Assemble the stairway framework by nailing the gussets in place between the outer stringers with 16d nails. Turn the framework upside down and attach the center stringer by nailing through the gussets.

Position the stairway framework against the deck rim joist, and attach with deck screws driven through the top gusset into the rim joist. Drill pilot holes through the bottom gusset into the concrete pad and attach with masonry screws.

Cut the stair railing posts (K) to length. Shape the top ends. Install the posts by clamping them into place against the stringers, drilling pilot holes through the stringers into the posts, and attaching with lag screws and washers.

Measure and cut the treads (L) to length, using a circular saw. The bottom treads are notched to fit around the posts.

INSTALL THE DECKING

If possible, buy decking (M) long enough to span the deck. When joints between deck boards are necessary, center them above joists so the ends of both boards are supported.

Position the first deck board along the outer 45° rim joist, and mark the railing post locations. Cut notches for the railing posts, using a circular saw, handsaw, and chisel. Attach the board by driving two deck screws into each joist.

Cut and attach the remaining deck boards, leaving a ⅛" gap between the boards for drainage.

INSTALL THE RAILING

The railing for this deck is assembled in sections and then installed. The balusters are first fastened between the inner rails, then the baluster assembly is cut to exact length and attached to the outer rails.

Verify the measurements between your railing posts. Measure, mark, and cut the top and bottom rails (N) to length.

Install the bottom rails by drilling angled ⅛" pilot holes into the posts at the ends, and attaching with deck screws. *Note: Where the railings meet the posts at a 45° angle, you'll need to notch the ends to fit.*

Measure, mark, and cut the top and bottom inner rails (O), leaving them several inches long for final trimming.

Measure, mark, and cut the deck balusters (P) to length.

Assemble each railing section by positioning the balusters between the top and bottom inner rails, drilling ⅛" pilot holes, and attaching them with deck screws. Trim the section to final length with an equal space at each end.

Position the baluster assembly on the bottom rail and nail in place.

Position the top rail above the baluster assembly, drill pilot holes through the top inner rail into the top rail, and attach with deck screws from below.

To determine the angle for the ends of the stairway rails and balusters, as well as the length of the inner and outer stairway rails, hold a straight 2 × 4 across one pair of stairway posts. With the top edge of the 2 × 4 crossing each post at the routed groove, mark the angle on the back of the board. *Note: The angle will be approximately 32°, but you'll get the best fit by marking it from your actual railing posts.*

Measure, mark, and cut the top and bottom rails to length, with the ends angled to fit against the posts. Install the bottom rails.

Cut inner rails and balusters to size with mitered ends.

Build the stairway railing assemblies using the same procedures as used for the deck railing assemblies, taking care that the space between balusters is 4" or less.

Install the stairway railing assemblies by positioning them on the bottom rails and nailing with 6d casing nails.

Install the stairway top rails by positioning them above the railing assemblies, drilling pilot holes through the top inner rails, and driving deck screws from below.

Drive deck screws up through the top inner rail to attach the top rail to the baluster assembly.

Square Platform Deck

A freestanding platform deck is a low-maintenance option for creating an outdoor floor. Because it can be constructed virtually anywhere, in almost any size, a platform deck works in nearly any landscape. The wood can be left natural, stained, or painted to blend with your house and other landscape elements.

You'll be able to build this deck over a single weekend. It uses lumber in standard lengths, so you won't need to do a lot of cutting. In addition, this deck uses precast concrete footings rather than poured footings. These precast footings are available at home improvement centers and lumberyards.

This 12 × 12-ft. deck rests on a 10 × 10-ft. base formed by 18 concrete footings arranged in three rows of six footings each. Joists are secured in slots in the tops of the footings, simplifying the building process.

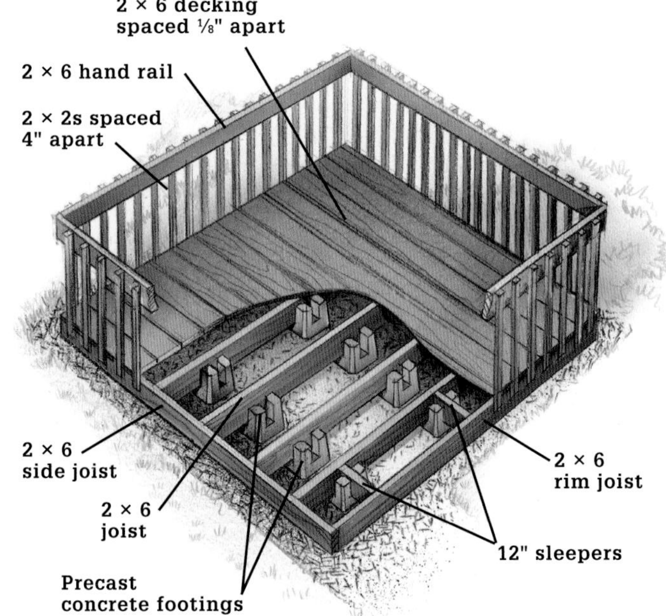

Framing Plan

Construction Materials

Precast concrete footings (18)
12-ft. 2 × 6s (38)
2 lbs. galvanized 3" deck screws

For optional railing:
42-in. 2 × 2s (75)
12-ft. 2 × 6s (4)

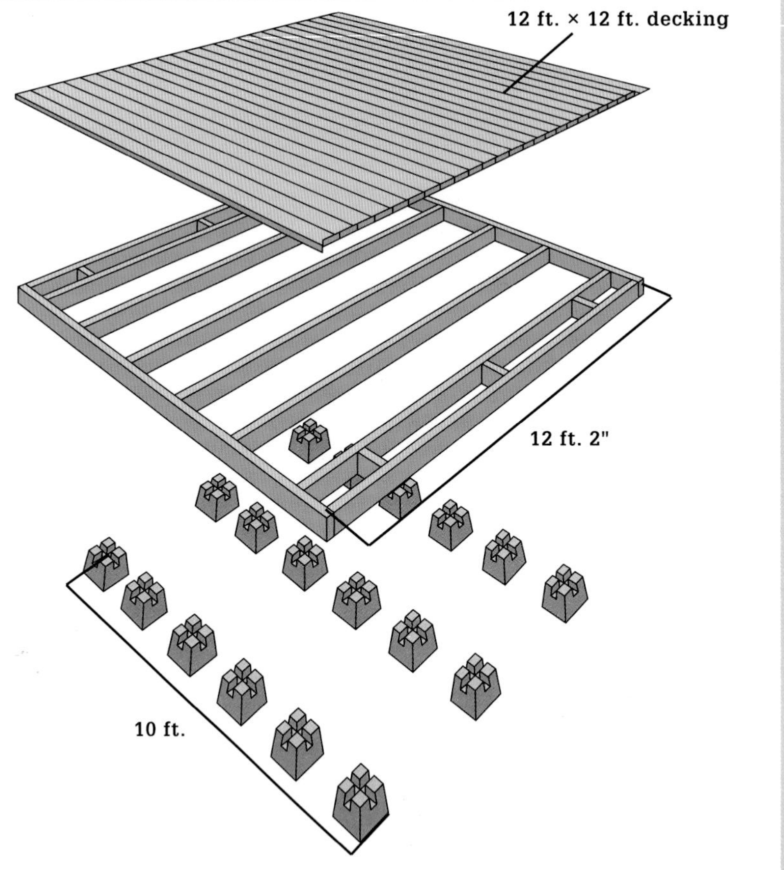

How to Build a Platform Deck

INSTALL & LEVEL THE FOOTINGS

Measure a 10 × 10-ft. area for the deck foundation, and mark the corners with stakes.

Position a footing at each corner, then measure from corner to corner, from the center of each footing. Adjust until the diagonal measurements are equal, which means the footings are square.

Place a 2 × 6 across the corner footings for the back row, setting it in the center slots. Check this joist with a level, then add or remove soil beneath footings as necessary to level it.

Center a footing between these corner footings. Use a level to recheck the joist, then add or remove soil beneath the center footing, if necessary. Remove the joist.

Repeat the process to set and level the footings for the front row.

Position the remaining 12 footings at equal intervals, aligned in three rows. Position a 2 × 6 from the front row of footings to the back, and adjust soil as necessary to bring the interior footings into alignment with the front and back rows.

INSTALL THE JOISTS

Seal the ends of each 2 × 6 with wood sealer/protectant and let them dry completely.

Center a 12-ft. joist across each row of footings. Using a level, check the joists once again and carefully adjust the footings if necessary.

ADD THE SIDE JOISTS & RIM JOISTS

Line up a 2 × 6 flush against the ends of the joists along the left side of the deck, with the ends extending equally past the front and back joists.

Attach the side joist by driving a pair of deck screws into each joist.

Repeat this process to install the right side joist.

At the front of the deck, position a 2 × 6 rim joist flush between the ends of the side joists, forming a butt joint on each end.

Attach the rim joist to the side joists by driving a pair of deck screws through the faces of the side joists, into the ends of the rim joist.

Repeat to install the other rim joist.

Position the corner footings and the center footing for the back joist. Remove or add soil beneath the footings to level them.

Position the remaining footings and insert the joists. Check to make sure the framework is level, and adjust as needed.

POSITION THE SLEEPERS

Measure and cut six 2 × 6 sleepers to fit between the front and back joists and the rim joists. Seal the cut ends with wood sealer/protectant and let them dry completely.

Position one sleeper in each row of footings, between the first joist and the rim joist. Attach each sleeper by driving a pair of galvanized deck screws through each of the joists and into the sleeper.

SQUARE UP THE FRAME

Once the framing is complete, measure the diagonals from corner to corner. Compare the measurements to see if they are equal.

Adjust the framing as necessary by pushing it into alignment. Have someone help you hold one side of the framework while you push against the other.

LAY THE DECKING

Seal the 2 × 6 decking boards with wood sealer/protectant and let them dry. Seal all exposed framing members as well.

Lay a 2 × 6 over the surface of the deck, perpendicular to the joists and flush with the rim joist. Secure this board with deck screws.

Repeat to install the rest of the decking. Use a framing square to set a ⅛" space between boards. Rip cut the last decking board if needed.

Install the front and back rim joists between the ends of the side joists, securing them with pairs of deck screws.

Position the sleepers in the slots of the footings, then attach them to both joists with pairs of deck screws.

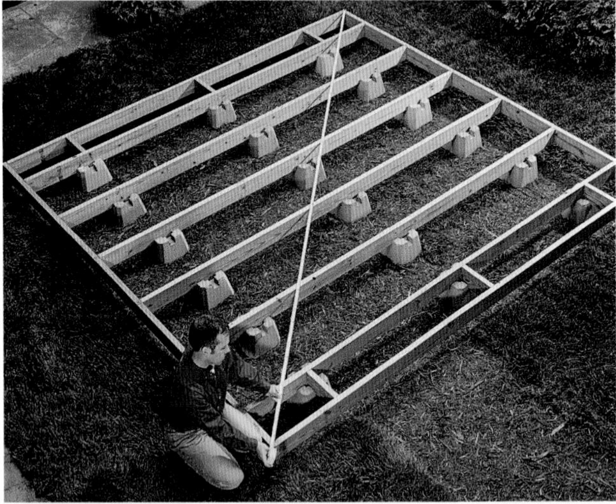

After the framing is completed, measure the diagonals and adjust the frame until it's square.

Install the decking by driving a pair of screws into each joist. Use a framing square to leave a ⅛" space between boards.

Variation: Adding a Railing ▸

Although this platform deck rests low to the ground, you may want to add a hand rail around two or three sides of the deck, especially if the deck will be used by young children or an elderly person. For each side of the deck to which you're adding railings, you'll need 25 2 × 2s, 42" long.

The wooden railing shown here is just one of many different railing styles to consider. For more railing options and material choices, see the Deck Railings chapter, pages 160 to 191. Or, you could install fixed benches with backrests, which would add functionality to the deck and double as railings.

Gang together the 2 × 2s, then drill a pair of pilot holes into the beveled ends, and a single pilot hole in the opposite ends.

PREPARE THE BALUSTERS

Place the 2 × 2s flush together, adjust them so the ends are even, and draw a pair of straight lines, 3" apart, across each board, 1½" above the beveled end. Repeat the process and draw a single line 2¾" from the top of the other end. Using the lines as guides, drill pilot holes into the 2 × 2s.

Apply wood sealer/protectant to the ends of the 2 × 2s.

Attach the 2 × 2s to the side joists, leaving a 4" gap between them.

ATTACH THE BALUSTERS

Position a 2 × 2 flush with the bottom of the joist, then clamp it in place to use as a placement guide.

Position the corner 2 × 2s against the side joists, beveled end down, 4" in from the corner. Check for plumb, then drive deck screws through the pilot holes.

Attach the remaining 2 × 2s for each side, spacing them 4" apart.

ATTACH THE HAND RAILING

Hold a 12-ft. 2 × 6 that forms the top of the railing in place, behind the installed 2 × 2s.

Attach the 2 × 2s to the 2 × 6 top rails by driving deck screws through the pilot holes.

Connect the top rails at the corners using pairs of deck screws.

Finish the railing by applying a coat of wood sealer, according to the manufacturer's directions.

Level the 2 × 6 railing behind the 2 × 2s, then attach it by driving screws through the pilot holes.

Multi-level Deck

This multilevel deck is ideal where you need access from different areas and levels of your home. The size and shape also provide many functional spaces for entertaining, privacy, or relaxation, as well as unobtrusive storage areas for recreational accessories.

The lower deck in this plan has been built around a patio. If you want this as a deck area instead, simply extend the lower ledger board across the house and run joists between the ledger and the center beam. You can remove the spa area from the plans and adjust the shape of the lower deck if you wish, too.

With some modification, this design also can help you make use of an otherwise unusable steep slope. However, you may need to eliminate or reduce the storage and small deck area underneath the landing. Some excavation of the existing slope area might also be required.

A large, multi-level deck such as this is ideal where you want to include many different recreation areas, such as an outdoor dining spot, a reading corner, and a spa retreat. Add a privacy fence for an even more secluded tubbing experience.

Cutaway View: Lower Deck & Tub

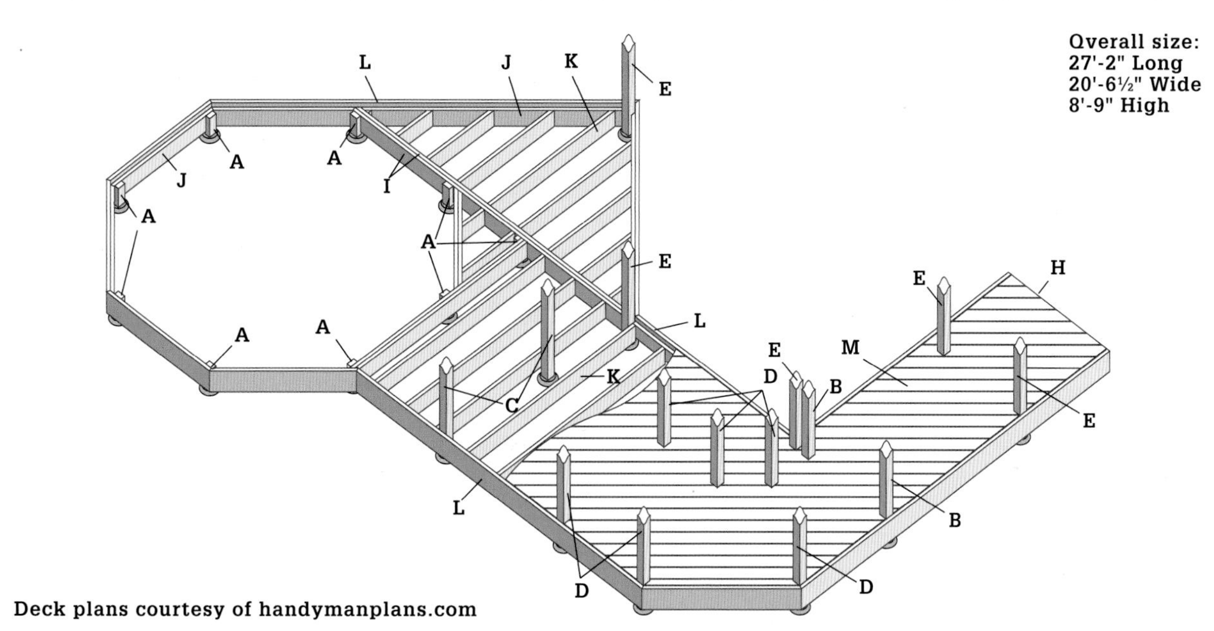

Deck plans courtesy of handymanplans.com

Supplies

2 × 6" metal joist hangers (138)
2 × 6" double metal joist hangers (2)
6 × 6" metal post anchors (28)
16d galvanized nails (3½", 25 lbs.)
10d galvanized nails (3", 30 lbs.)
3" galvanized screws (15 lbs.)
60 lb. dry concrete in bags (62)
½ × 6" galvanized carriage bolts, washers, and nuts (26)
½ × 4" galvanized lag screws (26)
½ × 6" galvanized lag screws (12)
½ × 4" galvanized expansion bolts (8)
Weather-resistant hinges* (4)
Weather-resistant door latch* (2)
Metal ledger flashing (34 ft.)
Decorative post cap* (19)
*optional

Lumber List

QTY.	SIZE	MATERIAL	PART
18	6 × 6" × 8'	Trtd. lumber	Post (A, B, C, D, F, G)
5	6 × 6" × 10'	Trtd. lumber	Post (E)
40	2 × 6" × 4'	Trtd. lumber	Rim joist (J), joist (K)
52	2 × 6" × 6'	Trtd. lumber	Beam (I), rim joist (J), joist (K), tread (O), kick plate (T)
27	2 × 6" × 8'	Trtd. lumber	Ledger (H), beam (I), rim joist (J), joist (K), cross bracing (N)
12	2 × 6" × 10'	Trtd. lumber	Ledger (H), rim joist (J), joist (K)
2	2 × 6" × 12'	Trtd. lumber	Beam (I)
76	2 × 6" × 16'	Trtd. lumber	Decking (M)
1	2 × 6" × 18'	Trtd. lumber	Rim joist (J)
6	2 × 8" × 4'	Trtd. lumber	Face board (L)
5	2 × 8" × 8'	Trtd. lumber	Face board (L)

QTY.	SIZE	MATERIAL	PART
3	2 × 8" × 10'	Trtd. lumber	Face board (L)
1	2 × 10" × 6'	Trtd. lumber	Stair hanger (U)
2	2 × 12" × 8'	Trtd. lumber	Stair face board (S)
1	2 × 12" × 10'	Trtd. lumber	Stair face board (S)
3		Trtd. lumber	7-tread precut Stair stringer (Q)
4		Trtd. lumber	5-tread precut Stair stringer (R)
16	2 × 4" × 4'	Trtd. lumber	Top & bottom rails (V)
8	2 × 4" × 6'	Trtd. lumber	Top & bottom rails (V)
2	2 × 4" × 8'	Trtd. lumber	Top & bottom stair rails (W)
2	2 × 4" × 10'	Trtd. lumber	Top & bottom stair rails (W)
12	1 × 8" × 6'	Trtd. lumber	Riser (P)
68	2 × 12" × 10'	Trtd. lumber	Balusters (X)

Cutaway View: Upper Deck & Landing

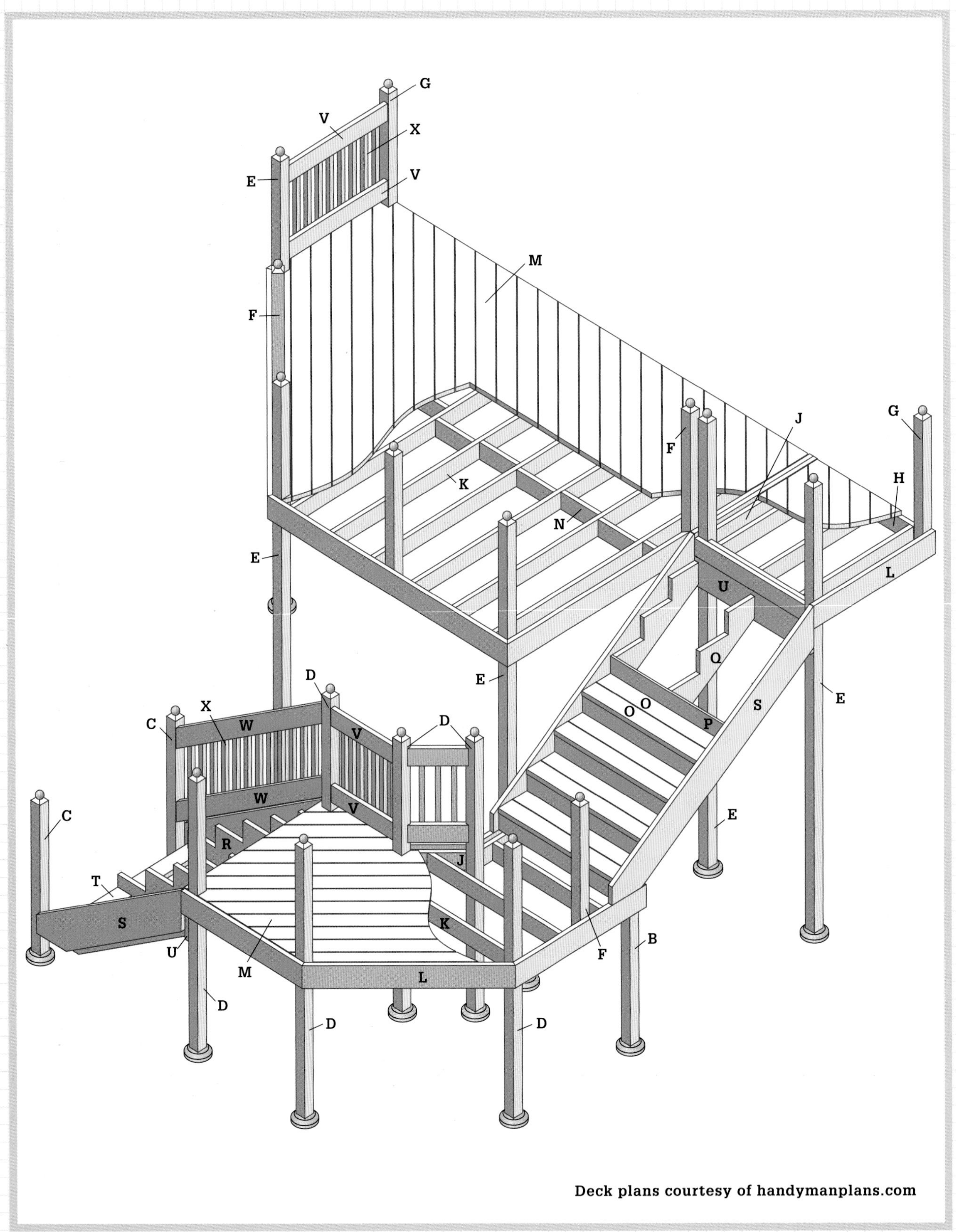

Lower Deck Framing Plan

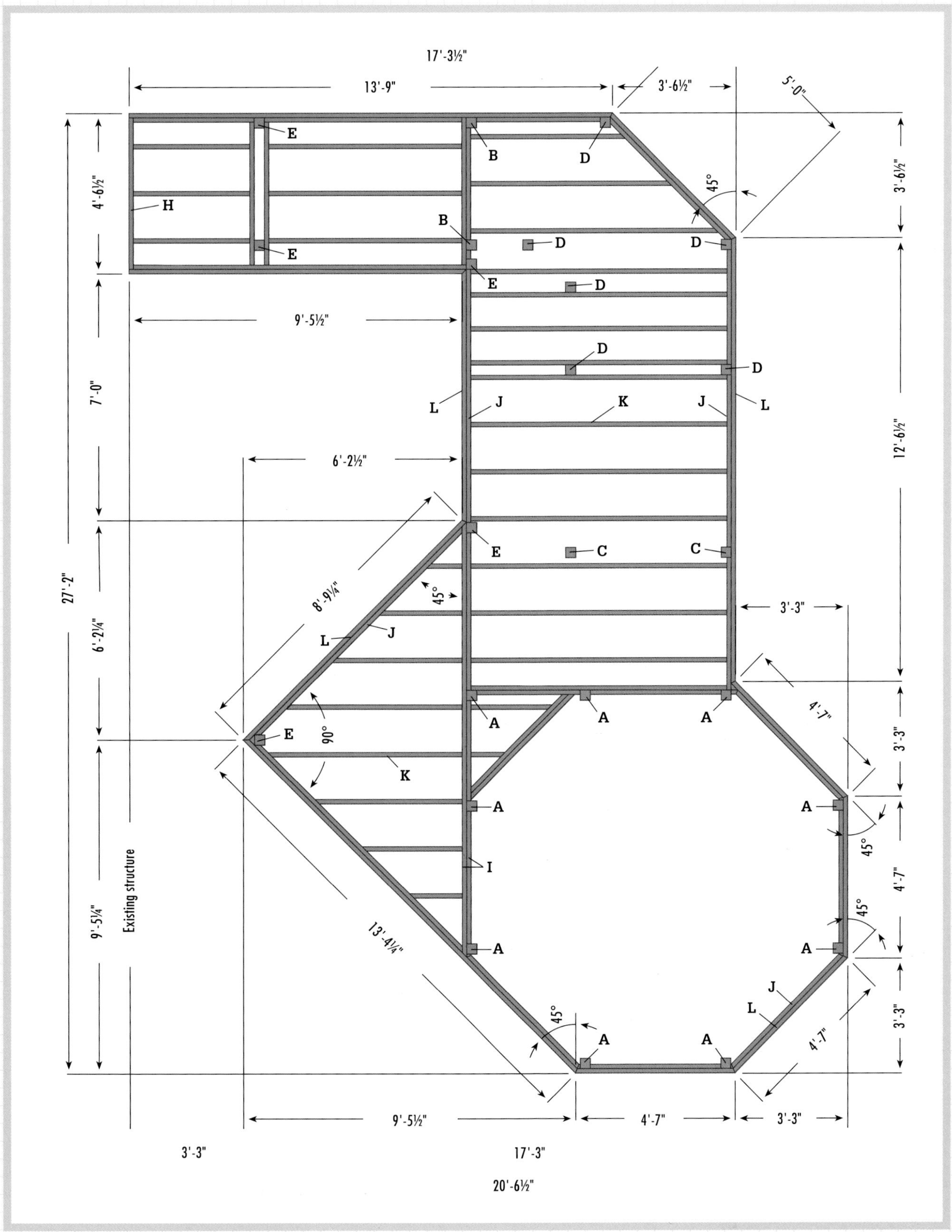

Upper Deck Framing Plan

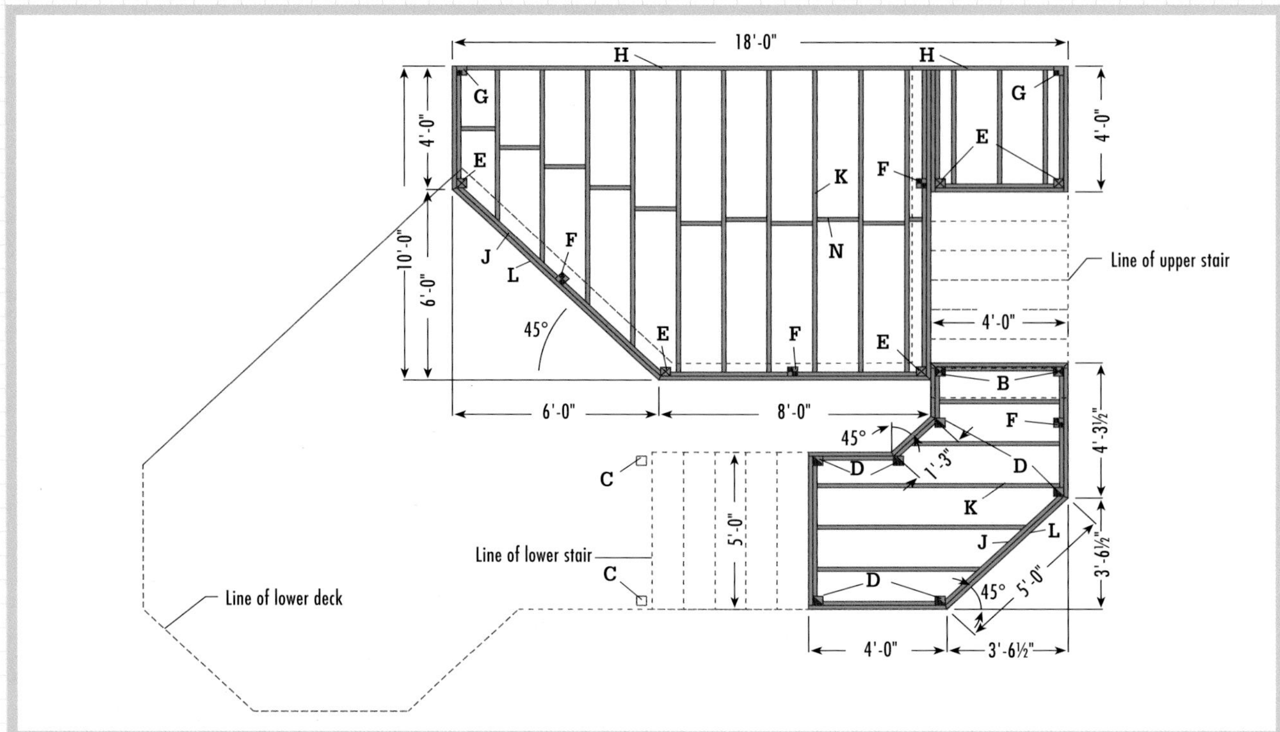

Front Elevation

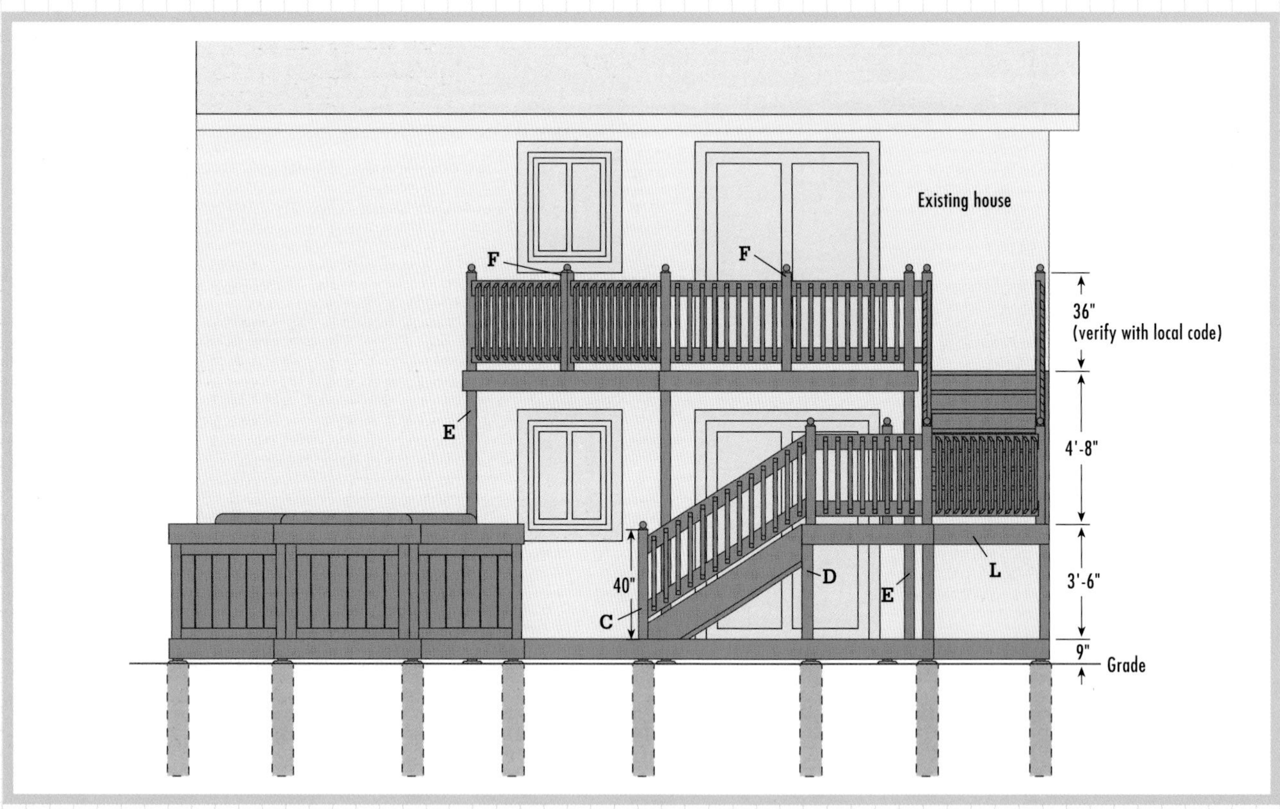

Post Location Plan

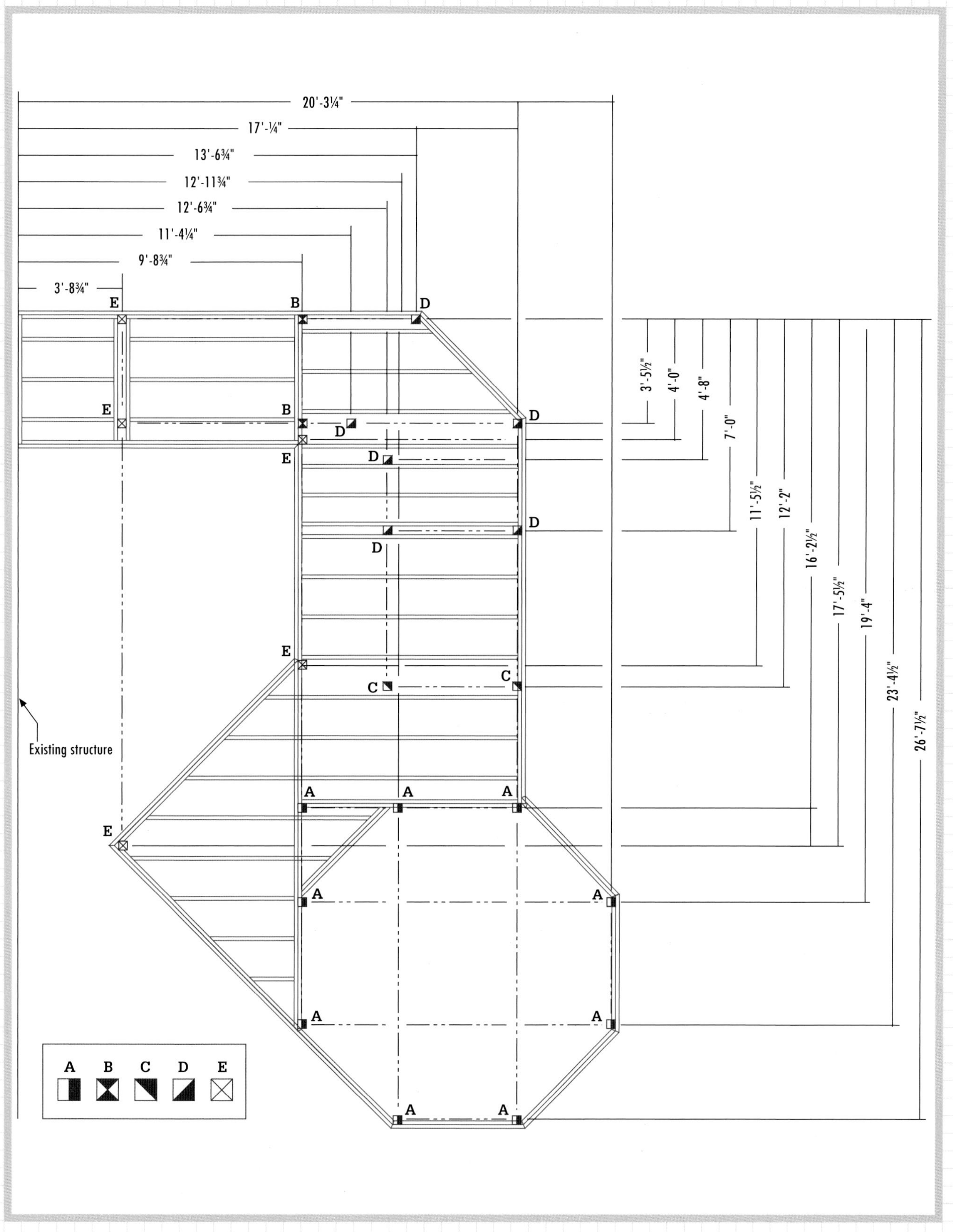

Lower Stair Detail

Upper Stair Detail

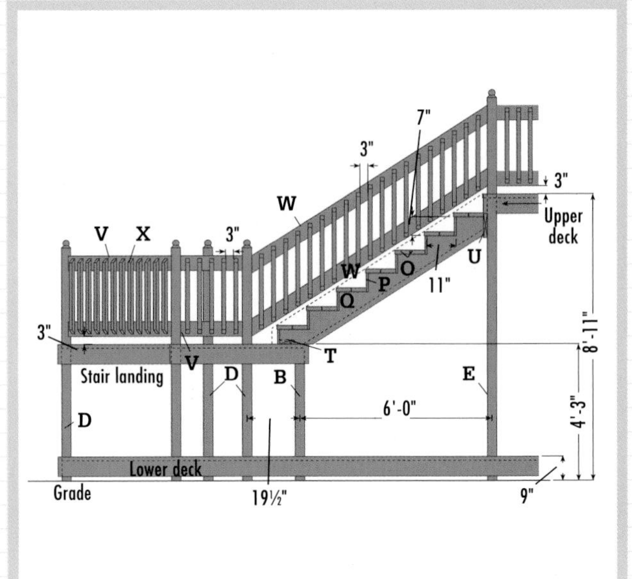

How to Build a Multi-level Deck

ATTACH THE LEDGERS

Draw a level outline on the siding in both locations to show where the ledgers and the end joists will fit against the house (See the Lower Deck Framing Plan and Upper Deck Framing Plan, pages 331 and 332). Position the top edge of each ledger so that the surface of the decking boards will be 1" below the indoor floor level. This height difference prevents rainwater or melted snow from seeping into the house.

Cut out the siding along the outline with a circular saw. To keep the blade from cutting too deeply into the sheathing underneath the siding, set the blade depth the same thickness as the siding. Finish the corners of the cutouts with a hammer and chisel, holding the beveled side in to ensure a straight cut.

Install new building felt over the existing felt exposed by siding removal. Cut galvanized flashing to the length of each cutout using metal snips, and slide it up under the siding.

Measure and cut the ledgers to length from pressure-treated 2 × 6 lumber. Center the ledgers in the cutouts, underneath the flashing, with space at the ends for the end joists. Brace ledgers in place, fastening them temporarily to the house with 3" deck screws.

Drill pairs of ⅜" pilot holes through the ledger and sheathing and into the house header joist at 16" intervals. Counterbore each pilot hole ½" deep, using a 1⅜" spade bit. Attach the ledgers to the wall with ½ × 4" lag screws and washers, using an impact driver or a ratchet wrench.

Apply a thick bead of silicone caulk between the siding and the flashing. Also seal the lag screw heads and any gaps between the wall and the ledgers.

POUR THE FOOTINGS

Referring to the Post Location Plan on page 333, stretch mason's strings across the site, using 2 × 4 batterboards. Check the mason's strings for square, using the 3-4-5 triangle method. Adjust as necessary until they are square. Measure along the strings to locate the centerpoints of the footings. Mark the locations with tape.

Drop a plumb bob at the tape locations and drive stakes into the ground to mark the centerpoints of the footings. Remove the mason's strings and dig holes for the footings, using a clamshell digger or power auger. Make certain the hole sizes and depths comply with your local building code, which may require flaring the footings at their base.

Pour 2" to 3" of loose gravel into each hole for drainage. Cut the footing tube forms to length, long enough so they will extend 2" above grade, using a reciprocating saw or handsaw. Insert the forms into the holes and backfill with soil. Lay out and mark the location for a concrete pad within the hexagonal spa area (see Lower Deck Framing Plan, page 331). Excavate and build forms for the pad.

Fill the tube forms with concrete in stages, tamping the concrete at each stage with a long stick to eliminate any air pockets. Screed the tops flush with a flat 2 × 4. Retie the mason's strings and drop a plumb bob to establish centerpoint of the footing. Insert a J-bolt into each footing, leaving ¾" to 1" of thread exposed. Clean the bolt threads before the concrete sets.

Pour concrete into the spa pad form and tamp to remove air pockets. Screed the top flush with the form (no other finishing techniques are necessary for this pad) and allow the pad to cure. *Note: Some codes do not allow securing a portion of a deck connected to stairs to a concrete pad. Check your local building code.*

SET THE POSTS

Lay a long, straight 2 × 4 flat across pairs of footings. With one edge tight against the J-bolts, draw a reference line across each footing. Do this in both directions for pairs of footings where necessary.

Place a metal post anchor on each footing, center it over the J-bolt, and square it with the reference line. Thread a nut over each J-bolt and tighten each of the post anchors in place.

Cut deck support posts A through E to their approximate length, adding several inches for final trimming (see Elevation, page 332, and Upper Stair Detail, page 334). Place the posts in the anchors and tack them into place with one nail each.

With a level as a guide, plumb the posts, using braces and stakes to hold posts B through E plumb. Once the posts are plumb, finish nailing them to the anchors.

INSTALL THE BEAM, RIM JOISTS & FACE BOARDS FOR THE LOWER & UPPER DECKS

Using a string, water, or laser level, mark the top edge of the lower deck rim joists and center beam locations on posts A and at the footing ends of appropriate posts B through E (see Lower Deck Framing Plan, page 331). Make a mark level with the top edge of the lower ledger.

Mark posts E for the upper deck rim joists, using the top edge of the upper ledger as the reference.

Measure, cut, and install rim joists for the upper deck from pressure-treated 2 × 6 lumber. Do this one piece at a time to ensure accurate measuring. Cut 45° miters at the ends of the pieces that meet posts at the 45° corners. Attach rim joists to the post faces, using 3½" deck screws.

Measure, cut, and install face boards from pressure-treated 2 × 8 lumber. Do this one piece at a time, as with the rim joists. Cut 22½° miters at the ends of the pieces that meet at the 45° corners. Attach face board pieces that fit flush with the post faces using ½ × 6" carriage bolts, washers, and nuts. Attach pieces that don't fit flush with the post faces at the 45° corners with ½ × 4" lag screws and washers. Make sure to stagger the bolt and/or screw locations on posts where two pieces attach. Attach the face boards to the rim joists with pairs of 3" deck screws driven at 24" intervals.

Build the center beam from doubled 2 × 8 pressure-treated lumber. Measure, cut, and attach it to the posts with ½ × 8" carriage bolts, washers, and nuts. Cut 45° miters in the ends of the pieces that will meet the rim joist face at a non-perpendicular junction.

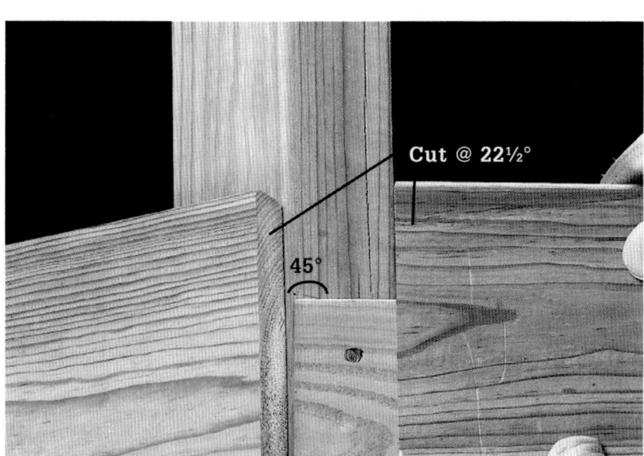

Cut 45° miters at the ends of rim joists that meet posts at a 45° corner. Cut 22½° miters at the ends of face boards that meet at a 45° corner.

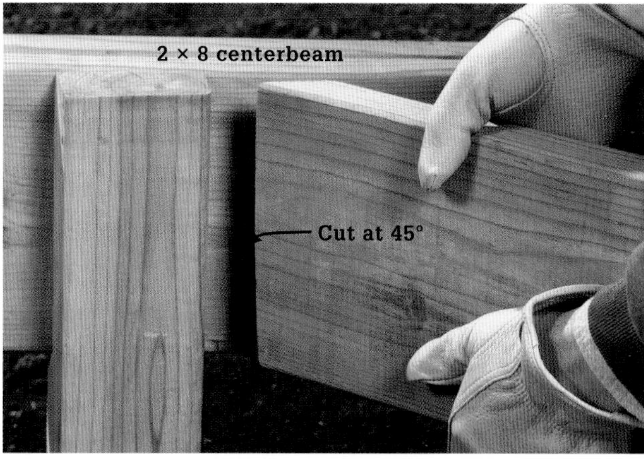

Cut a 45°-miter at the ends of rim joists and face boards that meet the center beam of the lower deck at a 45° corner.

Measure, cut, and install the rim joists and face boards for the lower deck in the same manner you followed for the upper deck. However, cut 45° miters in the ends of the pieces that will meet the center beam face at a non-perpendicular junction. Cut the tops of posts A flush with the top edges of the rim joists and center beam using a reciprocating saw.

INSTALL THE RIM JOISTS & FACE BOARDS FOR THE LANDING

Measure 42" up from the top of the lower deck rim joists attached to posts B and D and mark the posts (see Upper Stair Detail, page 334).

Measure, cut, and attach the landing rim joists, aligning their top edges with the 42" marks, and add the face boards in the same manner you followed for the lower and upper decks. Cut the tops of posts B flush with the top edges of the rim joists.

INSTALL THE JOISTS

Measure and mark the outlines for joist locations spaced 16" on center on the ledger and rim joists of the upper deck (see Upper Deck Framing Plan, page 332). The spacing of the joists measured along the 45° angled rim joist will be 22⅝" on-center. Measure and mark the outlines for joist locations for the stair landing.

Measure and mark the outlines for joist locations spaced 16" on center on the ledger, rim joists, and center beam of the lower deck (see Lower Deck Framing Plan, page 331). The joist spacing will be 22⅝" on-center measured on the 45° angled rim joist.

Attach the joist hangers to the ledgers, rim joists, and center beam with 10d joist hanger nails, using a scrap 2 × 6 as a spacer to maintain the correct spread for each hanger. Use 45° joist hangers of the proper direction where joists meet the angled rim joists.

Measure, mark, and cut 2 × 6 pressure-treated lumber for the joists.

Insert the joists into the hangers with crown side up, and attach at both ends with 10d joist hanger nails. Be sure to drive a nail in every hole in the hangers. Add cross bracing for the joists in the upper deck as necessary.

INSTALL THE RAILING POSTS

Cut railing posts F and G to their approximate length, adding several inches for final trimming.

Clamp each post in place to the inner face of the rim joist. Drill pilot holes for two ½ × 6" carriage bolts through the rim joist and the post. Counterbore the holes in the rim joist ½"-deep, using a 1⅜" spade bit. Attach the posts to the rim joists with the carriage bolts, washers, and nuts.

INSTALL THE DECKING

Position a deck board along the outer 45° rim joist on the upper deck, overhanging the rim joists at both ends. Mark the railing post locations.

Cut notches for the railing posts, using a jigsaw. Test fit the board: its leading edge should be flush with the front face of the 45° rim joist. Adjust as necessary. Attach the board by driving two deck screws into each joist.

Cut and attach the remaining deck boards, again letting ends overhang the rim joists. Leave a ⅛" gap between the boards for drainage. Cut notches for railing posts.

Mark and snap lines across the overhanging board ends that are aligned with the outer faces of the rim joists. Set the depth of the circular saw blade

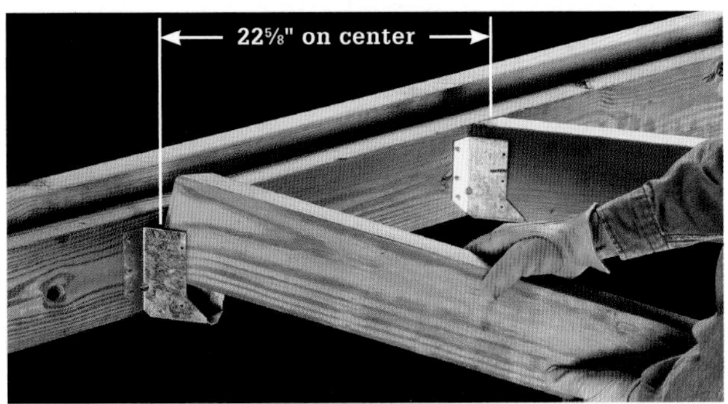

Use 45°-angled joist hangers where joists meet the angled rim joists. Space joists 22⅝" on center.

Attach the railing posts to the upper deck rim joists with carriage bolts, washers, and nuts. *Note: check your local codes; most codes now prohibit notched railing posts. You may have to adjust the plans to mount the post entirely on the outside of the rim joist.*

⅛" deeper than the thickness of the decking and cut along the line, and complete cuts at corners or walls with a jigsaw, and a hammer and sharp chisel. Remove all braces and stakes supporting posts. Install the decking on the stair landing and lower deck following the same methods.

BUILDING THE STAIRS

Cut the stair stringers for the upper stairs to length and use a framing square to mark the rise and run for each step. (See Upper Stair Detail, page 334. If you need to alter the plans to accommodate the height of your deck, see pages 146 to 149.) Cut the notches and the angles at the ends of the stringers with a circular saw, then complete the cuts at corners with a jigsaw.

Measure and cut a stair hanger and attach it to the posts E at the stair location with deck screws. Its top edge should butt against the bottom edge of the rim joist.

Position the middle stringer so the bottom end is flat against the middle of the stair landing and the upper end is against the stair hanger. Mark where the front edge of the stringer meets the landing. Measure and cut a 2 × 6 kick plate to fit between the outer stringers. Align the front edge of the kick plate with the mark so the board is parallel to the near edge of the landing. Fasten with deck screws. Cut a notch for the 2 × 6 kick plate in the middle stringer.

Position each outer stringer against one end of the kick plate and against the stair hanger. Drive a screw through each stringer into the kick plate. Square each stringer to the hanger, using a framing square, and mark its position. Attach the upper ends of the stringers to the hanger with angle brackets. Position the middle stringer evenly between the outer stringers. Attach it to the stair hanger with a skewable joist hanger, and to the kick plate using deck screws driven at an angle.

Measure and cut riser boards from pressure treated 1 × 8 lumber. Attach the riser boards to the stringers with two deck screws per stringer. Drill pilot holes for the screws at the ends of the boards.

Measure and cut two 2 × 6 stair treads for each step. Their ends should be flush with the outer faces of the stringers. Attach the treads with two deck screws per tread at each stringer, leaving a ⅛" gap between treads. The back tread should touch the riser on each step.

Measure, layout, cut, and install the lower stairs following the same methods.

INSTALL THE RAILING

For railing installation, refer to the Upper Stair Detail on page 334. For additional railing installation techniques, refer to pages 161 to 191.

ENCLOSE THE SPA & STORAGE AREAS

Install the spa on the pad and connect it to the utilities following the manufacturer's instructions. Have a professional do the installation if you are not comfortable working on plumbing, wiring, or gas systems.

After the spa is installed, follow the methods on pages 266 to 269 for enclosing the framing. You can use the same basic techniques to create storage enclosures beneath the stairway landings.

Cut notches in the decking boards that meet the railing posts. Test fit the board: the leading edge should be flush with the face boards.

Attach the center stair stringer to the kick plate, using deck screws driven at an angle.

Cut and install railings in notches cut into the inner faces of the railing posts.

Casual Curve Deck

Gentle, sweeping curves define this delightful design. Enclosed wraparound steps give a feeling of solidity to the deck. Easily adapted to other dimensions, this plan offers a great deal of functional appeal without a large outlay of time or money. The deck pattern is a simple "flying V" design that also adds enormous visual interest.

Stair railings should not be necessary with the height and step design of this plan, but check with your local building inspector. A simple metal railing could be installed without affecting the visual allure of the design. A built-in planter and matching bench provide both increased function and greater aesthetic appeal to what is a very simple deck design.

This small deck is basic in design but still very stylish due to the enclosed steps. They make the deck appear as a solid structure. The deck itself is made even more interesting with the flying V pattern of the deck boards.

Cutaway View

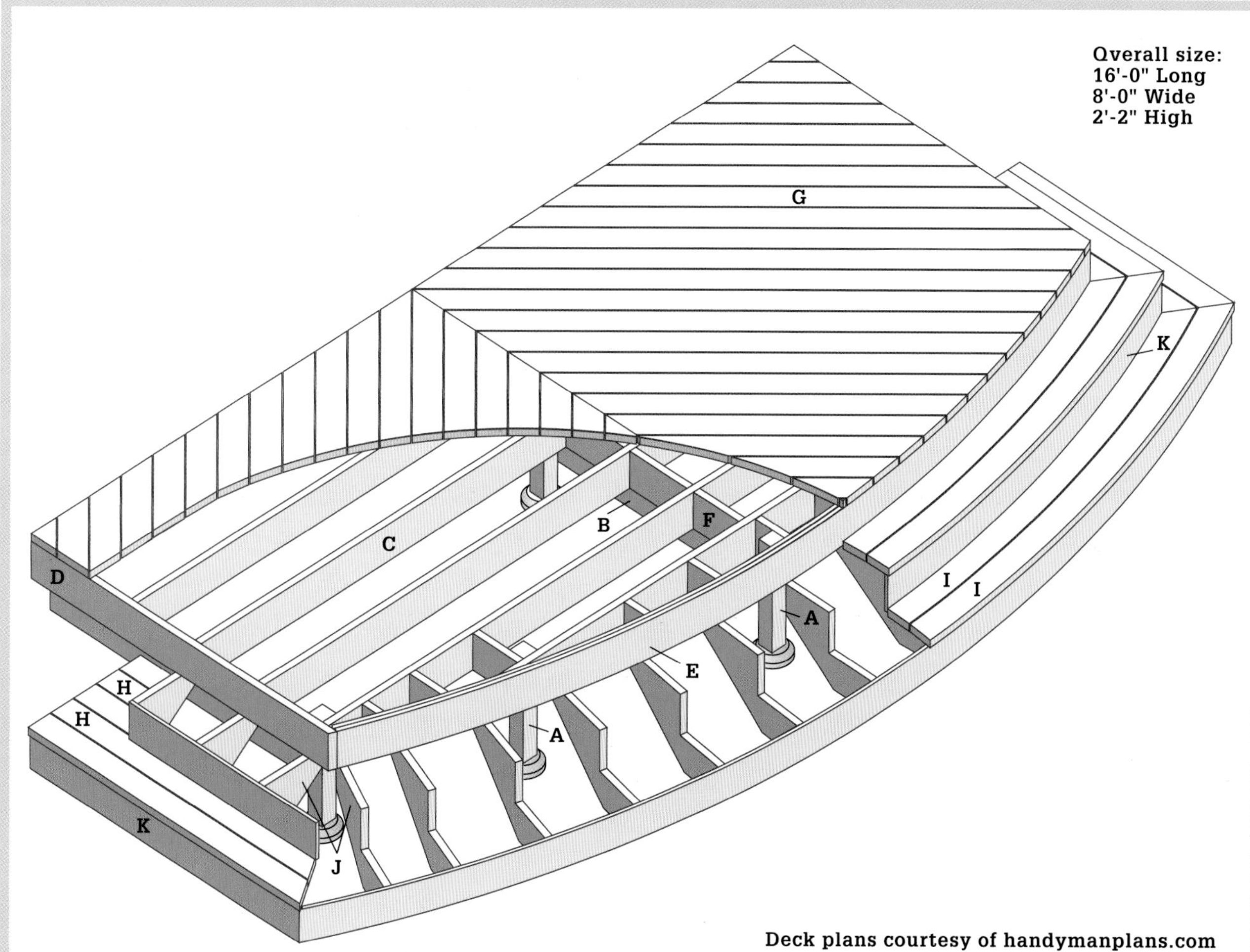

Deck plans courtesy of handymanplans.com

Supplies

10"-diameter footing forms (9)
3" direct bearing hardware (6)
2 × 8" double joist hangers (4)
2 × 8" joist hangers (72)
2½" decking screws
Joist hanger nails
16d galvanized nails
12d galvanized casing nails
½ × 4" carriage bolts, washers, and nuts (12)
½ × 4" lag screws (22)
Exterior silicone caulk (3 tubes)
Concrete as required

Lumber List

QTY.	SIZE	MATERIAL	PART
3	6 × 6" × 8'	Trtd. lumber	Posts (A)
6	2 × 8" × 8'	Trtd. lumber	Beam (B), rim joists (D)
3	2 × 8" × 8'	Trtd. lumber	Beam (B), blocking (F)
1	2 × 8" × 12'	Trtd. lumber	Joists (C)
6	2 × 8" × 16'	Trtd. lumber	Joists (C), rim joist (D)
7	1 × 8" × 10'	Trtd. lumber	Curved rim joist (E), stair risers (K)
2	1 × 8" × 12'	Trtd. lumber	Stair risers (K)
32	1½ × 6" × 8'	Trtd. lumber	Decking (G)
4	1½ × 6" × 10'	Trtd. lumber	Decking (G)
8	1½ × 6" × 12'	Trtd. lumber	Decking (G)
3	2 × 6" × 10'	Trtd. lumber	Stair treads (H)
9	2 × 12" × 8'	Trtd. lumber	Stair stringers (J)
8	2 × 12" × 10'	Trtd. lumber	Curved stair tread (I)

Framing Plan

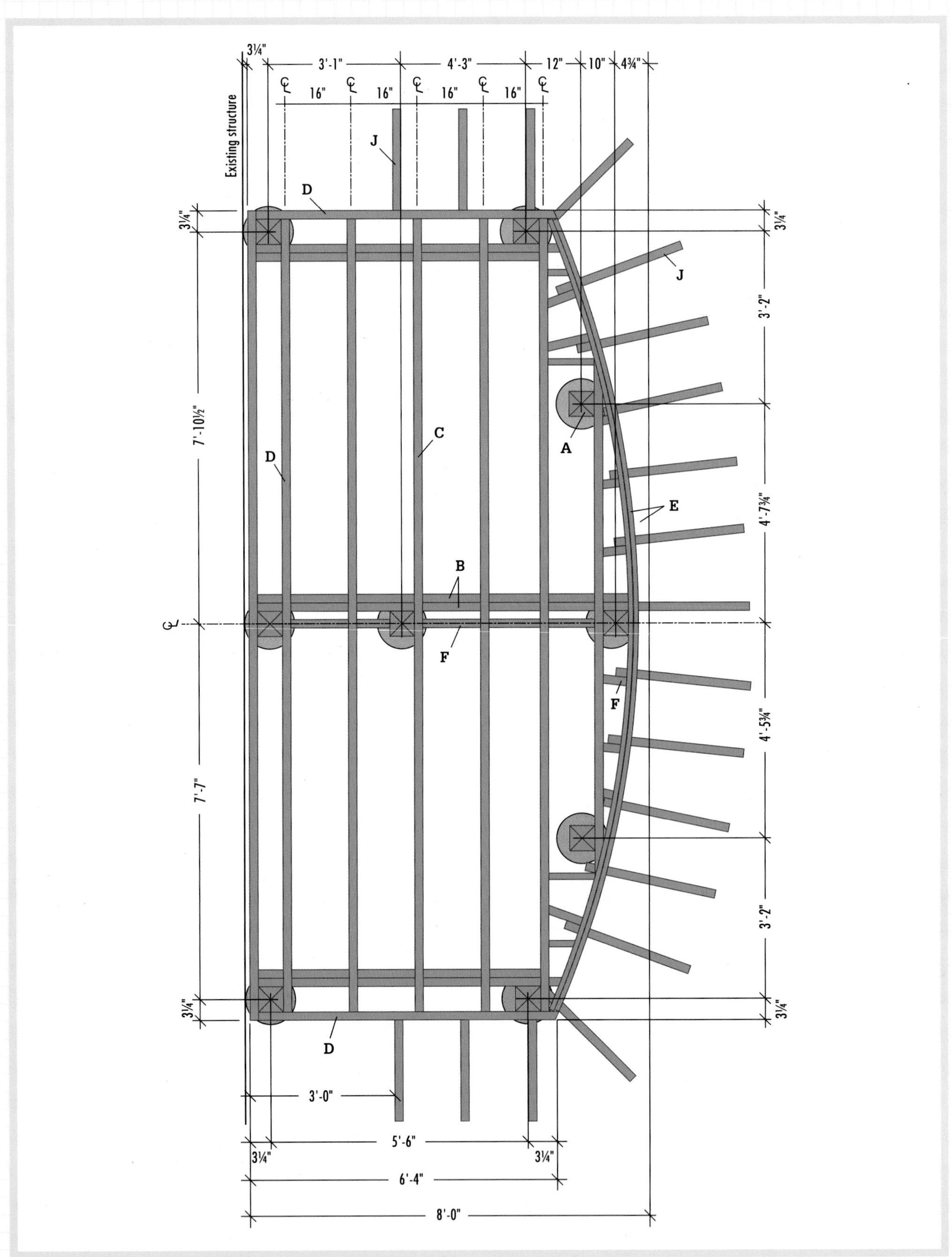

How to Build a Casual Curve Deck

POUR THE FOOTINGS

A ledger isn't used for this deck plan. If you alter these plans to include a ledger board, see pages 62 to 69 for ledger installation methods.

Mark the deck location on the wall of the house (see Framing Plan), then stretch mason's strings across the site, using 2 × 4 batterboards. Temporarily attach batterboards to the wall with deck screws. Check the mason's strings for square, using the 3-4-5 triangle method. Adjust as necessary until they are square. Measure along the strings to locate the centerpoints of the footings and mark each with tape. *Note: Allow yourself room to dig the footings at the house wall; the centerpoint of the posts can be up to 16" from the end of the beam.*

Drop a plumb bob at the tape locations and drive stakes into the ground to mark the centerpoints of the footings.

Remove the mason's strings and dig holes for the footings, using a clamshell digger or power auger. Make certain the hole sizes and depths comply with your local building code, which may require flaring the footings at their base.

Pour 2" to 3" of loose gravel into each hole for drainage.

Cut the footing tube forms to length, so they extend 2" above grade, using a reciprocating saw or handsaw. Insert the forms into the holes and backfill with soil.

Fill the tube forms with concrete in stages, tamping the concrete at each stage with a long stick to eliminate any air pockets. Screed the tops flush with a flat 2 × 4.

Retie the mason's strings and drop a plumb bob to establish the centerpoint of the footing. Insert a J-bolt into each footing, leaving ¾" to 1" of thread exposed. Clean the bolt threads before the concrete sets. *Note: Another option is to install threaded rods with epoxy after the concrete has cured.*

SET THE POSTS

Start by laying a long straight 2 × 4 flat across pairs of footings. With one edge tight against the J-bolts, draw a reference line across each footing. Do this in both directions for pairs of footings where necessary.

Place a metal post anchor on each footing, center it over the J-bolt, and square it with the reference line. Thread a nut over each J-bolt and tighten each of the post anchors in place.

Cut 30"-long posts from pressure-treated 6 × 6 lumber. Place each post in a post anchor and tack it in place with one nail. With a level as a guide, plumb the posts, using braces and stakes to hold them in place. Finish nailing the posts to the anchor.

At the centermost post along the wall, measure down from the door, allowing 7¼" for the joists, 1½" for the decking, and 1" between the decking surface and the interior floor, then mark the post at this measurement.

Use a string, water, or laser level to transfer this mark to the other posts. Each mark will be level with the top edge of the beams.

INSTALL THE BEAMS

Measure and cut two pressure-treated 2 × 8s to length for each of the three beams (see Framing Plan, page 340). Place their faces together so that their crown sides are aligned and attach them together with pairs of galvanized nails or deck screws driven in a zig-zag pattern every 12".

Position the crown (top) edge of each beam against the level marks on the appropriate posts and clamp it in place. Mark and then notch the posts 3" deep for the beams. Drill pairs of holes for ½ × 6" carriage bolts through the beam and post at each location. Attach each beam to the posts with the carriage bolts, washers, and nuts, inserting the bolts through the beam.

INSTALL THE RIM JOISTS

Measure and cut the two outer rim joists. Provide a 1 × 2" space between one end of each joist and the wall and a 2" extension beyond the outer corner post at the other end. Position their bottom edges so they are level with the top edges of the beams and attach them to the posts with 3" deck screws.

Measure, cut, and attach the wall-side rim joist between the ends of the outer rim joists. Align the wall-side rim joist face that is nearest the wall so it is flush with the ends of the outer joists. Drill pilot holes through the outer rim joist and drive deck screws through into the wall-side rim joist ends.

Cut and install the inner joist between the outer rim joists on the front faces of the outer corner posts. Attach it to the posts with deck screws and to the beams with rafter ties.

INSTALL THE CURVED RIM JOIST

Measure and cut a pressure-treated 1 × 8 a few inches longer than needed to span from the outer rim joist to the centerpoint of the middle post at the front of the deck. This will be the first piece of the curved rim joist. Cut numerous ½"-deep kerfs along the back width of this board. See page 120 for more information on cutting kerfs.

(continued)

Cut ½"-deep kerfs along the back width of the first 1 × 8 for the curved rim joist. Bend and attach it to the posts, using clamps to hold it in position.

Install the next layer of kerfed 1 × 8s, driving pairs of screws every 12" and at each post location.

Place one end of the board in the intersection of an outer rim joist and inner joist at an outer corner post, with the kerfed face against the inner joist and its top edge flush with the top edges of the joists. Drill pilot holes and drive 3" deck screws through the end of the board into the joist and post.

Bend the other end of the board until it meets the face of the center post and attach it to the post with deck screws driven 1" from the centerpoint. Make sure the bottom edge of the curved joist is level with the top edge of the beam. Mark a straight cut line at the centerpoint of the post on the curved joist, using a speed square. Cut the board with a circular saw with its blade set ⅛" deeper than the thickness of the board.

Measure, cut, and kerf another 1 × 8 a few inches longer than needed to complete the span. Attach one end in the intersection of the other outer rim joist and corner post. Bend and clamp the board into position. Mark a cutting line for the board to meet the other curved joist at the center post. Cut it with the circular saw, drill pilot holes, and drive deck screws to attach it to the post before removing the clamps.

Measure, cut, and kerf another pair of 1 × 8s. Clamp them to the first layer, staggering the joints so they do not fall on the center post and aligning the ends so they protrude past the rim joists. Drill pilot holes and fasten with deck screws every 12" and at post locations, then trim the ends of the rim joists flush with the outer face of the curved rim joist, using a reciprocating saw.

INSTALL THE JOISTS

Measure, cut, and install the remaining inner joists with 16" on-center spacing beginning at the wall side of the deck.

Select a 2 × 8 for the inner joist closest to the curved rim joist that is about 12" longer than necessary. Position it so its ends overlap the curved rim joist with its inner face aligned with the adjacent posts. Mark the profile of the inner face of the curved rim joist at each end of the inner joist. Cut the inner joist at these marks with a reciprocating saw, then install it with deck screws driven through it and into the curved rim joist.

Cut and install 2 × 8 blocking at the midpoints of the joist spans to provide support for the diagonal decking. Also install blocking between the curved rim joist and adjacent joists as necessary to help support the curved profile. Cut the tops of the posts flush with the top edges of the joists. Remove all braces and stakes supporting posts.

BUILD THE STAIRS

Cut the stair stringers to length from pressure-treated 2 × 12 lumber and use a framing square to mark the rise and run for each step. Cut the notches and the angles at the end of the stringers with a circular saw, then use a jigsaw to complete the corners.

Attach the side stair stringers to the joist ends. Attach the stringers for the curved stair to the blocking between the inner joists and the curved rim joist. Install additional blocking as necessary. Rip ¼"-thick plywood sheets into 2 × 8-ft.-long pieces and trace the profile of the curved rim joist onto them. Cut out this profile, using a jigsaw, and use the plywood templates to mark the inside curve for the inner tread of the top step onto 10-ft.-long pieces of 2 × 12 lumber. Cut a 2"-wide piece of 2 × 6 lumber and use it as a spacer to mark the outside curve for the inner tread. Guide one end of the spacer along the inside curve line while holding a pencil point at the other end.

Cut the curved inner tread pieces using a jigsaw. Use the outside curved edge of the inner tread to mark the inside curve of the outer tread for the top step. Use the spacer to mark the outside edge, then cut the treads using a jigsaw.

Use the outside curved edge of the outer tread for the top step to mark the inside curved edge on the inner tread of the bottom step. Repeat the process used to mark and cut the top step treads to complete the bottom step treads.

Install the curved treads, drilling pilot holes and using deck screws. Make sure joints between tread pieces are supported by stringers.

Measure and cut the side treads from 2 × 6 lumber, and attach them to the side stair stringers.

INSTALL THE DECKING

Cut a 45° angle at the end of a deck board and position it with the long point ¼" from the wall and centered on the midpoint blocking. The other end should overhang the rim joists at the opposite corner. Attach the board by driving two deck screws into each joist.

Cut and attach the rest of the deck boards on this side of the deck.

Cut and attach the deck boards for the other side of the deck, again letting ends overhang the rim joists. Trim the ends of the deck boards.

Mark and snap chalk lines across the overhanging board. Set the depth of the circular saw blade ⅛" deeper than the thickness of the decking and cut along the lines. Complete the cuts at the wall with a jigsaw, and a hammer and sharp chisel.

Use the plywood templates you cut for the stair installation to mark the curve on the ends of the decking boards overhanging the curved rim joist and trim, using a jigsaw.

Cut a 2"-wide piece of 2 × 6 lumber and use it as a spacer to mark the outside curve for the inner tread.

Mark the profile of the inner face of the curved rim joist on each end of the 2 × 8 for the inner joist at the curve. Cut the joist at the marks, then fasten to the posts with carriage bolts and to the curved rim joist with deck screws.

Use a jigsaw to trim the decking boards overhanging the curved rim joist.

Deckbuilding Glossary

Baluster — a vertical railing member.

Batterboards — temporary stake structures used for positioning layout strings.

Beam — the main horizontal support for the deck, usually made from a pair of 2 × 8s or 2 × 10s attached to the deck posts.

Blocking — short pieces of lumber cut from joist material and fastened between joists for reinforcement.

Cap — the topmost horizontal railing member.

Cantilever — a common construction method (employed in some of the deck plans in this book) that involves extending the joists beyond the beam. The maximum overhang is specified in the Building Code.

Corner-post design — a construction method that incorporates posts at the outside edges of the deck, so the joists do not overhang the beam.

Decking — the floor boards of a deck (also known as deck boards).

End joists — the joists that are at each end of a series of parallel joists.

Face board — attractive wood, usually redwood or cedar, used to cover the rim joists and end joists.

Footing — a concrete pier that extends below the frost line and that bears the weight of the deck and any inset structures or furnishings.

Horizontal span — the horizontal distance a stairway covers.

Inset — an area of a deck that has been cut out to accommodate landscape features such as trees or to provide access to fixtures.

Joist — dimensional lumber, set on edge, that supports decking. Joists on attached decks hang between the ledger and rim joist.

Joist hanger — metal connecting pieces used to attach joists at right angles to ledger or header joists so that top edges are flush.

Ledger — a board, equal in size to the joists, that anchors the deck to the house and supports one end of the joists.

Open step — a step composed of treads mounted between stair stringers without any risers.

Post — a vertical member that supports a deck, stairway, or railing.

Post anchors — metal hardware for attaching deck posts to footings and raising the bottom of the post to keep it away from water. The end grain itself can be protected with sealer as added protection from rot.

Rim joist — a board fastened to the end of the joists, typically at the opposite end from the ledger. Rim joists attach to both ends of a free-standing deck.

Rise — the height of a step.

Riser — a board attached to the front of a step between treads.

Run — the depth of a step.

Span limit — the distance a board can safely cross between supports.

Stair cleat — supports for treads that are attached to stair stringers.

Stair stringer — an inclined member that supports a stairway's treads. A stair stringer may be solid, with treads attached to cleats mounted on the inside face, or cut out, with treads resting on top of the cutouts.

Tread — the horizontal face of each step in a stairway, often composed of two 2 × 6 boards.

Vertical drop — the vertical distance from the deck surface to the ground.

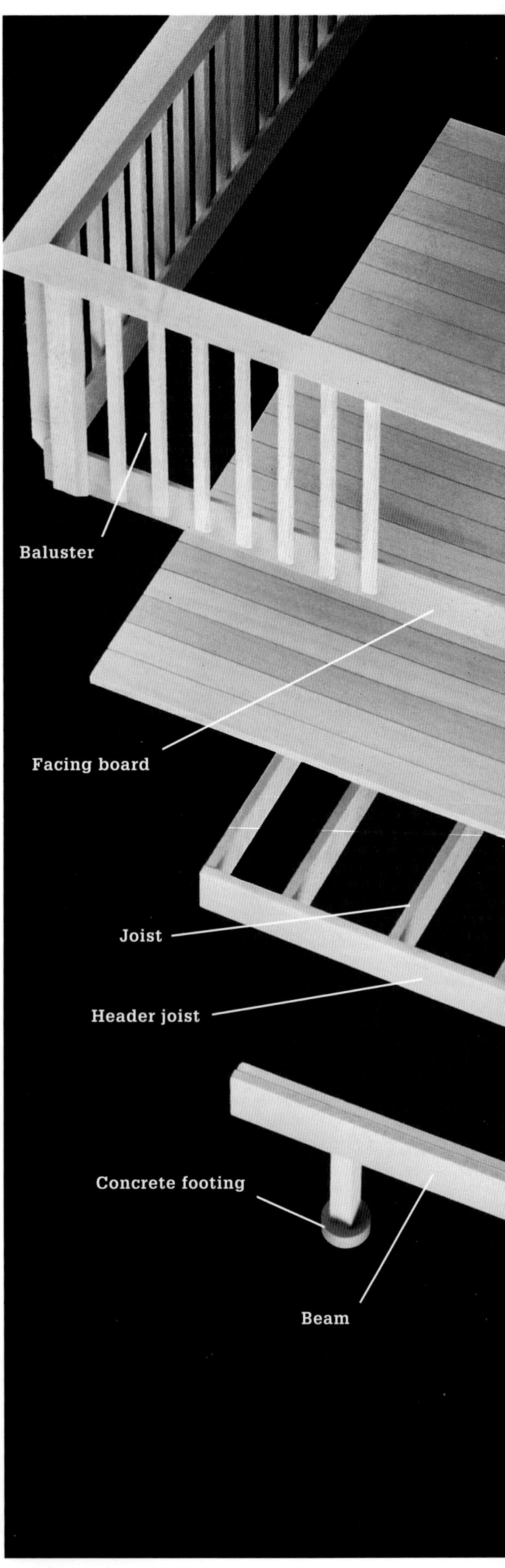

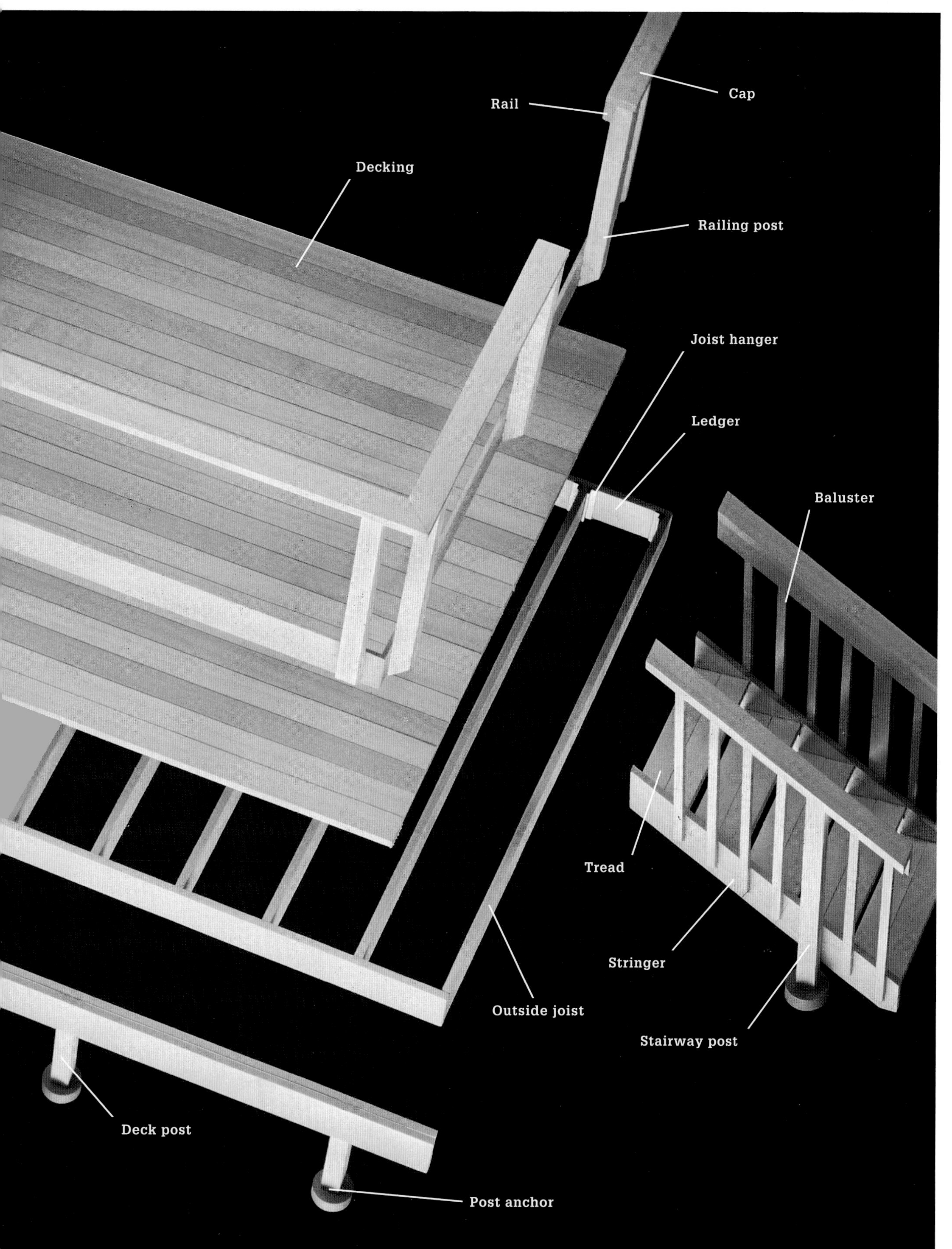
Cap
Rail
Decking
Railing post
Joist hanger
Ledger
Baluster
Tread
Stringer
Outside joist
Stairway post
Deck post
Post anchor

Reference Charts

Metric Conversions

TO CONVERT:	TO:	MULTIPLY BY:
Inches	Millimeters	25.4
Inches	Centimeters	2.54
Feet	Meters	0.305
Yards	Meters	0.914
Square inches	Square centimeters	6.45
Square feet	Square meters	0.093
Square yards	Square meters	0.836
Ounces	Milliliters	30.0
Pints (U.S.)	Liters	0.473 (Imp. 0.568)
Quarts (U.S.)	Liters	0.946 (Imp. 1.136)
Gallons (U.S.)	Liters	3.785 (Imp. 4.546)
Ounces	Grams	28.4
Pounds	Kilograms	0.454

TO CONVERT:	TO:	MULTIPLY BY:
Millimeters	Inches	0.039
Centimeters	Inches	0.394
Meters	Feet	3.28
Meters	Yards	1.09
Square centimeters	Square inches	0.155
Square meters	Square feet	10.8
Square meters	Square yards	1.2
Milliliters	Ounces	.033
Liters	Pints (U.S.)	2.114 (Imp. 1.76)
Liters	Quarts (U.S.)	1.057 (Imp. 0.88)
Liters	Gallons (U.S.)	0.264 (Imp. 0.22)
Grams	Ounces	0.035
Kilograms	Pounds	2.2

Converting Temperatures

Convert degrees Fahrenheit (F) to degrees Celsius (C) by following this simple formula: Subtract 32 from the Fahrenheit temperature reading. Then, multiply that number by 5/9. For example, 77°F - 32 = 45. 45 × 5/9 = 25°C.

To convert degrees Celsius to degrees Fahrenheit, multiply the Celsius temperature reading by 9/5. Then, add 32. For example, 25°C × 9/5 = 45. 45 + 32 = 77°F.

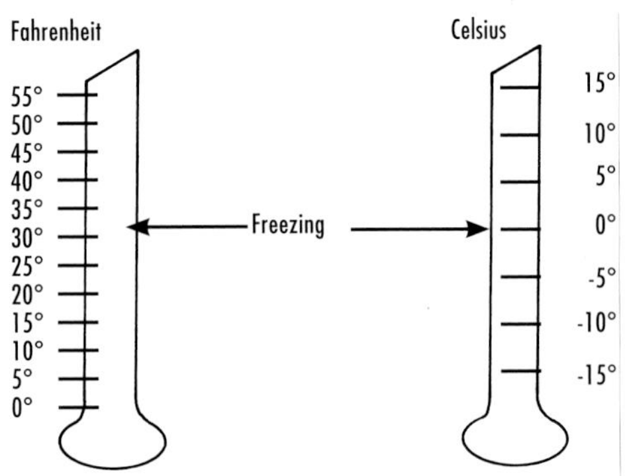

Metric Plywood Panels

Metric plywood panels are commonly available in two sizes: 1,200 mm × 2,400 mm and 1,220 mm × 2,400 mm, which is roughly equivalent to a 4 × 8-ft. sheet. Standard and Select sheathing panels come in standard thicknesses, while Sanded grade panels are available in special thicknesses.

STANDARD SHEATHING GRADE		SANDED GRADE	
7.5 mm	(5/16 in.)	6 mm	(4/17 in.)
9.5 mm	(⅜ in.)	8 mm	(5/16 in.)
12.5 mm	(½ in.)	11 mm	(7/16 in.)
15.5 mm	(⅝ in.)	14 mm	(9/16 in.)
18.5 mm	(¾ in.)	17 mm	(⅔ in.)
20.5 mm	(13/16 in.)	19 mm	(¾ in.)
22.5 mm	(⅞ in.)	21 mm	(13/16 in.)
25.5 mm	(1 in.)	24 mm	(15/16 in.)

Lumber Dimensions

NOMINAL-U.S.	ACTUAL-U.S. (IN INCHES)	METRIC
1 × 2	¾ × 1½	19 × 38 mm
1 × 3	¾ × 2½	19 × 64 mm
1 × 4	¾ × 3½	19 × 89 mm
1 × 6	¾ × 5½	19 × 140 mm
1 × 8	¾ × 7¼	19 × 184 mm
1 × 10	¾ × 9¼	19 × 235 mm
1 × 12	¾ × 11¼	19 × 286 mm
1¼ × 4	1 × 3½	25 × 89 mm
1¼ × 6	1 × 5½	25 × 140 mm
1¼ × 8	1 × 7¼	25 × 184 mm
1¼ × 10	1 × 9¼	25 × 235 mm
1¼ × 12	1 × 11¼	25 × 286 mm
1½ × 4	1¼ × 3½	32 × 89 mm
1½ × 6	1¼ × 5½	32 × 140 mm
1½ × 8	1¼ × 7¼	32 × 184 mm
1½ × 10	1¼ × 9¼	32 × 235 mm
1½ × 12	1¼ × 11¼	32 × 286 mm
2 × 4	1½ × 3½	38 × 89 mm
2 × 6	1½ × 5½	38 × 140 mm
2 × 8	1½ × 7¼	38 × 184 mm
2 × 10	1½ × 9¼	38 × 235 mm
2 × 12	1½ × 11¼	38 × 286 mm
3 × 6	2½ × 5½	64 × 140 mm
4 × 4	3½ × 3½	89 × 89 mm
4 × 6	3½ × 5½	89 × 140 mm
6 × 6	5½ × 5½	140 × 140 mm

Liquid Measurement Equivalents

1 Pint	= 16 Fluid Ounces	= 2 Cups
1 Quart	= 32 Fluid Ounces	= 2 Pints
1 Gallon	= 128 Fluid Ounces	= 4 Quarts

Resources

Absolute Concrete
360 297 5055
www.absoluteconcreteworks.com

American Wood Council
(Download a PDF copy of "Prescriptive Residential Deck Construction Guide" at http://www.awc.org/Publications/DCA/DCA6/DCA6-09.pdf.)

BEHR
800 854 0133, ext 2
www.behr.com

©Black & Decker
Portable power tools & more
800 544 6986
www.blackanddecker.com

Capital
562 903 1167
www.capital-cooking.com

Deckorators
www.deckorators.com

Dekmate
www.2x4basics.com/dekmate-products.asp

Dek-Block
800 664 2705
www.deckplans.com

Distinctive Design
423 505 7457
www.distinctivedesigns4you.com

Feeney Architectural Products
Glass panel railing (Design Rail), Cable railing (Cable Rail)
800 888 2418
www.feeneyarchitectural.com

GeoDeck
877 804 0137
www.geodeck.com

HandyDeck
866 206 8316
www.handydeck.com

LB Plastics
704 663 1543
www.lbplastics.com

Napoleon
705 726 4278
www.napoleongrills.com

Red Wing Shoes Co.
Work shoes and boots shown throughout book
800 733 9464
www.redwingshoes.com

Trex
Composite deck rail system
800 289 8739
www.trex.com

TimberTech
800 307 7780
www.timbertech.com

Underdeck
www.underdeck.com
(877) 805-7156

Viking
662 455 1200
www.vikingrange.com

Wolf / Subzero
800 222 7820
www.subzero.com

Wolmanized® Wood
770 804 6600
www.archchemicals.com

Photo Credits

Absolute Concrete: page 239, top right; 240, bottom left

Archedeck, www.archadeck.com, (888)OUR-DECK: page 13, top

CA Redwood Association, www.calredwood.org/photo: page 10, top right (by Ernest Braun); 12, top; 17 top

Capital: page 236, top; 240, bottom right

CertainTeed Corporation: page 11, top right and bottom

Clemens Jellema, Fine Decks, Inc. www.finedecks.com: page 13, bottom; 14, top right; 15 bottom; 17 bottom; 194; 213

Clive Nichols: Photo © page 15, top (designer Sarah Layton); 16, top left (designer S. Woodhams); 243, bottom left (designer Clare Matthews); 264 (Design Boardman Gelly & Co.)

Consentino: page 240, top left

Deck Builders, Inc., www.artistryindecks.com: page 16, top right; 212

Deckorators: page 14, top left and bottom; 183 top left, middle right, lower two; 243, top right

Distinctive Design: page 21, top left; 183 top right and middle left; 265, bottom right

Fiberon Composite Decking, www.fiberondecking.com: page 6, 8

FotoSearch: page 243, top right

GeoDeck: page 16, bottom; 235, top right

HandyDeck: page 235, top left

Hickory Dickory Decks, www.hickorydickorydecks.com, (800) 263-4774: page 195

iStock: page 21, bottom right; 242 (Stephanie Philips)

Marvel: page 237, top right

Robert Agli: page 237, bottom left; 240, top right; 243, top left

TAMKO Building Products, Inc., www.evergrain.com: page 12, bottom; 21 top right

Trex Company, Inc., www.trex.com: page 10, bottom; 11 top left; 21 bottom left; 244, top left; 245 (all)

Viking: page 234; 235 bottom; 237, bottom right; 238

Wolf/Subzero: page 237, top left

Wolmanized® Wood: page 10, top left; 244, bottom right; 265, top and bottom right

Index